Strategic Survey 2018
The Annual Assessment of Geopolitics

published by

Routledge
Taylor & Francis Group

for

The International Institute for Strategic Studies

The International Institute for Strategic Studies

Arundel House | 6 Temple Place | London | WC2R 2PG | UK

Strategic Survey 2018
The Annual Assessment of Geopolitics

First published November 2018 by **Routledge**
4 Park Square, Milton Park, Abingdon, Oxon, OX14 4RN

for **The International Institute for Strategic Studies**
Arundel House, 6 Temple Place, London, WC2R 2PG, UK

Simultaneously published in the USA and Canada by **Routledge**
52 Vanderbilt Avenue, New York, NY 10017

Routledge is an imprint of Taylor & Francis, an Informa business

© 2018 The International Institute for Strategic Studies

DIRECTOR-GENERAL AND CHIEF EXECUTIVE Dr John Chipman

EDITOR Dr Nicholas Redman

ASSOCIATE EDITOR Alex Goodwin
EDITORIAL Thomas Adamson-Green, Sara Hussain, Jill Lally, Jack May, Sam Stocker, Jessica Watson, Carolyn West
MAP RESEARCH Emma Bapt, Guillermo Perez Molina, Tom Waldwyn
COVER/PRODUCTION/CARTOGRAPHY John Buck, Kelly Verity
COVER IMAGES Getty Images

British Library Cataloguing in Publication Data
A catalogue record for this book is available from the British Library

Library of Congress Cataloguing in Publication Data

ISBN 978-1-85743-957-1
ISSN 0459-7230

Contents

Preface

Strategic Survey is now in its sixth decade. Over time, its form has changed but its purpose has not. It aims to record and analyse the important changes in the international system and the foreign policy of leading states, and to help readers think about questions of international security and order.

In this year's edition, we have changed the format somewhat. We retain the same organising principle as before, with one section for transnational or global issues, and the rest devoted to regions of the world. Within the regional sections, we present a shorter, more selective review of the important changes over the 12 months to mid-2018 than in preceding editions. Alongside, we have thematic essays on pertinent and pressing regional questions. They are a mix of those that you might expect to see – such as the North Korean nuclear issue, Iran and the Middle East following the US withdrawal from the Joint Comprehensive Plan of Action (JCPOA) nuclear deal, China's promotion of an export variant of its politico-economic system and South Africa under a new president – together with others that we regard as important but underexamined. Examples of the latter include the possibility of an 'African Spring' in sub-Saharan Africa; the success of the US in meeting its Paris commitments on cutting greenhouse-gas emissions; and the emergence of a new regional order in Central Asia.

We asked our authors to write these essays with a forward-looking perspective, so that they offer a guide to what readers should look out for, or expect, in 2019. They are not exercises in forecasting; rather, they aim to track developments over the last few years, to analyse the drivers of change, and to chart a trajectory or identify where the next fork in the road might lie. We hope that you find this useful and stimulating; we do not all think alike, but we all like to think.

Chapter 1

Selected Key Events

July 2017–June 2018

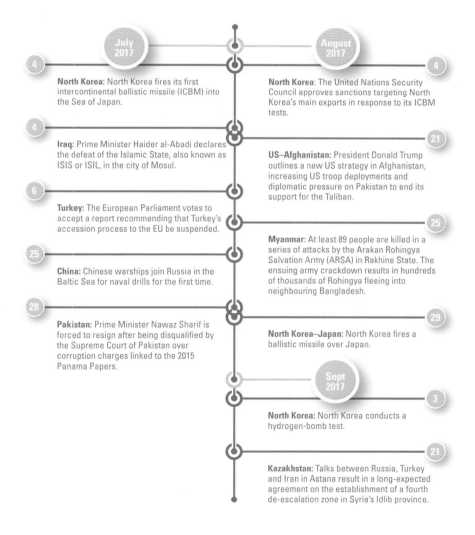

July 2017

4
North Korea: North Korea fires its first intercontinental ballistic missile (ICBM) into the Sea of Japan.

4
Iraq: Prime Minister Haider al-Abadi declares the defeat of the Islamic State, also known as ISIS or ISIL, in the city of Mosul.

6
Turkey: The European Parliament votes to accept a report recommending that Turkey's accession process to the EU be suspended.

25
China: Chinese warships join Russia in the Baltic Sea for naval drills for the first time.

28
Pakistan: Prime Minister Nawaz Sharif is forced to resign after being disqualified by the Supreme Court of Pakistan over corruption charges linked to the 2015 Panama Papers.

August 2017

4
North Korea: The United Nations Security Council approves sanctions targeting North Korea's main exports in response to its ICBM tests.

21
US–Afghanistan: President Donald Trump outlines a new US strategy in Afghanistan, increasing US troop deployments and diplomatic pressure on Pakistan to end its support for the Taliban.

25
Myanmar: At least 89 people are killed in a series of attacks by the Arakan Rohingya Salvation Army (ARSA) in Rakhine State. The ensuing army crackdown results in hundreds of thousands of Rohingya fleeing into neighbouring Bangladesh.

29
North Korea–Japan: North Korea fires a ballistic missile over Japan.

Sept 2017

3
North Korea: North Korea conducts a hydrogen-bomb test.

21
Kazakhstan: Talks between Russia, Turkey and Iran in Astana result in a long-expected agreement on the establishment of a fourth de-escalation zone in Syria's Idlib province.

21

Russia–China: Russia and China begin joint naval drills in the Sea of Japan and the Sea of Okhotsk.

24

Germany: Angela Merkel wins the German general election. The far-right populist party Alternative for Germany (AfD) makes significant gains, winning 94 seats in parliament and 12.6% of the vote.

25

Iraq: The Kurdistan Region of Iraq holds an unauthorised referendum on independence amid tensions with the federal government. The results show that 92% of Iraqi Kurds favour independence for the region.

October 2017

1

Spain: The Catalan regional government holds an unauthorised referendum on independence, with Catalan officials claiming that 90% of voters were in favour of secession.

12

Palestine: Fatah and Hamas sign a landmark agreement in Cairo giving the Palestinian Authority control of borders in the Gaza Strip, thus ending an 11-year split between the two factions.

14

Somalia: Truck-bomb explosions in central Mogadishu kill at least 237 people and injure more than 300 others.

17

Philippines: President Rodrigo Duterte declares the liberation of Marawi city after a four-month siege by the Philippine security forces to remove the occupying ISIS-linked Maute militants.

18

China: At the 19th National Congress, the Chinese Communist Party incorporates 'Xi Jinping Thought on Socialism with Chinese Characteristics for a New Era' into the party's constitution, placing Xi Jinping on a par with Mao Zedong and Deng Xiaoping.

23

Japan: Japan's ruling coalition, led by Prime Minister Shinzo Abe's Liberal Democratic Party, wins a snap election and secures a two-thirds majority in parliament.

Nov 2017

8

US–Ukraine: The US Congress approves the draft National Defense Authorization Act (NDAA), which allocates US$350 million for military aid and lethal weapons to Ukraine in 2018.

21

Zimbabwe: Zimbabwe's armed forces compel Robert Mugabe to resign, ending his 37-year rule. He is succeeded by his former deputy Emmerson Mnangagwa.

22

Europe: The International Criminal Tribunal for the Former Yugoslavia sentences former Bosnian Serb Army commander Ratko Mladic to life imprisonment for genocide and crimes against humanity.

Dec 2017

4

Yemen: Former president Ali Abdullah Saleh is killed by his erstwhile Houthi allies near the capital, Sana'a.

6

US–Israel: US President Donald Trump recognises Jerusalem as the capital of Israel and announces his intention to move the US Embassy there. This decision is widely criticised around the world and sparks a wave of protests in Palestine.

10

Sri Lanka: Sri Lanka cedes its southern port of Hambantota to China on a 99-year lease, after Colombo failed to repay debts to Beijing associated with the port's construction.

20

Poland: In an unprecedented move, the European Commission triggers Article 7 of the Lisbon Treaty against Poland over its controversial judicial reform.

January 2018

11

Tunisia: Police arrest 328 people on the third night of protests across the country. Protests broke out over the high living costs in the country after the ruling coalition announced VAT hikes.

20

Turkey: Turkey launches *Operation Olive Branch* against Kurdish-held Afrin in northwestern Syria, with support from Turkish-backed Syrian rebels.

February 2018

9

North Korea–South Korea: South and North Korean athletes march together under a single flag at the opening ceremony of the Pyeongchang Winter Olympics.

13

Asia-Pacific region: One of the Asia-Pacific region's largest multinational military exercises, *Cobra Gold*, begins in Thailand. It involves 11,000 personnel from 29 countries, including the US, Japan, Singapore, South Korea, Indonesia and Malaysia.

15

Ethiopia: Hailemariam Desalegn resigns as Ethiopian prime minister and chairman of the ruling Ethiopian People's Revolutionary Democratic Front (EPRDF). He is succeeded by Abiy Ahmed, who introduces a wide range of reforms.

28

Afghanistan: President Ashraf Ghani announces that his government will recognise the Taliban as a legitimate political party and enter into negotiations without preconditions.

March 2018

4

Italy: Populist parties triumph in Italy's general election. Anti-establishment Five Star Movement and far-right Northern League become Italy's largest parties and form a government.

4

UK: Former Russian military officer and British spy Sergei Skripal and his daughter are poisoned in Salisbury, England with the Novichok nerve agent. The attack is attributed to Russia and triggers a wave of expulsions of Russian diplomats from Western countries. Russia retaliates by expelling 189 foreign diplomats.

4

Germany: The German Social Democratic Party (SPD) agrees to form another 'grand coalition', ending nearly six months of uncertainty in German politics and securing Angela Merkel's fourth term in office.

15

Philippines: The Philippines formally withdraws from the International Criminal Court.

18

Russia: President Vladimir Putin is re-elected following a presidential election, receiving 76.6% of the vote.

April 2018

2

China: Beijing announces new tariffs on 128 food imports from the US, days after Washington imposed taxes of 25% on steel imports and of 10% on aluminium imports from China.

2

Egypt: Egypt's election authority announces that President Abdel Fattah al-Sisi has won the 26 March presidential election with 97.08% of the vote.

3

US–China: The US government threatens a 25% tariff on 1,300 Chinese products worth US$50billion. China responds with plans to impose a 25% tariff on 106 US products worth US$50billion.

8

Hungary: Prime Minister Viktor Orbán's Fidesz party wins the parliamentary elections with 49% of the vote, claiming 133 of the 199 seats in the National Assembly.

11

Azerbaijan: President Ilham Aliyev wins a fourth term, receiving 86% of the vote in an election boycotted by the major opposition parties.

27

North Korea–South Korea: North Korean leader Kim Jong-un and South Korean President Moon Jae-in hold a summit at the Joint Security Area of the Panmunjom truce village. They issue a joint statement in which they agree to turn the armistice into a peace treaty, as well as to work towards the complete denuclearisation of the Korean Peninsula.

ratification from both countries' parliaments and by a referendum in Macedonia, under the deal Macedonia, whose official name is the Former Yugoslav Republic of Macedonia, will become the Republic of North Macedonia.

May 2018

21

2

Basque region: ETA – the Basque terrorist group responsible for the deaths of more than 800 people since the 1960s – announces its dissolution and abandons its campaign for Basque independence.

US–North Korea: President Donald Trump meets North Korean leader Kim Jong-un in Singapore. The two countries agree to work towards the denuclearisation of the Korean Peninsula and to collaborate for the recovery of POW remains from the Korean War. Trump later pledges to end joint military exercises between the US and South Korea.

6

Lebanon: Hizbullah makes gains in Lebanon's first parliamentary election since 2009, winning (along with its allies) a small majority.

21

US: President Donald Trump announces plans to impose 25% tariffs starting on 6 July on US$50bn of imports from China, claiming that these new restrictions are justified by Beijing's long-standing theft of US companies' intellectual property. China retaliates the next day by imposing its own 25% tariff on US products worth US$34bn, and threatening to add a further US$6bn at a later date.

8

US: US President Donald Trump announces that the United States is withdrawing from the JCPOA Iran nuclear deal.

21

Hungary: The Hungarian parliament passes a series of laws to limit the influx of asylum seekers.

10

Malaysia: Mahathir Mohamad becomes prime minister for the second time after his Pakatan Harapan coalition wins 113 seats in the general election.

24

European Union: The EU introduces retaliatory tariffs on €2.8bn (US$3.2bn)-worth of US goods such as bourbon, motorcycles and orange juice.

19

Iraq: The radical Shia cleric Moqtada al-Sadr is announced as the winner of the 12 May election, closely followed by the political branch of the Popular Mobilisation Forces, with Prime Minister al-Abadi in third.

24

Turkey: President Recep Tayyip Erdogan wins Turkey's general election with 52.59% of the vote, amid claims of election fraud.

June 2018

27

4

Jordan: Prime minister Hani al-Mulki resigns days after nationwide protests against a new income tax and price hikes on fuel and electricity.

Pakistan: The Financial Action Task Force (FATF) puts Pakistan on its grey list for failing to tackle terror financing within its borders.

29

12

Greece–Macedonia: Greece and Macedonia reach an accord on their long-standing dispute over the name of the latter. Pending

European Union: EU leaders agree to create new centres in Europe for housing and processing asylum seekers. Germany also reaches a trilateral agreement with Spain and Greece to relocate thousands of refugees in Germany to those countries.

Chapter 2

Prospectives

In 2018, the fraying of key international and regional institutions, the dissipation of the so-called 'rules-based order', the boldness of China and Russia, the persistence of intractable regional conflicts and the unpredictable leadership of the United States were some of the dominant themes in commentary and debate about the international situation. Statecraft is back. States that are unhappy with the international order, or wish to create their own, are finding weaker resistance to their efforts to change things in their favour. Countries that relied on institutional arrangements or on external security guarantees are discovering that they need to revive their national strategic skills to protect their interests. Strategic dexterity is taking many different forms. The techniques used to gain advantage or to combat opponents in the technological age are various: blending cyber power and disinformation campaigns with the classic instruments of military force is commonplace for states as well as for international terrorist groups. The methods by which countries gain strategic advantage are often both innovative and brazen. The ways in which such state action can be deterred or countered are still in development. Uncertainty is heighted by the fact that some geopolitical moves have no obvious or immediate counter. 'Tolerance warfare', a style of geopolitical challenge that appears to be a preferred technique of the status quo disrupters, is becoming more prevalent.

Tolerance warfare can be defined as the persistent effort to test the tolerances for different forms of aggression against settled states. It is the effort to push back lines of resistance, probe weaknesses, assert rights unilaterally, break rules, establish new facts on the ground, strip others of initiative and gain systematic tactical advantage over hesitant opponents. The purpose of tolerance warfare is to stress-test the ability of the target to deter and defeat these efforts, and then to win advantage either by diverting the target's resources away from a central strategic purpose, or by creating new conditions that cannot be reversed except by expensive strategic effort that is perhaps disproportionate to the loss otherwise sustained. Sometimes tolerance warfare is conducted overtly and is in effect 'declared'; often tolerance warfare is conducted through proxies or partners, especially in the most immediate theatres of operations.

Iran conducts tolerance warfare in the Gulf and Levant, using partners and proxies to affect political agendas in the target states, gain a foothold for information operations and insinuate its style of warfare in neighbouring geographies. It is these 'other activities' of Iran that have posed in the past (and continue to do so today) more immediate challenges than its nuclear programme. A confirmed nuclear-weapons capacity would naturally pose a huge danger, including the prospect of further proliferation, but it is the political- and military-influence operations of the Iranian Islamic Revolutionary Guard Corps that creates daily pressures on the regional states affected.

Tolerance warfare, with its indirect and tactical elements, is in effect becoming a favoured strategy for those countries who cannot easily challenge their biggest rivals symmetrically. Most obviously, President Vladimir Putin's Russia is seeking asymmetrically to gain advantage in its weakened position by regular use of these kinds of tolerance-warfare stratagems. In the Cold War, proxy wars were fought by the Soviet Union against the US in tertiary theatres of operation: in Africa, Southeast Asia and Central America. In today's era of tolerance warfare, Russia's proxy- and tolerance-warfare tactics are being conducted significantly in the 'primary theatre' of operations: Europe and North America.

Putin's regime aims now to exploit the openness and weaknesses in Western democracies whose instincts for statecraft have been tempered by geopolitical failures abroad and constraints imposed by domestic public opinion on hard-power deployment internationally. Resentful of Western states for presuming to tutor Russia in the development of its political system, and angered by their attempts to draw Russia's closest neighbours into the Western political and economic orbit, Putin has used a raw form of state power in an effort to shake the European institutional order. He wishes to disturb the domestic calm of European states to undermine their strategic self-confidence, deter them from any further efforts to export Western styles of governance further eastwards and remind Europeans that Russia is a power to be dealt with on its own terms, not a country to be lectured to on the virtues of liberal governance.

In a way, the 2014 annexation of Crimea (under the false flag of a controlled referendum) and the intervention in eastern Ukraine (thinly disguised by 'green men' said not to be Russian soldiers) represented the first bold implementation of 'tolerance warfare' tactics. The fast creation of facts on the ground, which did not elicit a symmetric Western response, suggested to Russia that the boundaries of acceptable action in Europe were perhaps softening. Since then, Putin's regime has sent military air-craft into others' airspace with transponders off; deployed submarines to others' shorelines; attempted to launch a coup in Montenegro; mar-shalled the forces of RT (the state television network) to spread eccentric interpretations of international events; used social-media trolls to inject venom into the debate over the secession of Catalonia from Spain; launched cyber campaigns to influence US elections; and much more.

Indeed, in 2018, the most ostentatious act of Russian tolerance warfare was its deployment of the Novichok chemical agent in the United Kingdom in an effort to murder a former Russian spy who had turned double agent, an act carried out by two men named by the UK as officers of the GRU, the Russian military-intelligence agency. The subsequent effort by Russia to insist they were merely tourists was implausible – and probably deliberately so. Indeed, an ancillary feature of tolerance warfare is the deliberate effort to create diversionary narratives that are aimed at obfuscating the facts and sowing confusion in international public opinion. All this will continue for the foreseeable future.

The strong UK response to this act – which contrasted sharply with its more restrained response to Russia's use of polonium-210 in London in 2006 to poison another Russian enemy (Alexander Litvinenko) – was meant to inspire a large Western pushback against Russian tolerance warfare. The expulsion of diplomats from many European Union countries, as well as from North America and Australia, was meant to send a strong message that such chemical-weapons use was unacceptable – that the tolerances for Russian behaviour of this kind had been met and that the dismantlement of Russia's external intelligence network would become a key goal of allies and partners. The subsequent identification in September 2018 of the two alleged culprits brought new calls in the UK for the use of 'Unexplained Wealth Orders' to be imposed on Russians who might be laundering money through the UK financial system. Generally, the goal was to hit back at individuals who may have some links to the Putin regime and to demonstrate that persistent tolerance warfare had now shown its limits and that the UK would respond asymmetrically. The year 2018 will be remembered as a turning point: new measures were found by Western states to drain power and capacity away from Putin and his circle, however difficult that might be.

Strategically, the challenge posed by Putin's Russia is that its tolerance-warfare tactics have no obvious rejoinder. Russian cyber operations, information-warfare activities, propaganda warfare and campaigns of misinformation are all potentially deeply destabilising. The targets of such activity need to be careful not to rely only on the tools of the past in dealing with the challenges of the present. The challenge for the West is to manage the way Putin's Russia seeks to insinuate itself in Western domestic life. Russia would prefer that its relations with the US and Europe were again simply regulated by arms control. One Russian strategist has even sought to seduce the West back into that realm by suggesting that both parties should be released from the constraints of the 1987 Intermediate-Range Nuclear Forces Treaty. Arms control remains a strategic garden that needs to be tended, but Russia's information warfare and disruptive tactics within Western societies need at least as much attention and fresh approaches. Disrupting Russia's tolerance-warfare reach will become at least as powerful a strategic objective as has unwinding the networks of terrorists over the last decade and a half. Many of Russia's capacities are developed covertly and deployed deniably. Western countries have to revisit their domestic legal frameworks and determine how they can adapt their laws and their external policies to defeat the opposition. That challenge requires education of domestic populations, new offensive tactics, caution in diplomatic engagement and an appreciation that political and economic inducements to a Russia that appears to take pride in relative isolation are not what they once were. Strengthening the NATO–Russia Council, or offering G8 membership, are no longer carrots that can induce changed behaviour. Life on the outside has its attractions for Putin, and so while Europeans need to calibrate their punishments for malign behaviour soberly, and keep open lines of communication, at present they cannot be optimistic about the prospects for incentivising changed behaviour. Resilience will be the watchword.

In the East, China has also taken up some tolerance-warfare tactics. Its steady encroachments on islands, reefs and features it identifies as its own in the South China Sea has led to widespread criticism and considerable anxiety in the other claimant states who, more modestly, have also been establishing infrastructure on the territories to which they have competing claims. The very assertive effort by China to militarise many of the islands, and their direct or implied military threats to other states who might seek, alone, to explore for natural resources in adjacent waters, has served to intimidate neighbours in the South China Sea and tame their ambitions. The Association of Southeast Asian Nations (ASEAN), the relevant regional organisation, has repeatedly called for a robust Code of Conduct (CoC) – a rules-based order – to govern activity in the region, but no compelling and balanced CoC has yet emerged from the discussions held. ASEAN statements on the matter have regularly been weakened by Chinese influence on some of the member states. The ability of ASEAN to develop and then uphold, in collaboration with

China, mutually agreeable norms to constrain unwelcome activity by claimant states appears to be negligible.

China has grown stronger and justifiably more confident in its international policy. It has gained in one generation what it could not do in ten, and its strategic arrival comes with the added weight of civilisational expectation. It has become a country that throws out hints of a generous global perspective, only to withdraw them in favour of a fierce national impulse. New to the responsibilities of its impending strategic maturity, it is resentful of any who might slight its character, doubt its purpose or challenge its core interests. This approach extends to companies internationally who may not use the approved nomenclature for Taiwan, as much as it would apply to states who do not see every exchange with China as 'win–win' and private scholars who express scepticism on sensitive issues. In this context, China is seeking to exercise more influence on overseas Chinese and extend the frontiers of understanding and consent for its new global role on terms that it thinks right. The patriotic call to national pride is an excellent device by which the Chinese Communist Party can bolster its domestic legitimacy at home so long as it continues so spectacularly to deliver on the economic front. In the last few years, however, state effort to animate overseas Chinese to support the national cause and call on them to champion Chinese perspectives and policies has become persistent. Such influence operations have also inspired legislation to contain it. The government of Australia passed revised laws on foreign financing of politicians and political groups, a decision in part inspired by concern that China was inserting itself in the Australian political process by suborning Australian nationals of Chinese descent and providing funds. It will be important for China to make judgements as to how far it can go in this sphere. There is a risk that excessive Chinese influence operations could disturb the delicately poised domestic balance of multi-ethnic states in Asia. A backlash against minority Chinese populations in ASEAN members is a strategic risk. As China grows, other states in Asia will feel the need to be on guard against these influence operations that may threaten the integrity of internal political processes and social compacts.

The shifting global order

Against this background, there will be a mixture of excitement and fear that continues to accompany China's Belt and Road Initiative (BRI) that formally extends to more than 60 countries in Africa, Asia, Europe and the Middle East, but actually has a near-global scope. It is the largest geo-economic project ever undertaken. The opportunities it offers are potentially vast, and if well executed, the infrastructure it will create will be a huge boon to development and international trade. On the other hand, alarm is also spreading that if poorly planned, especially by recipient states, the BRI could earn the moniker of the greatest 'debt-for-equity swap' in history, and stress more than just the capacity to repay debt. Even in Europe, China has sought special economic relations, as it were, in Eastern Europe; invested in the Greek port of Piraeus and the Belgian port of Zeebrugge; and looked at rare-earth mines in Greenland to support its interests in the High North, an investment proposition that has created tensions between the autonomous administration in Nuuk and the central government in Denmark. Europeans will increasingly find themselves having to regulate the impact of the BRI on their own economic-development model and find ways to ensure that the BRI does not alter standards of fiscal responsibility or infrastructure quality. In Argentina, a Chinese commitment to finance two additional power plants has been postponed by the Macri government to avoid too great a debt burden and facilitate continued IMF support. In every continent, the extent of the BRI is causing governments to think carefully about debt burdens and the political impact of BRI projects domestically. Strategists will have a duty to analyse which countries along the BRI may be vulnerable to having their financed infrastructure projects come under direct Chinese ownership if they are unable to pay, and which countries may suffer if they cannot properly engage with Chinese BRI approaches.

For the moment, China and Russia appear to be offering reserved strategic comfort to each other. They vote similarly at the UN, conduct joint military exercises and preach the desirability of global multi-polarity, even as they themselves each prefer unipolar impulses in their immediate neighbourhoods. But a declining Russia and a rising China are not obvious long-term allies, except in their mutual distaste for the remnants of a Pax Americana world order.

That order is shaky in Asia, uncertain in Europe and fragile in the Middle East. The divisions in the Gulf Cooperation Council (GCC) – which has seen Saudi Arabia and the United Arab Emirates (with Bahrain and Egypt in diplomatic support) isolating Qatar – have only ossified. Iran, Iraq, Turkey and Qatar appear in more regular diplomatic dialogue, a trend that may only create further distrust with the states sanctioning Qatar. The US has been unsuccessful in compelling a reunification of the GCC. Despite this, in May 2018 the US National Security Council began circulating plans for a prospective Middle East Strategic Alliance (MESA) that would initially comprise the six GCC countries along with Jordan, and eventually also Egypt, to which other countries might later subscribe. MESA would have military, diplomatic and trade features. This ambitious proposal was part of the attempt to convene a summit of GCC heads of state to heal the wounds within the organisation, but the vision of regional harmony on which it depended was not shared by the states concerned. In particular, Saudi Arabia and the UAE have pursued daring regional policies, such as standing up to Iran and prosecuting the war in Yemen, that they would not wish to have subject to formal alliance arrangements.

Even if the White House's vision for MESA was more practical in the current environment, Gulf Arab actors are not minded to think in terms of formal regional architecture or to propose their own framework. Saudi Arabia and the UAE, each in its own way, are seeking to shore up support for their national visions: Saudi Arabia is absorbed by its enormous domestic modernisation projects initiated by Crown Prince Mohammed bin Salman, the UAE by fashioning its own extra-regional diplomacy. While China has extended the BRI to Africa, some Gulf countries have also sought to gain footholds in different adjacent maritime spaces. The UAE has invested in ports in Djibouti and Somaliland, and the competing interests of Turkey and Qatar in the Horn of Africa, as well as the goals of China, have made port investments part of the political competition within the Horn and between other Middle East actors operating there. Proxy conflict in the Middle East has long been part of the strategic scene and persists in the Syrian tragedy. Now, even as Ethiopia and Eritrea have reconciled, international competition has returned with vigour to the Horn of Africa.

In the midst of all this hectic strategic activity, Western politicians have come to lament the passing of the rules-based order. It is clear that they would prefer that Russia be constrained by Europe's own recently established customs of post-modern domestic and inter-governmental relations; that China accept the principles of international law in Asia; and that Middle East states prosecute their regional policies with less absolutist aims. Yet in the West, too, there has been a disturbing return to simplistic and crude foreign-policy choices that run counter to established rules and norms, not least in the Trump administration's trade war with China; its decision to abandon the Iran nuclear deal without the support of allies or having identified a superior alternative; the closing of the Palestine Liberation Organization (PLO) embassy in Washington; the casual approach to NATO and other alliance relations; and the general 'shock and awe' style of diplomatic engagement that the president appears to favour.

A criticism was recently levelled against former US president Barack Obama to the effect that he 'was better at explaining the meaning of democracy than he was defending it against its opponents'. That may have been both an unkind and an unjust rebuke, but its framing suggests a warning to all who speak about the rules-based order. It is feckless to repeat the importance of maintaining a rules-based order without being inventive and determined in sustaining it against its opponents or usurpers. That effort cannot be borne by the US alone.

In Europe, the challenge for Germany and its EU partners is to identify ways in which Russian and Chinese policies may chip away at democratic and liberal values. Interference in domestic politics; influence operations and geo-economic projects with neo-colonial geostrategic aims; unilateral actions under the guise of creating multi-polarity: these are the features of Russian and Chinese policy that need to be dealt with and on which Europeans need to be in constant dialogue with the US and its other partners. The Brexit negotiations could fail to lead to a new financial, diplomatic and security partnership between the UK and the EU, a failure that would weaken both parties. There is no meaningful European strategic or defence autonomy without the UK's expeditionary military power, and the UK has a less credible claim to global influence if it is unable to play a leadership role with willing partners on the European continent. Within NATO, the challenge is not only to boost the credibility of Article 5 commitments and those on deterrence and defence, but also to arrive at a determined strategy on how to deal with threats below armed aggression, the so-called Article 4 contingencies, at which Russia is becoming adept. In Asia, Australia has taken brave positions on Asian security matters but it lacks company. ASEAN's claims to 'centrality' within the regional-security architecture will require it to break free of lowest-common-denominator positions in foreign policy. In South America, regional states have engaged in much talk but little action concerning the centrally planned suicide of Venezuela, which has caused such misery and a huge outflow of refugees. Efforts in autumn 2018 to refer Caracas to the International Criminal Court may perhaps portend an overdue change. Regional institutions similarly have borne witness, but not acted, as President Daniel Ortega's regime in Nicaragua faced ever more dramatic protests.

There are, in short, many examples of institutions and diplomatic practices being hollowed out from within, ignored with impunity or left unmodernised. Until these trends are reversed, and foreign policy in various regions can safely be channelled again through multilateral institutions, the mitigation of conflict and maintenance of regional orders will depend on responsible national statecraft.

Good statecraft will be in high demand as the next two years will see the denouement of a number of important strategic plays that had fitful starts or surprising intervals this year. In Asia, the Republic of Korea is pursuing détente with the North at a pace that seems unmatched by the Democratic People's Republic of Korea's (DPRK) steps towards complete and irreversible disarmament. There will soon come a point when diplomatic entreaty will appear insufficiently reciprocated, yet reviving a 'maximum pressure' campaign will be immensely difficult. The DPRK appears to have concluded that the US will not take umbrage at what it cannot see, so Pyongyang has stopped nuclear and missile tests in favour of a stealthier approach. If those tests are revived, or if the US becomes frustrated with Chairman Kim Jong-un's delaying tactics, then the risks of conflict return. In the Gulf, Iran is continuing its version of tolerance warfare in Iraq, Syria, Yemen and elsewhere, testing the limits of its extraterritorial influence. The military conflicts in Syria and Yemen continue to provide the main theatres for overt proxy warfare. Diplomatic resolutions to these two conflicts will be huge agenda items for 2019. Yet even if some stability and political process returns to these two countries, containing Iran's regional policies will continue to shape the strategic priorities of Saudi Arabia and the UAE. Should Iran choose to withdraw its compliance with the terms of the nuclear deal that the US exited, the tensions in the Middle East will rise hugely. Europe, China and Russia will all need to weigh in more diplomatically and the US will carry large responsibilities to keep the region from boiling over.

The simmering trade war between the US and China perhaps creates the most consequential geopolitical and geo-economic flashpoint for the medium term. The US has legitimate concerns about what it styles as China's 'predatory trade' practices that the World Trade Organisation, with its existing rules and institutions, is poorly suited to tackling. US President Donald Trump's dramatic imposition of tariffs on China is a frontal attack and direct challenge to China to accept a US definition of a fair trading order. The risk is that China's attention span in this domain may be longer than that of the US, and that the need to 'keep face' will make escalation more probable than compromise. An extensive trade conflict between the US and China is an immensely troubling propect and would constitute another deep wound for the already struggling forces of globalisation. The multilateral trading system, after all, is a rules-based platform on which the majority of international relations is conducted. It is here that statecraft will be most in demand. For the rest of the world, it matters little if that responsible statecraft comes first from the US or from China.

Chapter 3

Strategic Policy Issues

Is There a Liberal International Order?

The term 'liberal international order' is being anxiously invoked by politicians from the United States and Europe who are desperate to sustain that order. But it is unclear what they actually mean – beyond the status quo that seems perilously tentative at present – by the liberal international order.

Political scientists have gleefully leapt into the debate over whether there is an order, whether it is liberal and whether it is international. Staunch realists such as John Mearsheimer, Patrick Porter and Paul Staniland argue that the order enforced by the US after 1945 is neither liberal, international nor an order. There is considerable truth to the challenge. After 70 years of American dominance, legitimate questions are being raised about US support for ruthless dictatorships, long-standing tariffs to protect US markets and producers, whole swathes of the globe to which the US remained indifferent and the frequency of violent crises that have been destructive to millions of people. At best, the US has been an inconsistent trumpeter of the Pax Americana.

Advocates of the order vary widely in their descriptions of it as well. Daniel Deudney and G. John Ikenberry – the most ardent defenders of liberal internationalism – describe the order simply as 'nation-states cooperating to achieve security and prosperity'. Michael Mazarr terms the current system a 'US-led, rules-based order', while Hal Brands considers the liberal order to include 'representative government and human rights; and other liberal concepts, such as nonaggression, self-determination, and the peaceful settlement of disputes'.

The reason political language is so messy and the academic arguments are so vehement is that the liberal international order has been used as a shorthand for three separate but related phenomena: the creation of a rules-based order enshrined in institutions; the establishment of alliance relationships with the US as security guarantor; and the propagation of liberal values. The US has championed all three of these elements and often considered them inseparable. However, each of these three elements – the rules-based order, the security order and the liberal order – has its own history, purpose and remit, which has often led to tensions. In other words, the liberal international order is not a monolithic ideology, but a complex system of interlocking (and sometimes clashing) mechanisms and motivations.

The rules-based order

At its most fundamental, the post-1945 international order is a set of agreed rules of behaviour, principally non-interference in the internal affairs of other states, outlawing the use of force other than for self-defence, delineating where territorial and economic rights extend and establishing means for peacefully resolving conflicts.

Institutions were created in 1943–44 to consult on the rules and mediate disputes, to foster prosperity and to ensure powerful states complied with the rules. The basic institutions were the United Nations and the international financial institutions of the Bretton Woods agreements (the IMF and the World Bank). We have lived so long with the order that we forget how remarkable an achievement it is that, at present, 193 of the 195 countries in the world are members of the UN (only the Vatican and Palestine remain outside it), and all the world's countries except those and Andorra, Cuba, Liechtenstein, Monaco and North Korea participate in the Bretton Woods institutions. Powerful countries may – and do –

ignore UN edicts, but doing so drives up the cost of their actions, which is itself a valuable element of the rules-based order. Linkages of mutual prosperity reinforce incentives for the peaceful resolution of disputes. Economic webbing was thickened in 1995 with the creation of the World Trade Organisation (WTO), in which 164 countries negotiate and adjudicate terms of trade.

This is the rules-based order. The US brought the order into being and has been its largest contributor, guarantor and stabiliser of last resort.

It was, however, interests rather than values that drove the US to construct an international order of rules and institutions after the Second World War. American interest in constructing an order of rules enshrined in institutions predates the Cold War; its early traces can be seen in Woodrow Wilson's 'Fourteen Points' and in the International Court of Arbitration established in 1923. However, the rules-based order took practical form only after the bitter losses of the Second World War. Just as Roosevelt had no compunction about making common cause with Stalin to defeat Hitler, the US curtailed opportunities to advance its values in order to gain voluntary adherence by adversarial states to rules of interaction.

US policymakers sought to institute the rules-based order after 1945 out of fear – the men who had fought Nazi Germany and Imperial Japan rued the sacrifices that had been necessary to achieve victory and were determined to establish patterns of state interaction that were conducive to the peaceful settlement of disputes and increasing prosperity. They were not so in thrall to their philosophy that they failed to see that authoritarian states could become rich and powerful; they became architects in order to forestall a repetition of their experience. They built institutions and cultivated norms not because they could not imagine successful authoritarian states imposing unbearable rules on the less powerful, but precisely because they could.

Other states have extended the reach of rules-based institutions even further. The European Union has woven together 28 countries into a common legal, regulatory and market space. A subset of EU states adopted a common currency and allowed free movement within their borders. Elsewhere, large numbers of states have come together to create global institutions and agreements: 168 countries have ratified the United Nations Convention on the Law of the Sea; 123 have acceded to the formation of the International Criminal Court; and 195 countries adopted the Paris climate agreement in 2016. Non-governmental organisations have become powerful forces in the creation of international conventions, taking both convening power and norm creation from the exclusive control of states.

The security order

After the establishment of the institutions that would constitute the rules-based order, the US quickly entered into alliance relationships to prevent insecurity spiralling into conflict. These alliances, too, germinated from the necessity of interest in the aftermath of the Second World War: the US was occupying both Germany and Japan, and the dimensions of Soviet threats were becoming clearer. While the rules-based order preceded the Cold War, alliance relationships were integral to it.

The North Atlantic Treaty Organisation of 1949 was the first Western security umbrella, bringing the countries of Western Europe into collective defence commitments. US security guarantees were the basic building block, contingent on cooperation between recipient states. The US bias toward cooperative security enabled the rehabilitation of Germany and (mostly) Japan among their neighbours. It also introduced predictability, transparency and an external mediator for disputes, all of which combined to produce stability among the participants and deter attacks from adversaries.

Similar security arrangements were envisioned for other geographic regions, but other countries could not be cajoled into cooperation – either with each other or with the US – as the Europeans were. To this day, the United States' alliance relations in Asia remain a geometry of hub and spokes, not by American design but as a result of regional unwillingness for any different arrangement. Nor could US voters be persuaded to undertake commitments to a broad expanse of countries whose political and social practices seemed remote from America's own.

As the first possessor of nuclear weapons, American security guarantees stabilised the post-1945 order against the magnitude of Soviet conventional forces, and allowed US allies to reduce defence spending and reconstruct their economies and societies. Managing proliferation has remained a central US responsibility both within its alliance relationships and outside them. There, too, the US has relied on a rules-based institutional solution, negotiating the Non-Proliferation Treaty and establishing the International Atomic Energy Agency, which the US supports with financing and expertise.

With the end of the Cold War, the US and its NATO allies extended membership to countries formerly of the Warsaw Pact and even to countries that emerged from the collapse of the Soviet Union. NATO's expansion fundamentally redrew the security map of Europe, shifting Germany from a front-line state to one comfortably protected behind the territory of others, while Russia was relegated from the centre of Europe to its margin. The transatlantic relationship was, and is, the geographic centre of the liberal international order, not only because the security order was thickest and most institutionalised in Europe, but also because European countries have the greatest overlap of shared values with the US.

Security gets tangled up in the academic debate over primacy, which is the aspiration for dominant power. Since the end of the Second World War, the US has had both the security of nuclear retaliation and a broad conventional military capability. It has also had a public willing to support more defence spending than its competitors, resulting in the US amassing a significant set of military advantages. Since the end of the Cold War, the US has had military superiority over any potential adversary or combination of adversaries.

As challengers rise and US technological and operational military advantages erode, preserving its security ought to reinforce the value of allies' participation. They share the burden of common defence, allow the US to station and flow forces through their territory and give US policies a bias in favour not just of support but also of participation. Former chairman of the Joint Chiefs of Staff Admiral Michael Mullen is fond of talking about America's thousand-ship navy, because allies add so significantly to US numbers. One of the curiosities of the administration of US President Donald Trump is how indifferent the leader of the free world is to the value allies bring to US efforts to preserve and advance its own security.

The liberal order

Hegemons recreate the international order in their domestic political image. For the US, this meant prejudicing the order in favour of its domestic political philosophy, namely that people have rights and that they loan these rights to governments in limited ways for consensual purposes. The philosophy is the extension of America's domestic political creed: a belief that the truths Americans hold to be self-evident domestically are universal – that a mother of five in the Pakistani Federally Administered Tribal Areas wants the same things her American counterpart wants. At a minimum, that entails personal safety, freedom of conscience and expression, the ability to determine her form of government and to engage in commerce.

Whether to foster those ideals in US foreign policy has been a roiling debate since the country's inception, when Thomas Jefferson favoured giving assistance to France's revolutionaries because of shared values, while George Washington and John Adams believed that US interests could not withstand the political and economic consequences of indulging such a luxury. Up until the end of the Cold War, conflicts between protecting American interests and advancing American values were generally resolved in favour of interests.

With the end of the Cold War, the US and its allies finally had the luxury to make choices that propagated their values, seemingly unconstrained by their interests. NATO expanded to incorporate new members, arguing over and above Russian objections to insist that states had a sovereign right to choose their allegiances, and democratic states had particular affinity for each other. However, cracks quickly began to appear in the coherence of the post-1991 liberal international order when the US found that its values-driven foreign policy was often unsupported by the institutions it had helped create, a process that was accelerated by the impact of 9/11. NATO allies intervened without a UN Security Council resolution to protect Kosovo's ethnic Albanian majority from Serbia in 1999. The US assembled a 'coalition of the willing' to intervene in Iraq without a UN Security Council resolution in 2003. NATO exceeded its UN Security Council mandate in Libya in 2011, embittering both Russia and China. In all these instances, advancing 'Western values' as universal rights has been a central component of the argument for using force to surmount the post-1945 rules.

If security choices driven by liberal values were seen by illiberal states as prejudiced against them, economic liberalism favoured at least some. Russia could muscle its way into European energy markets, while Russian oligarchs could secret their money out of the country and into property in the US and Europe. Most spectacularly, China benefited from being brought into the WTO in 2001 without having to meet the rules its competitors were constrained by. Western states believed inclusion in the liberal political, economic and security order would create convergence in ideals, prosperity and policies across the world.

The idea originates with the German philosopher Georg Hegel, who argued that good things go together and that as basic needs are met people become more demanding political consumers. The theory was applied to the end of the Cold War by Francis Fukuyama in his 1992 book *The End of History and the Last Man*, wherein ennui would be the great problem of the last man because political and economic liberalism would not only produce prosperity, but also ensure the satisfactory distribution of resources in free societies. The magnetism of prosperity (assumed to be exclusive to economic liberalism) would pull all governments toward political liberalism.

Policies designed to advance Western values have not succeeded in Russia or China, and are struggling against cultural and political backlash even in some countries added to the Western fold since the end of the Cold War. The economic success of authoritarian governments adopting some free-market practices is a bracing challenge for the West, calling into question the inevitability of history bending its arc toward their values. But values-led policies are now deeply entrenched in the policymaking apparatuses of the US and its major allies in Europe and beyond; wrenching back toward interest-driven policies even in security will require major efforts by governments of the West.

Even in the post-Cold War penumbra of Western dominance, values have been unevenly applied – never pressed consistently on friendly countries such as Saudi Arabia, Indonesia or Turkey, ignored in places of little strategic significance, clumsily advanced in Mexico, and covertly advanced by overthrowing legitimate governments in Chile and Iran.

The inconsistencies and failures resulted from not taking opportunities when they presented themselves; writing off engagements that became too costly or politically unsupportable; making compromises when values and interests came into conflict; accepting the obduracy of opposition by countries across some policy portfolios coupled with cooperation on others; and policy bungles, hubris, ignorance and even malevolence.

As Porter argues, ideas about liberal internationalism have been pervasive among Americans working in national security since 1945. But those same ideas are also pervasive among countries with the power to impede US interests. States that realists predict would work to counteract US designs mostly do not. That is the material advantage of its political philosophy: US power is more palatable to other countries, which has reduced challenges to the US-led order.

The other material result of its political philosophy, as Tom Wright argues, is that adversaries rightly believe regime change is the ultimate purpose of American policy. China, Iran, North Korea and Russia cannot believe palliative assurances to the contrary because the values that drive US and Western policy are ultimately incompatible with authoritarian governance.

Liberalism may also be moving beyond the provenance of the nation-state – that is, becoming self-propagating in the West. Despite the Trump administration's withdrawal from the Paris climate agreement in 2017, UN Secretary-General António Guterres announced in March 2018 that the US was still on track to meet its agreement commitments. This achievement was driven by US states, cities, businesses and individuals working in tandem toward the goal of reducing emissions despite overt hostility by the federal government.

Non-state action is more difficult in the security realm because states mostly retain the monopoly on use of inter-state violence. But even there, civil activism forced most Western governments' hands to support a ban on anti-personnel landmines. Responsive governance in the West may prove an asymmetric disadvantage in security, as technology advances into artificial intelligence, since illiberal states can make choices that provide first-mover advantages or speed to the detriment of societies where consent of the governed is required. Yet public concern about environmental degradation or safe food and medicine supplies may prove an effective tool for advancing liberalism in repressive societies.

Challengers to the order

Russia, China and the US all pose different kinds of challenges to the existing order. Russia rejects the liberal order, the security order in Europe and aspects of the rules-based order. It seeks to re-establish the 1945 UN Charter of non-interference in state sovereignty, but uses military force to impose or uphold its preferred governments and suborns the domestic politics of others.

Like Russia, China rejects the liberal order, the security order in Asia and aspects of the rules-based order. It is in some cases subtler – building islands in disputed areas rather than invading neighbours outright – and has the great advantage of money to create illiberal alternatives. China has created new institutions, such as the Asian Infrastructure Investment Bank, and is creating potential vehicles for greater economic cooperation with the Belt and Road Initiative (BRI). The BRI may prove to be a gigantic debt-for-equity swap, with China repossessing valuable infrastructure, but participation is voluntary and the prospect of abundant credit for distressed borrowers has proven difficult to resist.

The US may be the biggest threat of all to the existing order. The US under Trump's leadership is doing more damage to the international order than America's enemies. It rejects the liberal order, verges on repudiating the security order and disregards the rules-based order. While American governments have previously had fractious disagreements with allies, every president before Trump seems to have believed in the fundamental elements of the order. Trump appears to believe the order is a scam perpetrated on the US, rather than a system instituted by the US for the perpetuation of peace and security on American terms.

Yet while the United States' many failures besmirch the record, they do not negate it. In the time of its primacy, the US consciously constructed a set of institutions, alliances, economic interconnectedness and norms of state behaviour that constitute not just a world view, but an inter-state system built on the foundations of that world view.

The US in the time of its primacy *has* behaved differently than other great powers in important ways. It voluntarily constrained its power through consensual institutions that gave less powerful states the ability to influence the rules and US choices. It gave those institutions some autonomy by propagating values and norms of behaviour to which the US mostly adhered. It provided security guarantees to countries that could not fully defend themselves. It encouraged its allies to adopt cooperative and integrated practices that became norms. It enforced the peaceful resolution of disputes and fought wars to advance not just its interests but also its political philosophy. It showcased the vitality of free markets in producing prosperity and advanced trade to mutual benefit. In short, the US shaped the international order after 1945 to a large extent in its image.

The most parsimonious proof that there is a liberal international order is the anxiety with which its beneficiaries worry about its disappearance. The United States' closest allies in Europe, North America and Asia are the most fraught at the prospect of sustaining the order without American leadership, or even perhaps against American opposition. Should the liberal international order disappear, the advantages it has brought much of the world may quickly follow.

The Impact of the ICT Revolution on International Relations

The development of information and communications technologies (ICTs) over the past 20 years has served as a powerful catalyst and accelerant for change in the distribution of power in the international system, as well as the ways in which that power can be used. Domination of ICTs and related technologies is increasingly determining where power lies, for technological capability and economic prowess appear to be inextricably linked. The emergence of cyberspace has added new terrain to a struggle between Western states and others over matters of global governance and the appropriate balance between individual freedom and state control. It has presented a challenge to states, in that their monopoly on some types of information has been eroded in favour of individuals and non-state actors. Yet states have also benefited from vastly increased opportunities for intelligence collection and the (deniable) subversion of rival states, as well as (in the case of authoritarian states) much greater capabilities to exercise social control over their own populations. The ICT revolution is also disrupting military affairs in ways that seem likely to reduce human agency in conflict and to blunt some of the advantages on which Western militaries have depended since the end of the Cold War.

Technology and state power

The development of ICTs has become a driver of economic growth and productivity among states. It is also accelerating the redistribution of economic power in favour of non-Western states. For the West, this transition is proving difficult to appreciate or accept. On the one hand, the speed with which it is taking place, especially in relation to China, has come as a surprise. On the other hand, for many in the West who are not directly affected by the immediate consequences (such as the loss of manufacturing jobs due to automation and other ICT-driven processes), this period probably feels more like the 'extended present' described in Albert Einstein's Special Theory of Relativity: a sense of being in an intermediate state between past and future where nothing is changing. This may explain why some Western policymakers appear still to be in denial about what is taking place as evidenced by a lack of discernible strategies for addressing this challenge.

The United States, which is confronting a future in which it can no longer be assured of global economic, scientific, technological and military supremacy, appears to be somewhere between denial and anger, as evidenced by its attempts – belated and of dubious effectiveness – to constrain China's technical development by excluding Chinese corporations from US markets and imposing limits on Chinese purchases of US technology companies, in what has come to be termed a 'new cold war'. The new situation is unlikely to prove a zero-sum game: developed economies may well find that possessing strong institutions, educational systems that privilege independent thought and creativity and cultures of scientific and technical excellence still confer advantages. However, the reality remains that power is being both transferred and redistributed around the planet with consequences that are hard to predict.

The key factors in the ICT revolution have been speed and cost. Previously, information had been a scarce and valuable commodity that conferred power on those who possessed it. Information has now become cheap and ubiquitous in ways that have challenged traditional power elites while empowering a growing range of actors. Since the 1970s, computing power has increased exponentially while costs have undergone a commensurate reduction. The cost of communications, now almost entirely ICT-enabled, has fallen more than one thousand fold since the 1970s. As Joseph Nye has observed, if something similar had happened in the automotive sector, the cost of a car today would be US$5.

In the economic sphere, one of the most significant consequences of the ICT revolution has been a dramatic reduction in the 'flash-to-bang time' between the emergence of a new idea and its commoditisation. Whereas in the Industrial Age such commoditisation often involved long and costly periods of trial and error, new ideas can now be quickly commercialised using sophisticated design and manufacturing capabilities that are highly automated and reliable.

As Willy Shih of the Harvard Business School has observed, 'young competitors can skip years of practice and experience-building and become competitive threats [to developed economies] almost instantly … [this approach] turns science into simply a matter of following a recipe. The tools make the process repeatable and take out the variability and risk.'

It was always to be expected that at some point Asian countries would become more globally preponderant once they had emerged from the shadow of Western imperialism and had abandoned ideologically driven policies that frustrated economic development, but the evolution of ICT has dramatically sped up that process. The Chinese leadership's appreciation dating from the early 1980s of the importance of ICTs for China's economic development was such that its development had to be pushed forward despite the risks of giving citizens access to information that challenged the Communist Party narrative.

ICTs have been especially prominent in China's effort to transition from an export-led growth model to one based on domestic consumption. The rapid expansion of China's digital economy over the past decade is helping to expedite the realisation of this challenging objective. E-commerce in China accounted for 0.6% of total global transactions in 2005; by 2016, its share had grown to 42%, greater than that of the US, Japan, France, Germany and the United Kingdom combined. The value of Chinese mobile payments in 2016 was US$9 trillion compared to US mobile payments of US$112 billion, and China is quickly transitioning towards becoming a cashless society. China's ICT champions – Baidu, Alibaba and Tencent (collectively known as BAT) – are rapidly catching up with their US competitors in terms of market valuation.

China's immediate objective is to reduce its dependence on US technology within its ICT sector, a vulnerability highlighted by the case of the Chinese telecoms company ZTE. In 2016, the US government sought to punish ZTE for having undertaken business activities in Iran and North Korea in breach of international sanctions. In 2017, ZTE agreed to pay a fine of US$1.2bn and punish some of its executives, but failed to do so. In response, the US imposed a seven-year ban on ZTE in April

2018 that denied the company access to US-produced microchips. As China is unable to produce microchips itself, this amounted to a death sentence for the company and seemed to constitute a significant point of leverage in the United States' emerging trade dispute with China. But in response to a direct intercession by Chinese President Xi Jinping, US President Donald Trump relented, opting instead for a solution that involved accepting a team of US compliance officers. This episode will only have reinforced China's conviction that continued reliance on foreign hardware and software represents a strategic vulnerability that must be overcome at all costs.

Looking to the longer term, China has begun to resource and implement an ambitious strategy to become the world leader and technical standard-setter for the next generations of technology, including 5G mobile communications, artificial intelligence (AI), the Internet of Things, quantum encryption and computing, robotics, nanotechnology, biomedicine and space exploration. These ambitions are couched within an unabashedly state-corporatist approach to economic development. In effect, China's ambitions have set the stage for a race with the US that will shape the geostrategic landscape for the twenty-first century, a race which will have economic, ideological, military and technical components.

ICT and statecraft

ICTs are shaping all aspects of statecraft, including diplomacy, intelligence and the use of force. Advances in ICT and the digitisation of information have made more pervasive intelligence collection possible, and by a wider range of actors. There is much more intelligence to collect in the form of large data volumes that are stored in inherently insecure databases, while social-media content serves as a repository of hitherto unobtainable personal information about potential intelligence targets. Major powers retain a significant advantage, but any state with a telecommunications agency potentially has the capacity to develop the kind of signals intelligence – SIGINT– collection capability that previously only major powers could have possessed. China is a prime example of a state whose foreign-intelligence capabilities have been dramatically transformed over the past 20 years through the use of cyber espionage for both commercial and statecraft purposes. Many states in Africa, Asia and Latin America are using greatly enhanced collection capabilities to monitor or suppress dissent among their own populations more effectively, while criminal groups use similar capabilities to frustrate the efforts of law enforcement. Meanwhile, North Korea has utilised its substantial cyber capabilities both to attack adversaries and to raise revenue through cyber criminality, a case in point being the theft of US$81 million from the central bank of Bangladesh in 2016.

The fact that levels of espionage have become so pervasive has arguably created a new and unprecedented set of circumstances. It has often been observed that when it comes to digital networks, the distinction between espionage and sabotage can be determined only by intent. This is not strictly true, given that any digital exploit that has sabotage as its purpose will necessarily have a specific sabotage component. Alternatively, exploits that are, for example, found on the networks of electricity grids or nuclear power plants and which appear to have only intelligence-gathering functions may well be intended as a prelude to sabotage activities. There will always be the fear that any exploit discovered – and average discovery time can range from 146 days in the US to more than 400 days in the EU – may have a sabotage component too sophisticated to be easily identified. States are increasingly using their intelligence capabilities (in the form of both state agencies and non-state proxies) to probe the networks of adversaries for vulnerabilities that can be activated in times of tension or conflict, with the aim of disabling that society's ability to function. Such exploits may also have a signalling function, designed to discourage states from taking hostile action for fear of a damaging response.

This presents a challenge for policymakers both in states that engage in cyber espionage and in those which are a target of such activities. The picture is further clouded by the risk of unintended consequences, as exemplified in 2017 when NotPetya, a particularly virulent ransomware virus directed primarily against Ukrainian government agencies,

China Takes the Lead in Technology

According to some measures, China appears to have assumed a position at the forefront of innovation, having surpassed both the United States and the European Union in total number of patent applications. Research and development (R&D) spending has also risen, along with gross national income. The US remains the highest spender in R&D, but has found itself in growing competition with China over the past few years, which is quickly closing the gap in R&D spending – the backbone of innovation.

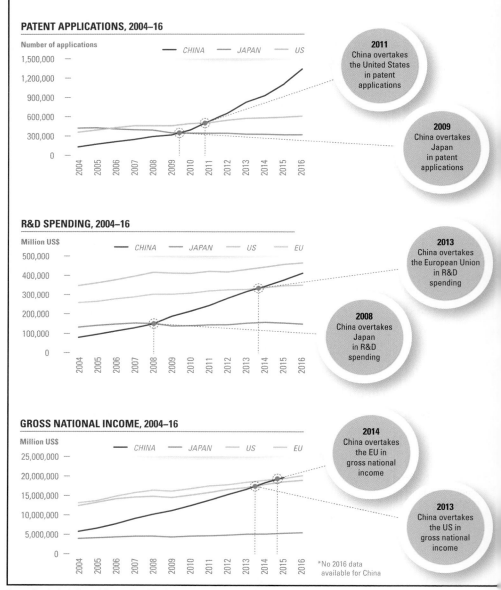

PATENT APPLICATIONS, 2004–16

Number of applications

CHINA — JAPAN — US

2011
China overtakes the United States in patent applications

2009
China overtakes Japan in patent applications

R&D SPENDING, 2004–16

Million US$

CHINA — JAPAN — US — EU

2013
China overtakes the European Union in R&D spending

2008
China overtakes Japan in R&D spending

GROSS NATIONAL INCOME, 2004–16

Million US$

CHINA — JAPAN — US — EU

2014
China overtakes the EU in gross national income

2013
China overtakes the US in gross national income

*No 2016 data available for China

Sources: Organisation for Economic Co-operation and Development, World Integrated Trade Solution, World Intellectual Property Organization

CHINA, MASTER OF PATENTS:

China's total number of patent applications in 2016 represents more than the US, Japan, Republic of Korea and the European Patent Office combined (42.8% of total applications worldwide).

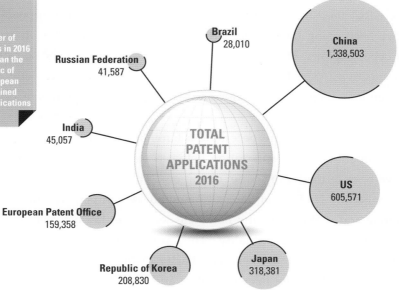

TOTAL PATENT APPLICATIONS 2016

Brazil
28,010

Russian Federation
41,587

China
1,338,503

India
45,057

US
605,571

European Patent Office
159,358

Republic of Korea
208,830

Japan
318,381

CHINA IS THE LEADING COUNTRY IN TERMS OF HIGH-TECHNOLOGY EXPORTS IN THE WORLD:

In 2016, Chinese high-tech exports were three times higher than those of the US in current US dollars. In descending order, the top five high-tech exporters in 2016 were: China, Germany, US, Singapore and the Republic of Korea. High-tech exports are products with high R&D intensity, such as computers, aerospace materials and equipment, scientific instruments, electrical machinery and pharmaceuticals.

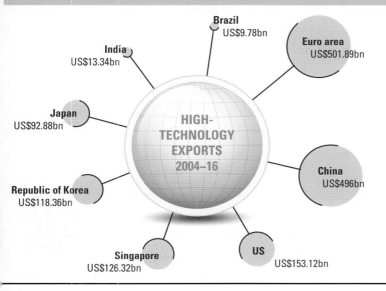

HIGH-TECHNOLOGY EXPORTS 2004–16

Brazil
US$9.78bn

India
US$13.34bn

Euro area
US$501.89bn

Japan
US$92.88bn

China
US$496bn

Republic of Korea
US$118.36bn

Singapore
US$126.32bn

US
US$153.12bn

spread widely throughout Australia, Europe, Russia and the US, causing billions of dollars in damage. The CIA attributed the virus to the GRU, the Russian military-intelligence agency, which appears to have been using the conflict with Ukraine as a test bed for an array of cyber exploits. The impact of such exploits highlights the so-called 'connectivity paradox', whereby the most advanced and network-dependent states are also those most vulnerable to significant cyber disruptions.

Such disruptions are becoming a familiar part of a new approach to competition and contestation between states in the form of what have been termed 'grey-zone' operations. These operations have been described by US Special Forces Command as 'competitive interaction among and within state and non-state actors that fall between the traditional war and peace duality'. They are characterised by ambiguity about the nature of the conflict, opacity of the parties involved and uncertainty about the relevant policy and legal frameworks. There is nothing intrinsically new about such operations, but ICTs have enormously facilitated them by enabling actors to undertake (at low cost and with a degree of deniability) a range of activities that cause damage without rising to a level that would easily justify a kinetic response. An example of this kind of operation is the attacks by entities acting on behalf of the Iranian state between 2011 and 2013 against the US banking and financial system undertaken in response to US sanctions related to the Iranian nuclear programme. The effect of such attacks, conducted by private actors operating under state direction, was made worse by the fact that those on the receiving end – not appreciating the subtle signalling coming from Iran and lacking any geostrategic context – undertook unauthorised 'hack-back' operations which increased the risks of escalation.

A more eye-catching example is the alleged Russian interference in the 2016 US presidential election, which centred on the skilful exploitation of social media. Russians purporting to be US citizens opened large numbers of fake social-media accounts, predominantly on Facebook and Twitter. These accounts were used to put out messages focusing on divisive social issues which were then amplified by bots (software applications that perform simple repetitive tasks at a much higher rate than humans can). This created the impression of a trending national debate on particular issues that could include anything from immigration and race relations to the behaviours of individual candidates, which US politicians then felt compelled to address and the traditional media to cover, thereby creating yet further amplification. According to Facebook, as many as 126m Americans were likely to have seen messages posted, as well as advertisements bought by this and other Russian troll factories. Days before the election took place, Russian hackers also attempted to breach US voting systems by sending malware-infected emails to the computers of state-election officials.

The aims of this Russian campaign evolved from an initial intention to discredit presidential candidate Hillary Clinton and generate distrust in the US political process to promoting the candidacy of Donald Trump as the person most likely to ease sanctions on Russia. This approach exemplifies the Russian concept of reflexive control, defined by Colonel Timothy Thomas as 'a means of conveying to a partner or an opponent specially prepared information to incline him voluntarily to make the predetermined decision desired by the initiator of the action'. In effect it enabled Russia, a reduced and limited power compared to its Soviet predecessor, to inflict significant damage on the integrity of the US democratic process at minimal cost through the digital exploitation of existing fissures in US society. Even though the US government was well aware of what was taking place and who was responsible, its ability to respond to such behaviour in a timely manner or effectively sanction it was limited.

Though China has not yet sought to emulate the kind of information operations practised by Russia, it too has used ICTs to extend its influence in a variety of ways and to shape the global environment along lines that are favourable to Chinese interests. In the diplomatic arena, China has taken the lead in advocating the concept of cyber sovereignty and the need for new forms of global governance of the cyber domain. China seeks to replace the existing multi-stakeholder governance model that evolved organically with the growth of the internet with a 'multilateral' model that gives a predominant role to national governments. Such arguments tend to resonate with states in the developing world, and China's approach has now extended to arguing that the entire global governance system established in the wake of the Second World War needs to be reformed to take account of the interests of states not represented, or even in existence, when the current model was established.

For China, ideology is a key driver for its efforts to reshape the global governance agenda: the need for explicit international acceptance of its political model as having equal validity with liberal democracy, and the need to be able to take action beyond China's own borders to defend against ideological attack. This involves both the monitoring and harassment of political opponents and dissidents and requiring foreign states and businesses to conform to China's public narrative, the latter point exemplified by the pressure put on foreign airlines to categorise Taiwan, Hong Kong and Macao as Chinese territory in their schedules and promotional literature. It also involves promoting China's 'discourse power' (*huayuquan*), namely its ability to promote its own narrative. China's growing digital presence around the world has been pressed into service for this purpose. In the words of the now-disgraced former head of the Cyberspace Administration of China Lu Wei, 'collection power decides communication power, communication power decides influence and influence decides soft power'.

The Information Age has witnessed a resurrection of ideology – not just China's version of Marxism, but also Islamism and right-wing ideologies – and increasing competition between narratives. Extremist groups such as the Islamic State, also known as ISIS or ISIL, have made effective use of social media to spread their ideology, and the question of whether service providers such as Facebook and YouTube are adequately policing their networks to eliminate such content has become a contentious issue of public policy. Western liberal democracies have struggled to engage in this ideological contention and have thus far failed to come up with convincing counter-narratives.

ICT and military power

Within the continuum of power projection, armed force still exercises a decisive role. As in other arenas, ICTs are shaping both the kinds of weaponry deployed by armed forces and the ways in which those weapons are used. ICTs and related technologies such as AI have enabled the development of a growing range of precision-guided conventionally armed weapons that can be deployed in an environment that offers an unprecedentedly granular view of the battlespace. At the same time, air-defence systems that are ICT-enabled (and increasingly AI-dependent) have become more sophisticated and more widely available, with the result that for the first time in many decades the air supremacy of the US and its allies can no longer be taken for granted.

The use of autonomous systems has become widespread to the point where even non-state groups are able to deploy them, albeit still in a relatively unsophisticated form. Experiments with the use of drone swarms to overwhelm defensive systems may in due course negate, or at least substantially alter, the utility of long-established capabilities such as the carrier battlegroup. Faced with a battlespace environment that is ever more data-rich, armed forces are having to look increasingly towards reliance on autonomous decision-making systems, which are, however, vulnerable to disruption and deception and raise difficult ethical issues. They are also having to prepare to fight in a digitally depleted environment amid the expectation that in advance of or during an actual conflict, the adversary will attempt to damage and degrade the ICT systems on which so many modern military capabilities depend. It is currently far from evident that the most digitally dependent militaries will in fact be able to function effectively in such an environment.

For the foreseeable future, the global geostrategic landscape seems set to be dominated by a growing competition and contestation between the US and China, with other states having to navigate an increasingly complex path between the two and, where possible, find common cause among themselves. This is not merely a competition between the incumbent and rising powers but also a competition between competing ideologies: liberal democracy versus authoritarianism; open markets versus state corporatism; and rules-based order versus unconstrained self-interest. It is a struggle that will be waged on many fronts, but mastery of ICTs and related technologies will play a major role in determining the outcome.

Winners and Losers from Higher Oil Prices

Oil prices have increased on average by more than 30% since the beginning of 2018. Tighter demand and supply conditions and heightened geopolitical risks saw average Brent prices rise by 53.1% in July 2018 to US$74.25 per barrel compared to July 2017 (US$48.48 per barrel). Oil supply did not keep up with the rise in oil demand as the synchronised recovery in global economic growth was under way. In fact, the successful implementation of the 2017 historical pact between the Organization of the Petroleum Exporting Countries (OPEC) and non-OPEC countries took 1.8 million barrels of oil per day (b/d) away from the market, and was compounded by unexpected supply disruptions in Canada, Libya, Nigeria and Venezuela. The impending US sanctions on Iranian oil exports due to enter into effect on 4 November 2018 will undoubtedly add to these pressures. While both supply and demand factors indicate a tighter market ahead, the return of volatility will likely become a dominant feature in the year ahead, complicating the economic and geopolitical fallout from higher oil prices.

Geopolitics support a tightening of oil-market fundamentals

According to the IMF, global economic growth remains strong in both advanced and emerging economies. This should augur well for continued growth in oil demand. Emerging signs of slowdown in the euro area, the United Kingdom and Japan notwithstanding, advanced economies' growth forecast remained unchanged at 2.2% year-on-year (y/y) as US growth remains above potential, while the IMF sees emerging economies' growth accelerating to 5.1% y/y in 2019 up from an estimated 4.9% y/y in 2018. Oil-demand forecasts by the International Energy Agency (IEA) echo this positive outlook, with expectations that world oil-demand growth of 1.4m b/d in 2018 will remain broadly constant in 2019.

But the brewing trade war, turmoil in emerging markets and proliferation of sanctions pose serious downside risks to growth. Escalating trade disputes between the United States and China are a direct threat to the fragile recovery of the global economy. According to the IMF, an escalation in international trade disputes could knock 0.5% off growth projections by 2020. The World Bank in turn estimates that 'tariff escalation, coupled with a shock to investor confidence, could reduce global exports by up to 3% (US$674 billion) and global income by up to 1.7% (US$1.4 trillion) with losses across all regions', adding a warning that firms may delay investments because of uncertainty over market access, reversing the ongoing recovery in global trade and investment growth.

As geopolitical and geo-economic risks continue to build up, the oil-supply outlook looks even more uncertain. The US decision to withdraw from the Iran nuclear deal – the Joint Comprehensive Plan of Action (JCPOA) – and strictly reimpose secondary sanctions on Iran makes the future of Iran's oil exports (which amounted to up to 2.4m b/d before sanctions were imposed) the biggest supply risk to energy markets, especially in light of the fact that output losses in Libya and Venezuela (around 350,000 b/d and 500,000 b/d respectively in July 2018 compared to a year earlier) were only partially brought back on line in August (rising by around 310,000 b/d and 20,000 b/d respectively). Moreover, OPEC production data for August reveals a drop of 240,000 b/d in Iranian oil production compared to a month earlier, as placement of Iranian exports is facing considerable hurdles. Refiners across the world are cutting back on Iranian oil purchases, notably in Europe, which accounts for about a third of Iranian sales. The cost of non-compliance with US secondary sanctions is just too onerous for refiners, oil-importing companies, tanker operators and insurance companies compared to the limited benefits and business opportunities that the Iranian market provides. Major Asian states, notably Japan and South Korea (the fourth- and fifth-largest consumers of Iranian oil) have also announced plans to eliminate those purchases. As for China and India (the top two importers of Iranian oil), the latter advised its domestic refiners to prepare for a 'drastic reduction' of imports from Iran, but is in the process of seeking waivers from the US Office of Foreign Assets Control. China, however, remains defiant, refusing to comply with US-imposed sanctions.

The ability of other oil producers to bridge this impending supply shortfall will be tested. OPEC agreed in June 2018 under US pressure to raise production in anticipation of these additional losses. Saudi Arabia already increased production by around 400,000 b/d in June, while the United Arab Emirates and Kuwait raised theirs by 60,000 and 40,000 b/d respectively. In July and August, however, Saudi Arabia brought its production level down. At higher prices, a strong rebound of shale oil will also likely continue. The US Energy Information Administration forecasts total average US crude-oil production to increase from 10.68m b/d in 2018, up 1.3m b/d from 2017, to 11.7m b/d in 2019, making the US the largest crude-oil producer in the world. But while cost cuts, technological improvements and productivity gains helped improve profitability and saw a rise in rig counts, pipeline infrastructure and transportation bottlenecks may delay production increases until 2019.

Oil exporters: the good, the bad and the ugly

Given the strategic importance of oil for both producing and consuming countries, the supply-driven rebound in prices could have significant economic, political and security implications, particularly in a turbulent and fast-changing geo-economic landscape with looming risks from trade wars and sanctions. For most oil-producing countries, the benefits of higher prices can be substantial. Major oil exporters in the Middle East and Africa, Latin America (Colombia, Brazil), as well as Russia will see a significant increase in commodity-export revenues. Their current-account fiscal positions will improve and profits in the energy sector will increase. According to the IMF's forecasts in June 2018 that anticipate an oil price of US$70.23 in 2018 and US$68.99 in 2019, the Arab Gulf states will see their collective budget deficit decline from 5.5% of GDP in 2017 to 3.5% and 2.3% of GDP in 2018 and 2019 respectively. For Saudi Arabia, the fiscal deficit will likely be reduced beyond the government's own target and register 3.8% of GDP, versus 6.7% of GDP outlined in the 2018 budget law. The Russian Ministry of Finance recently issued a budget amendment in which oil and gas revenues were expected to generate the equivalent of US$44.4bn in 2018, up from previous forecasts of US$8.5bn, which had been based on an average Urals crude price of US$40 per barrel. It now expects a budget surplus of 0.45% of GDP – its first surplus since 2011 – compared to original forecasts of a deficit of 1.3% of GDP.

This reversal of fortunes will relieve strains after several years of austerity. The sharp fall in oil prices since 2014, coupled with rising concerns about a 'lower for longer oil price', forced producers to adopt drastic fiscal-austerity measures, including a public-sector employment freeze, subsidy cuts, utility-price hikes (Bahrain, Iraq, Kuwait, Oman, Saudi Arabia) and currency devaluations (Azerbaijan, Iran, Kazakhstan, Nigeria, Russia), in order to stem the deterioration of public finances and stop the rapid depletion of foreign reserves. These measures were met with strong resistance and criticism in many states, especially as public-spending cuts resulted in a sharp slowdown of economic activity and higher unemployment. Protests erupted in Iraq and discontent was widespread in Bahrain, Kuwait, Oman and Saudi Arabia. Higher prices will thus provide an opportunity in the short term for states to loosen their grip on the public purse in order to regain some of the waning political support, despite the fact that policymakers are convinced that the rentier state is proving to be an unviable and unsustainable model. In Saudi Arabia, where economic growth is struggling to pick up (1.7% and 1.9% y/y in 2018 and 2019 respectively according to the IMF), Crown Prince Mohammed bin Salman faces strong demands for a redistribution of windfalls. The kingdom's 2018 budget saw a public-spending increase of 32% y/y, including a significant push of investment spending to help create much-needed jobs for young Saudis. In Russia, however, the surpluses resulting from an imminent fivefold increase in oil and gas revenues will serve to replenish the Reserve Fund, which is almost depleted after years of low oil prices. Reserve funds tided Russia through two recessions and supported Russian sovereignty, which in Russian President Vladimir Putin's view depends partly on not being beholden to the IMF or global bond markets.

In theory, higher oil prices may weaken the resolve to curb military spending, heightening the risk of conflicts and insecurity. Key oil-producing countries are heavily involved in direct military operations or in supporting paramilitary groups fighting proxy battles, and many are among the largest spenders on defence. But a return to largess and military adventurism is unaffordable, as rising debt levels during periods of low oil prices have weakened sovereign balance sheets. Debt levels of oil-exporting countries in the Middle East and North Africa (MENA) region have risen the most, from 35% in 2015 to almost 60% of GDP in 2018 according to the IMF, while the debt build-up of African oil exporters went from 32% to 45% during the same period. Accordingly, a reversal of fiscal discipline both to accommodate domestic political demands and support expensive military engagement abroad is unlikely to be affordable or sustainable for many oil exporters.

Rather, a slowdown in the pace of painful structural reforms is most likely. Concerns about a 'lower for longer' oil-price outlook have been instrumental in allowing the implementation of critical and long-delayed structural reforms, as well as initiating ambitious plans for economic transformation centred around the private sector. In Saudi Arabia, the launch of 'Saudi Vision 2030' – aimed at modernising and diversifying the Saudi economy – has initiated unprecedented changes at both the economic and social levels. In Nigeria, where the oil industry has suffered from theft on a large scale (an estimated 84.4m barrels of crude were stolen in 2013, at a cost of US$6.7bn), the government was forced to advance sectoral reforms and parliament managed to pass the new Petroleum Industry Bill in early 2018, after 17 years of delays, to help with taxation and investment incentives for its industry. As oil prices rise, the sense of urgency across oil-producing countries may wane, and the risk that these reforms will come to a halt or be postponed may increase. In particular, a sharp rise in prices will make recent fuel-subsidy reform more difficult politically. In Kuwait, for example, the removal of fuel subsidies has already been suspended, while the introduction of value-added tax in several Gulf Cooperation Council countries announced last year seems to be indefinitely postponed.

Venezuela is an exception as its economy will likely deteriorate further even if oil prices rise. Despite holding the largest proven oil reserves in the world, state intervention and weak governance has undermined the sector and severely reduced Venezuela's oil production. From 3.5m b/d in 1998, the country's output fell below 1.3m b/d in July 2018, and is expected to fall below 1m before long. After being among the top suppliers to the US, Venezuela is unable to serve many of its customers as the majority of the small amount of oil that the Venezuelan state oil firm PDVSA is producing is being allocated for domestic consumption and for the payment of debt to China and Russia. The sharp fall in output has even obliged Venezuela to import oil from Russia in order to honour past agreements that mandate selling heavily discounted oil to Cuba. Venezuela's exports to China have also sunk to an eight-year low, prompting the latter to throw them a US$5bn lifeline to secure increased production. With increased dependence on Chinese and Russian loans to sustain even small production levels, Venezuela's ability to benefit from a recovery in oil prices will thus be limited.

Iran's economic and social crisis will also worsen as sanctions enter into force, eroding the benefits from higher oil prices. Besides an expected sharp fall in oil exports, the determination of the US administration to implement the renewed secondary sanctions strictly and aggressively will aggravate socio-economic conditions in Iran. In particular, Iran's economy will suffer from the withdrawal of planned European investment in the key strategic sectors of oil, automotive and infrastructure, as witnessed by recent decisions by Total, Peugeot and Siemens to stop operations in Iran. This will deprive the economy of much-needed financing and technology transfer that are necessary to bolster the country's economic potential amid biting demographics. Indeed, sanctions in 2012–13 led to a contraction of the Iranian economy by 6.6% y/y, while inflation shot up to 39% and youth unemployment reached a historical high of 37%. The EU and the United States' severing of ties with Iran's financial sector and central bank will only add to the sharp devaluation of the currency and heighten inflationary pressures, exacerbating public discontent and possibly inciting further protests against the regime's inability to curb corruption and address socio-economic grievances.

As pressures intensify, Iran will likely seek deeper economic integration with China and Russia. The inability of the EU, despite colossal efforts, to circumvent US sanctions and advance an economic package that reassures Iran is accelerating Iran's eastward integration strategy. Iran remains a strategic partner for China and a cornerstone of its energy-security strategy, far from US influence. It is also a critical node in China's Belt and Road Initiative. However, while China and Russia seem determined to support the JCPOA and defy the Trump administration's unilateral move, their ability to do so will be tested. Filling the vacuum left by European companies as they exit the Iranian market may not be straightforward, as many of the key Chinese companies (notably CNPC, Sinopec and CNOOC) could be targeted by the secondary sanctions, impacting the scale and quality of potential investments. However, other companies might engage in barter deals, resort to settlement in renminbi or work with banks which do not operate or do business with the US. Russia will look towards reinstating an oil-for-goods programme to Iran and has announced it wants to invest up to US$50bn in Iran's energy sector. Such an engagement may not be enough to dampen the sanctions' shock but will allow Tehran to avert a full-fledged economic collapse, albeit at the expense of increasing its reliance on China and Russia.

Oil importers: trouble ahead?

Higher oil prices will hurt countries that remain heavily dependent on crude-oil imports. Those will see their current-account and fiscal positions worsen, their currencies weaken and inflation soar, which will threaten much-needed growth recovery. The Asia-Pacific region will be affected the most, as the region's oil demand accounts for over 35% of the world's total consumption. While China is the largest consumer, the exposure of other Asian countries to high oil prices remains elevated, notably in India, the Philippines and Vietnam. Cheap oil and continued reforms had helped these countries achieve higher rates of growth, rein in finances and improve standards of living over the last two years. The fear is that higher oil prices will threaten those achievements as countries will have to absorb a much larger crude-oil import bill and cope with the inflationary impact of oil prices on millions of poor people. Ahead of elections next year, India – which imports almost 80% of its oil – has warned about its high degree of sensitivity to oil prices.

States delivering large and costly energy subsidies and social-welfare programmes will be under particular strain. In Indonesia, where approximately 20% of the government's budget is spent on energy subsidies, the bill for subsidies will almost double, being expected to reach 163.5trn rupiah (US$11.4bn) in 2018, up from the original budget estimate of 94.5trn rupiah (US$6.7bn). This will inevitably constrain the government's ability to tackle other policy priorities such as critical social and infrastructure projects ahead of next year's general elections, but also maritime-security ones. Similarly, in the MENA region, countries' efforts to phase out energy subsidies are still under way and the burden of subsidies continues to be significant in Egypt, Jordan, Lebanon, Morocco and Tunisia. As higher oil prices hit, inflationary pressures will add to budgetary strain, making the implementation of structural reforms more difficult to achieve and driving popular unease, notably in Jordan and Tunisia, both of which witnessed protests in the first half of 2018.

Turkey will be most at risk as higher oil prices exacerbate an unfolding currency crisis. Turkey's dependence on oil imports is one of the highest in the world and a major drag on the country's large twin deficits. According to the Central Bank of Turkey, the country's annual external-financing requirements exceed US$180bn per year, posing huge refinancing risks amid tightening global financial conditions. Higher oil prices will thus add further pressures on an already battered local currency, stoking further inflation. While the sharp depreciation of the lira could dampen the negative impact on economic growth as tourism activity picks up, two factors will complicate Turkey's outlook: the uncertain exit strategy from the ongoing stand-off with the US and the unpredictability of Turkish President Recep Tayyip Erdogan's policies, in particular his defiance of the Trump administration and his efforts to undermine the central bank's independence.

Escalating confrontation with the US could aggravate the geopolitical spillovers of Turkey's deepening financial turmoil. The restrictions imposed by the US for reducing imports of Iranian oil to zero will exacerbate Turkey's energy-security risks. Iran accounts for almost 50% of Turkey's oil imports, with the rest coming from Iraq, Russia, Kuwait and Saudi Arabia. Compliance with US sanctions and concerns about the reliability of Iraqi supply could significantly increase Turkey's strategic reliance on Russia. Russia could become the major supplier of both oil and natural gas to Turkey. (Rosatom, Russia's state-owned nuclear-energy agency, is already building – and will operate – Turkey's first nuclear power plant.) Accordingly, the US refusal to accommodate Turkey's demands to maintain commercial ties with Iran to meet its energy-security needs leaves Turkey little choice but to come closer to the Russia–Iran fold, complicating matters among NATO allies.

As the world's largest importer of oil, China's energy-security concerns will also come to the fore and shape its policy response. China accounts for almost 10% of global oil consumption: in April 2018, China imported around 9.6m b/d at a cost of US$768m per day, or US$280bn per year. Low oil prices in 2014–17 have helped to boost consumer spending, lower the cost of doing business and support growth. Higher energy prices could reverse these trends, hit Chinese manufacturers and dampen private consumption, which would complicate Beijing's plan to transition China's economy away from an investment-led model and towards a service- and consumption-led growth model. As such, and in the face of mounting risks from US tariff escalation, China's determination to continue buying Iranian oil, fill the demand gap left by Japan and South Korea, and benefit from highly discounted Iranian oil prices will only grow stronger. Whether this could come at the expense of other rival producers, namely Russia and Saudi Arabia, remains to be seen. Driven by the need to lock in as cheap a price as possible, China will use its buying power to encourage competition among suppliers to its own advantage. A recent decision by Sinopec, China's largest state-run refiner, to reduce purchases from Saudi Arabia as the latter raised its prices is a case in point. Moreover, renewed episodes of sanctions will reinforce China's focus on reducing its vulnerability to oil-price volatility, including through investing in the electric-vehicles industry, among others.

As for the US, higher oil prices represent a double-edged sword, and weathering the impact of Iran sanctions on US consumers is the key challenge. On the one hand, the US economy is benefiting from the rise in oil prices by allowing an increase in domestic energy production as it strives to achieve greater energy independence. This acceleration of business investment in the oil and gas sector, as well as along the supply chain, helped the US to become one of the world's top producers. Higher oil prices are also helping to expand the opportunities for US shale-oil exports and outward investment in oil-exporting countries across the world. However, the US still imports more than 10m b/d. As prices continue to rise or witness sharp moves, this could have profound distributional effects within the US economy as higher prices will negatively affect investment and consumption by the non-oil sector and households. The ability to withstand the negative impact of higher oil prices will depend on the ability of shale producers to raise output, and on ensuring key allies in OPEC do the same so that they can keep the lid on prices. Supply flexibility and availability of alternatives were essential to contain the impact on prices, and therefore rally European and Asian countries' support for sanctions in 2012. However, the reality is different this time around as many allies are not uniformly adhering to the sanctions, spare capacity is very thin and infrastructure bottlenecks stand in the way of shale in the short to medium term.

The spillover from heightened geopolitical risks as the US attempts to contain Iran through renewed waves of sanctions is causing a noticeable rise in oil prices along with higher volatility. While oil-producing countries – including many US allies – are expected to benefit from a higher price of oil, several other countries with significant reliance on oil imports will be negatively affected, including possibly the US itself in the short run. The challenges faced by the Iranian economy are no doubt significant, but the collateral damage to many oil-importing countries, many of which are critical allies of the US, is non-negligible.

The Speed of War: Faster Weapons; Faster Organisations

Western military dominance has been eroded across land, sea, air, space and in the electromagnetic spectrum. Advanced military capabilities are proliferating, and systems that were previously the preserve of Western states, such as armed uninhabited aerial vehicles (UAVs) and high-precision guided weapons, are increasingly operated by others, including potential adversaries, who are also developing new types of capabilities for themselves. There is now contestation in all domains, and the pace of change is accelerating. In 2017, US Secretary of Defense James Mattis said that it took several thousand years of war on sea and land, and around 100 years in the air, for those domains to be brought to the current position, but only ten years for space and cyberspace to mature into war-fighting realms.

Weapons are being developed that can travel faster, farther and with greater precision than was previously possible. Developments in hypersonic flight, for instance, are opening new possibilities in offensive operations. The pace of technological change will accelerate the speed of battle and raise the demand for yet quicker weapons.

Supporting this process is the growing spread of technology and related know-how that has enabled states (and empowered individuals) to develop, acquire and adapt hardware and software. Amid an increasingly data-infused world, technology developments either originating in or driven by the civilian sector will be integrated into war-fighting organisations in order to help leverage and exploit data, provide an advantage over an adversary and enable weapons to be used more quickly and targeted more precisely.

Integrating advanced technologies into command-and-control systems will enable quicker decisions and, coupled with faster weapons, put pressure on an adversary's decision space: there will be less time to take decisions. The state that is best able to exploit these changes may find opportunity. The problem for Western states is that they are now not the only ones seeking such advantages, and in other countries there may be fewer bureaucratic hurdles to fielding relevant systems. It means that, in the West, attention is focused on a different kind of speed: the pace at which organisations can buy relevant weapons and systems as well as innovate, adapt and integrate change. It is by improving in these areas, as well as in developments in technology and weapons, that the West might be able to reinforce its capability edge.

New capabilities bring new promise

New information and communications technologies (ICTs) carry the potential to improve some existing military systems and reduce the utility of others; the challenge is in discerning which can be adapted and which will be genuinely superseded. ICTs will also deliver new capabilities. Cyber power is one example: it is now a military competence in its own right. Greater use is also being made of artificial intelligence (AI) and machine learning in order to augment human capacity, to process increasing volumes of data more rapidly than before and to improve the effectiveness of weapons and other military systems.

During the US-led campaigns in Afghanistan and Iraq, rapid progress in intelligence, surveillance and reconnaissance (ISR) capabilities were fused with the emerging capability to exploit large datasets in order to bring actionable information more rapidly to military personnel. (Discerning changes to pattern-of-life movements and mapping adversary networks by tracking their use of ICTs are but two examples.) Over the same period, there were rapid developments in the technical capacities needed to transmit data quickly over distance and in large volumes. Chairman of the US Joint Chiefs of Staff General Joseph Dunford noted in early 2017 that data and imagery could now be delivered by satellite to a deployed platoon in Afghanistan at a volume that would only have been possible at divisional level five years before. The volume of data that can be amassed by modern sensor suites, and the speed with which this needs to be processed and disseminated, already surpasses the processing power of the human mind. This is as true for combat platforms as it is for command, control, communications, computers, intelligence, surveillance and reconnaissance (C4ISR) systems. This had led to the introduction of levels of autonomy. Frank Hoffman notes that the US Navy and US Army 'now field defensive missile systems with degrees of autonomy built into their controls'.

Other areas of technological progress include:

- robotics and uninhabited land, sea and air vehicles – including integrating these with AI systems and teaming with existing weapons;
- quantum cryptography and quantum computing;
- artificial intelligence, and autonomous control;
- nanosciences and materials science, which are important for seeking processing futures beyond current chip designs;
- space, to which more nations now have access and where there will in future be greater competition;
- directed energy, where advances in power supply have enabled greater progress; and
- developments in hypersonic flight.

Of course, some of these have been discussed for years; in many cases they have long been the 'next big thing'. Nonetheless some are in use, such as the autonomy example mentioned by Hoffman, while artificial intelligence is used for some decision-support functions. And others, like directed energy and hypersonics, are now on the cusp of service entry. This is in some measure because technical capacities have improved, but also because aspirations for use have been reassessed. For instance, some analysts explain the progress in exploiting AI because algorithm-based technologies capable of tasks such as pattern recognition in large data-sets are not seen as intrinsically reliant on progress in the search for AI that can mimic human decision-making.

As well as opportunity, this process brings risk. Greater integration of advanced ICTs within armed forces and states will improve the capacity of military systems but will also make those systems vulnerable to the actions of adversaries, such as cyber attack, jamming or spoofing. While

ICTs may hold the promise of increasing the speed with which information might be gathered and assessed and an engagement might take place – thus compressing the time in which an adversary has to consider a response – the same might hold true in reverse. Adversaries might have similar capabilities in systems and in weapons. Furthermore, ICTs may also drive yet more automation and autonomy in defences in order to minimise an adversary's first-strike advantage, possibly increasing the risk of miscalculation in response. According to Dunford, 'information operations, space and cyber capabilities and ballistic missile technology have accelerated the speed of war, making conflict today faster and more complex than at any point in history'. Other capabilities, including hypersonic weapons, could be added to his list.

Hypersonics

The US, Russia and China are the main actors pursuing developments in hypersonic weapons. These are generally taken to include weapons capable of speeds above Mach 5 (that is, above 6,125 kilometres per hour, although the speed of sound varies with altitude and temperature). Current developments are focused on boost-glide vehicles (where air vehicles are boosted to altitude and speed by more traditional rocket motors and then glide unpowered at high altitude), and hypersonic weapons with air-breathing engines that are able to maintain powered flight until impact. However, the ambition to achieve hypersonic flight is not new; from their early days in the Second World War, ballistic missiles attained hypersonic velocities, and both the US and Russia examined new hypersonic designs at least from the 1970s.

Despite these attempts, hypersonic flight was for years a victim of a conspiracy of optimism. The scale of technical challenges and the lack of maturity of the technology hampered early attempts to introduce operational systems, but progress in this area is now picking up speed for a number of reasons. For one, aspirations have been reshaped. There is now more focus on hypersonic flight for missiles rather than on more sweeping ambitions for applications that might lead to hypersonic passenger aircraft. At the same time, progress has been made in overcoming earlier technical challenges in hypersonics, including in air-breathing propulsion, materials technology, an adequate understanding of high-speed flight aerodynamics, heat-management challenges for guidance systems at hypersonic speeds, a lack of adequate wind-tunnel facilities and immature computer-modelling technologies.

Developments in hypersonic weapons

Russia's announcement in March 2018 of its *Avangard* hypersonic weapon attracted much attention. *Avangard* is a hypersonic glide vehicle (HGV), possibly intended to be launched from the *Sarmat* heavy intercontinental ballistic missile (ICBM) or the existing *Satan* ICBM. It is intended to circumvent Western missile defences and possibly deliver either a nuclear or non-nuclear payload. Moscow said that *Avangard* will enter service around the turn of the decade.

At the same time, Russia also went public with *Kinzhal*, a weapon based on the *Iskander* surface-to-surface ballistic missile and designed to be air-launched from a MiG-31 interceptor. *Kinzhal* may have anti-ship and land-attack roles. It has a shorter range than *Avangard* but when combined with the carrier-aircraft's range could lead to targeting at ranges of around 2,000 kilometres. At a tactical level Russia is pursuing the 3M22 *Zircon* hypersonic anti-ship missile. Moscow is also developing the *izdeliye* 75 (also known as GZUR), with a range of 1,500 km. This is possibly an air-launched air-to-surface weapon in the Mach 6 range.

China too is pursuing an HGV, which was termed 'Wu-14' by US intelligence analysts. China began testing this around 2014 and a system could be fielded by 2020. It might be dual-capable. Like *Avangard*, Wu-14 is understood to be an unpowered glider, which would offer only limited options for defensive manoeuvres during flight. China also has air-launched ballistic-missile projects in development.

In the US, the Defense Advanced Research Projects Agency (DARPA) has tested Hypersonic Test Vehicles (HTVs) in the past. Tests in 2010 and 2011 of a research vehicle called HTV-2 ended in the vehicle's destruction in both instances but generated valuable information about hypersonic heating issues. The services have been active too, working closely with DARPA. The US Army has in the past tested an Advanced Hypersonic Weapon Concept (a glide vehicle), and the US Air Force tested the X-51A *Waverider*. In the public domain, current efforts are centred on two projects for which contracts were awarded in April 2018. Lockheed Martin was awarded a US$928-million contract to develop the air-launched Hypersonic Conventional Strike Weapon and – it emerged later – a second project called the Air Launched Rapid Response Weapon. Derived from a DARPA tactical boost-glide vehicle project, this reportedly has the designation AGM-183A.

The advent of hypersonic weapons may radically change both the speed and potential range of engagement. Hypersonic weapons may simply arrive too quickly for the adversary to organise an engagement, while current defensive systems might be too slow to shoot them down. And they will bring greater targeting options for time-critical and distant targets, offering strategic reach and precision. As an example, on a test flight in 2013 the US experimental X-51A *Waverider* hypersonic air vehicle 'traveled more than 230 nautical miles in just over six minutes', reaching a peak airspeed of Mach 5.1, according to the US Air Force (USAF). Indeed, 'hypersonics overcomes the constraints of distance, time and defence that already limit conventional aerospace power projection', according to senior US defence adviser Richard Hallion. When combined with the benefits of faster C4ISR, enabled by improved processing capabilities and augmented by artificial intelligence, not only will weapons themselves be faster but so too will the capacity to find a target and process all the information necessary to decide whether or not to engage.

Implications for decision-making

Hypersonic systems, once fully integrated into war-fighting inventories, will have implications for the future utility of some military platforms, including bombers and aircraft carriers. They will afford nations an advantage by delivering more and faster targeting options on a global scale and will pose problems for an adversary's defensive engagements and command and control. Hypersonic systems can create 'dislocating effects' by compressing and disrupting an opponent's decision-making cycle. Other new technologies, such as AI, will have the same effect; these faster weapons and faster systems might, in turn, potentially enable greater capability in each other.

Military leaders strive to make quicker and better-informed decisions than their adversary. Former USAF Colonel John Boyd tried to synthesise military decision-making cycles in his OODA (observe, orient, decide, act) loop. In this case, employing hypersonic systems would rapidly condense the time available for an adversary to effectively observe and orient, creating problems for clear-sighted decision-making. Integrating advanced ICTs like AI brings a new challenge. This will, according to Will Roper, US Assistant Secretary of the Air Force for Acquisition, Technology and Logistics, 'likely draw this loop into a knot of unprecedented decision speed at global scale'.

But while challenges exist, so too do opportunities. For the side able to employ the more advanced technology, information might be processed faster and fed into the observe and orient stages, enabling a quicker and better-informed decision than would be available to an adversary. AI, for instance, can sift vast quantities of available information ('big data') and manage complex sensor feeds in order to provide options up to the decision-making level more rapidly. Doing this at increasing speed might provide more time to make the right decision and enact it more quickly than the adversary. According to Hoffman, 'in such situations, the necessity for preplanned delegation and engagement authorities is clear'. Even so, as Frank Partnoy of the University of San Diego observed in 2012, acting fast might not necessarily mean acting first: 'those able to step back and think about the big picture,' he said, 'have a major advantage'. Indeed, using technical means to increase the time available to make decisions could, when coupled with fast and accurate weapons (themselves augmented by improved ICTs), create the space to outfox an opponent by waiting for an adversary to move first or even by detecting and engaging a threat before it is launched (engaging 'left-of-launch'). With system speed in some cases outpacing human capacities, there has been sharpened focus on developments in autonomous control – an area that opens up many other questions in the legal and ethical realms relating to the degree of human involvement, particularly when it comes to weapons release.

Implications for organisations

One of the principal problems for Western states in tackling these questions is that they are no longer the only states setting the pace in areas such as hypersonics and AI. In order to maintain a lead, speed needs to be picked up in some areas, including the pace at which organisations

Hypersonic Weapons

A number of nations, principally China, Russia and the United States, are actively engaged in the development of hypersonic weapons capable of flight at speeds of Mach 5 and above. When combined with developments in command, control, communications, computers, intelligence, surveillance and reconnaissance (C4ISR), their use holds the potential to drastically reduce the strike time against a broad target set. For those defending the target, these systems compress the time available to adequately identify, assess, track and engage an incoming weapon. Enhanced defensive-focused C4ISR systems might improve matters, but any defence will also need more capable missile defences.

The concept of hypersonic weapons that fly within the atmosphere is not new, but technology and funding are now catching up with former aspirations. Developments tend to fall into two types: boost-glide systems and those that remain powered for the duration of flight. Boost-glide vehicles include Russia's *Avangard*, the Chinese system designated WU-14 by the US and may also include the future US 'Air-launched Rapid Response Weapon' project.

The graphic on the right illustrates the range- and time-to-target challenges that hypersonics might bring. For a notional system launched from China's eastern seaboard, a subsonic weapon would take 18 minutes to reach Taiwan travelling at Mach 0.8; a Mach 5 hypersonic weapon makes the same flight in three minutes, reducing to 1 minutes 30 seconds for a Mach 10 weapon. A subsonic weapon travels 2,500 kilometres in 2 hours 30 minutes at Mach 0.8; a hypersonic weapon traveling at Mach 5 might transit the same distance in 25 minutes.

MARITIME CHALLENGES

E-2D Hawkeye AEW
Altitude 9,100 m*

Distance to horizon 350 km***
Mach 5 time to impact: 3 minutes 25 seconds
Mach 3 time to impact: 5 minutes 42 seconds

Distance to horizon 25.7 km***
Mach 5 time to impact: 15.1 seconds
Mach 3 time to impact: 25.2 seconds

AN/SPS-67 RADAR
Altitude 27m*

MYANMAR

LAO

M2.5

50 min

THAILAND

MA

* Figure given is nominal service ceiling, operational altitude may vary.
** Figure given is an estimated height of the surface search RADAR above the waterline.
*** Figure given is calculated by taking the tangential distance from the observational altitude in metres above mean sea level (MAMSL) to the missile altitude in MAMSL. This does not take into account the refraction of light as a result of atmospheric temperature changes.

Current anti-ship weapons such as *Brahmos* are capable of achieving Mach 3 in sea-skimming (3-5 MAMSL) profiles. Future systems may achieve velocities of Mach 5 or higher at the same altitude, although at these speeds they will face significant challenges in terms of control and buffeting and airframe heating. This graphic illustrates the difference in reaction time between such systems. Ships will also face high-speed and hypersonic threats adopting different flight profiles, such as dive-attack.

High-speed weapons will alter the concept of operations for naval vessels. Alone, this *Arleigh Burke*-class destroyer can identify sea-skimming threats only as far away as the horizon, as viewed by its highest placed search-and-surveillance radar – the AN/SPS-67. From this position, a sea-skimming threat may be picked up 25.7 km from the vessel.

Currently, threats in this area are from supersonic systems. Should hypersonic sea-skimming systems enter service, these challenges sharpen. If an incoming weapon is travelling at Mach 5 (1.72 km/second), this leaves just 15.1 seconds for the destroyer to engage the threat before impact. If the destroyer is operating under the surveillance cover provided by an E-2D *Hawkeye* airborne early warning (AEW) aircraft, the direct line of sight to the horizon is extended to 350 km. In this case, an incoming missile, at Mach 5, would still strike the vessel 3 minutes 25 seconds from detection.

Source: IISS

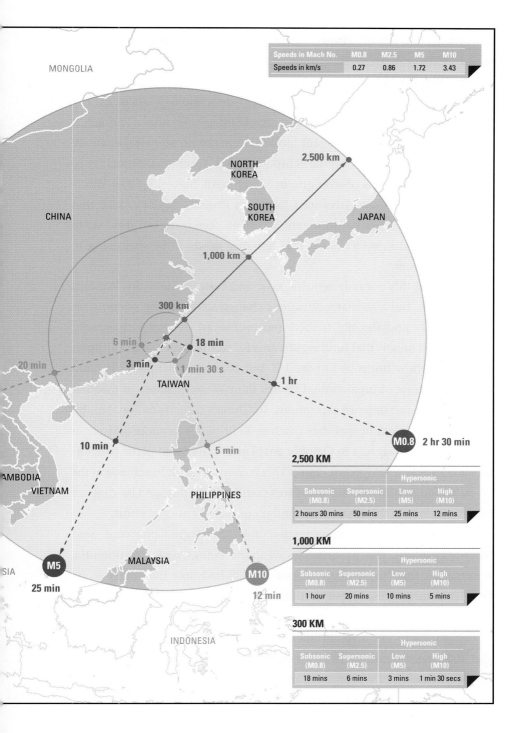

Speeds in Mach No.	M0.8	M2.5	M5	M10
Speeds in km/s	0.27	0.86	1.72	3.43

2,500 KM

			Hypersonic	
	Subsonic (M0.8)	Supersonic (M2.5)	Low (M5)	High (M10)
	2 hours 30 mins	50 mins	25 mins	12 mins

1,000 KM

			Hypersonic	
	Subsonic (M0.8)	Supersonic (M2.5)	Low (M5)	High (M10)
	1 hour	20 mins	10 mins	5 mins

300 KM

			Hypersonic	
	Subsonic (M0.8)	Supersonic (M2.5)	Low (M5)	High (M10)
	18 mins	6 mins	3 mins	1 min 30 secs

can buy and field relevant weapons and systems, as well as the speed with which defence ministries and armed forces are able to adapt, innovate and integrate change.

The West could look to maintain a technological lead, and it is likely that investments will increase in advanced-technology areas as key Western states try to retain or obtain an advantage. Another approach is to accept contestation while still looking to maintain advantage, aware that dominance might only be temporary. Yet another approach is to focus on specific areas of strength. In March 2018, Steven Walker, director of the US Defense Advanced Research Projects Agency, said that 'the US can no longer be dominant across all scenarios, but it needs to be highly lethal in select ones. This lethality needs to be surprising to peer competitors.'

Achieving this not only requires new and better systems for Western armed forces, but also that institutions change so that these systems are more rapidly and flexibly fielded and employed. A changed security environment means that funding streams for technologies such as hypersonics have now improved in the US, but countries such as China and Russia face fewer bureaucratic hurdles than Western states in meeting their security and defence aspirations. In China's case, its national ambitions are made clear in speeches (such as Xi Jinping's keynote address at the 19th Party Congress in October 2017) and in national plans (such as July 2017's 'AI Development Plan'). This is more difficult to achieve in the West, although other useful measures could still be pursued by defence establishments in the absence of similar concerted national effort.

General John Hyten, commander of US Strategic Command, said when discussing the progress in weapons being made by potential adversaries, that 'in so many places' the US had 'lost the ability to go fast'. To remedy this, Hyten thought change was required in five areas: the budget; requirements (where he said it should take 'no longer than three months to get a requirement for anything'); acquisition; testing; and risk assessment. Losses during test phases should not constrain the development of a promising programme, and programme directors should be allowed to take risks, accepting that failure is a necessary part of the process of fielding improved systems. The current US approach to testing hypersonic systems might point the way. At the 2018 Farnborough International Air Show, Roper said that recent progress stems from a decision to reshape the hypersonic project and view it as an experimental test programme where risk is accepted.

Acquisition processes also need to move faster. Rapid-capabilities offices – tasked with introducing capabilities faster than normal procurement cycles allow – have in some states helped to bring new systems into service relatively quickly. However, the question remains as to whether governments are willing to allow these offices to operate in the long term alongside more traditional acquisition structures. This raises questions over the level of reform needed to mainstream faster ways of working in acquisition structures and how to achieve this. Improving the requirements process might be one way; another might be to increase the mission flexibility of military platforms. Yet another would be to speed up procurement decision-making. In recent years, the US began a process of moving decision authority for some programmes away from the Office of the Secretary of Defense. Pentagon chiefs think that this will allow them to move ahead more quickly as each decision has fewer review stages.

Also, defence organisations need to work better with the private sector, where an increasing amount of militarily-relevant technology is developed. This would allow defence organisations to more rapidly identify innovation and benefit more quickly from technology developments. The US 'must leverage commercial technologies and adapt at their pace', as Roper put it when he was head of the Strategic Capabilities Office. At the same time, defence organisations need to maintain contacts beyond the primes, with small- and medium-sized enterprises (SMEs) where much defence-relevant innovation originates.

Using faster systems to best effect means that organisations will have to consider how to recruit and retain the best people, so that agility and innovation is a personal as well as institutional proficiency. If individuals have the right skills, adjustments might have to be made to military structures and processes to attract and retain them. After all, military leaders, says Dunford, need to prioritise adaptability and innovation and be capable of 'thriving at the speed of war'.

What difference does it make?

The technical developments described here matter greatly for armed forces. Faster weapons and faster C4ISR systems will change the way military leaders operate on the battlefield as well as how they plan and execute missions. They will also allow a broader range of targeting options than hitherto, with hypersonic weapons allowing more fleeting targets to be engaged than was previously possible. The application of technology will compress decision space; this will be worrisome for an adversary but an advantage for the state able to best harness and integrate these technologies. And while general AI – machines able to think for themselves and perhaps act autonomously – may still be some time off, perhaps now is the time to consider AI's legal, moral and ethical dimensions and, as Hoffman wrote, 'think about its effect on war and warfare'. That said, the current level of AI and machine-learning augmentation of C4ISR systems indicates that at least a degree of autonomous control is already in place.

But while these technologies might change the way conflict is fought, it is questionable whether they will necessarily make war any easier or more predictable, certainly when it is fought on land or in complex cultural and political contexts. While they may in some ways be revolutionary (with the side that is able to use, for instance, AI-enabled C4ISR systems being able to benefit from more options more quickly), the course of recent wars should temper views over the effect new technologies can have. In any case, with potential adversaries pursuing the same or similar systems, or measures designed to blunt Western advantage, any edge they bring may be short-lived: these periods of relative advantage are also being compressed. Nonetheless, the increasing speed of weapons and of the decision-making cycle will challenge military professionals. In order to cope with a collapsing decision space, more use will likely be made of technological assistance, as well as reliance on planned routines to enable faster responses at times of operational stress. Meanwhile, mindful of the 'Clausewitzian elements that frame our understanding of war's nature', Hoffman argues that autonomy will change the nature of war. Greater delegation 'to lower echelons for faster forms of attack' might, he says, weaken political direction while 'deep-learning forms of AI will augment the intuition and judgement of experienced commanders'.

It is likely that technological innovation will challenge current conceptions of what conflict is, with a further blurring likely of the line between peace and war and kinetic and non-kinetic action. At the same time, greater progress in robotics, AI and autonomy will have the potential to alter national risk calculations. New technologies will enable ever more sophisticated and disruptive 'grey zone' operations. The objectives of these actions may not be intrinsically new, but the use of ever more technically complex means might not only boost the speed at which any potential effect may occur but also increase the difficulty for states seeking to respond in a timely fashion. If anything, these challenges place a premium not just on the need to procure and integrate faster weapons and improved C4ISR systems, but also to increase the speed with which military systems are procured and organisations and personnel can adapt in the face of military demands in peace, war and in the increasingly indistinct area between. Successfully achieving all this is not a given.

Chapter 4

Asia-Pacific

2017–18 Review

As was evident at the IISS Shangri-La Dialogue in Singapore in June 2018, three major concerns dominated thinking in the region and beyond about Asia-Pacific security: the crisis provoked by nuclear and ballistic-missile tests carried out by the Democratic People's Republic of Korea (DPRK); China's arrival as a major strategic actor; and heightened anxiety among US allies and partners over the durability of American commitments in the region.

There was high drama surrounding the North Korean security crisis. During the second half of 2017, this derived from the Kim regime's sequence of ballistic-missile tests as well as its first alleged hydrogen-bomb test in September. The US strategy was one of 'maximum pressure', and hostile rhetoric escalated from US President Donald Trump as well as the DPRK. Washington lobbied hard to gain international support for UN Security Council resolutions imposing even tighter economic sanctions on Pyongyang, and even China – the DPRK's main economic partner – appeared to enforce these more rigorously. More ominously, it was reported that US defence planners were assessing a range of potential military options intended to deny Pyongyang the capability to deliver nuclear warheads to the continental United States. It seemed quite possible that war would break out during the coming months. During the first half of 2018, however, it was the quite sudden move towards dialogue between the key actors – the DPRK, the Republic of Korea and the US – that drew international attention. These developments culminated in the Singapore Summit between Trump and North Korean Chairman Kim Jong-un on 12 June. The summit did not result in the agreement on CVID that the Trump administration had sought (and notably there was no unanimity as to what the 'D' in the CVID acronym implied: both 'dismantlement' and 'denuclearisation' were cited along with the criteria 'complete, verifiable, irreversible'). Indeed, there is evidence that – despite some largely symbolic gestures towards disarmament – the DPRK has continued both its nuclear and its missile programmes. Moreover, Trump made concessions – notably, to suspend US military exercises with South Korean forces – that concerned those in the US and its allies who saw continuing US military commitments and readiness as vital for security in the region. Nevertheless, the opening of dialogue had removed the threat of conflict for the time being and, despite the shortcomings of the summit's outcomes, it seemed possible that Kim Jong-un's prioritisation of economic development could provide the basis for a continuing peace process.

As international attention focused on the North Korean security crisis, China's Communist Party leaders intensified their drive to make their country the foremost power in the Asia-Pacific. The 19th Party Congress in October 2017 was significant not just in terms of its incorporation of 'Xi Jinping Thought on Socialism with Chinese Characteristics for the New Era' into the party constitution, but also because it highlighted China's growing international confidence. In the Asia-Pacific particularly, the Trump administration's revision of US foreign policy (including its rejection of multilateral approaches to trade) provided an opportunity for Beijing to assert a stronger regional leadership role in support of free trade. Behind the scenes, though, the Chinese geostrategic policies which had so troubled its neighbours for the previous half-decade continued. China repeatedly claimed that the situation in the South China Sea had calmed down, but satellite imagery and Western countries' intelligence reports painted a different picture: construction of military infrastructure on Chinese-occupied features there continued unabated, and the People's Liberation Army was deploying missile systems.

China's growing international heft has been evident in its successful promotion of multilateral institutions – such as the Shanghai Cooperation Organisation and the Asian Infrastructure Investment Bank – that provide alternatives to the Western-dominated groupings that have been pre-eminent for decades. In the Asia-Pacific, Beijing's Belt and Road Initiative (BRI), though vaguely defined, appears to provide immense economic opportunities to regional states. Governments in the region, seeking to boost their transport and communications infrastructure rapidly and relatively cheaply, initially engaged enthusiastically in the initiative. However, by 2017, many observers – in the region as well as in the West – were expressing concern over the risk of smaller countries, in particular, becoming ensnared in debt traps and effectively ceding control of critical national infrastructure to the Chinese. In December 2017, Sri Lanka granted China controlling equity in, and a 99-year operating lease on, its Hambantota port, emphasising that these risks potentially carried strategic implications for the wider region as well as the countries concerned. But while it was clear that Southeast Asian governments were aware of potential pitfalls relating to the BRI, most were also evidently reluctant to deny themselves access to its potential economic benefits. While they were often also interested in taking advantage of the alternative infrastructural-development options offered by India, Japan and the West, these seldom offered the scale of investment or rapidity of implementation potentially provided by the BRI.

China has not been alone among Asia's major powers in becoming more assertive. The continuity provided by Shinzo Abe's lengthy premiership since 2012 has allowed Japan to develop a new paradigm for its foreign and external-security policies. The emerging 'Abe Doctrine' envisages economic revival through the implementation of policies often referred to collectively as 'Abenomics'; the restoration of Japan's great-power status, particularly in response to China's strategic arrival and the challenges this poses; the removal of obstructions – such as Article 9 of the constitution – that prevent Japan from using its military power in the same way as other countries; and a degree of historical revisionism. But while broadly attractive to many Japanese as well as some of Japan's international partners, this new approach has encountered important obstacles: the economy has not proven easy to revive; Article 9 of the constitution remains unchanged; and historical revisionism has provoked protests from countries which were victims of Japan during the Second World War, notably China and the Republic of Korea. Trump's presidency has also complicated matters. The Abe Doctrine had assumed that Japan could rely on continued US leadership in the Asia-Pacific, in both economic and security spheres. But, despite Abe's courting of the new US administration, Trump's withdrawal of the US from the proposed Trans-Pacific Partnership and subsequent failure to take seriously Japan's security concerns in the context of summit diplomacy with the DPRK were among the important indications that Japan might now need to keep its strategic options open, not least by edging towards rapprochement with China.

Asia-Pacific: Drivers of Strategic Change

- China is projecting an increasingly confident image across the world through its more assertive foreign policy and growing global economic presence.
- Japan under the premiership of Shinzo Abe is seeking to redefine itself as a contemporary great power, but Abe's efforts to revise Article 9 of the Japanese Constitution to allow a greater role for the security forces remain frustrated.
- Concerned by debt and its strategic implications, some Southeast Asian states are re-evaluating their commitment to China's Belt and Road Initiative, either suspending or looking to renegotiate the terms of major infrastructure projects.
- US–North Korean relations remain unclear after a turbulent 18 months in which the countries' leaders oscillated between sabre-rattling and rapprochement, with the landmark June 2018 meeting between US President Donald Trump and North Korean leader Kim Jong-un offering little in the way of tangible steps towards addressing the DPRK's nuclear arsenal.

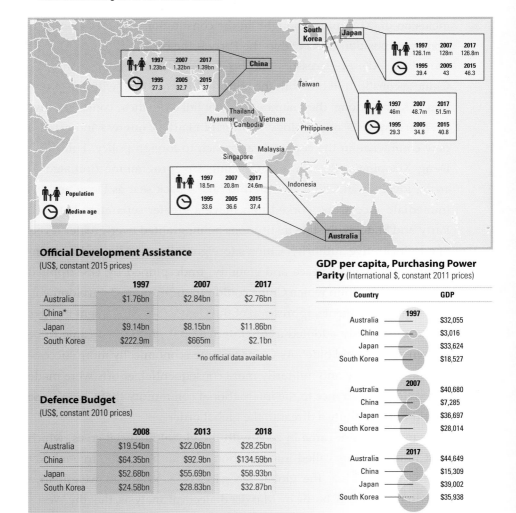

Official Development Assistance
(US$, constant 2015 prices)

	1997	2007	2017
Australia	$1.76bn	$2.84bn	$2.76bn
China*	-	-	-
Japan	$9.14bn	$8.15bn	$11.86bn
South Korea	$222.9m	$665m	$2.1bn

*no official data available

Defence Budget
(US$, constant 2010 prices)

	2008	2013	2018
Australia	$19.54bn	$22.06bn	$28.25bn
China	$64.35bn	$92.9bn	$134.59bn
Japan	$52.68bn	$55.69bn	$58.93bn
South Korea	$24.58bn	$28.83bn	$32.87bn

GDP per capita, Purchasing Power Parity (International $, constant 2011 prices)

Country	GDP
1997	
Australia	$32,055
China	$3,016
Japan	$33,624
South Korea	$18,527
2007	
Australia	$40,680
China	$7,285
Japan	$36,697
South Korea	$28,014
2017	
Australia	$44,649
China	$15,309
Japan	$39,002
South Korea	$35,938

Sources: IISS; OECD; UN Department of Economic and Social Affairs (Population Division, 2017); World Bank

China: Renewed Ideology, New Foreign Policy

China's 19th Party Congress, held in October 2017, was noteworthy for several reasons, but especially the high profile given to ideology. A new political doctrine – 'Xi Jinping Thought on Socialism with Chinese Characteristics for a New Era' – was incorporated into the constitution of the Chinese Communist Party (CCP). 'Xi Jinping Thought' reasserted the centrality of the CCP to Chinese political life, with Xi proclaiming at the Congress that 'north, south, east, west, the Party controls everything'. The inclusion of 'Xi Jinping Thought' in the constitution also formalised the dominant position of Xi within the Party – the contributions to Marxist thought of Xi's predecessors had been similarly incorporated into the Chinese constitution but with the critical difference that, with the exception of Mao Zedong, their names were not linked to these contributions.

The emphasis on ideology at the 19th Party Congress indicated a new confidence in the country's approach to foreign policy. Following Deng Xiaoping's 'Reform and Opening Up' programme (initiated in 1978), ideology in China appeared to take a back seat as Deng and his immediate successors worked to achieve a greater separation between Party and State, with state institutions being granted ever-greater levels of administrative authority. China's foreign policy was limited to maintaining a climate of peace and stability, underpinned by US-supplied public goods, within which China could pursue economic development. Following the violent suppression of the Democracy Movement in 1989, China consciously adopted a low international profile that came to be known as 'hide and bide'. As China became economically more successful and politically and militarily more consequential, efforts were made to provide reassurance to the international community that China's rise would not constitute a threat to the global order.

A turning point came in 2008 with the global financial crisis, which for China's leaders called into question the validity of the free-market approach. In China, the global recession of 2008 added weight to a growing conviction, borne by Marxist dialectical analysis, that the West's seemingly terminal decline and China's rise were ineluctable products of historical forces. The 19th Party Congress set the seal on this process by signalling that 'hide and bide' was dead and that China would henceforth pursue a more assertive and expansive foreign policy, a policy that would be identifiably 'Chinese'. At the Congress, Xi offered the Chinese model of development as an option for developing states to pursue and 'Chinese wisdom' as something that could be drawn on for the benefit of humanity as a whole. In the aftermath of the Congress, Chinese state media published extensive commentary which sought to highlight the perceived shortcomings of Western intellectual traditions and governance systems. It also argued for changes to the post-Second World War order to accommodate the interests of states with different cultures and value systems from those of the Western liberal democracies which, China claimed, had unfairly exploited their dominant position as rulemakers to serve their own interests.

China, in other words, does not want merely to participate in a Western political and economic framework that cannot be relied upon to promote Chinese interests. Instead, it wishes to project its own vision, driven by its own revived brand of socialism. Efforts to promote the study of Marxism in schools and universities have been reinforced, while China Central Television (CCTV) ran a series of programmes with the title 'Marx Had It Right' ('*Makesi Shi Duide*'), in which eager, clean-cut young students respond to hagiographic footage depicting the life and works of Karl Marx and demonstrate why his economic and social prescriptions were – invariably – correct. Much effort has also been devoted to reframing Marxist theory in the context of Chinese thought. In his speech to the Congress, Xi spoke of the need to

> dig deeply into the thought and concepts, humanistic culture and ethical norms to be found in China's excellent traditional culture, link continuity and creativity in line with the demands of the era and permit Chinese culture to demonstrate its eternal attraction and contemporary charisma.

In effect, Xi was seeking to recast Marxism as an ideology that represents the next development in China's historical and cultural evolution, and one that has global application by virtue of its recourse to Confucian humanistic traditions. By collapsing the distinction between Marxism and traditional Chinese identity, Xi was attempting to rehabilitate a declining belief in Communism within China and to bolster the ideological drive behind China's expansion onto the world stage.

Countering Western influence

The emergence of 'Xi Jinping Thought' represents the culmination of an extensive intellectual debate both inside and outside the CCP, the outcome of which was far from a foregone conclusion. In an article in *Open Times* in January 2018, Jiang Shigong, a professor at Peking University's School of Law and a subtle and articulate exponent of Xi's ideology, wrote that there were political forces in the period preceding the 18th Party Congress in 2012 (at which Xi Jinping was nominated as Hu Jintao's replacement) that

> hoped to use the Reform and Opening line created by Deng Xiaoping to negate the socialist system established during the Mao Zedong era, and that advocated undertaking subversive reforms of the political system following the economic reforms … The goals of their so-called 'reforms of the political system', it goes without saying, were to gradually weaken and eventually eliminate the leadership of the Party on the basis of a separation of Party and government and to bring about a Western democratic system.

Since the collapse of the Soviet Union – which the West portrayed as a victory of liberalism over communism – China has had to contend with what it perceives as the threat of 'peaceful evolution' – the subversive effect of Western liberal values promoted by a Western-dominated international discourse enabled by information and communications technologies (ICTs). In recent years, Chinese-language media have published numerous articles talking about the threat from 'hostile foreign forces' seeking to contain China's rise and bring about the overthrow of the CCP (intriguingly, Chinese policy-makers appear to believe that if such articles are published only in the Chinese language their Western counterparts will somehow not notice). The United States' system of regional alliances is decried as 'redolent of Cold War thinking' and aimed at containing China. Since 2016, China has instituted an annual National Security Week, during which citizens are shown posters and films illustrating the threat from foreign spies.

China has gone on the counter-attack by manipulating various levers of national power. These include: efforts to shape the international environment and international institutions in pro-China directions; promoting a 'China discourse' both positively (through the international expansion of China's broadcast media) and negatively (by denying access within China to content that challenges the CCP narrative and seeking to silence critics overseas); and the use of the United Front Work Department (UFWD) to leverage an increasingly influential Chinese diaspora to pursue and promote pro-CCP policies and to cultivate potentially sympathetic non-Chinese individuals of influence. In so doing, China seeks to exploit its growing economic and financial influence in the form of both access to Chinese markets and Chinese inward investment projects.

Shaping the global environment

China is seeking to shape the global environment both by reforming existing institutions and by creating new ones. These aims have been facilitated in part by the Trump administration's increasing disdain for multilateralism, as exemplified by its withdrawal from the Paris Agreement on Climate Change and blocking of key appointments to the World Trade Organisation's (WTO) Appellate Body, which handles the resolution of trade disputes. In the context of US retrenchment, China has been able to present itself as the global leader in advocating multilateralism and free trade whilst also pushing back on key issues such as human rights where, together with Russia and other like-minded states, it seeks to diminish the degree to which the international human-rights agenda is able to constrain state power. Taking advantage of the United States' desire to limit funding to the United

Nations and its withdrawal from the UN Human Rights Council, China and Russia have sought cuts in the numbers of UN peacekeeping staff dealing with human rights and sexual violence in conflict zones, and have orchestrated a refusal by the UN General Assembly to fund the UN Secretary-General's human-rights cell. China has also sought to bar human-rights advocacy groups from speaking at UN human-rights sessions. In addition, it has promoted a multilateral governance model for the internet that seeks to give states primacy in matters of internet oversight while also engaging in foot-dragging in discussions in the UN Group of Governmental Experts on whether and how existing international law – and in particular the Law of Armed Conflict – should apply within the cyber domain. China has also actively promoted the role of the Shanghai Cooperation Organisation, a joint economic and security mechanism established in 2002 which now has eight members, including Russia and India.

Moreover, China has begun to create new institutions and to seek to repurpose existing ones. An example of the former approach is the Asian Infrastructure Investment Bank (AIIB), which was established in response to the refusal by the US Congress to approve enhanced voting rights for China within the International Monetary Fund to reflect the country's increased economic and financial clout. It must also be recognised that the AIIB does not seek to displace but rather to supplement existing Bretton Woods institutions. An example of the latter is China's effort, together with Russia, to secure an overarching role for the International Telecommunication Union (ITU) on issues of cyber governance. While not an institution, China's ambitious Belt and Road Initiative (BRI) has multiple objectives that include the extension of Chinese influence overseas. China has used the BRI to promote its normative behaviours by teaching the security forces of states to which it has supplied information and communications networks to use these networks as a means of social control involving the monitoring and suppression of dissent. China has sought to present the BRI as a significant Chinese contribution to the provision of global security goods, including an attempt to have the BRI equated with international peace and security in a draft resolution at the 2017 UN General Assembly, although this effort was thwarted by a coalition of states led by India.

Controlling the message

During the Mao years, all written and broadcast media were under state control. Deng's period of Reform and Opening Up gave rise to a much more diverse and lively media scene characterised by many independent outlets such as the highly respected economics and financial magazine *Caixin* and the recently closed political magazine *Yanhuang Chunqiu*, which had been an influential advocate of political reform among China's intelligentsia. Investigative journalism flourished in this period of relative liberalisation. The advent of the internet seemed to constitute an irresistible tide moving in the direction of political liberalisation.

That tide has now turned. Under Xi, the CCP has made strenuous efforts to impose control over the internet by excluding externally gen-erated content seen to be opposing CCP messaging and also by closely monitoring internally generated content, to the point where individual social-media posts can be taken down within minutes of being gener-ated. In 2016, Xi made it clear that, in the words of the *People's Daily*, the role of China's media was 'the dissemination of the Party's policies and proposals'. Following the 19th Party Congress and as part of a general strengthening of Party control over state agencies, the CCP Central Propaganda Department – now rebranded in English as the Central Publicity Department – has taken over responsibility for all state media formerly overseen by the State Administration of Press, Publication, Radio, Film and Television. A new broadcasting service, Voice of China, was launched in March 2018 with the aim of 'propagating the party's theories, directions, principles and policies' and 'telling good China stories'. Party control over the film industry includes strictly rationing the number of foreign films that can be shown in China, with Hollywood seemingly willing to accept some degree of Chinese editorial control as the price of access to 1.3 billion viewers.

The public promotion of China's image overseas has, however, been accompanied by more insidious techniques designed to discourage externally generated criticism of China. Such techniques include using China's growing engagement with Western academic institutions (including those with an academic presence in China) to limit critical analysis of Chinese policies. A major component of this strategy has been the global network of Confucius Institutes attached to universities and schools with the purpose of promoting the teaching of the Chinese language. Such institutes have come under increasing scrutiny in Western countries for seeking to interfere in and constrain academic debate on China, and in some cases universities have severed their connections with these institutes. There is also some evidence that Chinese students in Western universities have been mobilised to protest against elements of curricula seen as anti-Chinese and have been encouraged to report on fellow students who default from the party line.

The CCP UFWD has exercised an increasingly important role in promoting the CCP's message overseas. Formerly a low-key organisation whose primary function was to combat the influence of Taiwan among Chinese diaspora communities, the UFWD has recently assumed greater prominence. In 2018, the UFWD was given responsibility for ethnic and religious affairs in addition to its overseas Chinese responsibilities, involving a substantial increase in its staff. Domestically, this is a recognition of the need to manage the challenges of a society that has, due to economic liberalisation, urbanisation and the emergence of a substantial middle class, become far more complex and diverse than was the case in the Mao era. The growing popularity of organised religion is a reflection of this complexity and has been met with redoubled efforts at Sinicisation. Internationally, the UFWD aims to expand Chinese influence through Chinese diaspora communities and non-Chinese individuals sympathetic to Chinese aims. In the case of the former, China has made it clear that under its concept of *ius sanguinis*, all ethnic Chinese, irrespective of their actual nationality, fall within the purview of the Chinese state.

The UFWD has attracted significant adverse attention for its attempts to leverage wealthy and influential Chinese diaspora communities for the purpose of influencing the politics of the states in which they reside in China's favour. Such leverage can include the offer of economic favours

– or the threat to withhold them – and pressure put on family members in China to ensure compliance. This issue has been especially salient in Australia and New Zealand. In Australia, a congressman resigned after it was found that he had accepted travel funding from a wealthy Chinese businessman. A report commissioned by Prime Minister Malcolm Fraser in 2016 found that 'the Chinese Communist Party had tried to influence Australian policy, compromise political parties and gain access to all levels of government' for over a decade. The report led to the introduction of draft legislation outlawing all forms of foreign interference in Australian politics and also strengthening anti-espionage laws, moves that were decried by the Chinese government as evidence of bigotry and Cold War thinking. In New Zealand, a report by one academic highlighted the extent of CCP penetration by making reference to the case of an ethnic Chinese parliamentarian who had worked at a university in China that serves as the principal feeder institute supplying linguists to the Chinese signals intelligence agency 3/PLA – a fact he omitted to mention in his residence application.

Under Xi, China has reoriented itself both nationally and internationally. China and the CCP are to be considered synonymous, meaning that every facet of Chinese state activity is inherently ideological. Chinese ideology is also promoted in the foreign-policy domain through vaguely defined and seemingly unthreatening concepts such as Xi Jinping's 'Community of Common Destiny' and by a continuous process of challenging the credibility of Western institutions and political concepts. China's views are not subject to direct critique from the Chinese population, allowing them to be presented as enjoying widespread support. Such an approach presents a significant challenge for Western liberal democracies which are only now starting to appreciate the scale of what is at stake, much less to mount a coherent response. China is not only waging war on the key pillars of the hitherto prevailing liberal democratic order – universal values, human rights, a free press, the rule of law, judicial independence, civil society – but is also seeking to erode the credibility of such ideas internationally. We are witnessing the first act of a drama which will define the twenty-first century.

In the short to medium term, progress towards China's goals is likely to be uneven. It is becoming clear that within China itself there are reservations about the advisability of the current assertive strategy and an awareness that China risks overplaying its hand. Such criticism must, however, be made *sotto voce* given the extent of Xi's domination of the policy process and national discourse. China can be expected to focus its efforts first and foremost in the developing world, where concerns about issues such as human rights are subordinated to the urgent imperative for economic development and where China's readiness to invest in infrastructure projects confers a significant advantage. For China, economic power is at the heart of its soft-power strategy, while the projection of an international image of a technologically advanced, prosperous and stable society is the rationale for the ideology it has adopted.

Japan: Abe's Legacy

When Shinzo Abe resigned in September 2007 as prime minister of Japan, few people expected to witness his return to the position five years later. His political obituary had already been written and Abe largely dismissed as a footnote in Japanese political history. The fact that he has now become one of the longest-serving prime ministers, and – subject to a leadership election within the governing Liberal Democratic Party (LDP) in September 2018 – might become *the* longest-serving Japanese prime minister, suggests that his legacy is worth serious consideration. Since his re-election in December 2012, Abe has brought stability to a previously dysfunctional political system, although at a cost to civil liberties. Internationally, he has overhauled a previously low-profile foreign policy and made Japan a more proactive and visible power in the world as part of a project to bolster Japan's great-power status, but at the expense of its traditional internationalism. Regardless of how long Abe remains in power – whether he steps down in 2018 or 2021 – a double-edged legacy seems assured.

The 'Abe Doctrine'

Abe's second term as prime minister has been characterised by the emergence of the so-called 'Abe Doctrine', which, although not an official policy, is set to define Japan's future role in the world in place of the previous and long-defunct 'Yoshida Doctrine'. Named after Shigeru Yoshida, Japan's long-serving post-war prime minister and the only other Japanese prime minister to serve two non-consecutive terms in office, the Yoshida Doctrine provided a road map for Japan through the period of post-war US occupation and the Cold War international order. By prioritising economic growth and engagement with regional neighbours while pursuing a low-profile foreign policy and restrained defence policies under the wing of a US security guarantee, Yoshida was able to steer Japan towards post-war reintegration in the international community and through an economic miracle that catapulted it to the status of second-largest economy in the world. However, with the end of the Cold War and the consequent demands placed upon Japan to play a higher-profile role in the world, epitomised by Japan's perceived failure to make a human contribution to the First Gulf War, this foreign-policy orientation no longer appeared to be fit for purpose.

Since then, Japan experienced two 'lost' decades of inertia and false dawns. Partly in response to this narrative of decline, Abe has promoted his eponymous doctrine in Japan's national-security policy and across a range of key bilateral relationships and multilateral forums. It is notable that much of the substance of the Abe Doctrine is little different from the agenda pursued during his brief and failed stint in power in the 2000s. However, the defining difference between the two Abe administrations has been the rise of China and the consequent perceived political, economic and security threats to Japan's position. This has created a more receptive audience within Japan for Abe's vision, which consists of four tenets.

Firstly – and most importantly – Abe believes that Japan needs to halt its perceived decline and secure its status as a contemporary great power, an ambition made particularly urgent in the context of the rise of China. In his New Year's reflection in 2015, Abe declared that 'our predecessors [made] Japan one of the greatest powers in the world. There is no reason whatsoever that the Japanese of that era could achieve this but the Japanese of today cannot.'

Secondly, Abe believes that Japan must shed a number of self-imposed constraints that have prevented it from making, in his words, a 'proactive contribution to peace'. Abe wishes to reform the post-war constitution of Japan, and in particular the peace clause of Article 9, by which Japan renounces 'war as a sovereign right of the nation and the threat or use of force as means of settling international disputes' and asserts that 'sea, and air forces, as well as other war potential, will never be maintained. The right of belligerency of the state will not be recognized.' In 2014, Abe succeeded in reversing Japan's traditional refusal to exercise the right of collective self-defence – Japan now can assist a foreign country with which it maintains a close relationship and that comes under attack by a third party. This is subject to a number of caveats. Any such attack must 'threaten Japan's survival and pose a clear danger to fundamentally overturn people's right to life, liberty and pursuit of happiness', 'when there is no other appropriate means available to repel the attack and ensure Japan's survival and protect its people; [and the] use of force [is] limited to the minimum extent necessary'. Although some regard these conditions as providing a high benchmark to be met, in reality they are open to considerable interpretation. Despite tabling (and then withdrawing in the face of opposition) a proposal to dilute Article 96 – which outlines the stringent conditions that need to be met in order to approve an amendment – Abe has so far been unsuccessful in revising the constitution, and Article 9 in relation to the legal status of the Self Defense Forces (SDF) in particular. Nevertheless, he has set 2020 as the year by which he will achieve this long-cherished goal. He has also incrementally jettisoned a number of other constraints relating to security, such as lifting restrictions on arms exports so that Japanese companies can develop markets in the United Kingdom and Australia.

The third tenet of the Abe Doctrine, and even more controversial than the second, is that Japan needs to revise its view of recent history. Abe has challenged the post-war narrative of Japan as an aggressor by paying respect to its war dead at the controversial Yasukuni Shrine, and questioning the evidence relating to the Japanese Imperial Armed Forces' use of 'comfort women' as well the 1993 Kono Statement in which the Japanese government recognised the role of coercion. This tenet is also a deeply personal matter for Abe as he seeks to rehabilitate the reputation of his grandfather Nobusuke Kishi, wartime minster of munitions, suspected Class-A war criminal and post-war prime minister. Although this third tenet may seem explicitly oriented towards a domestic audience, at the same time it threatens to sow doubt among Japan's regional neighbours and close allies as well as undermine any of the positive intentions behind Japan making a 'proactive contribution to peace' and providing international public goods in its role as a contemporary great power.

Finally, Japan must be economically strong. Abe's signature policies for achieving this objective have been collectively dubbed 'Abenomics' and consist of the 'three arrows' of monetary easing, fiscal stimuli and structural reform – all to be fired simultaneously (in contrast to previous attempts to kick-start the Japanese economy). Abenomics is partly a pragmatic response to the criticisms levelled at his first, failed administration for pursuing an ideological and nationalist agenda at the expense of economic and social welfare. However, it is equally a requirement for pursuing and realising the other three tenets, one that harks back to the Meiji-period slogan of *fukoku kyohei* (rich country, strong army). A high-profile corollary of Abenomics has been a concerted effort to increase the participation of Japanese women in the general workforce and in leadership positions, known as 'Womenomics'.

The strategies by which Abe has pursued these tenets include 'values-oriented diplomacy' based on the promotion of democracy, freedom, human rights, the rule of law and the market economy, thereby establishing an 'Arc of Freedom and Prosperity' involving countries from Northeast Asia through Central Asia to Eastern Europe. This arc, however, is seen by China as an attempt at encirclement.

The pursuit of an Abe Doctrine has not been straightforward. The performance of the Japanese economy under Abenomics has been modest at best and Abe's attempts to empower women represent a meagre legacy. In fact, according to the World Economic Forum's Global Gender Gap reports, Japan slipped from 101st in 2012 (when Abe returned to power) to 114th in 2017, just ahead of Ethiopia. The tenets also present some obvious contradictions that are difficult to reconcile, especially the historical revisionism, which raises international concerns of resurgent Japanese nationalism. This pursuit of an overtly nationalist agenda in the doctrine has also resulted in a decline in Japan's traditional internationalist behaviour. This development can be seen in the Abe administration's response to the G8's agenda on the role of women in conflict under the 2013 UK presidency, when it emphasised a future-oriented approach in an attempt to deflect attention from the issue of comfort women, and when it considered suspending contributions to UNESCO for supporting China's view of the 1937 Nanjing Massacre in 2015.

Moreover, the election of US President Donald Trump in 2016 presented Abe with a considerable challenge in managing what Mike Mansfield, the former US ambassador to Japan, once described as 'the most important bilateral relationship in the world, bar none'. Abe rose to this challenge with a strategy of carving out the role of 'Trump whisperer'. To this end, he was the first world leader to meet with Trump after his election and the second leader to visit Trump after his inauguration. Since then, a number of official visits and bilaterals have taken place, especially in light of the Singapore Summit between Trump and Kim Jong-un in June 2018 as Abe sought to ensure Japan and its immediate security concerns were not frozen out of discussions.

At the same time, Japan has hedged its bets by promoting the idea of a 'Free and Open Indo-Pacific' (FOIP) as an attempt to connect Asia (broadly defined), the Middle East and Africa and maintain an international rules-based order that supports free trade at a moment when the US appears to be actively undermining these arrangements. Abe expended considerable political capital on supporting the Trans-Pacific Partnership, only to see Trump announce unilateral US withdrawal in January 2017. However, the appointment of Taro Kono, perceived to be progressive on history issues and well connected to US officials, as foreign minister in August 2017 provided a valuable resource in managing future turbulence in the relationship.

Domestic stability

Abe is likely to be remembered as having provided relative stability at home. Japanese politics was characterised by a 'revolving door' of Japanese prime ministers prior to the LDP's landslide victory in the House of Representatives election of December 2012, which also brought to an end the now-defunct Democratic Party of Japan's brief period in power. The dominance of Japanese conservatism was reinforced by further landslide victories for the LDP in two snap elections for the House of Representatives in December 2014 and October 2017, and electoral victories in the elections of July 2013 and July 2016 for the House of Councillors. Even losing the July 2016 election for the governorship of Tokyo to Yuriko Koike did little to dent this dominance as she was still an LDP member, just not its favoured candidate. (Following her election as governor, Koike established her own national political party to challenge the LDP in the October 2017 election, but stepped down as leader of the new party after suffering a heavy defeat in the election.) Although public-opinion polls throughout his time in office suggest that Japanese people do not particularly care for Abe as an individual but broadly support the LDP, in terms of electoral politics, his place in history is assured and it is difficult to discern any effective opposition from outside his own party.

As a result, since 2012, the Abe administration has been able to pursue a conservative agenda largely unchallenged. Learning lessons from his scandal-tainted first period in power, Abe has been more robust in his selection of cabinet and senior bureaucrats and has required cabinet members to have their speeches approved. In the absence of an effective opposition within the Diet or his own party, the fourth estate in Japan has also proved to be ineffective. Despite overwhelming public disapproval, the Act on the Protection of Specially Designated Secrets, passed in December 2013, threatened journalists and whistle-blowing bureaucrats with hefty fines and possible imprisonment should they disclose

Japan Under Abe: State of the Nation

Shinzo Abe's reform programme aims to have a profound and lasting impact on Japanese society. 'Abenomics', the agenda of economic reform that has become the spearhead of Abe's leadership, has been generally successful, although some of Japan's biggest structural problems, such as the deflation spiral, remain deeply rooted. Abe's reforms to foreign policy have also become a source of acute tensions with Japan's neighbours, as Tokyo has turned towards historical revisionism and 'proactive pacifism'.

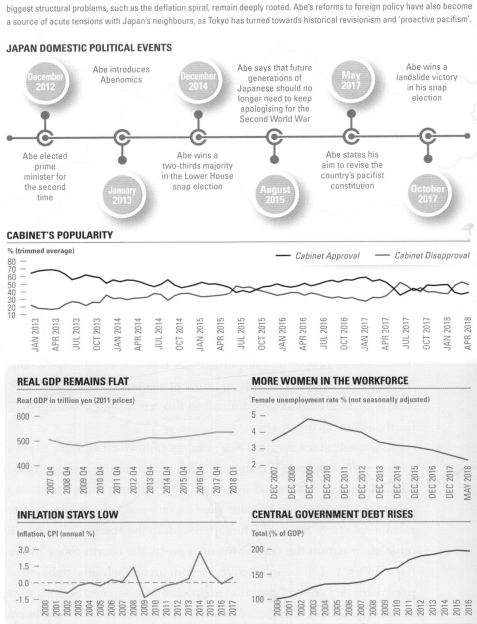

JAPAN DOMESTIC POLITICAL EVENTS

December 2012 — Abe introduces Abenomics

December 2014 — Abe says that future generations of Japanese should no longer need to keep apologising for the Second World War

May 2017 — Abe wins a landslide victory in his snap election

Abe elected prime minister for the second time

January 2013

Abe wins a two-thirds majority in the Lower House snap election

Abe states his aim to revise the country's pacifist constitution

August 2015

October 2017

CABINET'S POPULARITY

% (trimmed average)

—— Cabinet Approval   —— Cabinet Disapproval

80 — 70 — 60 — 50 — 40 — 30 — 20 — 10 —

JAN 2013, APR 2013, JUL 2013, OCT 2013, JAN 2014, APR 2014, JUL 2014, OCT 2014, JAN 2015, APR 2015, JUL 2015, OCT 2015, JAN 2016, APR 2016, JUL 2016, OCT 2016, JAN 2017, APR 2017, JUL 2017, OCT 2017, JAN 2018, APR 2018

REAL GDP REMAINS FLAT

Real GDP in trillion yen (2011 prices)

600 — 500 — 400 —

2007 Q4, 2008 Q4, 2009 Q4, 2010 Q4, 2011 Q4, 2012 Q4, 2013 Q4, 2014 Q4, 2015 Q4, 2016 Q4, 2017 Q4, 2018 Q1

MORE WOMEN IN THE WORKFORCE

Female unemployment rate % (not seasonally adjusted)

5 — 4 — 3 — 2 —

DEC 2007, DEC 2008, DEC 2009, DEC 2010, DEC 2011, DEC 2012, DEC 2013, DEC 2014, DEC 2015, DEC 2016, DEC 2017, MAY 2018

INFLATION STAYS LOW

Inflation, CPI (annual %)

3.0 — 1.5 — 0.0 — -1.5 —

2000, 2001, 2002, 2003, 2004, 2005, 2006, 2007, 2008, 2009, 2010, 2011, 2012, 2013, 2014, 2015, 2016, 2017

CENTRAL GOVERNMENT DEBT RISES

Total (% of GDP)

200 — 150 — 100 —

2000, 2001, 2002, 2003, 2004, 2005, 2006, 2007, 2008, 2009, 2010, 2011, 2012, 2013, 2014, 2015, 2016

Sources: BBC, Bloomberg, CNN, The Diplomat, Guardian, Japanese Government, Japan Macro Advisors, New York Times, Organisation for Economic Co-operation and Development, World Bank

JAPANESE TERRITORIAL DISPUTES

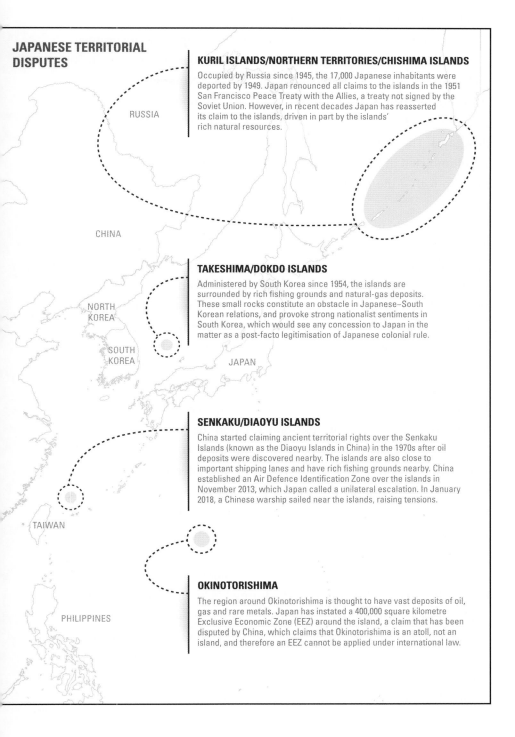

KURIL ISLANDS/NORTHERN TERRITORIES/CHISHIMA ISLANDS

Occupied by Russia since 1945, the 17,000 Japanese inhabitants were deported by 1949. Japan renounced all claims to the islands in the 1951 San Francisco Peace Treaty with the Allies, a treaty not signed by the Soviet Union. However, in recent decades Japan has reasserted its claim to the islands, driven in part by the islands' rich natural resources.

RUSSIA

CHINA

TAKESHIMA/DOKDO ISLANDS

Administered by South Korea since 1954, the islands are surrounded by rich fishing grounds and natural-gas deposits. These small rocks constitute an obstacle in Japanese–South Korean relations, and provoke strong nationalist sentiments in South Korea, which would see any concession to Japan in the matter as a post-facto legitimisation of Japanese colonial rule.

NORTH KOREA

SOUTH KOREA

JAPAN

SENKAKU/DIAOYU ISLANDS

China started claiming ancient territorial rights over the Senkaku Islands (known as the Diaoyu Islands in China) in the 1970s after oil deposits were discovered nearby. The islands are also close to important shipping lanes and have rich fishing grounds nearby. China established an Air Defence Identification Zone over the islands in November 2013, which Japan called a unilateral escalation. In January 2018, a Chinese warship sailed near the islands, raising tensions.

TAIWAN

OKINOTORISHIMA

The region around Okinotorishima is thought to have vast deposits of oil, gas and rare metals. Japan has instated a 400,000 square kilometre Exclusive Economic Zone (EEZ) around the island, a claim that has been disputed by China, which claims that Okinotorishima is an atoll, not an island, and therefore an EEZ cannot be applied under international law.

PHILIPPINES

sensitive information related to issues of Japanese national security – the definition of which is the prerogative of the Japanese government without independent oversight. In addition, a number of Abe sympathisers have been appointed to the public broadcaster Nippon Hoso Kyokai, including its chair Katsuto Momii and board members Naoki Hyakuta (the nationalist novelist) and the historical revisionist academic Michiko Hasegawa. The result is that in terms of international reputation, Japan has plummeted in the Reporters without Borders' World Press Freedom Index to 67th – the lowest among G7 countries – having been 11th in 2010.

Many aspects of the Abe Doctrine have impacted on government structures and policies in Japan, such as the creation of a US-style National Security Council (NSC) in December 2013 that places the prime minister in a central position of influence in the coordination of national security. At the same time, the Abe administration released a revised National Security Strategy that argued for an expanded role for the SDF, and has overseen a series of steadily increasing defence budgets, returning Japan to 2002 levels of spending and contrasting with the cap of 1% of GDP on military spending established during the Cold War. These developments were followed by measures that were perceived to erode civilian control over military personnel within the Ministry of Defense (which was upgraded from bureau to ministry status during Abe's first period in power). The Abe administration intends to introduce a revised national curriculum over the next few years that emphasises a disciplinarian approach focusing on state-defined national interests and instilling a moral and patriotic education in Japanese children. This is already raising concerns among more liberal sections of Japanese society that Abe's reforms are redolent of pre-war Japan and hark back once again to his failed nationalist agenda during his first period in power.

Abe has tempered his nationalist agenda by responding to the Japanese people's concerns over welfare. He was also lucky in that the intervening time between his first and second terms also saw the perceived threat of China embed itself within Japanese society, thereby making his nationalism more palatable. However, this should not be regarded as part of the global shift towards populism and anti-politics. Abe was born and bred within the Japanese political establishment – his father Shintaro Abe served as foreign minister and was prime minister assumptive, while his grandfather Kishi, as mentioned above, also served as prime minister – and in many ways his style of governance represents business as usual in the Japanese body politic.

However, Abe has faced several challenges during his premiership. His assumed successor and prominent nationalist Tomomi Inada was forced to resign in 2017 as defense minister over a cover-up of the true extent of danger to Japanese peacekeepers operating in South Sudan. Abe himself has spent a considerable amount of time and effort responding to accusations of financial impropriety and favouritism that may continue to threaten his position. In addition, Abe's goal of revising the Japanese constitution remains unfulfilled.

Abe's lasting legacy?

Abe may end up being synonymous in the public imagination with the 2020 Tokyo Olympics, having played a role in its award, projecting Japan's soft power by appearing as Super Mario at the 2016 Rio Olympics (and he may possibly remain in power to host the actual event). He may also be remembered as the prime minister who saw Japan through a generational shift, as a number of other high-profile events are due to coincide with the Olympics, including Emperor Akihito's abdication – the first emperor to do so for two centuries – and the first Japan-hosted G20 summit, due to take place in 2019 in Osaka. However, Abe is more likely to be remembered as the 'comeback kid' of Japanese politics and for his longevity, with the contrast between his two terms representing a fascinating example of political redemption. Domestically, despite his inability to connect directly with the electorate, he is likely to be remembered for having provided stability as a result of a series of landslide election victories, benefitting from some of the lowest voter turnouts in Japanese political history and the extreme fragmentation of the opposition. However, this stability has been established at the expense of freedoms, whether in government or Japanese society more broadly. In terms of foreign policy, the Yoshida Doctrine has now been replaced by the Abe Doctrine, one that is likely to continue to define Japan's role in the world after Abe steps down. Ultimately, the need to respond to external uncertainties and the lack of a credible alternative suggest that Abe's vision is likely to remain in place beyond his tenure as leader.

DPRK: Desiring Peace?

The always-tense Korean Peninsula seemed to be heading to war in 2017. An unprecedented flurry of testing by the Democratic People's Republic of Korea (DPRK) – including three intercontinental ballistic missiles (ICBMs) and its first credible claim of a hydrogen-bomb test – prompted the United States to threaten a military response. No one imagined that 2018 would see a turn to peace. Yet by early July the DPRK's young leader Kim Jong-un – who in his first six years in power met with no other head of state – had held no fewer than six summit meetings: three with China, two with South Korea and, most notably, his meeting with US President Donald Trump in Singapore on 12 June. However, it was far from guaranteed that the rapprochement between the DPRK and the US would endure, or that it would bring about a significant change in conditions on the ground.

Fire, fury, diplomacy?

Nine tests of 12 ballistic missiles by the DPRK in the first half of 2017 were followed by a further six tests of eight ballistic missiles in the second half. As anticipated, these included Pyongyang's first ICBM launches: two *Hwasong*-14s in swift succession on 4 July and 28 July, then on 28 November a *Hwasong*-15 believed to be capable of striking the entire continental US. On 3 September the DPRK appeared to have exploded its first hydrogen bomb – its third nuclear test in two years and sixth overall. In August, Kim explicitly threatened to fire four missiles into US waters near Guam, but ultimately did not do so.

In his maiden address to the United Nations General Assembly on 19 September, Trump – who had previously warned that DPRK threats would be met with 'fire and fury' – threatened to 'totally destroy' North Korea, whose leader he derided as 'Little Rocket Man'. On 22 September Kim responded, issuing a highly unusual personal statement whose final sentence read: 'I will surely and definitely tame the mentally deranged US dotard with fire.' Washington pointedly refused to rule out military options. Victor Cha – director for Asian Affairs on the National Security Council between 2004 and 2007 and adviser on North Korea to then-president George W. Bush – saw his nomination as US ambassador to South Korea withdrawn in January 2018 after criticising the idea of a pre-emptive strike on the DPRK. That post, vacant for 17 months, went instead to Harry B. Harris, a retired admiral and then commander of the United States Pacific Command, who was sworn in on 30 June.

The UN Security Council responded too. To the eight main resolutions (all unanimous) since 2006 that have censured and sanctioned the DPRK, three more were added in the past 12 months: Resolution 2371 (adopted on 5 August 2017), condemning July's ICBM tests; Resolution 2375 (adopted on 11 September 2017), responding to September's nuclear test; and Resolution 2397 (adopted on 22 December 2017), with reference to November's ICBM launch. These new resolutions further tightened sanctions on the DPRK. Chinese trade figures for early 2018 suggested more rigorous enforcement than before: Pyongyang's exports to its main partner (China accounts for some 90% of DPRK trade) fell sharply, although puzzlingly imports from China were little changed. This pressure was one factor, but not the sole one, in Kim Jong-un's strategic shift to diplomacy in 2018.

The first hint of change came on 29 November, when Kim Jong-un hailed the previous day's *Hwasong*-15 test as having 'realised the great historic cause of completing the state nuclear force'. A clearer shift came a month later in Kim's New Year address. While stern towards the US – 'the nuclear button is on my office desk all the time' – Kim's speech contained an unexpected olive branch for Seoul. Having ignored all Moon Jae-in's overtures since Moon's election as president of the Republic of Korea (ROK) on 9 May 2017, Kim now congratulated the ROK on hosting the upcoming Pyeongchang Winter Olympic Games, and said the DPRK was ready to participate. Pyongyang had evinced no prior interest in Pyeongchang; indeed, the tensions of the peninsula had led some competing nations to fear for their athletes' safety.

Moon accepted with alacrity. The two Koreas marched together at Pyeongchang and fielded a hastily trained joint women's ice-hockey team, but otherwise competed separately. The DPRK also sent its famously demure cheerleaders, a taekwondo squad and a light orchestra. More importantly, the opening and closing ceremonies were an opportunity to invite senior DPRK delegations, led by two of Kim Jong-un's key aides: his sister Kim Yo-jong, and Kim Yong-chol, in charge of South Korean affairs as head of the ruling Workers' Party (WPK)'s United Front Department. The latter was controversial. A Korean People's Army (KPA) general, in his former role as director of the Reconnaissance General Bureau Kim Yong-chol is regarded as having masterminded the sinking of the ROK Navy corvette *Cheonan* in March 2010, with 46 lives lost. Conservative demonstrators tried to block his entry at the Demilitarised Zone, but he used a different crossing. Both Kim Yo-jong and Kim Yong-chol were studiously ignored by US Vice President Mike Pence and Ivanka Trump, respectively, in the VIP box at Pyeongchang. Off-camera, both Kims held intensive and unpublicised talks in Seoul with a wide range of ROK government interlocutors.

On 5 March an ROK delegation flew to Pyongyang, led by Chung Eui-yong, director of the National Security Office in the Blue House (the presidential office) and Suh Hoon, director of the National Intelligence Service and a veteran negotiator with the DPRK. They went straight into a cordial meeting and banquet with Kim Jong-un at the WPK headquarters, hitherto off-limits to South Koreans; by contrast, his late father Kim Jong-il (who ruled between 1994 and 2011) would keep ROK visitors waiting with no known schedule. The radical idea of a US–DPRK summit was broached, which Chung conveyed to Washington on 8 March and Trump accepted on the spot without consulting his staff. The end of May was the initial target date, but this eventually became 12 June, with Singapore chosen as the most suitable venue.

Events then moved quickly on several fronts. The first inter-Korean summit for 11 years, and only the third ever, was held on 27 April. The first two summits, in 2000 and 2007, had been held in Pyongyang. This time the venue – one of several masterstrokes in an event carefully choreographed for television – was located on the ROK side of Panmunjom, which straddles the Military Demarcation Line between the two countries, thereby repurposing a site redolent of conflict as a place of peace. A long and varied day went smoothly, burnishing the image of both leaders. Kim Jong-un appeared personable and assured in his debut on the global stage. Yet this was much more than just a lengthy photo opportunity. The Panmunjom Declaration, signed by Kim and Moon, is substantial, with many specific commitments and deadlines. In the two months after the summit, the two sides met often to discuss a wide range of issues, including family reunions, sports exchanges, reconnecting roads and railways, easing military tensions, environmental and forestry cooperation, and opening a liaison office in the former Kaesong Industrial Complex. A second brief summit, initially secret, was held on 26 May on the DPRK side of Panmunjom, but came at a difficult moment in the new US–DPRK outreach. On 24 May, Trump cancelled the Singapore summit, citing Pyongyang's hostility, only to declare that it was back on again the following day.

The Kim–Trump summit: an uncertain legacy

That this unprecedented meeting – the first between a serving US president and a North Korean supreme leader – took place is remarkable. Yet it has thus far proved more symbolic than substantive. Unlike the Panmunjom Declaration or the Clinton era's 1994 US–DPRK Agreed Framework – or indeed the multilateral accord with Iran on nuclear development from which Trump withdrew the US on 15 May, calling it 'horrible [and] one-sided' – the Singapore joint statement is brief and vague, containing no concrete agreements or deadlines. There were, however, unexpected developments which caught many off guard.

At his post-summit press conference Trump abruptly cancelled the upcoming US–ROK defensive exercises (which Trump described as 'war games'), labelling them as 'provocative' – echoing a charge often laid by Pyongyang – and costly. Neither the ROK, the Pentagon nor the United States Forces Korea had apparently been consulted or warned, but all fell into line. On 18 June, the Department of Defense said it had halted planning for the annual *Ulchi Freedom Guardian* manoeuvres, scheduled for August. On 22 June, it confirmed that Defense Secretary James Mattis had 'indefinitely suspended select military exercises on the Korean Peninsula', including *Ulchi Freedom Guardian* as well as two Korean Marine Exchange Program training exercises due in the next three months. Any further cancellations, however, would 'depend upon North Korea continuing to have productive negotiations in good faith'.

Much hinges upon future talks bearing fruit, but Trump's conviction that he has secured peace for our time – on 3 July he tweeted: 'If not for me, we would now be at War with North Korea!' – is widely doubted, including by usually supportive outlets such as Fox News. There is speculation that the Singapore summit reached additional understandings that for whatever reason were not included in the published statement. However, given the DPRK's history of breaking or even repudiating agreements, such tacit trust is clearly a far from adequate basis for diplomatic or security progress unless much more detail is provided without undue delay.

So far Pyongyang has done two things. On 20 April, at a plenary of the WPK, Kim Jong-un declared that no further nuclear or ICBM tests 'are necessary for the DPRK now', and 'the mission of the northern nuclear test ground has thus come to an end'. A few foreign journalists were invited to witness large explosions at the Punggye-ri test site on 24 May. Those who had brought radiation detectors had them confiscated; the party included no nuclear experts, and no verification was possible. While both this and the testing moratorium are significant and welcome, they are at best initial steps in what, to be credible, must soon become a comprehensive, detailed, verified, time-bound and public denuclearisation process.

In 2017, Beijing proposed a 'dual freeze': US–ROK joint exercises were to be suspended if the DPRK halted nuclear and ICBM tests. Washington rejected this due to the implicit suggestion that illegal ICBM tests and legitimate routine defensive exercises were tradable equivalents, yet by mid-2018 this was the de facto position. In a parallel retreat, the US now echoes Pyongyang's formula of 'denuclearisation of the Korean Peninsula', with its implication that both sides must make concessions. The Trump administration's initial demand for CVID – complete, verifiable, irreversible [nuclear] dismantlement – (coined under George W. Bush in the Six-Party Talks held between 2003 and 2008) was absent from the Singapore statement. By July 2018 the State Department spoke of 'final, fully verified denuclearization', insisting this was not a softening. 'Maximum pressure' is another vanished slogan, though Washington still says sanctions will remain until full denuclearisation. Also gone is the demand for immediacy, absurd for technical as well as political reasons. In a report published in May, Siegfried Hecker – a former director of the US Los Alamos weapons laboratory and the only foreign scientist to have had a glimpse of Pyongyang's still largely unknown and wholly undeclared second nuclear programme, based on uranium enrichment – wrote that full denuclearisation would take at least a decade. In urging immediacy, National Security Advisor John Bolton – who now admits that the process may require a year or so – cited the precedent of Libya: hardly reassuring (as he must have known) to Kim Jong-un, given the grim ultimate fate of Muammar Gadhafi and his regime. Elsewhere, in yet another retreat, Washington has fallen silent on Pyongyang's human-rights abuses, which were catalogued in depth in 2014 by a special UN Commission of Inquiry and were often highlighted by Trump in 2017, such as when he called North Korea 'a hell that no one deserves'.

North Korean sincerity?

Predicting whether the new fledgling Korean peace process will prove durable entails teasing out the motives of the major protagonists, some of which are clearer than others. Nothing Kim Jong-un has yet said or done suggests a radical departure from the policy stance he inherited from his father Kim Jong-il and grandfather Kim Il-sung, in a political system where loyalty and fidelity are paramount. Efforts to assess Kim Jong-un's goals often neglect this domestic dimension. Pitched into power in 2011 with scant preparation, Kim's first task was to secure his own position. This involved reining in the KPA which had grown overweening under his father's '*Songun*' (military-first) policy, restoring Party control – its top organs had atrophied – and eliminating rivals, most notably Jang Song-thaek, his powerful uncle and Beijing's friend, in 2013.

Having secured the home front, from 2016 Kim moved to doing the same externally: seeking to render the DPRK impregnable with an accelerated process of nuclear tests and missile and rocket launches. As he said in November 2017 and reiterated in April 2018, that phase is now complete, as is the '*Byungjin*' (parallel development) policy, proclaimed in 2013, of the simultaneous pursuit of nuclear weapons and economic development. Henceforth the latter alone is the top priority. On that basis the new switch to diplomatic outreach does not break with past policy, but rather builds upon it. With his nuclear-defended realm secure, and new leaders in Seoul and Washington open to dialogue, it made sense for Kim to emerge from a seclusion hitherto much misunderstood. No hermit, he was simply biding his time – as in fact his father also did at the outset of his reign.

Kim's debut on the global stage has begun well for him, with much gained at little cost. What remains unclear is how far he is really ready to go on the road of denuclearisation, and what will happen if Trump decides his new friend is not, after all, sincere or fast enough. Satellite imagery from June 2018 showed that infrastructural development is continuing at Yongbyon, the main nuclear site north of Pyongyang; meanwhile, the Defense Intelligence Agency reportedly assessed that, far from preparing any kind of complete nuclear and missile inventory, the DPRK was instead taking steps to conceal the full extent of its nuclear activities.

Moreover, nuclear and ICBM concerns, while urgent, are by no means the only threat which Pyongyang poses. As highlighted by the use of a nerve agent in the flagrantly public murder of Kim Jong-un's older half-brother Kim Jong-nam at Kuala Lumpur airport in February, the DPRK's arsenal also includes chemical and biological weapons. (UN inspectors have alleged that the DPRK exports dual-use chemicals to its close ally Syria.) The DPRK has also been linked to some major world-wide cyber attacks in recent years, most notoriously on Sony Pictures in 2014, but also including the WannaCry ransomware attack in May 2017 as well as bank cyber-heists in Bangladesh, Taiwan and indeed South Korea, which has been under continuous assault for over a decade. On 5 July, the quasi-official ROK news agency Yonhap reported that such hacking is ongoing, despite the Panmunjom Declaration's pledge to halt mutually hostile acts. This hardly suggests that Kim Jong-un is sincerely seeking peace. Perhaps this area too will eventually go on the negotiating table – presumably not in public – to be halted if and when the price is right.

The optimistic view is that the DPRK will drive a hard bargain, as always. Domestically, Kim Jong-un may still be vulnerable if he is perceived as giving away too much too soon, but the more immediate risk to the nascent peace process is that he will be – indeed already is – seen as giving up too little to sustain trust and credibility in Washington. The Singapore summit was preceded by several days of intensive talks at Panmunjom (on the DPRK side) between Sung Kim – a former special representative for North Korea Policy and US ambassador in Seoul, now posted to Manila – and DPRK vice-foreign minister Choe Son-hui. Washington would surely have liked more substance in the Singapore declaration, but Pyongyang was unyielding, perhaps judging that, after his earlier cancellation ploy, Trump was committed to the summit. Hopefully Kim and his advisers are no less adept in judging that now, by contrast, it is time to engage in meaningful and constructive conversation directed at achieving tangible results.

Given the political capital both leaders have invested in their new relationship, there is a fair chance that the process will remain on track in the short term. Indeed, Trump's intense self-belief may sustain his faith even if Kim continues to yield nothing much or very specific. The president's folksy quip on 27 June to supporters in North Dakota – whose trust in him appears undimmed even by his embrace of Kim Jong-un –

that to go too fast would be 'like rushing the turkey out of the stove. It's not going to be as good … The longer we take, the better' – could render him patient for some time, at least until past the mid-term elections in November 2018.

Conversely, if at any point Trump decides Kim has betrayed his trust, it may not be easy for him simply to revert to 'fire and fury'. The Korean Peninsula has moved on. In South Korea, Moon Jae-in has taken care to flatter Trump despite what must be deep misgivings, but as the new inter-Korean peace process deepens and acquires its own momentum, Moon will not sacrifice his core beliefs and signature policy to placate a mercurial ally. A key question here, once again, is Kim Jong-un's sincerity. Despite the lamentable persistence of cyber attacks, and the ambiguous precedent of the 'sunshine' policy – though it was the ROK, not the DPRK, who abandoned that earlier decade of engagement (1998–2007), which included illicit secret payments by Seoul and was criticised by Southern conservatives for failing to insist that the North reciprocate – in all probability this time Pyongyang under the young leader is serious about improving ties with the ROK, its motive being to bring Seoul onside as a further bulwark (with China), counterweight and hedge in case the US does backtrack. Even in Tokyo, where Abe backed Trump's earlier hardline approach and is uneasy with his turn to peace, this is tempered by an acute awareness of Japan's geography. Japan is on the front-line, along with South Korea, and therefore vulnerable even to smaller missiles which do not seem to be on anyone's agenda. In sum, there is no appetite now anywhere in the region for a return to last year's sabre-rattling.

Overall, Trump may deserve credit for his boldness in initiating dialogue with the DPRK, despite the inconsistencies and self-deception this has entailed. A best-case scenario now is for this to continue, with just enough concessions by Pyongyang to keep the process on track. Even before Trump's first year, a decade of escalating sanctions and pressure, while richly merited, had signally failed to deter successive Kims from the nuclear path. Meanwhile, deterrence in the traditional sense nonetheless kept the peninsula peaceful. If what is now unfolding is a policy which works with rather than against the grain of Kim Jong-un's desire and need for economic development, and if he yields enough for sanctions to be gradually eased, then despite the obvious misgivings – moral hazard, rewarding bad behaviour and so on – North Korea may be enticed into a virtuous circle whose chances of ultimately neutralising the Kim regime look no worse than the ineffectual vicious cycle – weapons tests, sanctions, more tests, more sanctions and so on – which has predominated in recent years.

Southeast Asia and the Belt and Road Initiative

Beijing's official rationale for its Belt and Road Initiative (BRI) – the vast infrastructure and investment master plan which was initially launched in 2013 under the name One Belt, One Road – has been economic: the BRI boosts regional development, upgrades Chinese industry while exporting Chinese standards and deals with excess capacity. Chinese President Xi Jinping has assured the international community that the initiative will be conducted on the basis of 'win–win cooperation' and that all countries should respect each other's 'sovereignty, dignity and territorial integrity'. Unofficially, though, Chinese analysts discuss using international assistance and the BRI as a pretext for pursuing China's grand strategy. The People's Liberation Army Naval Research Institute, for example, has pushed for the gradual infiltration by China of 'select locations'. Analysts also highlight the dual-use nature of port facilities on the Belt and Road. While countries in Southeast Asia are cautious about the economic costs and strategic implications of the BRI in the region, in most cases this apprehension has not translated into rejecting or cancelling BRI projects.

The big idea
Xi opened the Belt and Road Forum for International Cooperation in Beijing in May 2017 to much fanfare, delivering a landmark speech that

represented the culmination of a four-year effort by China to promote its grand geostrategic infrastructure and economic-stimulus plan across Eurasia. In his speech, Xi identified several important global challenges: global growth lacked impetus; development needed to be more inclusive; and the gap between rich and poor remained too wide. The international, and particularly regional, response was strong and positive. According to Chinese state reports, 29 foreign heads of state and government and representatives from more than 130 countries, not to mention 70 international organisations, attended the opening ceremony. At the Belt and Road Forum, Xi stressed that development – encompassing economic growth, integration and interconnectivity – was the 'master key' to solving all problems, including security. Many heads of state agreed with Xi's link between security and development. Pakistan's then-prime minister Nawaz Sharif, for example, described the BRI as 'a powerful tool for overcoming extremism and terrorism'.

From China's perspective, the liberal global economic order sponsored by the United States and its allies since the 1940s should be replaced by an improved form of global governance, and the BRI is at the heart of that drive. At the 19th National Congress of the Chinese Communist Party (CCP) in October 2017, the BRI was enshrined into the party's constitution. The congress resolved that China would 'actively promote international cooperation through the Belt and Road Initiative, and continue to take an active part in reforming and developing the global governance system'. At a time when the rules-based international system is under question, the CCP has exploited the BRI in such a way that it positions Xi as a saviour of global economic growth. The BRI is one element of a carefully choreographed 'China Plan' by China across military, diplomatic and economic spheres that will challenge the existing, Western-dominated rules-based international order.

Despite the profusion of information on the official Belt and Road website (*yidaiyilu*), it is nevertheless difficult to get a clear sense of the full scope of BRI projects. China has announced a multitude of new projects since the Belt and Road Forum while also bringing older projects within the initiative's purview, such as the Kyaukpyu deep-sea port in

Myanmar's western Rakhine State and the Chinese mega-project in the Koh Kong province in Cambodia – both projects predate the BRI but are listed on the official website. Geography also plays a part: the BRI appears most clearly defined in China's immediate region where the BRI connects Chinese provincial nodes to those on the country's western periphery and eastern seaboard. This lends credence to critics of the BRI who suggest that the initiative is (at least initially) aimed at stimulating China's domestic economy through extending infrastructure and economic links to the immediate neighbourhood and thus offloading Chinese excess capacity from state-owned enterprises. To its detractors the BRI project becomes more nebulous and ill-defined as the distance from China increases, with almost any Chinese joint venture west of China categorised as a BRI project.

The BRI has been eyed with scepticism, particularly in the West. International observers have criticised the lack of transparency regarding planned BRI projects and have urged China to publish more data on its financial support for the initiative with regard to the amounts lent to each country and the terms of these loans. Sri Lanka has been in the spotlight since 2017 after allowing China a controlling equity in, and a long-term operating lease on, its Hambantota port after struggling to make payments on the debt it had taken on to develop it. The Sri Lankan case has highlighted the risks involved in the BRI, which some observers fear could result in strategic facilities, such as ports or railways, in Southeast Asia being surrendered to Chinese control in the event of loan defaults. Following the defeat of Malaysia's then-prime minister Najib Razak in the May 2018 elections by Mahathir Mohamad amid corruption allegations, Mahathir has placed the East Coast Rail Link project and pipeline projects worth US$23 billion on hold, stating that the terms of the project offered by Chinese funders were 'lopsided' and warning of the threat of neo-colonialism by 'rich countries'.

Southeast Asia's response

Bad cases notwithstanding, there is no denying that the BRI holds substantial economic potential, particularly for meeting infrastructure needs in Southeast Asia. (The Asian Development Bank estimates that the sub-region needs to invest 5.7% of its aggregate GDP in infrastructure during the period to 2030 to 'maintain its growth momentum, tackle poverty, and respond to climate change'.)

For this reason, the response in Southeast Asia has been more nuanced than most reporting on the BRI has allowed for. Such reports correctly observe 'push back' across Southeast Asia. However, this has not taken the form of rejecting the BRI as a whole but, rather, examining the economic viability of each project and seeking better terms.

Myanmar, for example, is scaling down the Kyaukpyu port project over concerns that it could leave the country heavily indebted, but it is nevertheless proceeding with the project due to the urgent need to develop Myanmar's weak infrastructure. Naypyidaw needs to keep its geo-economic and -political options open given growing criticism – particularly from the West but also from nearby Southeast Asian countries (such as Indonesia and Malaysia) – over its treatment of the Rohingya minority community. China acknowledges that BRI projects in Myanmar, including the China–Myanmar Economic Corridor, have been affected by violence in Rakhine State, but maintains that lack of development is the core problem for the afflicted country. Flourishing trading links between Yunnan province and a growing Chinese presence in Mandalay, for example, are viewed by Beijing as an important land link for the BRI in Myanmar. Meanwhile, China has taken a strong stance over ethnic conflict in Shan State, where in 2016 cross-border conflict flared between the ethnic Chinese Kokhang militants and Myanmar forces, prompting the Chinese People's Liberation Army to mount a show of force there.

Like Myanmar, Thailand cannot afford to turn its back on China, particularly in light of diplomatic strains with the West over its military government which came to power in a coup in 2014. Thailand is at the heart of a BRI project – a pan-Asian railway line intended to improve connectivity between southern China and Southeast Asia. In July 2017, Thailand's cabinet approved the 252-kilometre-long stretch of the line between the capital Bangkok and the northeastern province of Nakhon

Ratchasima. The project has been dogged by disagreements with China over design, funding and technology transfer, but construction nevertheless commenced in December 2017. Pursuing BRI options has not, of course, stopped Thailand from further hedging. It has sought to convince Cambodia, Laos, Myanmar and Vietnam to set up a regional infrastructure fund for the Mekong region. In June 2018, at the eighth summit of the Ayeyawady–Chao Phraya–Mekong Economic Cooperation Strategy (ACMECS), Thailand proposed the establishment of an ACMECS fund to support infrastructural development in mainland Southeast Asia.

Even countries benefiting from warmer relations with the West are eager to proceed with BRI projects, though they might seek to negotiate better terms. Foremost among these is the Philippines. In August 2017, Philippine Secretary of Finance Carlos Dominguez III said that the BRI – and especially the 21st Century Maritime Silk Road component of the BRI – could be integrated with the Philippines' plans for major domestic-infrastructure construction and help the country to open new markets for its products. Under the Duterte administration, Manila has made an about-turn in how it approaches the South China Sea dispute, which has long been a source of tension in relations with China, particularly during the previous administration led by Benigno Aquino III from 2010–16. The Duterte administration has studiously avoided mention of a 2016 United Nations tribunal ruling in a case brought by the Philippines against China over the latter's claims and activities in the South China Sea, though the ruling was a major victory for the Philippines. In November 2017, Beijing rewarded Manila for its discretion with promises of major infrastructure deals, including the Chico River Pump Irrigation Project, the New Centennial Water Source Project (and associated Kaliwa Dam Project) and the Philippine National Railway South Long Haul Project. In August 2018, Duterte adopted a harsher public tone in response to Chinese threats to the Philippine Air Force in the South China Sea. If rhetoric escalates between the Philippines and China, some of this financing could be unilaterally withdrawn by Chinese funders.

In Indonesia, the Jakarta–Bandung rail project has stalled because of problems with land acquisition and concerns about affordability, but Jakarta is hopeful that it can reach agreement with Beijing on how to 'reduce the costs' of the rail link. More broadly, Beijing's funding is important to one of the main pillars of President Joko Widodo's 'Global Maritime Axis' vision, which he announced in June 2014 with the aim of reinforcing maritime-transport links across the sprawling Indonesian archipelago of more than 17,000 islands. In August 2017, Chinese Foreign Minister Wang Yi announced that Beijing was willing to 'promote synergy' between the BRI and Indonesia's Global Maritime Axis, and was positively considering participation in the building infrastructure to support Indonesia's three planned maritime 'corridors'.

Similarly, while the recently elected government in Malaysia is reviewing large infrastructure projects and in May cancelled the Kuala Lumpur–Singapore High Speed Rail project, Mahathir has made clear that he is not in principle against the BRI. Indeed, in an interview in June 2018, he appeared to claim credit for the idea, saying that he had 'suggested long ago improving the Silk Road'. Instead, Mahathir's government is seeking to negotiate better terms for Chinese projects, including the US$13.8-bn East Coast Rail project, to ensure that Malaysia as well as China reap the benefits of the BRI. Kuala Lumpur aims to persuade Beijing that debt traps are detrimental for China as well as regional countries, because projects that go sour may do damage to China's reputation.

Even Singapore, a highly developed city-state, has been working to ensure that it is not left out of the BRI after Beijing failed to invite Singaporean Prime Minister Lee Hsien Loong to the Belt and Road Forum in May 2017. In April 2018, Lee said that Singapore was an 'early and strong supporter' of the BRI and emphasised the potential for China and Singapore to cooperate on developing infrastructural and financial connectivity. Moreover, he suggested, Singapore could play a role in arbitrating cross-border commercial disputes. In August 2017, the Singapore Business Federation and China Enterprises Association jointly launched the BRI Connect Platform at the Singapore Regional Business Forum. The platform is intended to connect parties interested in potential collaboration on BRI projects and facilitate the role of regional businesses in implementing such projects. One month later, Singaporean and Chinese mediation centres signed a memorandum of understanding to work together on BRI-related business disputes. However, there has been little sign of subsequent progress on this initiative, and in mid-2018 China established international courts in Shenzhen and Xi'an to arbitrate disputes on BRI maritime and land projects, respectively.

Vietnam is possibly the most cautious country in Southeast Asia with regard to the BRI. Memories of the 1979 Sino-Vietnamese war, as well as the South China Sea dispute, continue to undermine bilateral ties. Anti-China sentiment is evident in Vietnam: in June 2018, there were anti-Chinese protests in several Vietnamese cities against special economic zones that some fear will favour Chinese investors. But even in Vietnam's case, the government has offered diplomatic support to the BRI – Vietnam's President Tran Dai Quang attended the Belt and Road Forum in Beijing – and has not ruled out encouraging private investors in Vietnam to apply for BRI loans. In July 2017, China's *People's Daily* reported that the Vinh Tan 1 Thermal Power Plant – an important BRI project in Vietnam's southern province of Binh Thuan – would help ease local electricity shortages after its completion at the end of 2018. The coal-fired power project will generate approximately 8bn kilowatt hours of electricity annually by 2019. With investment in the project totalling US$1.76bn, the Vinh Tan 1 Thermal Power Plant is the largest Chinese investment in Vietnam, as well as the first BOT (build–operate–transfer) project by China in the country.

The BRI is still at an early stage of what China evidently intends to be a long-term programme. Many projects have not yet materialised; some might never come to fruition. Nonetheless, the BRI has generated a sense of geo-economic momentum that underpins China's growing strategic clout in Southeast Asia, both bilaterally and within the Association of Southeast Asian Nations (ASEAN). While most Southeast Asian countries have hedged their options by remaining open to Japanese and Western initiatives – for example, Japan's bidding for the Bandung–Jakarta high-speed rail project and the Kuala Lumpur–Singapore high-speed rail link – there has been a perceptible shift towards closer alignment with China's policies and priorities. If Southeast Asia continues along the current trajectory, China will be able to consolidate its already rapidly growing geo-economic influence in the region under the banner of the BRI.

However, this is by no means a foregone conclusion. The broader implications of the unfolding US–China trade war are still unclear, as is whether the US, its allies and partners are able to provide a convincing response to the BRI. There are several alternative strategic visions: Japan's Southern Strategy (whereby Tokyo seeks to strengthen its economic and security relations with Southeast Asia); India's Act East policy (in large part an attempt to foster greater economic and strategic ties with the countries of Southeast Asia); and the United States' Free and Open Indo-Pacific, a strategy that seeks to win the support of other democracies in the region (Australia, India and Japan in particular) in balancing China's growing influence. The Free and Open Indo-Pacific strategy, however, is facing challenges, not least in terms of India's cool response and the need to ensure a strong economic component. How these diverse visions are translated into concrete policies and whether they may be synergised with each other, or even with the BRI – China and Japan, for instance, agreed in early August to encourage deeper economic cooperation in the private sector, targeting infrastructure projects in the region as part of the BRI – will play a critical role in shaping the region's strategic as well as geo-economic landscape over the coming decade. Much of the debate about the BRI has focused on Southeast Asian countries facing invidious choices between Chinese and Western geostrategic interests, and some experts argue that China is moving into a vacuum left by the US as a result of US President Donald Trump's abandonment of the Trans-Pacific Partnership. China has consistently stressed that the BRI is designed to be complementary to existing initiatives in the region and to be fully inclusive. Renewed attention by the US in Southeast Asia combined with the weight of the BRI could, if managed well by regional countries, offer more opportunities to improve infrastructure than ever before.

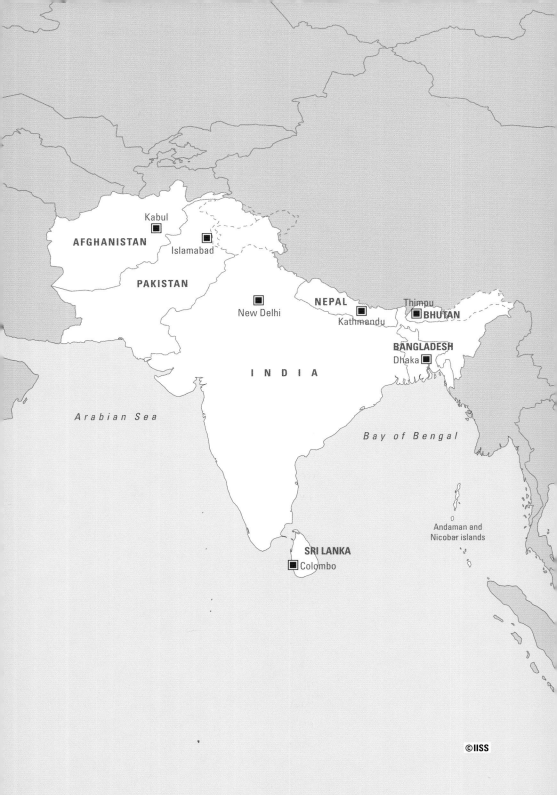

Chapter 5

South Asia and Afghanistan

2017–18 Review

US President Donald Trump announced a new 'Afghanistan and South Asia' strategy on 21 August 2017, which aimed to apply a much-needed wider regional approach to Afghanistan in an attempt to end the 17-year conflict. However, the Taliban remained strong in the year to mid-August 2018, attacking the western city of Farah and threatening to take Ghazni, though a three-day truce between the Taliban and the government in June 2018 gave some hope for peace talks after earlier setbacks.

The United States also unveiled a new approach to its relations with Pakistan, pursuing a tougher line towards Islamabad. At the start of 2018, Washington suspended military assistance worth approximately US$2 billion to prompt 'decisive, sustained action' by Pakistan against Taliban and Haqqani-network personnel and infrastructure inside Pakistan. In February, the US led an effort at a meeting of the Financial Action Task Force to 'grey list' Pakistan, who were formally placed on the list in June. Consequences of the 'grey listing' could include an impact on Pakistan's economy, affecting imports, exports and access to international lending. US economic assistance continued, however, as did political and security engagement at the top levels of government. As Pakistan's relations with the US became strained, its ties with China strengthened. China's portfolio of investments in Pakistan has grown, most notably as part of the China–Pakistan Economic Corridor (CPEC). Domestically, however, tensions between the military and the government increased. In April 2017, Pakistan's Supreme Court established a group – including officials from Pakistan's Inter-Services Intelligence and Military Intelligence – to investigate corruption allegations against then-prime minister Nawaz Sharif and his family following the release of the Panama Papers. Sharif resigned in July 2017 after the Supreme Court disqualified him from holding public office for being dishonest in disclosing his earnings.

After considerable political jostling, the prime minister and leader of the opposition agreed on the appointment of former chief justice Nasir-ul-Mulk as the country's caretaker prime minister to preside over the elections, which took place on 25 July 2018. The Pakistan Tehreek-e-Insaf (PTI) party won the most seats in the election, upsetting the establishment forces of the Pakistan Muslim League–Nawaz (PML–N) and the Pakistan People's Party (PPP). The PTI won 149 of the 342 seats in the National Assembly, Pakistan's lower house, while the PML–N won 82 and the PPP 54. Imran Khan, the PTI leader and former cricketer, was sworn in as prime minister of Pakistan on 18 August. The election marked only the second time that a civilian government in Pakistan had completed its five-year term and transferred power to another elected government (the first happened in 2013). The PML–N and PPP both accused the military of interfering in the election in favour of the PTI. The relationship between Khan and the Pakistan military, especially in the first year of the PTI government, will be crucial for how Pakistan's key foreign-policy relationships develop. In his first speech following the elections, Khan highlighted his desire to strengthen relations with China, especially through CPEC, while he also wished to address ties with Afghanistan, India, Iran and the US. His first foreign visit as prime minister was to Saudi Arabia, shortly after he was sworn in as prime minister.

In April 2018, Pakistan's high-level political and security engagement with Afghanistan was enhanced through the finalisation of a joint action plan 'to bring more cooperation and coordination' between the two countries, called the Afghanistan–Pakistan Action Plan for Peace and Solidarity (APAPPS). During the inaugural meetings of the APAPPS in Kabul in July, the two sides discussed enhancing cooperation on political, military, intelligence, economic, trade and refugee-repatriation issues. Elsewhere, Pakistan's relations with India remained tense, with regular exchanges of fire across the international border as well as across the Line of Control that divides the Kashmir region.

In India, Prime Minister Narendra Modi's Bharatiya Janata Party (BJP) strengthened its position by winning nine state elections, most notably in Uttar Pradesh, Gujarat and the northeastern state of Tripura. As a consequence, it held power in 19 of India's 29 states. However, the BJP faced a setback in Karnataka, where its attempt to form a minority administration failed and the Congress and Janata Dal parties formed a coalition government. With the general election due in mid-2019, the main opposition and regional parties explored the possibility of an anti-BJP alliance. Although Modi and the BJP are strong politically, there is some concern over the impact of his economic reforms on small businesses. He has replaced 17 central, state and local taxes with a single tax and in July 2017 the government introduced a goods and services tax (GST), the most significant tax reform in the history of modern India, which required amendment of the constitution. The economy recorded high single-digit growth and was forecast to expand by 7.4% in 2018–19, but the government remained well short of its target to create 10 million jobs a year for the rapidly expanding workforce. There were also concerns over investment, as the growth in foreign direct investment (FDI) fell to a five-year low of 3% in 2017–18.

In mid-2017, there was a tense 73-day military stand-off between Indian and Chinese security forces in the disputed Doklam area in Bhutan – the longest and most serious confrontation between the states for decades. It ended on 28 August 2017 after several rounds of closed-door bilateral negotiations and discussions. In late April 2018, Modi met Chinese President Xi Jinping for an 'informal summit' in Wuhan, at which they agreed to restore relations and 'speed up' economic cooperation in the Bangladesh–China–India–Myanmar (BCIM) Economic

Corridor. However, they continued to disagree on items such as China's Belt and Road Initiative (BRI) and its Pakistan offshoot, CPEC. In a thinly veiled criticism of China, Modi emphasised the importance of a rules-based international order and spoke against infrastructure projects that were not 'based on respect for sovereignty and territorial integrity, consultation, good governance, transparency, viability and sustainability' in his keynote address at the IISS Shangri-La Dialogue in Singapore in June 2018.

Elsewhere in South Asia, domestic politics took a turbulent turn. In Sri Lanka, the opposition leader and former president Mahinda Rajapaksa called on the government to resign after his party, the Sri Lanka People's Front, scored a resounding victory in local elections, gaining control of 239 of the 340 municipal, urban and divisional councils. The ruling coalition between Prime Minister Ranil Wickremesinghe's centre-right United National Party (UNP) and President Maithripala Sirisena's centre-left Sri Lanka Freedom Party (SLFP) has failed to deliver anti-corruption measures and economic reforms. Elections are not due until late 2019, with the political crisis between the ruling coalition of Sirisena and Wickremesinghe set to dominate the domestic political discourse in the coming year.

In Bangladesh, which is due to hold a general election in 2018, there were country-wide protests after Khaleda Zia, the former prime minister and current leader of the main opposition party, the Bangladesh National Party (BNP), was found guilty of corruption and jailed for five years. The conviction stoked fears among the opposition that Prime Minister Sheikh Hasina and her ruling Bangladesh Azami League would not allow a free and fair general election (the next of which is scheduled for late December 2018). Zia's imprisonment also raised fears about the security situation in the country ahead of the general election. Bangladesh's relations with neighbouring Myanmar were severely strained by Myanmar's crackdown on Rohingya Muslims in Rakhine State. In the year from August 2017, nearly 700,000 Rohingya Muslims – an ethnic category that is not recognised by the Myanmar government – fled the Myanmar armed forces' brutal military operations, causing a major humanitarian crisis in Bangladesh. In June 2018, Myanmar and the United Nations signed an agreement to repatriate the Rohingya refugees, although the prospects for implementation remained slim, as the agreement was rejected by Rohingya community leaders who stated that it did not address their concerns and would not help with the repatriation of refugees.

As the Maldives prepared for its presidential elections in September 2018, a political and constitutional crisis erupted. On 5 February, President Abdulla Yameen Abdul Gayoom declared a state of emergency that lasted until 22 March after the Supreme Court ruled to reinstate 12 opposition members of parliament (who had been barred for defecting from the ruling party), and overturned verdicts against nine opposition figures (including former president Mohamed Nasheed, elected in the country's first contested democratic election in 2008, who had been charged with allegations of attempting to overthrow the government).

During the state of emergency, key opposition leaders were either arrested or imprisoned, including the chief justice and the president's half-brother, Maumoon Abdul Gayoom, who had ruled the country as president continuously for 30 years from 1978. The measures caused mass protests across the country. Restoring the political process in the Maldives and ensuring the country's security and stability has been a major concern for international organisations and regional powers. Although Nasheed has been barred from standing in the election, his Maldivian Democratic Party (MDP) has nominated lawmaker Ibrahim Solih to contest the election as a joint opposition candidate, backed by the rest of the opposition parties.

In contrast to Bangladesh and the Maldives, electoral politics ran smoothly in Nepal. Communist parties triumphed in the December 2017 parliamentary elections, which were held under the country's new federal constitution, marking the end of Nepal's transition from monarchy to federal republic. The Communist Party of Nepal–Unified Marxist–Leninist (CPN–UML), led by Khadga Prasad Sharma Oli, topped the poll and formed a majority administration with the Communist Party of Nepal–Maoist Centre (CPN–MC) in the lower house of the national parliament and six of the country's seven newly created provinces. The CPN–UML and the CPN–MC (led by Pushpa Kamal Dahal, also known as Prachanda) subsequently merged under a joint Communist Party of Nepal (CPN). Nepal has had ten prime ministers in as many years, but new constitutional rules prohibit a no-confidence motion for the first two years of the parliament, ensuring a period of some much-needed stability in the country. Balancing relations with its two giant neighbours, India and China, will be the major geopolitical challenge for the Oli government over the next year.

South Asia and Afghanistan: Drivers of Strategic Change

▪ Pakistan's estrangement from the United States has become more pronounced following the suspension of US military aid worth US$2billion, drawing Pakistan into China's orbit. Domestically, Pakistan's general election on 25 July 2018 marked the breaking-up of the political duopoly in the country, with the Pakistan Tehreek-e-Insaf party (led by former cricketer Imran Khan) winning a majority victory.

▪ India and China are engaged in regional outreach, although such efforts are likely to conflict with each other. China's Belt and Road Initiative remains a particular obstacle in relations between the states.

▪ The Bharatiya Janata Party has made further gains in several by-elections in India, further cementing its grip on power ahead of the general election in 2019.

▪ The conflict in Afghanistan continues to witness high levels of violence, despite a 2017 US strategy that involved a troop surge and increase in airstrikes. Peace negotiations may see a breakthrough, however, with news of a July 2017 secret face-to-face meeting in Doha between a US State Department official and members of the Taliban.

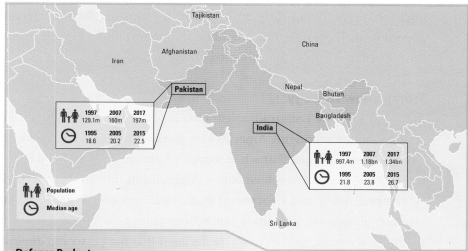

Defence Budget
(US$, constant 2010 prices)

	2008	2013	2018
India	$31.34bn	$46.12bn	$62.9bn
Pakistan	$4.79bn	$6.22bn	$7.77bn

GDP per capita, Purchasing Power Parity (International $, constant 2011 prices)

Country		GDP
India	1997	$2,195
Pakistan		$3,384
India	2007	$3,699
Pakistan		$4,288
India	2017	$6,427
Pakistan		$5,035

Imran Khan, Pakistan's cricketer-turned-politician and head of the Pakistan Tehreek-e-Insaf party, was elected the country's new prime minister in the general election on 25 July 2018

Sources: IISS; UN Department of Economic and Social Affairs (Population Division, 2017); World Bank

Prospects for Peace in Afghanistan

Afghanistan remains locked in a ferocious civil war, 17 years after the US-led invasion of the country and four years after the International Security Assistance Force handed over responsibility for the country's security to the Afghan government forces. However, 2018 witnessed the roll-out of a new US military strategy in the country, the first nation-wide ceasefire since 2001 and the first-ever talks between the US and the Taliban. Parliamentary and presidential elections in Afghanistan, scheduled for late 2018 and early 2019, will be a major test for the Afghan government. Thereafter there might be an opportunity to explore again the possibility for talks that emerged briefly in mid-2018.

Trump's new strategy

In August 2017, the Trump administration announced a new Afghanistan strategy, aimed at bringing America's longest war to a close. US President Donald Trump argued that while Barack Obama had set artificial time-tables for American involvement in Afghanistan, his strategy would be comprehensive and he stressed that 'conditions on the ground, not arbitrary timetables will guide our actions from now on', and vowed that the US would 'fight to win'. He declared that the US would deploy more US military personnel to Afghanistan, increase the number of Afghan security forces and intensify aerial bombing against the Taliban and other militant groups. Although Trump did not specify the number of additional personnel to be deployed, in June 2018 the US Defense Department stated that the surge had brought the current total of US military personnel in Afghanistan to approximately 14,000, up from 8,400 in January 2017 when Trump was sworn in as president.

Trump's strategy in Afghanistan aims to exert pressure on the insurgents in three ways in order to break the stalemate with the Taliban and push the group to the negotiating table. Firstly, the US would apply maximum military pressure to roll back the Taliban from the vast areas of the country it controls – the Taliban is openly active in 70% of Afghanistan according to a BBC study published in January 2018 –

and to expand the government's territorial writ, especially in densely populated areas. The strategy aims to reverse significantly the Taliban's territorial gains made over the past few years, especially since NATO formally concluded its combat mission at the end of 2014. In October 2017, General John Nicholson, commander of the US-led *Operation Resolute Support* in Afghanistan, pledged that a 'tidal wave of air power' would be unleashed in the war against the Taliban and that 'this is the beginning of the end for the Taliban'. As operations against the Islamic State, also known as ISIS or ISIL, in Syria and Iraq drew to a close towards the end of 2017, extra resources were shifted to Afghanistan, resulting in a dramatic escalation in the number of bombs dropped by the US Air Force.

Secondly, Trump's strategy focuses on targeting the financial sources of the Taliban, which mainly involves bombing heroin factories in Taliban-controlled areas, especially southern Helmand province, the source of most of the opium produced in Afghanistan. The Taliban usually taxes the opium industry in Afghanistan – although there are no exact figures, estimates of the Taliban's annual income from the drugs economy range from tens of millions of dollars to US$400m. Thirdly, the strategy aims to increase social and religious pressure on the Taliban by encouraging religious scholars to question the legitimacy of the Taliban's insurgency on religious grounds. As part of this approach, religious scholars held various meetings in Afghanistan in the first half of 2018 and condemned the Taliban's campaign of violence, labelling it 'un-Islamic'. Meetings of religious scholars were also held outside Afghanistan, including ones in Saudi Arabia and Indonesia. The Taliban denounced the conferences as an 'American process' to 'justify occupation' and urged clerics to reject the gatherings.

Despite the new US strategy, the first half of 2018 witnessed sustained Taliban activity. In April 2018, the group announced the launch of its 2018 spring offensive, which it said would include 'guerrilla, offensive, infiltrated and various other new and intricate tactics against the new war strategy of the enemy'. The insurgents carried out numerous deadly attacks throughout the country in the first half of 2018, including several in the capital Kabul. In May, the Taliban entered the capital of Farah province in western Afghanistan, close to the Iranian border, although they were ejected the day after a team of American special-forces commandos, accompanied by armed drones and jets, was dispatched to help Afghan forces. Several other provincial capitals including Ghazni, Kunduz, Lashkar Gah (Helmand province) and Tarin Kot (Uruzgan province) were threatened by the Taliban, where the group has a permanent presence on the outskirts and controls or contests several districts around the city centres.

US military officials have repeatedly given the impression that the new strategy is delivering. On 3 May 2018, Pentagon chief spokesperson Dana White explained that the uptick in violence was a sign that the Taliban was 'desperate' because it was 'losing ground', yet it was evident that the group was resilient in the face of heavy casualties. Overall, the new US strategy has shown very little progress in achieving the stated goal of pushing back the Taliban and forcing them to join peace talks with the Afghan government. Although the increased military pressure has slowed the expansion of Taliban territorial control and many Taliban fighters (including a few important commanders) have been killed, the group has largely managed to hold its territory and retain its operational capacity to launch devastating attacks.

The intensive aerial bombing campaign has also been criticised for causing civilian casualties. On 2 April 2018, an Afghan Air Force attack on a madrassa (religious seminary) in the Taliban-controlled district of Dasht-e Archi in northern Kunduz province killed at least 36 people, mostly children, and injured 71, according to the UN. The attack – which took place during a traditional graduation ceremony recognising the memorisation of the Koran by students – raised questions about US and Afghan strategy and supplied propaganda for the Taliban. Many more civilians have been killed and injured in attacks claimed by the Taliban and ISIS. According to the UN, more than 10,000 civilians were killed or injured in the violent attacks in the war in Afghanistan in 2017. The UN Assistance Mission in Afghanistan (UNAMA) released a report in July 2018 stating that the number of civilians killed in Afghanistan had reached a record high in the first half of the year. According to the report, 1,692 civilians were killed in the first six months of 2018, which is the highest January–June count in the ten years for which records have been kept.

Mutual ceasefires and secret meetings

In June 2018, the Afghan government announced a unilateral ceasefire around the time of the Muslim festival of Eid ul-Fitr. It did so to signal to society that it was open to peace; to offer its army and population some respite from the fighting, which had exacted a heavy toll; and to pressure the Taliban to make a decision whether or not to reciprocate. Afghan President Ashraf Ghani told the security forces to cease operations against the Taliban 'from the 27th of Ramadan until the 5th day of Eid' (12–19 June), although he added that fighting against other armed groups such as ISIS and al-Qaeda would continue. The US supported the announcement and agreed to abide by the terms of the ceasefire.

On 9 June, the Taliban announced that it too would observe a three-day ceasefire over the Eid ul-Fitr holiday, although the group would continue to target foreign forces and defend itself against any attack. The leadership did so in order to demonstrate that it continued to exert control over all fighters, and to put pressure on the government to extend its own ceasefire. Ghani duly obliged, announcing that the government would extend its ceasefire beyond 20 June for another ten days. However, the Taliban refused to extend its ceasefire beyond the three days of Eid, and thereafter it resumed attacks on the Afghan security forces. Nevertheless, the three-day truce was the first since the US-led invasion in 2001. It allowed hundreds of Taliban members to visit Kabul and other cities, where they openly socialised with government security forces and civilians. Meanwhile, several government employees and members of the Afghan security forces managed to visit their villages in Taliban-controlled areas. The government ended its 18-day unilateral ceasefire on 30 June and intense fighting soon resumed.

To date, all attempts at finding a political settlement for the conflict in Afghanistan have failed. There have been several instances of contact between the Afghan government and the Taliban over the past few years, but none have resulted in the establishment of an official peace process. At the core of the impasse is a disagreement about who should be at the negotiating table. The Taliban has repeatedly stated that it believes negotiations are a legitimate way of achieving its main objective – ending the 'occupation' of Afghanistan by foreign forces – but the group does not recognise the Afghan government as a legitimate negotiating party. The Taliban considers the Afghan government a puppet regime of the United States, viewing it as weak, divided and unable to effect major decisions, such as the full withdrawal of foreign forces from Afghanistan. The Taliban insists on talking only to the US, at least in the initial phase, whom it considers the main party to the conflict. The group says that it would be willing to talk to all Afghan sides once the issue of foreign forces is settled.

Until recently, Washington had refused to enter into direct talks with the Taliban. According to Washington, the war in Afghanistan is primarily between the two Afghan sides (the Afghan Taliban and the Afghan government), and Washington cannot substitute for direct negotiations between Kabul and the Taliban. Washington says that it supports and is prepared to facilitate an 'Afghan-led and Afghan-owned' peace process, and there have been indications that the two Afghan sides have exchanged views informally on a few occasions, although actual progress has been difficult to ascertain. In late May 2018, General Nicholson claimed that mid- to high-ranking figures in the Taliban had held secret meetings with Afghan officials to discuss a possible ceasefire, but the Taliban rejected Nicholson's statement as a 'false claim' and reiterated its position that it did not 'want to waste time in the name of talks' with the Afghan government 'in the presence of the occupying forces'.

In July 2018, the US reiterated that its policy in Afghanistan had not changed, but by late July, it emerged that a US delegation led by Alice Wells, deputy assistant secretary in the State Department's Bureau of South and Central Asian Affairs, had secretly held face-to-face talks in Doha with members of the Taliban's political office (which has been based in Qatar since 2013). Taliban sources described the first direct talks between the group and the Trump administration's officials as a 'preliminary' discussion, and added that the two sides had agreed to meet again soon. In early August, Afghanistan's Chief Executive Abdullah Abdullah confirmed that US officials had had 'direct contact' with members of the Afghan Taliban in Qatar.

The regional dimension

Both US and Afghan officials say that progress in negotiations, or on the battlefield, depends on Pakistan, where the insurgent leaders are alleged to have sanctuaries. Military pressure within Afghanistan alone is not thought to be sufficient to force the Taliban to negotiate while the group enjoys access to those safe havens. Effective pressure by Islamabad – such as arresting or expelling Taliban leaders – would prove much more disruptive and detrimental to the Taliban than killing its foot soldiers in Afghanistan. The Trump administration has articulated a harder policy towards Pakistan in setting out its new Afghanistan strategy: in January 2018, it suspended security assistance and aid to Pakistan until Islamabad takes action against the Afghan Taliban on its soil. Some US officials have said they have seen some positive indications from Islamabad – such as the Pakistan government signalling that it will help start a peace process – but there are few signs of a paradigm shift in Pakistan with regard to the Afghan Taliban. Indeed, some analysts believe that Islamabad will try to help the Taliban fully exploit its battlefield successes at the negotiating table. In addition, although other regional countries (especially Iran and Russia) too have their own agendas, they also have substantial influence in Afghanistan and can help stabilise the situation.

Various regional actors have attempted to further the Afghan peace and reconciliation process, albeit with varying results. The Quadrilateral Coordination Group (QCG) of Afghanistan, China, Pakistan and the US met five times in the first half of 2016 before momentum stalled. A follow-up meeting was held in the Omani capital of Muscat in October 2017, but it appears that the QCG process has come to a halt without any sign of tangible progress having been made.

Russia had been unhappy at being sidelined from the QCG process and in response launched a rival 'Moscow Format' of regional consultations aimed at finding a political settlement to the conflict in Afghanistan. The first round of talks, held in December 2016, was attended by China and Pakistan but did not include any representation from Afghanistan. The next round of talks was attended by six countries: Afghanistan, China, India, Iran, Pakistan and Russia. The format was further expanded for the third and last round which was held in Moscow in April 2017. The US and five Central Asian states were also invited to attend, although the US declined the invitation. (The US accuses Russia and Iran of support-ing the Afghan Taliban, raising concerns that increased tensions between Washington, Moscow and Tehran might negatively impact the situation in Afghanistan.) Zamir Kabulov, the Russian president's special envoy for Afghanistan, announced in mid-July that another Moscow Format meeting on Afghanistan would be held before the end of the summer of 2018, and added that the Taliban would also be invited to attend.

The so-called 'Kabul Process', which involves around 25 countries, offers yet another forum for pursuing the Afghan peace process. Speaking at the second conference on 28 February 2018, Ghani offered peace talks 'without preconditions' to the Taliban and held out the possibility that the Taliban could eventually be recognised as a legitimate political group. Ghani also proposed a ceasefire and exchange of prisoners. In return, the Taliban would need to recognise the Afghan government and respect the rule of law. However, Ghani did not mention foreign forces or when they might leave Afghanistan, thereby ignoring the central demand of the Taliban. Instead, it was clear that Ghani wanted to put pressure on the Taliban by telling the Afghan people and the rest of the world that the ball was now in the Taliban's court. Russia, Turkmenistan and Uzbekistan have all offered to host direct talks between the Afghan government and the Taliban, but without a shift in the key parties' nego-tiating positions, there are few signs of a major breakthrough in peace talks in the near future.

There is increasing recognition among US and Afghan officials as well as most analysts that military victory is beyond reach. The costs for all sides, both in terms of blood and treasure, are rising: the casualty figures of the Afghan security forces, which are already overwhelmed and over-stretched, are alarmingly high. Although casualty figures are not made public, media reports suggest that dozens of members of the Afghan security forces are killed or injured on a weekly basis. Meanwhile, US officials estimate that the war in Afghanistan will cost US taxpayers more than US$45 billion in 2018. The emergence and expansion of militant groups, such as the Islamic State in Khorasan Province (ISIS–KP) and the Islamic Movement of Uzbekistan (IMU), is making the security situation worse and the conflict even harder to resolve, with US and Afghan officials stating that around 20 local, regional and international violent extremist groups are active in Afghanistan. Since the formation of ISIS–KP in the Afghanistan–Pakistan region in January 2015, the group has claimed responsibility for a series of attacks in Afghanistan which, according to government statements and media reports, has resulted in the killing or wounding of more than 1,000 people in different parts of the country. However, the Taliban still remains the dominant insurgent group in the country. In February 2018, Afghan National Security Adviser Mohammad Hanif Atmar said there were more than 55,000 terrorists in the country, of which 30,000–40,000 were Afghan Taliban fighters with the remainder belonging to regional and international groups such as ISIS-KP, which had around 3,000 fighters in Afghanistan.

Parliamentary polls (already delayed by three years) scheduled for October 2018 and presidential elections due to take place in early 2019 will test the political stability and strength of government institutions in Afghanistan. Thereafter, there may be the opportunity for further exploration of the possibilities for peace talks. Direct talks between the US and the Taliban may pave the way for trilateral talks involving the US, the Taliban and the Afghan government, and eventually bilateral talks between the Taliban and the Afghan government to settle the country's political future.

One potential risk factor concerns US policy, as there were signs in mid-2018 that the Trump administration – following the appointment of a new secretary of state and national security advisor – might waver in its renewed military commitment to the conflict. Psychologically and materially, this would be a huge blow to the government of Afghanistan and its army. It would perhaps strengthen the conviction among the Taliban that military victory was achievable. Other militant groups would also draw encouragement. However, the departure of the US and its allies might prompt some Taliban fighters to consider their objective achieved and return home; this happened in the late 1980s, after the Soviet Army withdrew.

If the US were to scale back and eventually pull out, the manner of it would matter a great deal. A precipitate withdrawal would create a destabilising vacuum that regional powers Pakistan, Iran, India, the Central Asian states and Russia would be impelled to fill. A planned withdrawal, in tandem with negotiations involving the regional players and the Taliban, might offer the best route to peace. The Taliban's exclusion from the 2001 Bonn conference, in hindsight, proved to be a costly error. Their involvement in 'Bonn II' would offer the best chance for a durable peace.

India and China: Prospects for Accommodation and Competition

In mid-2017, China and India were engaged in a military stand-off on the Doklam plateau that lasted for 73 days. The stand-off marked the nadir of a two-year deterioration in bilateral relations and required the direct intervention of Chinese President Xi Jinping and Indian Prime Minister Narendra Modi to bring the crisis to an end. Thereafter, the two states undertook a seemingly remarkable reset of diplomatic relations and committed to expanding cooperation in new areas. However, a residual element of contest between Asia's two rising giants seems guaranteed. Not all their interests can be reconciled and the power gap between the two states is growing, which presents several dilemmas for India as the weaker state. The relationship may also be vulnerable to the rise in strategic manoeuvres by China and the United States in the Indo-Pacific region.

Contained competition

While India and China are neighbouring states with an established overland trading history, the geographical barrier of the Himalayas has limited their interaction. Neither state has therefore been the other's principal concern, a situation which has arguably helped to keep relations cordial, although some points of contention have endured. China's support for Pakistan became an irritant for India at an early stage in the post-colonial relationship, while China's successful test of a nuclear weapon in 1964 established a second area of concern for India that deepened with China's accession to the Nuclear Non-Proliferation Treaty (NPT) in 1992. China, for its part, is discomfited that India has given refuge to the Tibetan spiritual leader the Dalai Lama.

However, the most testing bilateral issue is the disputed border between the two states, which runs for 3,488 kilometres according to India and 2,000 km according to China. In places, India's view of where the frontier lies differs from China's by up to 30 km. In 1962, the two states fought a brief war over the border. (India's defeat in the conflict was so damaging that India still refuses to declassify its official history on grounds of 'national interest', although some documents have been leaked.) A subsequent border stand-off in 1988 prompted the two states to refocus on less contentious areas where cooperation could proceed. Trade ties subsequently flourished, but by the start of the new century Indian officials began to fret about the strategic consequences of China's economic transformation, powered by high rates of GDP growth. Despite the rapid growth of India over the same period, it has been unable to keep up with China. Indian real GDP has in fact grown more quickly than China's since 2016, but the higher base of the Chinese economy means that the gap between the two economies has continued to widen in China's favour.

The dynamics of the two states' respective relationships with the US have added further strain to bilateral dealings. Since 2000, the US has sought a strategic convergence with India with an eye to the challenge that China could pose to the US in Asia and beyond in the twenty-first century. In 2008, then-president George W. Bush convinced China to agree to a waiver allowing India to enter into civil nuclear trade – India had previously been excluded from such trade under the terms of the NPT – meaning that India could choose to reallocate its domestic nuclear fuel for the production of nuclear weapons. This affected strategic competition with China, which pursued its own robust nuclear deterrent primarily against the US and Russia, but also against India.

In the wake of Xi's accession to power in 2013, Beijing adopted an overtly assertive foreign and security outlook, setting the US as China's priority peer-competitor. China increased its ties with India's neighbours (including Pakistan), while its navy deployed with greater regularity to the Indian Ocean, which for China is a maritime gateway to the Western hemisphere. All these factors increased India's fears of encirclement and inspired a concomitant rapprochement with the US. This, in turn, stoked China's own fears of a US-engineered encirclement with India's support. As a consequence, the old formula of managing differences and cooperating economically came under growing strain.

The road to Doklam

From 2015 onwards, calculated risk-taking by both sides threatened to undermine the relationship. China's selective dismissal of Indian concerns about terrorists originating from Pakistan in the wake of the 2008 Mumbai attacks (which China had otherwise condemned) caused increasing resentment in New Delhi. By June 2016, China had also thwarted Modi's high-profile campaign to join the Nuclear Suppliers Group. India was further unsettled by China's encroachments in disputed border areas during important bilateral meetings. One significant incident occurred in 2014 during a state visit by Xi to India, which Modi intended to use as a showpiece casting China as a partner for India. However, while Modi hosted Xi in Gujarat, Chinese and Indian troops faced off in Kashmir's Ladakh region to defend small road and irrigation projects on what each side regarded as its own territory. This incident, combined with several others, reinforced a perception among Indian decision-makers that China had departed from past practice in its dealings with India.

By early 2016, some Indian officials privately admitted that New Delhi was willing to antagonise China in defence of core Indian interests on the border and to demonstrate India was not a pushover. For its part, China perceived that the US–India strategic convergence under the Obama administration increasingly threatened Chinese interests. Although publicly India continued to cleave to its strategic autonomy, it appeared to China that India had become more receptive to US influence, especially after the signature of a pan-Asian US–Indian Joint Strategic Vision in New Delhi in 2015. According to the Stockholm International Peace Research Institute, US arms exports to India increased by 557% in volume between 2008–12 and 2013–17, with the result that the US has become India's second-largest arms supplier.

These developments undermined trust in a bilateral relationship where form – the routine of regular high-level meetings and reciprocal visits – is often a complement to or partial substitute for substance. The regularity and importance of bilateral governmental meetings is a good barometer of the state of the relationship. From late 2016, dialogue between Indian and Chinese defence ministers and senior military officers was suspended. The respective national-security advisers continued to meet annually on border matters, but for three years Xi and Modi only met on the sidelines of regional or international meetings.

The Doklam stand-off began when China extended the construction of a road into the territory of Bhutan, a state with which China does not maintain full diplomatic relations. India deployed troops to defend Bhutan – which is tied to India by a 2007 friendship agreement – and the two forces faced off directly. During the stand-off, India and China exchanged rhetorical accusations that were unprecedented in a generation. Only the direct intervention of Xi and Modi on 29 August ended the crisis (Modi's threat to snub a Xi-hosted international summit may have been the trigger, although both claimed that the other had pulled back). The two leaders called for a restoration of the pre-2015 diplomatic situation. India's change of tack with China was nothing less than spectacular, as suddenly the language of cooperation and understanding returned to the fore of public statements. India agreed to resume relations unconditionally, saying privately that it had made its point to China by standing up to and surprising it by sending troops into Bhutan. Publicly, India returned to highlighting the positives in the relationship.

From September 2017 to April 2018, Indian and Chinese officials restored ministerial-level bilateral dialogues, allowing for Xi to host Modi at an unprecedented 'informal summit' in Wuhan. Alongside delegation talks, the summit witnessed a heightened version of the personalised brand of diplomacy which Xi and Modi had trialled in 2014–15. What they agreed is not entirely clear, but a decision appeared to have been made that mutually beneficial cooperation across 20 policy dialogues should proceed, regardless of disagreements in other spheres. Some of those differences were to be set aside for discussion in the future. Others could be resolved, but recuperations (within limits) or provocations (largely symbolic) for reasons of national status or even domestic political mobilisation were understood to remain possible.

Cooperation and competition

There is scope for considerable cooperation between India and China in the spheres of global economic governance and trade. India is the largest beneficiary of the Asia Infrastructure Investment Bank, which was established by China in 2015. In July 2018, China agreed to reduce non-tariff barriers on Indian pharmaceutical exports, which, alongside greater Chinese investment in Indian manufacturing, may help to narrow India's huge trade deficit with China (which was US$63 billion in 2017). However, Modi has agreed to focus less on the deficit and more on the target (originally set for 2015) of pushing trade volumes above US$100bn annually (by comparison, India–China trade totalled US$84.4bn in 2017). Officially, both states recognise that there are complementary aspects between Xi's 'Made in China 2025' high-tech investment programme and Modi's 2014 'Make in India' initiative to attract foreign investment and deepen India's integration into global supply chains. Both countries stood to export more without necessarily competing as they could make products with different added value. Unofficially, however, and in common with many Western economies, India also looked to China's global industrial-leadership plans in several strategic technology-heavy sectors with a degree of apprehension.

India and China also have common interests in the international sphere. Both states advocate the maintenance of the multilateral trading system in the face of US threats to undermine the operation of the World Trade Organization. By mid-2018, both China and India had retaliated against US tariffs on imported steel and aluminium. At the United Nations Climate Change Conference in Copenhagen in December 2009, Beijing and New Delhi resisted attempts to impose cuts on their carbon emissions due to their status as developing economies, while placing faith in civil nuclear energy and renewables, including solar electricity. The US withdrawal from the 2015 Paris climate agreement – an agreement which India and China had played a critical role in bringing about – was an opportunity for India and China to join European states in supporting the agreement. Yet greener energy may also be a source of tension between the two states, given China's dominance of global production for such items as LED lights and solar panels, which India also wishes to manufacture.

The two states have explored ways to mitigate the so-called 'Asian premium' on oil prices, possibly through coordinated purchases. Mutual recognition of the need to secure the supply of energy by sea – particularly from the Persian Gulf – inclines both states to tolerate each other's naval presence in the northwestern Indian Ocean and surrounding areas. There are also plans to resume joint counter-terrorism drills in 2019 and to participate in a multilateral military exercise led by the Shanghai Cooperation Organisation, which admitted India and Pakistan in 2017. In the wake of the Wuhan summit, China no longer expects India to join the Belt and Road Initiative (BRI), but the two powers may cooperate on infrastructure development in South Asian nations using '2+1' high-level coordination mechanisms (where New Delhi and Beijing can jointly hold a dialogue with a third country in South Asia). Indeed, some commentators have argued that the combination of China's investment forays into South Asia and India's rising engagement with Southeast Asia under its 'Act East' policy means they are destined to cooperate, however much they might also compete.

Economic cooperation and engagement will be vital in maintaining the current state of the relationship, especially given the pressures stemming from different security interests and shifts in Asia's strategic balance. For both states, the cost of conflict far outweighs the potential benefits. Despite the high tension, the Doklam stand-off maintained the countries' proud record of no shots fired over the border. However, the stand-off also underlined the danger of escalation, as well as illustrating how one aspect of the India–China relationship could damage the whole. In part this relates to the perception that, not unlike in the case of the South China Sea, one side could undertake actions to change the facts on the ground through use of hybrid activities in a grey zone (as Indians analysts sometimes characterise it). While the two governments insist the relationship is robust, this assurance does not offer any guarantee that the relationship will be accident-free. India in particular must be pragmatic and imaginative about its attempts to influence the balance of the relationship. Because of the power asymmetry, India cannot readily seek to roll back China's influence in South Asia in a comprehensive manner; rather, it must pick its battles. Rhetorically, Indian officials are embracing the notion of 'Southern Asia', by which they mean South Asia plus China. At the same time, India exerted little or no effort to arrest the decline of democratic politics in Maldives in 2017.

Strategic trust is scarcely possible in a situation where some obvious points of disagreement are acknowledged but no effort is being made to resolve them, and cooperation in the absence of strategic trust will be fraught. It will, for example, be difficult to finesse the sharp differences over the BRI. Despite the lack of explicit comment from Modi himself, India's opposition to the scheme is well known. India particularly objects to the China–Pakistan Economic Corridor and the transformation of the Pakistani port of Gwadar into an inter-regional transhipment hub designed to link China to the Indian Ocean (and perhaps in time to support Chinese naval operations in the Indian Ocean). India also regards Chinese development projects in Kashmir as illegitimate third-party interventions in India's dispute with Pakistan.

India has restrained itself from using its early opposition to the scheme to seek diplomatic advantages in the 2018 context of a rising global backlash against the BRI. However, while eschewing direct confrontation with China, India has explored bilateral and trilateral cooperation, particularly with Japan, to counter Chinese influence in South Asia. This includes a trilateral mechanism launched in 2015 with Japan and the US involving the respective foreign ministers, as well as the Asia–Africa Growth Corridor, a bilateral initiative with Japan initiated in 2017 to collaborate on infrastructure development in the Indo-Pacific.

Military tensions persist

The Wuhan pledge to enhance strategic communication between the armed forces of China and India, especially on land, will be difficult to implement. While sporadic contacts resumed after the Wuhan meeting, there is no sign that either army will make more frequent use of the hotline for operational commanders that was first announced in 2013. Moreover, because the Doklam incident was not strictly a bilateral matter (because India deployed troops on behalf of Bhutan), neither side has sought to revise understandings regarding the management of the border question; rather, they continue to rely on the subjective notion of continuing to uphold the status quo while both sides continue to develop military infrastructure close to the frontier. India began building transport and military infrastructure in the late 2000s and Modi's government has accelerated the modernisation of old Himalayan airstrips. India has also planned to station some of its foreign-acquired strike aircraft and artillery nearby. Although India has reportedly frozen the creation of new units for at least part of the Mountain Strike Corps on budgetary grounds, it continues to accumulate long-range, second-strike nuclear-attack capabilities, with the expected introduction of the 5,000-km-range *Agni-5* missile by 2019, and completion of at least four nuclear-powered submarines by 2035 that are all understood to be ranged primarily against China rather than Pakistan. Satellite imagery shows that China too has developed permanent staging military posts in the Doklam region. Since 2016, China has been modernising civilian and military infrastructure in other sections of the border under a unified Western Theatre Command.

The greatest source of uncertainty and opportunity in the bilateral relations concerns the maritime domain. A diplomat-led maritime dialogue resumed in July 2018 after a two-year hiatus, raising hopes that an agreement to prevent incidents at sea, between military vessels over- or under-water, might eventually be concluded. However, the two navies are competitors. Modi has funded the Indian navy modestly but he has demanded that it stay ahead of China's military reach in the Indian Ocean. He has struck a number of bilateral and trilateral agreements with Australia, France, Indonesia, Japan, the Philippines, Russia, Singapore, the United Kingdom and the United States, as well as some Gulf countries, to broaden India's networks and to improve its situational awareness in the Indian Ocean. Modi is seeking to craft developing partnerships in an increasingly competitive Asia while maintaining India's freedom of action, especially toward China.

Modi had great hopes for the relationship with China; thus far, the returns have been relatively modest. Each state acknowledges the economic potential of the relationship, but as both states adopt a more extrovert stance in the Indo-Pacific and elsewhere, the challenge of insulating their relations from broader currents of strategic competition will become more difficult. Relations between the two may take a back seat as India's focus shifts inward to domestic affairs ahead of its general election in 2019. However, provided no security-related incident occurs, the post-Wuhan rapprochement between India and China looks set to continue.

Pakistan: Seeking a Strategic Space Between the United States and China

Pakistan, flanked by instability in Afghanistan to the west and a perceived existential threat in the shape of India to the east, as well as
facing domestic political turmoil and impending economic problems,
is seeking a tolerable strategic space between China and the United
States. Although Washington and Beijing have represented the book-
ends of Pakistani foreign and security policy for many years, current
circumstances are challenging Pakistan's ability to calibrate its external
relations. Most salient is the downturn in US–Pakistan ties over 2017–18,
but questions concerning the costs and benefits associated with the
signature China–Pakistan Economic Corridor (CPEC) signal a debate,
albeit quiet, concerning the degree to which Pakistan can rely solely on
China. Meanwhile, India, as always, looms on Pakistan's horizon, inter-
secting with all facets of the US–China–Pakistan triangle and colouring
Islamabad's views of its ties with Washington and Beijing.

US–Pakistan tensions

Tensions in US–Pakistan relations are not new. Indeed, the relationship has often been described as a rollercoaster, with dramatic and
publicly visible low points (such as the imposition of US sanctions for
nuclear and missile proliferation or military coups) alternating with high
points, such as the bilateral cooperation to counter the Soviet invasion
of Afghanistan in the 1980s. These high points are often exaggerated in
retrospect, masking underlying differences between the two countries –
during the Cold War, the two sides maintained fundamentally different
conceptions of the relationship: where Pakistan sought an external ally
against rival India, the US was focused on the global struggle against
communism and had no interest in alienating New Delhi. Although
the communist threat vanished in 1990, Pakistan's nuclear and missile
activities and its support for terrorist proxies raised US fears that a terrorist incident might spark a war between India and Pakistan – including
the risk of a nuclear confrontation – or that extremists might come into

possession of nuclear materials. From the Pakistani perspective, however, the US was an inconstant and insensitive ally, a global hegemon which discarded Pakistan when it was no longer useful and ignored Pakistan's security interests, especially with regard to India.

Relations seemed to start afresh in 2001 as Pakistan, albeit reluctantly, assisted the US intervention in Afghanistan. However, Pakistan's support for the Taliban regime (which included the provision of safe havens to Afghan Taliban fighters and their families within Pakistan) and apparent reticence to assist in the capture of Osama bin Laden created additional frictions, especially in 2011 when US special forces killed bin Laden in a compound located less than a mile away from Pakistan's military academy. While Pakistan has historically feared an Indian presence in Afghanistan and the possibility of an anti-Pakistan government in Kabul, the US has seen Pakistan's tolerance for the Taliban as perpetuating instability in Afghanistan and causing casualties among its own forces as well as those of its NATO and Afghan allies. Despite repeated assurances from Islamabad that it was supporting neither the Taliban nor other militant groups, Washington detected no consequential change in Pakistani actions as the conflict in Afghanistan dragged on. US frustration with what was seen as Pakistani duplicity grew more intense and public from the latter years of the George W. Bush administration and through the Obama presidency, and found its most direct and open expression in the new US strategy for Afghanistan and South Asia, announced by US President Donald Trump in a speech on 21 August 2017. Trump acknowledged Pakistan's losses in fighting terrorists who had targeted the Pakistani state, but pointedly stated that 'we have been paying Pakistan billions and billions of dollars at the same time they are housing the very terrorists that we are fighting. But that will have to change, and that will change immediately.'

Islamabad was taken aback by the tone of the speech and especially by a presidential tweet on 1 January 2018 that claimed Pakistan had 'given us nothing but lies & deceit'. Particularly galling were Trump's recognition of India's 'important contributions to stability in Afghanistan' and his statement that a key part of the US strategy for South Asia and

Afghanistan was the development of the 'strategic relationship' between India and the US. In the same month the US suspended military assistance worth approximately US\$2 billion as an incentive to prompt 'decisive, sustained action' (in the words of US Assistant Secretary of Defense Randall Schriver) against Taliban and Haqqani network individuals and infrastructure inside Pakistan. Washington, however, has continued to state its interest in finding 'common ground' and 'not walking away from Pakistan' and civilian assistance has not been cut. Given that the US is no longer the principal source of Pakistan's weaponry, the effect of the US suspension will be limited to select end-items such as F-16s, *Harpoon*s and air-to-air missiles; the psychological and political impact of reduced military interaction is probably greater. Additional pressure came in February 2018 when the US led an initiative at the meeting of the Financial Action Task Force (FATF) to place Pakistan on that organisation's 'grey list' as of June 2018. Being added to the 'grey list' is a warning step with few immediate practical consequences, but it will be a caution to potential investors and could lead to serious sanctions if Islamabad fails to address the FATF's concerns and thus ends up on the 'black list'.

Closer relationship with China

As Pakistan's relations with the US have deteriorated over the past decade, its ties to China have deepened. Historically, Islamabad has viewed China as a supplement, or sometimes as an alternative, to the US (increasingly opting for Chinese military hardware such as tanks, frigates and fighter aircraft over the years, for instance), while Beijing has used Pakistan to contain and distract India. China has at times disapproved of Pakistani behaviour, but criticism is usually delivered in private or, if in public, only in muted tones, a diplomatic style much appreciated in Islamabad. More commonly, bilateral ties are extolled with phrases such as 'sweeter than honey' and 'higher than the Himalayas'. Pakistan also values China's supportive diplomatic interventions, such as blocking India's entry into the Nuclear Suppliers Group in 2016 and repeatedly vetoing the designation of Jaysh-e-Mohammad leader Masood Azhar as a global terrorist under UN Security Council Resolution 1267. Azhar, residing openly in Pakistan, is one of India's most wanted men, accused of being the organiser behind an assault on an Indian air base in January 2016, among other attacks.

In practical terms, China has been Pakistan's primary arms supplier since the 1990s and has supported Pakistan's nuclear and missile programmes. Pakistan also relies on China for economic assistance and commerce. China has become Pakistan's largest trading partner and has pledged approximately US$62bn in loans and investment as part of CPEC. Inaugurated in 2015, this keystone of President Xi's Belt and Road Initiative is a collection of projects aimed at linking China's western regions to the Arabian Sea via the small port of Gwadar on Pakistan's Makran coast. Through infrastructure development, power generation and the establishment of special economic zones, CPEC is perceived as a potential 'game-changer' for Pakistan, creating thousands of jobs and transforming the country into a regional economic hub.

Although the bilateral relationship is important for Beijing and central to Pakistan's aspirations, the rhetorical hyperbole associated with Sino-Pakistani collaboration can mask serious concerns on both sides. Some Pakistani economists, for instance, question Islamabad's unbridled enthusiasm for CPEC, citing a lack of transparency and fears that Chinese loans (many carrying interest rates of up to 7%) will leave Pakistan ensnared in a debt trap. There are also doubts about Pakistan's ability to meet Chinese expectations regarding the creation and maintenance of a stable, prosperous and efficiently managed commercial corridor. Compounding the indebtedness to Beijing are additional loans estimated to be as high as US$4bn that Pakistan negotiated in the first half of 2018 to forestall a foreign-exchange crisis. Bilateral trade is another problem area as the balance is heavily tilted in China's favour, with Chinese exports to Pakistan (US$13.68bn) greatly exceeding Chinese imports from Pakistan (US$1.59bn) in 2016–2017. This trend seems to be accelerating and Pakistani businessmen complain that local markets are inundated with inexpensive Chinese products which undermine local manufacturers.

China has interests and concerns of its own. Beyond the success of CPEC, Beijing's foremost worry is that jihadists and separatists might find inspiration and support among the many extremist groups that shelter in Pakistan to foment unrest among the ethnic Uighur Muslims of China's Xinjiang province. Direct terrorist threats to CPEC projects and Chinese workers are also a worry as many of its planned routes as well as the port of Gwadar lie in violence-ridden Balochistan province. Pakistan has deployed a 15,000–man security force comprised of army and police personnel to protect CPEC projects and the Chinese labour force, but this threat is likely to endure unless Islamabad can address local grievances in a comprehensive manner. Most troublesome are Baloch complaints that they derive few benefits from CPEC or from their province's mineral wealth (claiming jobs and contracts go to outsiders), but Pashtun groups have also conducted persistent peaceful protests against mistreatment and alienation over the past year as well. Furthermore, terrorism and instability inform Chinese attitudes towards Pakistan at the geopolitical level. Although committed to strong relations with Pakistan, Beijing has no desire to be called in to rescue Islamabad from its own mistakes, especially on issues relating to terrorism. China's efforts to balance the desire to enhance relations with Pakistan while resisting the perception that it is underwriting Pakistani adventurism can lead to some delicate decisions. While Beijing, for example, has thus far protected Masood Azhar at the UN Security Council, in September 2017 it agreed to a leaders' declaration at the BRICS (Brazil, Russia, India, China and South Africa) summit in Xiamen that specifically named Azhar's organisation as a security concern. More significantly, China voted to add Pakistan to the FATF grey list during that institution's February 2018 plenary session.

Also relevant for Pakistan is China's interest in broader regional stability. Although Afghanistan is not a top-tier issue for Beijing, China has played a major role in convening the Quadrilateral Coordination Group (QCG) with Afghanistan, Pakistan and the US, as well as a China–Pakistan–Afghanistan–Tajikistan counter-terrorism coordination mechanism and trilateral China–Pakistan–Afghanistan meetings.

These are in addition to its bilateral relations with the Kabul government and occasional interactions with Taliban representatives. Protecting CPEC, quelling instability on its southern borders and insulating Xinjiang from extremism are thus fundamental Chinese interests that involve Pakistan.

India and domestic politics

Two other factors are essential in interpreting Pakistan's interactions with the US and China: India and domestic politics. The prism through which Pakistan views all of its foreign relationships is India, and Islamabad sees cause for concern in New Delhi's recent interactions with both Washington and Beijing, although the state of US–India relations is by far the most alarming from a Pakistani perspective. Some Pakistani officials and many commentators routinely mischaracterise the US–India relationship as an 'alliance', especially in the wake of the 2008 US–India Civil Nuclear Agreement. Similarly, many Pakistanis are convinced that the US is pursuing a policy of 'containment' vis-à-vis China (even though the close intermeshing of the US and Chinese economies means that a Cold War-style containment is hardly a realistic option for Washington). Rather, as US Defense Secretary James Mattis stated in June 2018, the US will cooperate with China where it can and compete where it must. Taken together, these erroneous assumptions about US policy towards India and China can result in faulty conclusions that may hamper the US–Pakistan relationship. One example is the mistaken belief that Washington opposes CPEC and may collude with India to undermine the promise of this enterprise that Pakistanis view as crucial for their country's future. Such unsound foundations do not augur well for the establishment of a relationship based on realistic expectations as both sides desire.

Given the strength of its own ties to Beijing, Pakistan is far less concerned about Sino-Indian relations. Nonetheless, Pakistanis are acutely aware that China is India's largest trading partner and that the volume of Sino-Indian trade, although heavily balanced in China's favour, was in 2016–17 five times larger (more than US$73bn) than that between

China and Pakistan (some US$15bn). On the foreign-policy front, Sino-Indian tensions have eased considerably since the extended Doklam border stand-off in 2017. An informal Xi–Modi summit in April 2018, Modi's bold initiatives to improve communications and China's desire to reduce US–India alignment highlight both sides' interest in expanding commercial opportunities and avoiding conflict. These Sino-Indian considerations are not an indication that Beijing is going to downgrade its close ties with Pakistan, but they do suggest the other regional interests Beijing will seek to accommodate as it pursues its goals in Pakistan.

Islamabad's domestic challenges are not as obvious as its international considerations. In formulating policy towards Washington, for example, the government has to account for widespread anti-Americanism, much of it promoted by the government and military for decades. A defiant stance towards the US thus guarantees popular acclaim but can impede efforts to repair relations as those seeking accommodation can be portrayed as unpatriotic or even un-Islamic. At the same time, the traditional orientation towards Europe and North America remains in culture, education, democratic values and especially in a millions-strong Pakistani diaspora. Despite perceptions of mistreatment by a supposedly declining US, few serious voices call for a complete break with Washington and most recognise that China cannot substitute for the US. Although Pakistanis routinely evince strongly favourable opinions of China, CPEC may spark societal tensions as Chinese goods flood local markets and thousands of Chinese workers take up long-term residence. Many Pakistanis will have to adjust to insular Chinese communities in their midst, potentially generating tensions that could tarnish the official bonhomie and pose awkward challenges for policymakers attempting to implement CPEC projects. Distributing the presumed benefits of CPEC equitably among Pakistan's four provinces will also be a difficult problem, with provincial politicians demanding their fair share while Chinese managers complain about delays owing to domestic disputes and bureaucratic torpor.

The most important aspect of Pakistan's internal politics, however, is the civil–military divide, where the military – and specifically the army

Pakistan's Pivot to China: Defence, Trade, Debt

For many decades the United States has been a significant supplier of Pakistan's military equipment. However, as US–Pakistan relations have become strained, the sale of equipment to Pakistan has been negatively affected. Over the past two decades China has stepped in to fill this gap and now supplies Pakistan with arms across a range of domains and equipment types and is China's primary defence-export market. Pakistan's arms arrangement with China differs from the US relationship in two ways. Firstly, the sale of military equipment does not come with political strings attached. Secondly, China has been willing and able to develop the Pakistani defence industry, which is something the US has had little interest in. Pakistan has now produced hundreds of Chinese-designed tanks, fighter aircraft and missile boats and will soon begin construction of Chinese submarines. As well as providing jobs for Pakistanis, this has also given Pakistan the capability to support and develop further that equipment. In recent years, Pakistan has begun to book export contracts of its own, providing a further boon to Pakistan's defence industry.

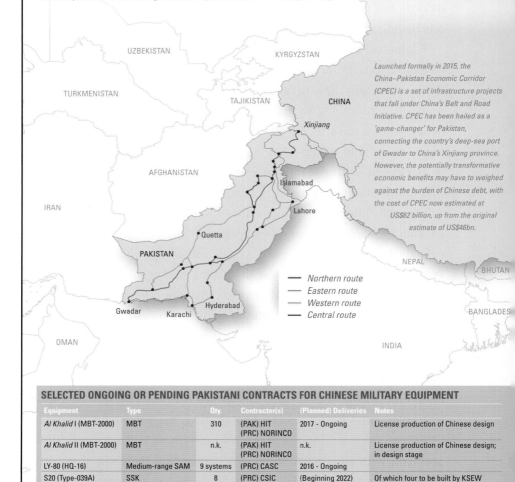

Launched formally in 2015, the China–Pakistan Economic Corridor (CPEC) is a set of infrastructure projects that fall under China's Belt and Road Initiative. CPEC has been hailed as a 'game-changer' for Pakistan, connecting the country's deep-sea port of Gwadar to China's Xinjiang province. However, the potentially transformative economic benefits may have to weighed against the burden of Chinese debt, with the cost of CPEC now estimated at US$62 billion, up from the original estimate of US$46bn.

— Northern route
— Eastern route
— Western route
— Central route

SELECTED ONGOING OR PENDING PAKISTANI CONTRACTS FOR CHINESE MILITARY EQUIPMENT

Equipment	Type	Qty.	Contractor(s)	(Planned) Deliveries	Notes
Al Khalid I (MBT-2000)	MBT	310	(PAK) HIT (PRC) NORINCO	2017 - Ongoing	License production of Chinese design
Al Khalid II (MBT-2000)	MBT	n.k.	(PAK) HIT (PRC) NORINCO	n.k.	License production of Chinese design; in design stage
LY-80 (HQ-16)	Medium-range SAM	9 systems	(PRC) CASC	2016 - Ongoing	
S20 (Type-039A)	SSK	8	(PRC) CSIC (PAK) KSEW	(Beginning 2022)	Of which four to be built by KSEW
Jiangkai II (Type-054A)	FFGHM	4	(PRC) CSSC	(To complete 2021)	
1,500-ton patrol ship Hingol class	PSOH PCO	2 4	(PRC) CSSC (PAK) KSEW	2016 - Ongoing	KSEW to build one of each class

Sources: Financial Times, IISS, Planning Commission of Pakistan, US Institute of Peace, Wall Street Journal, World Integrated Trade Solution

Aligned with the West during the Cold War, Pakistan has subsequently grown increasingly enmeshed with China not only in matters of defence, but also trade and debt. Overall imports have more than tripled since 2003, with China capturing most of the increasing Pakistani market for foreign goods by quadrupling its share of Pakistan's imports in the same period, resulting in Pakistan carrying a large trade deficit with China. China has also risen to become Pakistan's second-most important export market after the US.

Against the backdrop of falling foreign-exchange reserves, Pakistan obtained a bailout estimated to be as high as US$4 billion from China in mid-2018. The repayments associated with the financing of the China–Pakistan Economic Corridor (CPEC) also look likely to increase the burden of Pakistani debt, indicating that the country's financial affairs will be tied to China for many years to come. However, Pakistan's Prime Minister Imran Khan, elected in July 2018, remains committed to delivering CPEC.

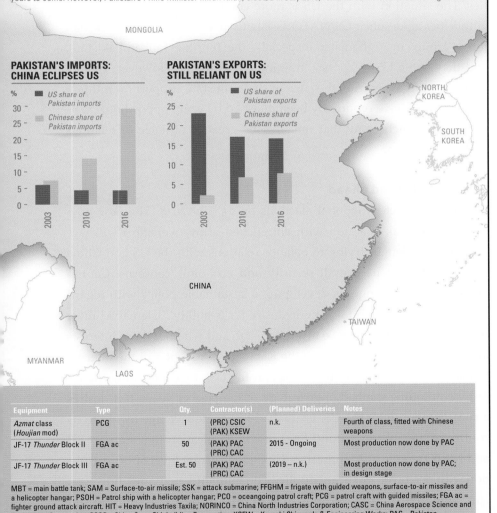

PAKISTAN'S IMPORTS: CHINA ECLIPSES US

%
- US share of Pakistan imports
- Chinese share of Pakistan imports

30, 25, 20, 15, 10, 5, 0

2003, 2010, 2016

PAKISTAN'S EXPORTS: STILL RELIANT ON US

%
- US share of Pakistan exports
- Chinese share of Pakistan exports

25, 20, 15, 10, 5, 0

2003, 2010, 2016

MONGOLIA

NORTH KOREA

SOUTH KOREA

CHINA

TAIWAN

MYANMAR

LAOS

Equipment	Type	Qty.	Contractor(s)	(Planned) Deliveries	Notes
Azmat class (*Houjian* mod)	PCG	1	(PRC) CSIC (PAK) KSEW	n.k.	Fourth of class, fitted with Chinese weapons
JF-17 *Thunder* Block II	FGA ac	50	(PAK) PAC (PRC) CAC	2015 - Ongoing	Most production now done by PAC
JF-17 *Thunder* Block III	FGA ac	Est. 50	(PAK) PAC (PRC) CAC	(2019 – n.k.)	Most production now done by PAC; in design stage

MBT = main battle tank; SAM = Surface-to-air missile; SSK = attack submarine; FFGHM = frigate with guided weapons, surface-to-air missiles and a helicopter hangar; PSOH = Patrol ship with a helicopter hangar; PCO = oceangoing patrol craft; PCG = patrol craft with guided missiles; FGA ac = fighter ground attack aircraft. HIT = Heavy Industries Taxila; NORINCO = China North Industries Corporation; CASC = China Aerospace Science and Technology Corporation; CSSC = China State Shipbuilding Corporation; KSEW = Karachi Shipyards & Engineering Works; PAC = Pakistan Aeronautical Complex; CAC = Chengdu Aircraft Industrial (Group) Co.

– dominates decision-making on key foreign-policy and security issues. With regards to China, the Pakistani military will want to ensure that its economic equities (such as construction and transportation) are protected, that the armed forces are not overtaxed in providing security for CPEC and that Beijing continues to meet its munitions requirements. If these demands are met, there is likely to be little dispute between civilian and military leaders with regard to the importance of Sino-Pakistani ties. The situation with the US is more complex. Civilian and military authorities alike solicit US/NATO assistance in eliminating anti-Pakistan terror groups in Afghanistan (especially the Tehrik-e-Taliban Pakistan), and they value US weaponry, training and funding. However, civilian efforts to shift away from the current stance of state support for militant organisations have reportedly been quashed by army opposition, creating a policy dichotomy that remains the greatest obstacle in relations with Washington.

An uncertain road ahead

Pakistan conducted national elections on 25 July 2018. The new government (a weak coalition with entrenched army oversight) will face daunting challenges trying to balance relations with the US and China in the context of its overall security and economic concerns. Central among those challenges is developing a sustainable policy with regard to Afghanistan. Beyond a generic desire for 'stability', Islamabad must decide where its interests lie in Afghanistan and whether those interests are best attained by supporting the Kabul government and the international community (including China and the US), by confronting the US or by continuing the hedging strategy of the past 17 years. If it desires a confrontation with the US, Islamabad has some leverage owing to its control of the air and ground lines of communication that support US and NATO troops in Afghanistan. Given the current level of US frustration with perceived Pakistani duplicity on militant sanctuaries, however, curtailing access to these lines of communication (as Islamabad did in 2011 in the wake of the bin Laden raid) could lead to a rupture with Washington.

Islamabad will likely seek to avoid such a drastic step. Instead, it will endeavour to do the minimum to meet US demands on tackling terrorist organisations sheltering in Pakistan, playing for time in hopes of out-lasting US ire and positioning itself as the key player in Afghan peace and reconciliation efforts. This hedging approach could be difficult to sustain, especially as Pakistan's impending foreign-exchange crisis will likely force a return to the International Monetary Fund, where the US wields significant influence. Islamabad will continue to rely on China for arms, diplomatic support and economic assistance as embodied in CPEC. However, the security of CPEC projects, Pakistan's capacity to absorb massive Chinese assistance and fear of debt-trap scenarios will remain sources of friction between Islamabad and Beijing. Though subdued in Sino-Pakistani public discourse, the highly visible presence of Islamic extremists in Pakistan will also persist as a potential point of tension.

The presence of militant groups within Pakistan will likely prove the key challenge for Pakistan in its attempts at strategic alignment. Pakistan's involvement with extremists and insurgents stems from a variety of factors: hopes of influencing events in Afghanistan where the Taliban, however recalcitrant, represents Pakistan's only ally; residual worries about Pashtun irredentism; their value as asymmetric tools against India; the supposed utility of some groups in countering other, more dangerous factions; sympathy for extremist worldviews among some in the establishment; and fear that targeting such elements would prompt unmanageable spasms of violence across the country. The Pakistani Army's recent efforts to 'mainstream' radical groups through the political process, however, while motivated by an interest in con-trolling them, also risks the (potentially irremediable) legitimation of violent intolerance. Many Pakistanis – including some in top leader-ship positions – recognise that the long-standing policy of supporting or tolerating violent extremist groups lies at the heart of many of the country's foreign-policy challenges, and that altering this would offer many benefits. In February, for example, Chief of Army Staff General Qamar Javed Bajwa told a private meeting of journalists that Pakistan would have to rid itself of violent extremist groups to be recognised as a normal state internationally; however, visible, irreversible progress in this direction has been scant. In addition to advancing Islamabad's relations with Washington and Beijing, a perceptible and irreversible shift away from sheltering militant groups or employing them as state proxies would also remove perhaps the most significant obstacle in Pakistan's relations with its South Asian neighbours. Eliminating the safe havens granted to the Afghan Taliban, the Haqqani network and others would not automatically end the fighting in Afghanistan, but applying pressure to leaders, fighters and their families would demonstrate that these insurgents stand alone and, it is hoped, would push key elements of the Afghan Taliban towards serious negotiations. A change in Pakistan's stance would also create new opportunities with India for reducing the current high level of cross-border fire, normalising relations and perhaps opening bilateral trade as well as commerce between India and Afghanistan. Pakistan stands to gain domestically as well from such a change. Curtailing violent extremists would reduce the level of terrorism inside the country, enhance its appeal as a destination for foreign investment and improve Pakistan's overall standing in the international community. Given their mutual interest in a stable, prosperous Pakistan and in regional peace, China and the US would both welcome such a strategic shift. The problem posed by militant groups has long been acknowledged in Pakistan, but consequential action has not been taken and it is not clear that the state has the will or the capacity to initiate such a fundamental shift in the near term. To effect such a change would require an individual or group with considerable political will and capital to initiate a change and remain in place to see the process through implementation, safeguarding the shift against the debilitating political inertia that has become ingrained since the 1980s.

Relations with the US are likely to be sorely tested over Islamabad's current approach to Afghanistan and its ties with radical groups, but the relationship with China may also be roiled by CPEC controversies (which might in turn bring to the surface long-standing concerns that trade with China has hurt Pakistan's domestic producers). A more constructive Pakistan policy on Afghanistan would be welcomed in Beijing and Washington, with benefits for both key relationships, but the prospects for such a change are slim.

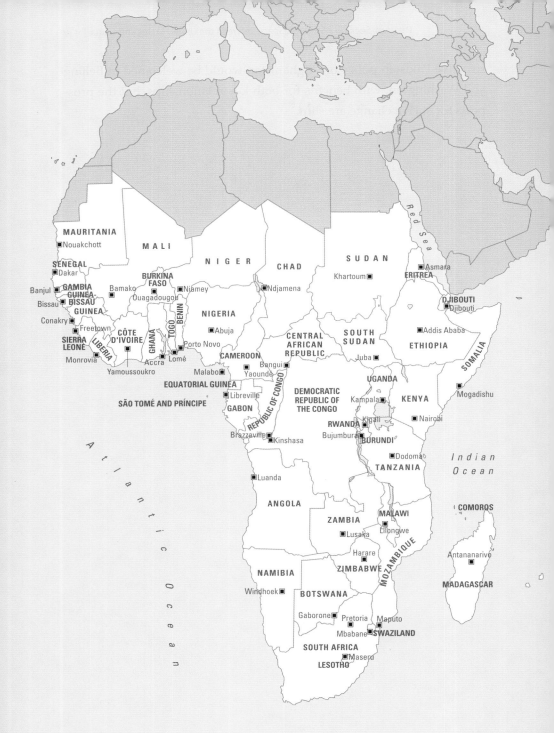

Chapter 6

Sub-Saharan Africa

2017–18 Review

Africa continued to be marginalised by the Trump administration, underscored by the truncated visit by then US secretary of state Rex Tillerson to Chad, Djibouti, Ethiopia, Kenya and Nigeria in March 2018. Although billed as an opportunity to discuss counter-terrorism, trade and investment, it was more realistically designed to smooth relations after a series of unfortunate comments by the US president, but was cut short when Tillerson was dismissed in the middle of the visit.

Even before the visit took place, the US administration emphasised that major announcements were unlikely and that Tillerson had no new US-led programmes to discuss. Nonetheless, the stated (security-first) order of priorities was deemed significant, since the Trump administration's putative military aggression in counter-terrorism operations has perhaps been the chief feature of its Africa policy. In pursuit of this, the US relaxed its rules of engagement in Somalia, and in August 2017 authorised the sale of almost US$600 million of military equipment to Nigeria to assist in Abuja's fight against Boko Haram. Much of the counter-terrorism activity centred on the use of uninhabited aerial vehicles (UAVs). In Somalia, for example, there were 16 confirmed US strikes using UAVs and piloted aircraft in the first half of 2018; this compares with 35 confirmed strikes in 2017, and just 14 and 11 strikes in 2016 and 2015 respectively. However, increased troop activity – and potential mission creep – were underscored by the deaths of four US troops in Niger in October 2017 and of a special-operations soldier in Somalia in June 2018. Following the Niger attack, US Secretary of Defense James Mattis stated that there would be 'more [military] actions in Africa, not less', but casualties proved domestically highly unpopular and prompted fierce political criticism of US troops becoming involved in fighting rather than training and advising.

Meanwhile, in early 2018 the Trump administration announced its reorientation of official defence policy away from counter-terrorism and towards efforts to compete with near-peer competitors such as Russia and China. In the context of this, and of criticism of US involvement in African missions, the US Africa Command (AFRICOM) was reportedly asked to plan for a potentially significant reduction in troop numbers in the region. Details have yet to be finalised, but this could involve the reduction of US special forces from current levels of around 1,200 by 25% over 18 months and 50% over 36 months. Such a drawdown – taking place in the context of warnings by senior commanders of the increasing threat posed by terrorist groups in the region, and West Africa in particular – would mark a notable further retreat from sub-Saharan Africa.

It is likely that the Trump administration's reordering of strategic priorities away from Africa and towards the global threat of Russia and China will actually open the way for Russia and China to increase their influence in sub-Saharan Africa. Russia already has strong security ties in North Africa, providing intelligence to Tunisia and support to Khalifa Haftar in Libya, for example. However, with Russian President Vladimir Putin seeking to restore Russia's influence throughout the developing world, 2017–18 saw increased Russian activity south of the Sahara. In December 2017, for example, Russia obtained an exemption to the United Nations arms embargo on Central African Republic, allowing it to supply light weapons, and also sent five military and 170 civilian instructors to help train the Central African Armed Forces (FACA). Wagner, a private Russian security company, is also thought to be active in the area. In part, engagement with FACA reflects Russia's concerns about the threat presented by Islamist militant groups. However, it is also intended to expand commercial opportunities: in March 2018, the Russian foreign ministry announced that it was working with the Central African Republic government to explore the country's natural resources on a concession basis. These resources are plentiful, and potentially include gem-quality diamonds (extraction of which has been undermined by civil strife) and gold. Russia appears to be seeking to replicate this model elsewhere in the region: in the year to mid-2018 it signed military-cooperation agreements with oil-rich Chad and Niger (which has the world's fourth-largest uranium reserves), and stated that it aims to boost military cooperation with, and potentially build a base in, Sudan. Given its existing presence in North Africa, this gives Russia a solid sphere of influence around the Sahel – and, potentially, a key role in the shifting strategic balance in the Horn of Africa.

The Russian authorities aim to consolidate relations by holding a high-level summit (most likely in 2019) to produce a comprehensive strategic road map for cooperation including concrete investment and trade opportunities in areas such as agriculture, energy and infrastructure. This is highly reminiscent of the Forum on China–Africa Cooperation (FOCAC), through which China has pledged billions of dollars to African states, including as part of its Belt and Road Initiative. This underscores the fact that increased engagement with Africa positions Russia in competition with China as well as the US. Indeed, China has been present in Central African Republic since 2007, and in June 2018 sought (but failed to obtain) UN dispensation to supply weapons to the country. However, in most respects China has remained ahead of Russia – and, in some respects, the US – in terms of strategic and security engagement with sub-Saharan Africa.

Reflecting the deepening complexity of Sino-African relations, China held its first China–Africa Defence and Security Forum in mid-2018. At the summit, which involved high-ranking military representatives from 50 African states, Chinese officials stated that China would provide 'comprehensive support' to African armies, as well as governments' anti-terrorism efforts, so as to promote regional stability. A number of factors are at play. There is also an obvious commercial opportunity: China's exports of military equipment to continental Africa were 55% higher in the period 2013–17 than in 2008–12, according to the Stockholm International Peace Research Institute, and China's share of total armament exports to sub-Saharan Africa increased from 16% to 27% over the same period. Nonetheless, there is substantial scope for further expansion: the US-based Center for Strategic and International Studies estimates that China exported weapons worth some US$3bn to continental Africa in 2008–17, whereas US and Russian weapons exports to the region (predominantly North Africa) totalled almost US$5bn and US$12.4bn respectively. Given the continuation of intra-state conflicts and ethnic and religious insurgencies, a large regional market for cost-effective Chinese weapons will clearly persist. Equally, China clearly wants to ensure the security of increasing amounts of Chinese-funded and -built infrastructure, of its resource supplies and of Chinese citizens living and working in the region. Such considerations will only increase as Sino-African cooperation enters what Chinese Foreign Minister Wang Yi described in early 2018 as a 'new stage'. This is likely to involve a more nuanced approach to African markets, with Chinese entities responding to individual market prospects, but industrial parks and ports will remain a high Chinese priority, meaning that Chinese involvement in the sensitive and rapidly changing Horn of Africa will persist.

Change in the Horn region is being driven by the March 2018 accession of a new prime minister, Abiy Ahmed, whose selection by the Ethiopian People's Revolutionary Democratic Front largely reflected an effort by the ruling group to soothe persistent social tensions by increasing representation of different ethnic groups. However, Abiy has shown far greater than expected appetite for reform, both domestically and abroad, and in June 2018 the Ethiopian authorities announced their acceptance of the Algiers peace deal signed after the 1998–2000 war with Eritrea. The July 2018 signing of an Ethiopian-Eritrean peace deal officially ending two decades of latent hostility has the potential to transform security in the Horn. Most obviously, normalisation of relations between Ethiopia and Eritrea could potentially foster cooperation on counter-terrorism and security in the area. However, there are broader implications, since the two states have also engaged in a proxy conflict in Somalia and, less directly, Djibouti. (Djibouti – one of Ethiopia's main economic allies – has been in dispute with Eritrea over a land and maritime border around Doumeira, one of the world's busiest shipping routes.) Somalia and Eritrea have already resumed diplomatic relations after a gap of nearly 15 years, and it is possible that UN sanctions against Eritrea – imposed in large part because of Eritrean support for various Islamist organisations opposed to the Ethiopian-backed Somali transitional federal government – will be reviewed.

The rapprochement also underscores the growing strategic influence of Gulf states such as the United Arab Emirates in the region. Eritrea's political and economic ties with Saudi Arabia and the UAE have deepened with Eritrea's support for the Saudi-led campaign against Houthi rebels in Yemen, and the government's decision to break diplomatic ties with Qatar after its allies in the Gulf did the same. Indeed, bases located in Eritrea, just across the Bab el-Mandeb Strait from Yemen's southwest coast, have proved vital in enabling the UAE to conduct military operations in southern Yemen. Ethiopia, meanwhile, has been the recipient of substantial UAE support: in mid-2018, for example, the UAE pledged to give Ethiopia US$3bn in aid and investment, while the two states have also sought to invest in and develop the port of Berbera in Somaliland. Development of Berbera is controversial, not least because Somaliland is not generally recognised as an independent state, and the deal was not authorised by the federal authorities in Somalia. Yet Berbera has obvious geostrategic importance. It has a deep seaport, and is positioned strategically on the Bab el-Mandeb Strait. The UAE and Saudi Arabia have already developed a series of sea bases along the coastline of the Red Sea, the Gulf of Aden and the Somali shore of the Indian Ocean. Gaining access to the Somaliland coastline would give the two states a commanding position in the area, with implications for the ongoing conflict with Yemen, for oil-transport routes (as recently as July 2018 Saudi Arabia temporarily suspended all oil shipments through Bab el-Mandeb after attacks on two crude-carrying vessels by Houthi rebels in Yemen) and for any attempts by Iran to secure a presence in the Red Sea. Of course, given the strategic nature of the area, interest is not limited to Gulf states. Djibouti has traditionally been a key location for multiple actors: it hosts the United States' only permanent military base in Africa and China's first permanent overseas military base, as well as French, Italian, German and Japanese military presences. However, the very profusion of interests presents potential concerns. China has made substantial investments in Djibouti, and its port area in particular, and there has been persistent speculation that the Djiboutian authorities, which in early 2018 terminated the concession of Dubai-based DP World for the Doraleh Container Terminal, will hand over control of the port to a Chinese entity. In March 2018, General Thomas Waldhauser, the commander of AFRICOM, warned that the United States' ability to resupply Camp Lemonnier and refuel naval vessels could be adversely affected should China place restrictions on the Port of Djibouti's use. In this context, the Somaliland coastline could prove an attractive alternative (or addition) to Djibouti. Such access is not guaranteed, given that the country's authoritarian regime remains highly suspicious of outside influences. However, given Eritrea's clear need for external funding, and some signs of a more outward-looking approach by the regime, it is possible that Eritrea will become the next area of competition for global powers seeking to maintain a presence in one of the world's most strategically significant waterways.

Sub-Saharan Africa: Drivers of Strategic Change

- Cyril Ramaphosa's election to the presidency of South Africa has been presented as an opportunity to halt the country's domestic and international decline. Ramaphosa's initial focus is likely to be domestic.
- Demographic changes continue to reshape sub-Saharan Africa, with a rise in young people and insufficient growth in new jobs in countries such as South Africa and Kenya portending higher levels of unemployment in the near future.
- Populist movements are on the rise in sub-Saharan Africa, with notable examples being the Economic Freedom Fighters party of South Africa and the political protests in Ethiopia and Zimbabwe. However, many regimes have proved adept at co-opting populist demands.
- Africa is moving closer to forms of regional economic integration that have boosted welfare in other regions with the African Continental Free Trade Area (AfCFTA) agreement, but Nigeria, one of Africa's largest economies, has yet to sign up.
- Despite recent political developments in Central Africa, the fundamental patterns driving insecurity in the region have not changed. President Joseph Kabila, for instance, announced that he would not stand for re-election in the Democratic Republic of the Congo, but looks likely to continue exerting influence through his nominated replacement Emmanuel Ramazani Shadary.

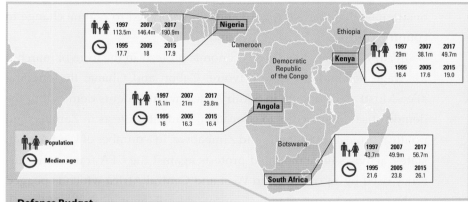

Defence Budget
(US$, constant 2010 prices)

	2008	2013	2018
Angola	$2.05bn	$4.7bn	$1.98bn
Kenya	$685m	$827m	$873m
Nigeria	$1.24bn	$1.91bn	$2.01bn
South Africa	$4.41bn	$4.66bn	$4.41bn

GDP per capita, Purchasing Power Parity (International $, constant 2011 prices)

Country	GDP
1997	
Angola	$2,840
Kenya	$2,179
Nigeria	$2,824
South Africa	$9,324
2007	
Angola	$5,443
Kenya	$2,395
Nigeria	$4,552
South Africa	$11,741
2017	
Angola	$5,819
Kenya	$2,993
Nigeria	$5,338
South Africa	$12,295

South African President Cyril Ramaphosa addresses an African National Congress party meeting on 19 May 2018

Sources: IISS; UN Department of Economic and Social Affairs (Population Division, 2017); World Bank

African Populism and the Possibility of an African Spring

Populism – a political philosophy that supports the rights and power of 'the people', broadly defined, in their struggle against a 'privileged elite' – is on the rise in sub-Saharan Africa, raising questions as to whether the region might experience an 'African Spring'. The region's ongoing democratic deficit, the demographic youth bulge, growing popular anger at corruption and crony capitalism and the gradual shift away from state largesse in many countries all echo the situation in the Middle East and North Africa that led to the Arab Spring, the series of protests and demonstrations that started in 2010 and ultimately led to regime change in countries including Egypt, Libya and Tunisia.

In 2017–18, there have been economic protests in the form of marches for wage demands in Côte d'Ivoire, Gabon and Ghana; the ongoing #FeesMustFall campaign in South Africa, with students demanding the democratisation of access to education; student protests in Zambia; and political protests in Ethiopia and Zimbabwe. In a number of West African states, activists have mounted protests against the CFA franc – the currency used by 14 countries in West and Central Africa which is pegged to the euro and supported by France – describing it as a relic of French colonialism. In Kenya, meanwhile, populist pressures prompted the introduction of legislation which set a cap on commercial lending rates and a floor on deposit rates, with Kenyan President Uhuru Kenyatta citing 'ordinary citizens' frustrations' about the cost of credit and earnings from deposits. The trend is perhaps most notable in South Africa, where the Economic Freedom Fighters (EFF) party is pursuing a radical agenda including the nationalisation of all land in the country. The EFF was formed only eight months prior to the 2014 election but won 6% of the vote, and concern about its potential performance in the 2019 polls, as well as its popularity among the disadvantaged, has seen its policies enter the political mainstream. However, African regimes have proven particularly adept at co-opting populist demands, and are much better prepared (and willing) to face down mass protests than their counterparts were at the onset of the Arab Spring. Protesters in sub-Saharan Africa are also divided, often on tribal lines, and have seen what happened to many of the states that participated in the Arab Spring.

The ongoing democratic deficit

A number of factors that led to the Arab Spring protests are apparent in sub-Saharan Africa, one being the region's ongoing democratic flaws. Democracy has seemingly become much more entrenched in sub-Saharan Africa in recent years. The incidence of coups – continental Africa has seen at least 200 successful and failed coups since the 1960s – has dropped substantially as democratic norms have taken hold, and several countries in the region (such as Ghana, Mauritius and Malawi) have undergone credible elections and peaceful transfers of power. However, it is also clear that elections do not automatically lead to representative governments. Numerous heads of state and ruling groups have learned how to sabotage the promise of genuine multiparty elections by undermining civil liberties and restricting the political space well ahead of the vote, as was the case in Ethiopia, where the ruling group and its allies won all 547 of the seats contested in the most recent (2015) election. Other governments have sought to manipulate registration lists and falsify vote counts in order to project the appearance of democracy while exploiting the fact that the institutions and election-monitoring mechanisms necessary to safeguard the democratic process are often absent or ineffective.

Above all, sub-Saharan Africa, which has the world's most youthful population, continues to have the world's oldest and longest-serving heads of government. Teodoro Obiang Nguema Mbasogo – Equatorial Guinea's president since August 1979 and the world's longest-serving leader – won a fifth seven-year term in 2016 and continues to dominate the political scene. Paul Biya has been in power in Cameroon for nearly 36 years, and seems set to stand for another seven-year term, notwithstanding the fact that he is already 85. In the Republic of Congo, Denis Sassou Nguesso – who has served 34 years (albeit not continuously) – repealed term limits in 2015, and is likely to run again in 2023, when his latest term expires. Sassou Nguesso is just one example of another anti-democratic trend in the region, whereby heads of state make every effort to extend their terms, often creating serious tensions. In Burundi, for example, there was substantial (mainly state-sponsored) violence ahead of the May 2018 referendum that allowed Pierre Nkurunziza to amend the constitution and extend the president's term from five years to seven. This will enable Nkurunziza, who has been in power since 2005, to rule for another 14 years when his current term expires in 2020. In this he followed the example of Paul Kagame in neighbouring Rwanda, who stood for and won a third seven-year term in 2017 following constitutional reforms that waived a previous two-term limit and was approved by 98% of voters in a referendum. The ruling group in Uganda also scrapped a constitutionally mandated age limit in 2017, enabling Yoweri Museveni (already in office for 32 years) to seek a sixth term in 2021 elections, while in the Democratic Republic of the Congo, Joseph Kabila has in effect ignored the end of his legal term, claiming that an election could not be organised in time. This is likely to lead to serious outbreaks of violence as the theoretical election date of the end of 2018 approaches. Given that long-term leaders (for example, Hosni Mubarak and Muammar Gadhafi) investing power in themselves at the expense of weakened institutions was one of the key drivers of the Arab Spring, this clearly highlights risks in the sub-Saharan region.

Of course, not all long-serving leaders have managed or sought to stay on. Indeed, 2017–18 was notable for the departure of a number of seemingly well-entrenched heads of state, including two of the region's dominant gerontocrats. However, such regime change was not generally achieved via entirely democratic means. The removal of Robert Mugabe (who had dominated Zimbabwe's political scene since 1980) in November 2017 was the result of a military coup, for all the authorities' attempts to portray it as a 'military-assisted transition'. The incumbent Zimbabwe African National Union–Patriotic Front (ZANU–PF) remained in power following the elections in July 2018, while Emmerson Mnangagwa, the new head of state, was a long-standing Mugabe loyalist prior to falling out with the president in 2017.

In Angola, the transition from José Eduardo dos Santos was at least via electoral means, but the populace did not have a direct vote on the change in leadership since presidential elections were abolished in 2010 (with the head of the largest parliamentary party automatically becoming head of state). In Ethiopia, meanwhile, public protests were clearly a factor in the resignation of the prime minister, Hailemariam Desalegn. However, the ruling Ethiopian People's Revolutionary Democratic Front remains in place, while the appointment of Abiy Ahmed was decided by a small ruling cadre, and it remains to be seen whether change at the top will lead to any genuine alteration in state policies. In all these cases, therefore, popular frustrations with government performance and desire for genuine change have not been fully addressed, and may yet re-emerge.

The youth bulge and end of state largesse

Demographic conditions could also present a potential threat to stability. At the time of the Arab Spring, the Middle East and North Africa regions were experiencing an unprecedented youth bulge, with around two-thirds of the 300 million or so combined population being younger than 29. The proportions are somewhat lower in sub-Saharan Africa – around one in six of the region's population is aged between 15 and 24, according to the African Development Bank – but the overall numbers are similar, and the median age of sub-Saharan Africa's population remains very low, at 19.5.

In theory, this offers the potential for a substantial demographic dividend: the World Bank has suggested that this dividend could account for 11–15% of GDP-volume growth by 2030, resulting in 40m–60m fewer people in poverty in 2030. This assumes, however, that there are steady improvements in educational outcomes, leading to an increase in overall skills levels (and the diversity of these skills) in the sub-Saharan labour force. It also assumes that jobs in the public and private sectors can be created at a sufficient pace to provide the growing youth population with jobs, and this is far from guaranteed. According to IMF projections covering the 2010–20 period, only 3m formal jobs are created for the 10m–12m young people entering the job market across the continent each year. Similarly, the International Labour Organization calculates that, over the past 25 years, there has been no improvement in young people's participation in the sub-Saharan African labour force.

This is not to say that three-quarters of young people are unemployed: underemployment is much more the issue. Figures vary between countries, but the World Economic Forum (WEF) has calculated that 90% (or more) of the sub-Saharan workforce is in the informal sector, such as subsistence agriculture and urban self-employment in petty services. Indeed, in Douala and Yaoundé in Cameroon, according to the WEF, about 96% of employment is informal. This phenomenon of youth unemployment/underemployment presents a clear potential security threat. A survey conducted by the World Bank in 2011 showed that around 40% of those joining rebel movements said they were motivated by a lack of jobs.

Large numbers of disaffected youth could easily fuel socio-political unrest and present a threat to democratic institutions, particularly as local authorities have struggled to come up with clear and viable strategies to tackle joblessness. One suggestion has been to increase youth participation in agriculture, but this does not tally with the well-documented demographic shift from rural to urban areas, nor is it clear how young people could gain access to land currently owned by established elites (whether foreign or local). Previous experience with land reform in Zimbabwe does not provide a particularly positive example, since many of those 'resettling' land have lacked the experience and inputs to attain viable living standards. However, this is unlikely to prevent the continued build-up of populist pressure to increase local access to land, whether in states such as South Africa (where it is likely to fuel resentment about the perceived enduring economic power of the white minority) or Ethiopia (where government ownership of land has been one of the drivers of persistent political unrest since 2015).

It has also been suggested that technology – notably artificial intelligence (AI) and associated automation – will transform sub-Saharan employment patterns. Again, however, it is far from clear that this will be wholly positive. Worldwide, the WEF predicts a net loss of 5m jobs to AI by 2020. In previous industrial evolutions, job losses from 'old' technologies have been largely outweighed by the creation of new positions. However, African states are not well placed to benefit from AI and related developments, given that these require substantial investment capital, research and development and highly skilled workers, and take relatively little account of sub-Saharan Africa's traditional economic advantages, such as low-cost labour and substantial natural resources. Indeed, even in South Africa – arguably the continent's most technologically developed state – 41% of all work activities are susceptible to automation, according to the WEF, while the related figures for Ethiopia, Nigeria and Kenya are 44%, 46% and 52% respectively. Official data in 2016 suggest that unemployment rates in these states range from 5.7% (Ethiopia) to 27.7% (South Africa), underscoring the substantial potential impact in some of the continent's major players. Equally, while a March 2018 survey by the Kenya National Bureau of Statistics puts the country's overall unemployment at 7.4%, the rate is heavily skewed towards younger Kenyans, with nine in every 10 unemployed Kenyans aged 35 years or less, and the average unemployment rate for 20–24-year-olds assessed at just over 19%.

The final factor suggesting that an African Spring is possible is the gradual shift away from state largesse in many countries. Oil prices remain well below the highs of 2011–14, notwithstanding the relative recovery in mid-2018, and oil exporters such as Nigeria and Angola can no longer afford to provide generous subsidies. This chiefly affects the poorer members of society, with the elite in many cases either retaining privileged access to goods or having accrued sufficient wealth not to need subsidised food or fuel. This situation is fuelling perceptions that state-led development in effect means crony capitalism benefiting only a small minority – a criticism increasingly levelled against the dos Santos regime in Angola prior to the president's departure in August 2017. Such perceptions are certainly not limited to oil exporters: anger at inequitable development is also one of the key reasons behind the unrest in Ethiopia and the growth in public discontent with the Mugabe regime in

Sub-Saharan Africa's Crisis of Youth Unemployment

Sub-Saharan Africa continues to undergo profound demographic changes, particularly in terms of city-population size, with several African megacities doubling in population over the last 20 years. Africa also has the world's most youthful population, and youth unemployment is a growing regional phenomenon.

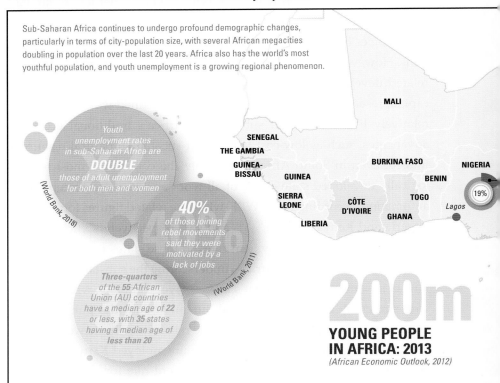

Youth unemployment rates in sub-Saharan Africa are **DOUBLE** those of adult unemployment for both men and women

(World Bank, 2018)

40% of those joining rebel movements said they were motivated by a lack of jobs

(World Bank, 2011)

Three-quarters of the **55** African Union (AU) countries have a median age of **22** or less, with **35** states having a median age of **less than 20**

MALI

SENEGAL
THE GAMBIA
GUINEA-BISSAU
GUINEA
SIERRA LEONE
LIBERIA

BURKINA FASO
BENIN
CÔTE D'IVOIRE
GHANA
TOGO

NIGERIA

Lagos

19%

200m
YOUNG PEOPLE IN AFRICA: 2013
(African Economic Outlook, 2012)

YOUTH UNEMPLOYMENT: A SOUTHERN PHENOMENON

The countries with the highest total and youth-unemployment rates in 2016 are located in the south: Swaziland, South Africa, Namibia, Mozambique and Lesotho.

Despite being one of the largest economies in Africa, South Africa has the second-highest percentage of unemployed young people in the region.

830m
YOUNG PEOPLE IN AFRICA: 2050 PROJECTED
(International Labour Organization)

CITY-POPULATION SIZE AND GROWTH

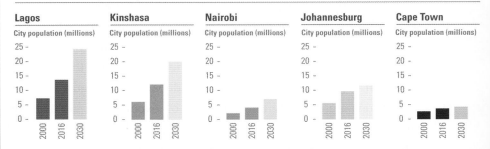

Lagos
City population (millions)

Kinshasa
City population (millions)

Nairobi
City population (millions)

Johannesburg
City population (millions)

Cape Town
City population (millions)

Sources: *African Economic Outlook/African Development Bank, CIA World Factbook, Index Mundi, International Labour Organization, United Nations Department of Economic and So Affairs – Population Division (2016), United Nations Development Programme, World Bank*

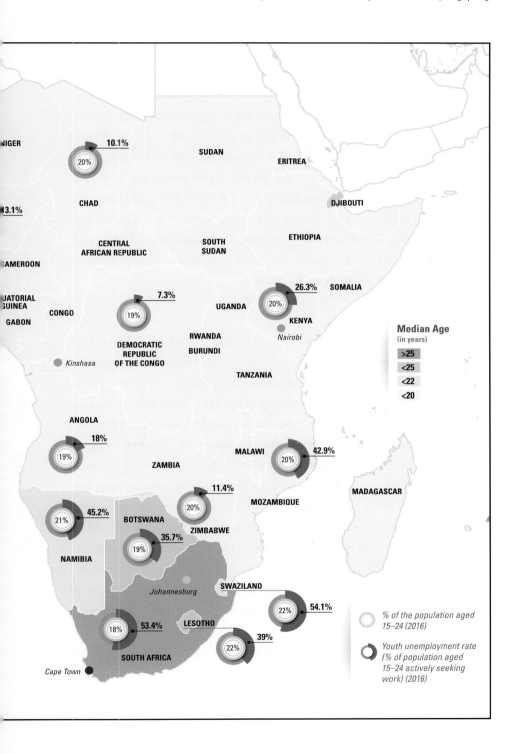

Zimbabwe in 2017. Equally, the move away from subsidies is not limited to oil exporters: a greater number of African states are recognising the need for fiscal restraint, not least because of the build-up of domestic and external debt (the median debt-to-GDP ratio in sub-Saharan Africa rose to 53% in 2017 from 48% in 2016, according to the World Bank). Overall economic growth rates remain somewhat muted: although the World Bank estimates that growth in sub-Saharan Africa rebounded from 1.3% in 2016 to 2.4% in 2017, overall incomes per capita continued to shrink, while investment remained weak and fiscal sustainability continued to fall. Between 2007 and 2016, four-fifths of countries in the region experienced a substantial deterioration in fiscal sustainability. The overall result is that many governments are finding it harder to use financial largesse to dampen inclinations to protest.

Populism co-opted

Despite the many parallels with the conditions that led to the Arab Spring, it is far from certain that sub-Saharan Africa will experience a wave of protests leading to substantial regime change. African governments have proven adept at co-opting populist demands and making them – or at least appearing to make them – part of national policy. For example, the Nigerian government now espouses the resource nationalism that was once the prerogative of militant groups in the Niger Delta, while in South Africa the ruling African National Congress is adopting elements of the EFF's land-acquisition proposals. Tanzania's president, John Magufuli, has championed populist causes ranging from tackling corruption to restoring the balance between the Tanzanian state and supposedly rapacious (and foreign) mining companies. Indeed, Magufuli's entire regime appears to be based on authoritarian populism, a trend that was also increasingly apparent in South Africa under Jacob Zuma's leadership.

Not coincidentally, former liberation movements built on populist support remain in power in Tanzania and South Africa. In countries where liberation movements continue to dominate decades after independence was achieved (such as Zimbabwe), ruling parties have sought to use populist rhetoric to legitimise their continued dominance by appealing to the continued struggle against foreign (i.e., colonial) powers seeking to maintain or regain power – one of the reasons why land ownership remains such a potent issue.

This co-option of populist demands is in part ideological, but also reflects regional governments' awareness of the risks of protests achieving a critical mass, and this is another factor militating against an African Spring. Protesters in Arab states benefited from the element of surprise, and from their regimes' inept responses. In contrast, sub-Saharan governments are much better prepared to meet large-scale protests (not least because some of them have already experienced such protests); in many of the states most obviously vulnerable to unrest, the authorities are prepared to take a vigorous, and often violent, approach to protest movements. According to a report by Ethiopia's state-affiliated Human Rights Commission in April 2017, 669 people died in the initial wave of anti-government protests that began in November 2015, with further deaths likely to have occurred since. According to the UN, at least 47 people were killed in 2007 and January 2018 in a government crackdown on demonstrations against Joseph Kabila in the Democratic Republic of the Congo, while in Guinea, at least 15 people have been killed and scores injured in clashes between the security forces, opposition supporters and pro-government protesters since the local elections held in February 2018. This type of strong state crackdown can often discourage citizens from engaging in protests, particularly as many people have relatively recent experience of violence in the form of armed conflicts, civil wars or coups on national territory.

Limited power of social media

Another factor mitigating against the possibility of a popular uprising in sub-Saharan Africa is the lack of widespread access to technology among the population. Sub-Saharan Africa has a much smaller urban, literate middle class than most of the countries of the Arab Spring, and their access to technology is much more restricted, making it harder to achieve mass mobilisation and turn protest into regime change. This is, of course, an oversimplification. Urbanisation is on the rise throughout the continent, while the numbers of the middle class are rising (albeit from a small base). Many people are dissatisfied with their existing political situations – according to pan-African research group Afrobarometer, only 40% of the population in 36 African countries believes that the last election in their country was free and fair – and are seeking to bypass state-dominated media. In Zimbabwe, the #ThisFlag and #Tajamuka movements presented an unprecedented threat to Robert Mugabe, not least because they were civic movements and the authorities struggled to use the tried-and-tested strategy of painting opponents as colonialist stooges.

Other notable campaigns driven by social media have included #Zumamustfall in South Africa, #TakeBackKenya (a movement geared towards denouncing corruption and bad governance within the Kenyan government) and the #BringBackOurGirls campaign in Nigeria (a response to the 2014 kidnapping of Chibok schoolgirls which reportedly contributed to the defeat of Goodluck Jonathan in the 2015 presidential elections). All of these movements have had varying levels of success, but have tended to take place in the more technologically advanced states on the continent. There is little doubt that coordinated, well-informed urban protest movements have the potential to have a substantial impact in the existing or incipient mega-cities of Addis Ababa, Johannesburg, Kinshasa, Lagos and Nairobi. However, given that informal-sector employment dominates in the cities, the widespread struggle to meet subsistence needs is likely to act as a partial constraint. (During the period of hyperinflation in Zimbabwe in 2007–08, for example, protests were limited in part because it was so difficult and time-consuming to secure basic items that citizens literally could not afford to take time to protest.) What is more, regimes are now more aware of the potential power of social media and have proved more adept at restricting access. In late 2017/early 2018, the Ethiopian government imposed a blanket internet shutdown in several regional states, while Cameroon introduced an internet shutdown after students sought to organise separatist protests via Facebook. Meanwhile, Sudan has employed 'cyber jihadists'

– a unit within the National Intelligence and Security Service – to infiltrate popular groups on Facebook and WhatsApp. Indeed, according to Freedom House's 2017 'Freedom on the Net' report, half of the sub-Saharan countries assessed had censored social-media-based efforts to mobilise for public causes. This is clearly designed to make it much harder for campaigns to secure enough mass appeal to drive genuine change.

The issue of heterogeneity, or rather lack thereof, is another potential constraint. The Arab Spring united secularists and Islamists, the middle classes and the poor, and left-wing groups and liberal economic reformers under a pan-Arab banner. Although pan-Africanism is growing in popularity in certain areas, it is questionable whether a similar phenomenon would occur in sub-Saharan Africa. Despite developments such as the proposed creation of an African free-trade area, the continent remains the least integrated in the world and continues to experience outbreaks of xenophobic violence. Given that tribal and linguistic differences are often entrenched within individual countries, politicians can easily use populist narratives regarding immigrants or tribal differences to marginalise opponents.

The Arab Spring: a cautionary tale?

Many Africans were broadly unaware of the events of the Arab Spring up to the point where leaders fell. According to a 2014 Gallup poll of people in 26 African states, more than two-thirds of respondents said that they had not followed the events of the Arab Spring 'closely at all'. However, there was more awareness of the aftermath – in part due to increased media coverage. In the Gallup poll, respondents in 18 of the 26 countries believed that the developments had a negative rather than positive impact for their country, and in states such as Sierra Leone and Madagascar (which experienced an unconstitutional transfer of power followed by a coup attempt in 2009–10), fewer than 10% of respondents approved of the Arab Spring.

This response is perhaps unsurprising given the long-term political developments in many of the countries involved in the Arab Spring.

Libya, Syria and Yemen have plunged into civil war; the military is playing an unprecedented role in Egypt; and many long-standing monarchical regimes have survived, in some cases because of a willingness to use heavy-handed security tactics. Closer to home, the Arab Spring was a contributory factor to religious and tribal instability in Mali. Regional governments have proven willing to use this narrative to deter protests: in Angola, for example, the ruling People's Movement for the Liberation of Angola (MPLA) has long portrayed support for the opposition National Union for the Total Independence of Angola (UNITA) or other protest movements as risking a return to civil conflict. Given that the country's civil war only ended in 2002 (having rumbled on, with some gaps, since 1975), this has proved to be a potent argument.

However, the region's regimes are not immune to popular protests and potential deposition. The political crisis in the Democratic Republic of the Congo will continue to deepen as the regime makes strenuous efforts to prolong the reign of Joseph Kabila, while rebel activity in the country increases. Togo's Faure Gnassingbé – in power since 2005 but part of a family dynasty that has ruled the country for 50 years – could also come under pressure: growing demands for political reforms in Togo have led to large protests, while wealth disparities are stark, with more than 80% of the rural population living on less than US$2 a day. Tensions are also building in Cameroon, which is facing security concerns arising from Islamist extremism, renewed violence in the country's restive anglophone regions and a deteriorating humanitarian situation in the Far North province. Anti-government sentiment is also set to rise in Uganda, where Yoweri Museveni, president since 1986, continues to demonstrate only lacklustre commitment to democratic reform. It is possible, though far from guaranteed, that some or all of these regimes could fall in the next year or two. However, the relative preparedness of regimes, the divisions between opponents and wariness of the potential impact in terms of conflict suggest that a contagious wave of instability across the region is unlikely to occur.

Central Africa: Chronic Instability, Entrenched Problems

Political stability in most of sub-Saharan Africa has improved steadily in recent years. Although military coups still take place, such as the 'military-assisted transition' in Zimbabwe in late 2017, their incidence has declined substantially as democracy has taken hold. Similarly, while a number of regimes are vulnerable to large-scale public unrest and potential overthrow, they remain in a minority in most sub-regions.

Central Africa is the exception to this regional trend. Whether defined narrowly as comprising the Central African Republic, the Democratic Republic of the Congo and the Republic of Congo, or more broadly to also include Gabon, Rwanda and Burundi, Central Africa is the continent's least stable sub-region, with countries affected by or attempting to recover from factors including sectarian and/or tribal conflict, unrest arising from political stasis and armed rebel activity. With porous borders and tribal links facilitating the spillover of political unrest and violence into neighbouring states, Central Africa acts as a constraint on the continent's political and economic progress. At the heart of the issue is the Democratic Republic of the Congo, where President Joseph Kabila's determination to rule by proxy threatens to lead to violence. A democratic poll in the country combined with coherent international action in the broader area would be an initial step towards bringing stability to the region, but neither seems likely.

Democratic Republic of the Congo looms large

There are a variety of reasons why Central Africa remains so troubled, but there is little doubt that the Democratic Republic of the Congo is the dominant factor, not least because it dwarfs its neighbouring states, both geographically – it is the size of Western Europe – and in terms of population size (it has a population of around 84 million people, compared with fewer than 5m in the Central African Republic). The intractability of the problems in the Democratic Republic of the Congo is hard to understand without some historical context. The country gained independence in 1960 after a notoriously brutal period of colonisation by Belgium and immediately entered a period of tribal and (as a proxy for the Cold War) ideological conflict. The mineral-rich provinces of Katanga and South Kasai both declared their secession from the central state, and when the prime minister, Patrice Lumumba, sought Soviet assistance he was toppled (and subsequently executed) in a coup led by Colonel Joseph Mobutu. Around 100,000 people are thought to have been killed during the crisis. Mobutu ran the country as a personal fiefdom, combining totalitarianism with kleptocracy – he is thought to have embezzled between US$4 billion and US$15bn during his 32 years in power – and having promised (but avoided) elections, was finally deposed in the First Congo War (1996–97). This conflict – in effect a Rwandan invasion of the country – was decisive in that it led to Mobutu's overthrow and replacement by rebel leader Laurent-Désiré Kabila, but in other respects brought little change, and little more than a year later the Second Congo War (1998–2003) began.

Eight African countries and around 25 armed groups were involved in a conflict so devastating that it is known as the African World War. It is thought that 5.4m people died in or as a result of the conflict (through disease and starvation, for example), while a further 2m were displaced. The conflict was fuelled by the Democratic Republic of the Congo's mineral wealth, with armed groups and foreign actors seeking to control diamond, gold and coltan mines, while ethnic divisions were stoked by warlords. The result was a military stalemate that left Joseph Kabila (son of Laurent, who was assassinated by his bodyguard in 2001) in power.

After Kabila, a Kabila proxy?

The key problem in the Democratic Republic of the Congo has been the president's desire to remain in office or buy time to put a succession plan in place. Kabila's term ended in December 2016, but he failed to step down as required by the constitution, exploiting his control of the security services and a tame judiciary to stay in power. These delays infuriated the opposition, triggered further international criticism (and sanctions) and exacerbated instability in the country: anti-Kabila sentiment has been extremely high in the Democratic Republic of the Congo, while the regime has become increasingly oppressive.

The announcement in August 2018 that Kabila would not seek to stand in the polls scheduled for December 2018 is unlikely to address all such concerns. Kabila has handpicked his successor, Emmanuel Ramazani Shadary, who is himself a controversial figure. Shadary served as interior minister during 2016–18 – a period of violent government crackdowns on protesters, and of a violent military suppression of an insurrection in the Kasai region. Moreover, in mid-2017 he was placed under EU sanctions (an asset freeze and travel ban) over serious human-rights abuses. The fact that Shadary does not appear to have a substantial support base of his own has fuelled perceptions that Kabila intends to remain the dominant political figure, but with a veil of international legitimacy, since he can claim to have respected the constitution (belatedly).

Around 25 candidates intend to stand in the polls, although only a handful are likely to secure more than a small proportion of the votes. Jean-Pierre Bemba – a former vice-president, and former rebel leader of the Congolese Liberation Movement (MLC) – is likely to be a key opponent. He is only in a position to stand because in June the International Criminal Court overturned on appeal his 2016 conviction for crimes against humanity in relation to the actions of troops under his command in the Central African Republic in 2002–03. Despite his initial conviction, Bemba has a strong support base in the north and the west of the Democratic Republic of the Congo as well as in the capital Kinshasa, and gained 42% of the vote to Kabila's 58% when he stood in the 2006 presidential election. His supporters see Bemba's arrest following the 2006 poll as an effort by Kabila to marginalise a rival, and the MLC leader's putative return will shake up the country's electoral scene.

However, a democratic transfer of power is far from guaranteed. Elections are unlikely to be free and fair, with the government aiming to use electronic-voting machines despite warnings from civil-society groups that they are vulnerable to hackers, and that their use threatens electoral transparency and the overall credibility of the vote. Thus the elections seem unlikely to produce a positive outcome. Opposition groups will certainly perceive Shadary to be a designated successor whom Kabila believes he can control from behind the scenes. Countries such as Angola have shown that this scenario does not always proceed as planned, but in any event Kabila's opponents would not regard a victory for a candidate of the ruling Alliance of the Presidential Majority (AMP) as credible, particularly if the opposition should unite around a single candidate. Widespread instability following the vote is thus likely.

It is also possible that Bemba or another opposition leader (such as Felix Tshisekedi) wins. This is unlikely given the ruling group's domination of the political space, but even if such a scenario were to occur, it is far from clear that the AMP or the security services would accept an opposition victory, potentially leading to open conflict. A victory for Bemba would also be likely to cause very serious tensions with neighbours, notably the Central African Republic. Even in the best-case scenario – a free and fair election producing a widely acceptable government that then pursues a genuine reform agenda – the country's almost overwhelming problems (including societal division, ethnic and other conflict, and the chronic weakness of central authority) would take years to address.

Regional instability

The political environment has changed since the beginning of the Second Congo War in 1998, when states including Angola, Rwanda, Uganda and Zimbabwe became directly involved in the conflict. Most regional powers are now concerned with domestic affairs. Rwanda is supportive of the Democratic Republic of the Congo's ongoing operation against the Democratic Forces for the Liberation of Rwanda rebels (formed by Rwandan Hutus linked to the 1994 Rwandan genocide) and seems unlikely to wish to disrupt this. Uganda is concerned with domestic issues, while Zimbabwe's new leadership is also focused on domestic problems, with the additional factor that direct intervention in the Democratic Republic of the Congo (unless as part of a mandated regional force) would be likely to sour Harare's efforts to achieve a rapprochement with Western states. Angola, meanwhile, is no longer in the throes of civil war – the National Union for the Total Independence of Angola (UNITA) is now an opposition party, albeit with little real political power – and is likely to take a hands-off stance unless its own stability is threatened by refugee flows. All of this suggests that while action under the aegis of a supranational group such as the Southern African Development Community (SADC) or the African Union (AU) is possible, intervention by various sovereign states on opposing sides is much less likely now than it was 20 years ago.

However, this is not to say that there is no danger of contagion. The Democratic Republic of the Congo borders a number of already fragile countries, and there is a clear risk that armed groups will pass through borders with, for example, Burundi, where President Pierre Nkurunziza has amended the constitution to extend presidential terms (while insisting that he does not intend to seek re-election in 2020), and South Sudan. South Sudan has been engaged in civil conflict for much of its seven-year existence, and fighters loyal to the ousted vice-president Riek Machar are known to have crossed into the Democratic Republic of the Congo, fuelling fears that they have formed a community-based militant group. Equally, security conditions in the Republic of Congo's restive Pool region remain poor.

There is also a potential risk of renewed civil war in neighbouring Central African Republic. Although there is a tribal dimension to the current tensions, they are chiefly driven by religious differences and date back to 2012–13, when the predominantly Muslim Séléka rebel movement entered the capital Bangui and overthrew then-president François Bozizé. Anti-balaka militias, mainly Christian, emerged to combat the Séléka, and violence then spilled over into the rest of the country. International interventions led to a peace deal, and reasonably free and fair elections, but large-scale inter-community violence has resumed since early 2017, particularly in rural areas. This is largely because two armed groups that were formerly part of Séléka, the Popular Front for the Renaissance of Central African Republic (FPRC) and the Union for Peace in Central Africa (UPC), are now engaged in a power struggle, although battles over resources also play a role. In the second half of

2017, serious conflict was in effect limited to the diamond-rich Haute-Kotto region, where the Lord's Resistance Army, the FPRC and other militias are competing to control access to diamond revenue. In 2018, however, there have been reports of increasing political violence in Ouaka, Basse-Kotto and in Bangui. This last is particularly concerning since the government's territorial control has hitherto been limited almost entirely to Bangui. In the context of increasing instability there too, and with the two main rebel groups yet to disarm, there is a clear risk that the government will be overthrown by rebels and the country will return to outright civil war.

Solutions in short supply

There are no easy or rapid solutions to the problems in Central Africa. Tribal and religious divisions are entrenched and domestic politics continue to be characterised by competing armed groups and, in many cases, kleptocratic governments. However, the minimum requirement for some sort of improvement in the sub-region is consistent international engagement. In the Central African Republic, a French-led international intervention force was put in place in December 2013 and helped stabilise the situation before withdrawing in 2016 following elections. Although the withdrawal was controversial given that the security situation remained volatile, the force was replaced by some 13,000 UN peacekeepers, which is probably the main reason why the current, democratically elected government has not been overthrown. Equally, the AU is promoting a road map for peace and seeking to mediate between the various groups.

In the Democratic Republic of the Congo, meanwhile, there was substantial international participation in the 2006 elections, which were the country's first multiparty polls in more than 40 years. The AU, European Union, SADC and UN took a coordinated approach, managing the technical and logistical aspects of the voting process, providing security at polling stations and mediating in election disputes. South Africa, which took the lead in mediation efforts during the Inter-Congolese Dialogue, provided support for the Congolese Independent National Electoral

Commission (CENI), even lending CENI some of its own electoral equipment. The result was elections that were widely regarded by both international and national observers as being technically sound, transparent and credible. In contrast, the 2011 elections were largely funded and managed by the Congolese authorities, and the level of international involvement was much lower, in part because of a growing consensus that the result was a foregone conclusion and also because the UN in particular was wary of repeating its experience in Côte d'Ivoire, where the local mission was drawn into acting as arbiter for the election and thus implicated in the resulting violence. The result in 2011 was a chaotic election process and an outcome that was immediately rejected by the losing candidate, triggering violent protests.

An undemocratic election in December 2018 in the Democratic Republic of the Congo would only serve to worsen problems in the sub-region. Although a Kabila candidacy would clearly have provoked heightened instability, and potentially derailed the presidential vote, his decision to stand down will almost certainly not lead to a free and fair vote. It is unlikely that the Congolese authorities will seek genuine 2006-style international participation in the election process, nor is it clear that international groups would be prepared to commit to this: there is an element of donor/international-community fatigue with the Central African region. The Democratic Republic of the Congo has not had a single peaceful transfer of power since independence, and none of the main possible outcomes of the next scheduled elections are particularly positive. Nor does the longer-term outlook appear sanguine: even if Kabila refrains from trying to retain behind-the-scenes influence, it is far from certain that Shadary will seek to do more than establish his own patronage network and plunder the country's remaining natural resources. Should the country somehow produce a Nelson Mandela-style figure who is capable of bringing opposing sides together, it would most likely take decades to address the entrenched inequalities.

Nonetheless, efforts to address poverty and economic inequality are clear prerequisites for an improvement in stability throughout the sub-region. The UN's latest Multidimensional Poverty Index reports that more than three-quarters of the Congolese population live below the poverty line, and poverty clearly increases the risk of violent protest and (in various states) of disaffected youth joining rebel groups. Boosting productivity and creating plentiful jobs for the overwhelmingly youthful population (more than 1.5m people enter the labour market each year) is vital if the Democratic Republic of the Congo is to start to make economic and thus political progress. In fact, the Congolese government already officially aims to increase so-called 'pro-poor' spending, boost public investment and strengthen governance in the mining sector, all of which would be steps in the right direction. In practice, however, such reforms would potentially undermine the personal interests of the current president and his entourage, and have thus tended to languish. Again, the possibility of rapid improvement appears slim.

It is possible that the Democratic Republic of the Congo as currently constituted is simply too big to succeed, both logistically and in terms of shared interests. The distance from Kinshasa to Kalemie in the east of the country is more than 2,200 kilometres – greater than from Paris to Minsk. Effective rule over such distances requires either much stronger central government or much greater devolution to regional administrations that share common goals with that government. Equally, the Democratic Republic of the Congo's heritage as an artificial entity that was largely created in the nineteenth century with little recognition of divergent tribal interests has long militated against stability. There have on occasion been suggestions that, if it cannot function as a viable nation-state, the Democratic Republic of the Congo should be partitioned. However, this would at the very least be a high-risk strategy, with the potential for a rise in violence. A less extreme version of this would be the development of federalism, but again this seems unlikely in the short to medium term. Historical events, such as attempted secession of the State of Katanga in 1960, are likely to make politicians wary of giving more power to regions, while genuine federalism would require the establishment of a regime that has the firm foundation of a legitimate mandate, and thus does not fear the development of competing interests. In the absence of such developments, instability looks set to persist.

Counting the cost

The cost of this continuing instability will clearly be high. In February 2018, the US Government Accountability Office calculated that the first 39 months of the UN peacekeeping operation in the Central African Republic had cost the UN around US$2.4bn. Meanwhile, the cost of deploying more than 18,000 UN peacekeepers in the Democratic Republic of the Congo since 1 July 2010 was US$8.7bn (as of June 2018). The economic cost to the states involved is also high. Real GDP in the Central African Republic declined by no less than 37% in 2013, and it will probably take years to return to its previous levels, particularly as persistent insecurity is likely to prevent the return of many internally displaced persons and thus hinders economic activity. In the Democratic Republic of the Congo, where economic growth averaged 7.7% between 2010 and 2015, largely because of mining-sector activities, growth has slowed substantially owing to the political crisis that has increasingly affected the country since late 2016. Indeed, this risks turning into a vicious circle: muted growth is likely to increase popular resentment of the regime, in turn boosting the risk of social instability and distracting from a more pro-growth reform agenda. Increased regional involvement in a renewed Congolese crisis would multiply the economic effect within Africa, but more systematic unrest in the Democratic Republic of the Congo would have a much broader international impact. Dislocation in the mineral-rich Katanga region, which contains between 50% and 60% of global cobalt reserves, could affect defence, automotive and electronics industries worldwide. As it is, cobalt prices have quadrupled since the beginning of 2016, driven by concerns regarding disrupted supply.

However, the cost of the problems in Central Africa will remain predominantly humanitarian. The Central African Republic's population was estimated at 4.6m people in 2016. As of May 2018, around 690,000 people were internally displaced, according to the UN High Commissioner for Refugees (UNHCR), while some 580,000 had fled to neighbouring states. The UNHCR also estimated that as of January 2018, some 4.5m people in the Democratic Republic of the Congo had been internally displaced (2.2m of them in 2017), and also reported that as of June 2018, there were some 780,000 refugees from the Democratic Republic of the Congo within sub-Saharan Africa (in part because of geography, the overall number of Congolese refugees in Europe and North America remains relatively small, in the tens of thousands). At the same time, the Democratic Republic of the Congo is itself hosting more than 530,000 refugees fleeing from violence in states such as Burundi, the Central African Republic and South Sudan. According to the Internal Displacement Monitoring Centre, the Democratic Republic of the Congo is second only to Syria in terms of the number of new internal displacements associated with conflict and violence, and many of the refugees from violence in the Central African region are fleeing to states that are themselves unstable, and poor. This increases the risk of tensions with host communities over already scarce resources, while tribal differences can also prove problematic. This problem looks set to persist, given that elections in the Democratic Republic of the Congo are likely to lack credibility in the current environment and will probably lead to increased violence in the country, and thus continued refugee flows. Central Africa will continue to represent a wellspring of instability at the very heart of the continent. It thus looks set to raise the risk profile of the region, dampening its prospects for investment and (in the case of East Africa) as a tourism destination, and casting further doubt on the already problematic 'Africa Rising' narrative.

Prospects for Free Trade in Africa

The African Continental Free Trade Area (AfCFTA), the legal framework of which was signed by 44 states in March 2018, will be one of the world's largest free-trade areas, by 2020 potentially covering more than 1.2 billion people and more than US$4 trillion in combined consumer and business spending across the 55 states of the African Union (AU). However, not all countries have signed up yet, and many governments remain protectionist in outlook and wary of the economic impact of a free-trade area. Given the challenges involved in integrating such diverse economies and regional priorities, it is far from clear that the establishment of one of the most ambitious trade groupings in the world is likely or even feasible within the mandated time frame.

A new vision for trade in Africa

On 21 March 2018 at a summit in Kigali, Rwanda, 44 of the 55 AU states signed the legal framework for the AfCFTA, arguably the most significant free-trade agreement since the establishment of the World Trade Organisation (WTO) in 1995. At the same gathering, 30 African countries signed a protocol on the free movement of people, while 47 states signed the Kigali Declaration, which sets the political goal of establishing a free-trade area.

The AfCFTA market is projected to include 1.7bn people with more than US$6.7trn of cumulative consumer and business spending by 2030. The draft agreement commits countries to progressively remove tariffs on 90% of goods-tariff lines (whose current average tariff is 6.1%); the remaining 10% of goods will have longer liberalisation periods, or may in some cases be excluded from liberalisation entirely. The agreement will also liberalise investment, intellectual-property rights and non-tariff barriers. In the longer term, a single currency may even be considered.

The AfCFTA has some ambitious objectives. As outlined by the AU, these include:

- Creating a single continental market for goods and services, with free movement of business travellers and investments, thus paving the way for more rapid progress towards the establishment of the Continental Customs Union and the African customs union.
- Expanding intra-African trade through improved harmonisation and coordination of trade-liberalisation and facilitation regimes and instruments across existing regional economic communities (RECs), and Africa in general. This forms part of

broader AU targets to more than double intra-African trade between January 2012 and January 2022.

- Resolving the challenges of multiple and overlapping memberships of such communities in order to hasten the process of regional and continental integration.
- Improving competitiveness at both the industry and company level by exploiting opportunities for scale production, continental market access and better reallocation of resources.

The time frame for implementing these wide-ranging objectives is, however, relatively brief. The trade area will come into effect 30 days after the agreement is ratified by the parliaments of at least 22 countries, with all signatories having 120 days after signing the AfCFTA framework to ratify it. AU leaders have suggested that the second phase of negotiations, covering issues including investment and intellectual-property rights, should begin by January 2019, with the aim of completing the entire process by the end of 2020.

Prospect of increased trade and new jobs

The most obvious potential benefit of the AfCFTA is increased trade within Africa. Total African trade levels are the lowest in the world, and statistics from the AU show that African states also trade far less with each other than is the case in other parts of the world. Intra-African trade represented about 16% of the total volume of African trade in 2014, according to the 2017 African Economic Outlook report, and while this was up from just 10% in 2000, it still compares unfavourably with 19% intra-regional trade in Latin America, 51% in Asia, 54% in North America and some 70% in Europe. Intra-African trade in manufacturing has actually declined, from 18% in 2005 to about 15% between 2010 and 2015.

Much intra-regional trade takes place on an informal basis and is therefore not captured in official statistics, but it is nonetheless clear that intra-African trade levels are well below those of other continents. There are a number of reasons for this, ranging from infrastructural and trade finance deficits to different production structures across countries.

High costs are also a significant factor: according to the United Nations Economic Commission for Africa (ECA), shipping a car from Japan to Abidjan, the Ivorian capital, costs US$1,500 (including insurance); shipping the same car from Ethiopia to Abidjan costs US$5,000. Trade is also constricted by the region's poor customs environment and its high tariffs and non-tariff barriers (NTBs). Indeed, with an average regional tariff of 6.1%, businesses currently face higher tariffs exporting within Africa than when they export outside it. Meanwhile, the burden arising from such NTBs as protracted customs procedures and excessive documentation is reflected in the World Bank's 'Doing Business' reports, which show that, on average, exportation in sub-Saharan Africa takes about eight days and costs US$807. In the East Asia and Pacific region, exporting takes some five days and costs just under US$500, while the figures for Latin America and the Caribbean are just under five days and US$637, and for South Asia 5.7 days and US$549.

Not all of these constraints can be addressed by the AfCFTA, at least in the short to medium term. However, modelling exercises by the ECA suggest that a regional free-trade area has the potential to lift intra-African trade by 52.3% between 2010 and 2022, relative to a baseline without it. The ECA also calculates that trade in industrial products will receive the largest boost, with an additional increase of 53.3% over the same period. Trade-facilitation measures, such as the further removal of NTBs, could lead to a further doubling of intra-African trade, according to the ECA, with industrial products again receiving the greatest stimulation. This should see intra-African trade reaching US$34bn by 2022, translating into real income gains of more than US$290m.

The projected disproportionate benefit for industrial exporters may help to diversify African trade, both with other African countries and with the rest of the world. Within Africa, cotton, maize, cocoa and live animals account for almost one-fifth of trade, and in a number of cases just one product accounts for almost all of a given country's exports to the rest of Africa. For example, traditionally, oil and seafood respectively account for more than 90% of Angolan and Seychellois exports to the rest of the continent. An increase in industry should also help fulfil the long-standing aim of many governments to move away from extractive and other commodities towards a more balanced and therefore sustainable export base. Extractive commodities (i.e., oil and minerals) accounted for more than three-quarters of Africa's exports outside the continent between 2012 and 2014, while petroleum alone accounted for more than 30% of intra-African trade and 35% of trade between the continent and the rest of the world. However, a dependence on extractive commodities exposes exporters to the volatility of international prices, as has been demonstrated by the substantial decline in international oil prices since 2014, which has had a marked negative impact on the fiscal and external balances of oil exporters such as Algeria, Angola, Gabon and Nigeria. Bolstering non-extractive exports via the AfCFTA would help such states to build up a trade portfolio less dependent on the fluctuations of commodity prices.

The development of manufacturing and other industrial sectors could have a positive impact on more than just the balance of payments for African states. At present, manufacturing represents, on average, around just 10% of total GDP in Africa. Boosting that proportion could ultimately drive the structural transformation of African economies from the current pattern of low productivity and labour-intensive activities to higher productivity and more highly skilled industrial and service activities, which should in turn lead to an improvement in GDP per capita and help alleviate poverty. Industrial development would also have a clear benefit in terms of job creation. Industry accounts for 25–33% of job creation in most regions of the world, but tends to be much lower in Africa. In Angola and Cameroon, for example, the World Bank calculates that less than 10% of the workforce is employed in industry, while the figure is only around 5% in Chad and Côte d'Ivoire. Even in larger economies such as Kenya and Nigeria, the figure is only around 13%, although South Africa (23%) is closer to the global norm.

Free movement and more negotiating clout

The free movement of people is a central part of the AfCFTA, and one that has the potential to transform the region. At best, reduced border controls would allow seamless migration of workers to fill skills gaps across the continent. The rise of populist movements in a number of European states suggests that completely unrestricted movement of people is probably overly ambitious, but even a relaxation of existing controls – at present, a visa is required in 54% of African countries to visit other African states – could make a substantial difference. Freer movement of people within Africa could potentially serve to improve relations with Europe in particular, since it could lead to reduced flows of migrants to Mediterranean states and the European Union in general. However, this will only be the case if sufficient well-paid job opportunities are created within the continent: failure to do so could actually lead to increased economic migration, since accessing the Mediterranean North African shore could prove easier.

An African trading bloc should also have substantially more clout when it comes to negotiating deals with other, non-African trading areas. At present, African trade interests are represented by no less than eight RECs: the Economic Community of West African States (ECOWAS), established in 1975; the Economic Community of Central African States (ECCAS), established in 1983; the Arab Maghreb Union (known by its French acronym, UMA), established in 1989, although largely dormant since 2008; the Southern African Development Community (SADC), established in 1992; the Common Market for Eastern and Southern Africa (COMESA), established in 1994; the Intergovernmental Authority on Development (IGAD), established in 1996; the Community of Sahel-Saharan States (CEN-SAD), established in 1998; and the East African Community (EAC), established in 2000.

Overall, 39 of 55 AU countries are members of more than one of the eight RECs, while Burundi, the Democratic Republic of the Congo, Djibouti, Eritrea, Libya, Sudan and Uganda are each members of three RECs and Kenya four. Multiple memberships impose high costs in time, energy and resources on African governments, which have to balance competing regulations. Multiple memberships also make it much more difficult for African states to present a unified negotiating position when dealing with existing, relatively homogeneous trading blocs such as the

EU, or to negotiate large-scale regional trade agreements such as the Trans-Pacific Partnership (TPP), the Transatlantic Trade and Investment Partnership (TTIP) or the Regional Comprehensive Economic Partnership (RCEP). The AfCFTA is coming into being during a period of significant change and uncertainty in the global trade environment. In mid-June, the United States confirmed that US$34bn-worth of China's goods would be subject to additional tariffs of 25%, with the possibility that goods worth a further US$16bn would be targeted after an extended period of public comment. China responded in kind. This is not the only challenge to the multilateral trading system. When the US first announced the imposition of import tariffs on steel and aluminium in March, Canada, Mexico and the EU were given temporary exemptions. However, the US removed these exemptions in early June, sparking a series of retaliatory tariffs from these trading partners, which have traditionally been US allies. In this context, combined with the US administration's notably sceptical attitude towards inter-regional trading agreements and the failure of the Doha Round of trade talks, Africa's move towards free trade goes against the current trend. However, the relative strength of the EU in negotiations with the UK over Brexit also underscores the strength of trading blocs vis-à-vis individual states, and African leaders remain optimistic that a bigger trading bloc could increase the region's negotiating power.

Potential constraints

The implementation of the AfCFTA will not be straightforward. This was apparent even at the much-heralded signing ceremony, because while 44 AU members did sign up, 11 did not. The abstainers included Botswana, Burundi, Eritrea, Guinea-Bissau, Lesotho, Namibia, Sierra Leone, Tanzania and Zambia, as well as the continent's two dominant economies, Nigeria and South Africa (although South Africa did sign the Kigali Declaration, signalling its intention to continue working on the AfCFTA process). There are a number of reasons why these states abstained: some requested additional time to conclude national consultations, while others needed to comply with domestic legislative procedures and secure ratification from parliament first.

However, some states have more deep-seated concerns, driven by the fact that the AfCFTA will join together countries with substantially different levels of economic development. Many of the smaller states are least-developed countries (LDCs) which depend upon income generated from tariffs. These LDCs are also concerned that their domestic markets will be flooded by lower-cost goods from bigger players. Indeed, such concerns are not even restricted to LDCs: pressure from unions is thought to have been a factor in Nigeria's decision not to sign the agreement. Nigerian President Muhammadu Buhari stated that 'continental aspirations must complement Nigeria's national interests', which includes not positioning the country as 'a dumping ground for finished goods'. In addition, countries signing up to the umbrella agreement would be committed to implementing any concessions agreed in future rounds of negotiations even before these negotiations took place. For states with relatively well-developed domestic-industrialisation plans (such as South Africa and Nigeria), this erosion of policy space is a significant concern.

The sheer scale of change required is another potential hurdle. Despite the fact that most African countries belong to the WTO, many adhere to broadly protectionist trade policies. Analysis by the Brussels-based Bruegel think tank shows that the declared most-favoured-nation (MFN) rate is much higher than in the EU and US. For example, the MFN tariff rate in Kenya is 12.4% and in South Africa 6.1%, as against rates of 2.7% in the US and 2.6% in the EU. Indeed, the weighted mean MFN rate exceeds 10% in more than half of African countries. There are further protectionist measures in the form of NTBs and technical barriers to trade (such as differing national requirements regarding packaging, testing and certification procedures). Unwinding these is likely to prove a mammoth task, even if the political commitment were there, and the process is likely to be further complicated by the lack of institutional capacity on the continent.

Well-designed regional institutions are also required to adjudicate on disputes, enforce existing agreements and facilitate fair bargaining between and among AfCFTA member countries, but the establishment of such institutions may well prove challenging, given that many of the pre-existing RECs have struggled to enforce compliance. For example, the SADC Tribunal – established with the purpose of ensuring compliance and resolving disputes with regard to the SADC treaty – found in favour of 79 white Zimbabwean commercial farmers who took the Mugabe government to court in 2007–08 in order to halt the compulsory acquisition of their farms. However, the Zimbabwean government refused to enforce the judgment and withdrew from the tribunal, which was in effect disbanded in 2012. This does not augur particularly well for the establishment of institutions that will independently enforce the rules of the AfCFTA, but such enforcement – notably regarding intellectual-property rights and anti-dumping and competition policy – will be vital to build confidence in the free-trade area, particularly in its early stages.

Above all, Africa's relatively underdeveloped transport and communication infrastructure will continue to act as a trade barrier – and potentially a more trenchant one than import tariffs or NTBs. The UN Conference on Trade and Development estimates that infrastructural deficiency in Africa reduces firms' productivity by 40%, and this infrastructural gap clearly has a negative impact on the potential for small and medium-sized enterprises in particular to engage in intra-African trade. There are some signs of progress: in January 2018, the Single African Air Transport Market initiative, a regional aviation agreement, was officially launched with the backing of 23 African countries. The deal will allow airlines from the signatory countries to access each other's aviation markets freely, and it is hoped that the agreement will lower costs and increase the number of direct flights between African states. However, many of the potential issues with the AfCFTA are apparent in the air-transport initiative, albeit on a smaller scale. It is questionable how many African airlines (many of which are state-owned, inefficient and unprofitable) will be able to invest in new routes and attract new customers. Indeed, many domestic airlines will struggle to defend their market share against major foreign airlines, and this is likely to make governments wary about opening their markets to competition.

Even if the air market is successfully liberalised, problems will persist since it accounts for only a small proportion of passenger and freight movement. Road transport dominates, accounting for around four-fifths of all passenger and freight movement in Africa, and road connections remain poor. According to a 2012 report by the Brookings Institution, Africa has a road density of only 16.8 kilometres per 1,000 square kilometres, less than half the average of 37 km per 1,000 km^2 in other low-income regions of the world, and only one-third of the region's rural population live within 2 km of a passable road. Similarly, rail density in Africa is 2.8 km per 1,000 km^2, as against 3.4 km per 1,000 km^2 in other low-income regions. Improving such links will be crucial to foster increased intra-African trade. In fact, several such projects are already under way or at the planning stage. Burkina Faso, Côte d'Ivoire and Mali announced in March 2018 that they were planning a special economic zone encompassing Sikasso (Mali), Bobo-Dioulasso (Burkina Faso) and Korhogo (Côte d'Ivoire), and are already discussing public–private partnerships for transport-infrastructure development. Indeed, the Abidjan–Ouagadougou rail line linking Côte d'Ivoire's commercial capital and Burkina Faso's capital is already being upgraded by France-based Bolloré. Other substantial transport schemes include the Maputo Development Corridor (launched in 1996) linking South Africa to Mozambique, and the Lamu Port–South Sudan–Ethiopia Transport Corridor (LAPSSET), which connects Kenya, Ethiopia and South Sudan. Other such schemes will be necessary to facilitate the increase in intra-African trade.

The AfCFTA offers potentially substantial benefits, initially for the continent's more diversified economies, which will be able to secure a large continental market for their manufactured products. In the longer term, the benefits could be more broadly based and could even help drive industrialisation across the continent. The AfCFTA must foster cooperation among multiple national and regional actors with trade interests that will inevitably diverge at times. Given the challenges posed by the heterogeneous size, openness and level of industrial development of African economies, the existence of numerous bilateral trade agreements with the rest of the world, and overlapping REC memberships, progress on regional integration is likely to remain slow. In this context, the AU's target of establishing one of the world's largest free-trade areas by 2020 looks overly ambitious.

South Africa: Foreign-policy Directions and Challenges for Cyril Ramaphosa

Cyril Ramaphosa assumed the presidency of South Africa in February 2018 against a troubled national, regional and global backdrop. The presidency of his predecessor, Jacob Zuma, had been defined by persistent corruption scandals, the capture of state institutions by patronage networks established around the president and policy inertia. The rapid deterioration of the country's socio-economic condition under Zuma was reflected by a near-stagnant economy, unemployment of 27.7% (as of late 2017), rising service-delivery protests and a downgrade of South Africa's credit rating to sub-investment or junk status by two of the three main ratings agencies. Zuma's foreign policy was equally problematic, being rooted in a hackneyed anti-imperialist discourse which frequently led to South Africa siding with authoritarian regimes on global issues. Combined with his ongoing domestic scandals, the net effect of Zuma's time in power was to bring South Africa's global reputation to a post-1994 nadir by the time the African National Congress (ANC) finally 'recalled' him from office and replaced him with Ramaphosa.

Zuma's presidency – which effectively represents a lost decade for South Africa – left Ramaphosa with a set of daunting challenges across the entire policy spectrum if he is to restore confidence in South Africa. Ramaphosa must rebuild the integrity and efficacy of state institutions and state-owned enterprises, and root out the corrupt networks that are now deeply embedded at the national and provincial levels. In foreign affairs, he needs to construct a coherent policy that not only facilitates his core objective of domestic transformation but also meets South Africa's regional responsibilities and rebuilds South Africa's global reputation.

With general elections slated for mid-2019, Ramaphosa must combine these domestic and foreign-policy reforms while dedicating sufficient time and energy towards securing a decisive ANC victory at the polls – an outcome that, in light of the relative decline of the ANC, is by no means guaranteed.

Ramaphosa's 'New Dawn'

In the space of a few months, Ramaphosa has succeeded in dispelling the air of fatalism and pessimism which pervaded discussion on South African politics under Zuma. The change may largely be attributable to Zuma's departure rather than any major successes for the new president himself – Zuma too was initially given a generous reception in 2009 largely based on his not being Thabo Mbeki. However, as the case of Zuma proves, the initial mood of goodwill is likely to prove ephemeral if not accompanied by a tangible record of policy achievement. That said, the new president has struck all the right notes, stressing the importance of accountability, of promoting constitutional values, and of economic reform and anti-corruption programmes.

His initial contribution to the debate on foreign affairs was much more limited. His first state of the nation address in February 2018 devoted only a few short lines to foreign affairs and there was no subsequent attempt to articulate a clear set of foreign-policy interests and priorities, still less anything which might be termed a 'Ramaphosa Doctrine'. Admittedly, in many aspects the new president's hands were tied: he inherited Zuma's position as chair of the Southern African Development Community (SADC) for 2017–18, chair of the BRICS (Brazil, Russia, India, China and South Africa) forum, and the chair of the Indian Ocean Rim Association, as well as co-chair of the Forum on China–Africa Cooperation. Ramaphosa will also have to work within the framework that has informed South African foreign policy since 1994: a commitment to Africa's advancement; solidarity with the Global South; and the reform of the architecture of global governance.

Despite these restrictions, three factors suggested that Ramaphosa was nevertheless intent on remodelling South Africa's foreign policy.

The first was his appointment of Lindiwe Sisulu as minister of international relations and cooperation on 27 February. An ANC heavyweight, Sisulu is intellectually formidable and well equipped to rebuild the institutional capability of the Department of International Relations and Cooperation (DIRCO), which lost its way under her predecessor and made only a very modest contribution to the foreign-policy discourse. Secondly, Ramaphosa has already demonstrated that he is highly sensitive to the nexus between domestic and foreign policy. His current investment drive – assisted by a range of trusted 'investment envoys' – is designed to secure US$100 billion in new investment over the next five years and is already producing some promising results, the message being that South Africa is now in more competent hands, is undergoing a 'structural reboot' and should not be judged by the various debacles associated with Zuma. Thirdly, Ramaphosa had already marked himself out as efficient and conversant in the language of international diplomacy and business, demonstrated by the ease with which he fitted in at the World Economic Forum in Davos in January 2018 while still Zuma's deputy, as well as his subsequent handling of his responsibilities as SADC chair.

Looking ahead, Ramaphosa's task is to map out the broad contours of a new foreign policy. In this endeavour he will be supported by a high-level review panel – made up of former diplomats and ANC foreign-policy officials and chaired by former deputy foreign minister Aziz Pahad – which Sisulu has appointed to provide a series of recommendations which will help inform a revamped foreign policy. Ramaphosa will be looking for this group to provide sophisticated input in three crucial areas of foreign policy: restoring South Africa's global reputation, implementing economic diplomacy and re-engaging with continental politics.

Restoring South Africa's global reputation

South Africa's reputation, which reached stratospheric heights during Nelson Mandela's one-term presidency (1994–99), has been in freefall since 2002–03 due to Mbeki's shift away from the dominant foreign-policy narratives of the Mandela era: South Africa as the 'good international citizen'; the North–South bridge-builder, mediator and problem-solver; and the champion of human rights in Africa and beyond. Mbeki favoured a foreign policy which was more overtly Africanist in character, rooted in solidarity with the Global South and drawing upon an often simplistic anti-imperialist discourse. South African foreign policy regressed to a position which was supportive of the traditional dogmas of sovereignty and non-interference, a clear departure from an emancipatory foreign-policy approach to one rooted in a defence of the interests and prerogatives of state elites, however egregious their behaviour. This manifested in expressions of support for authoritarian regimes in the Democratic Republic of the Congo, Sudan and Zimbabwe, and, beyond Africa, in a reluctance to censure regimes in Belarus, Iran and Myanmar. Zuma persisted with this more ideological approach to foreign affairs, in which considerations of human rights were eclipsed by hostility to Western conceptions of international relations and intervention, impacting the formulation of policy on Iran, Libya, North Korea, Sudan and Syria. Zuma's indulgent approach to authoritarian regimes in Africa brought South Africa into disrepute with human-rights non-governmental organisations and internal critics such as Archbishop Desmond Tutu, who viewed Zuma's stance as incompatible with the ideals expressed by Mandela. South Africa was also accused of disregarding the lessons of its own struggle for democracy, during which time state sovereignty and non-interference were considered secondary to a population's right to human dignity, equality and freedom.

Precisely how Ramaphosa will approach this issue remains to be seen, but three factors point towards a revival of idealism and support for human rights under his leadership above and beyond a mere change of tone. Firstly, since becoming president he has consistently invoked the spirit of Mandela and sought to cast his own leadership in that mould, the implication being that South Africa has descended from the moral high ground under Mandela's successors at considerable cost to its soft power and the values enshrined in its own constitution. This message has been amplified by Sisulu, who has spoken of South Africa's 'responsibility to regain the status that he [Mandela] left for us'. Secondly, Ramaphosa's background during the struggle period as an internal activist in the trade-union movement and United Democratic Front – organisations which adhered to rigorous internal democratic procedures – is likely to have given him greater empathy with grassroots democratic movements elsewhere. This offers a striking contrast to Mbeki and Zuma, who both hailed from the ANC movement in exile with its traditionally more closed and hierarchical approach to politics and its close affinity with supportive neighbouring states. That said, Sisulu was also part of the ANC movement in exile, and it remains to be seen if she will act as a counterweight to Ramaphosa in this regard. Finally, Ramaphosa's experience as the senior ANC negotiator in the early 1990s and subsequent role as chair of the Constituent Assembly (which drafted the country's final constitution in 1996) has given him a strong commitment to constitutional values and rights which will be difficult for him to ignore in other contexts.

His thinking on these issues will become clearer in 2019, as South Africa will be compelled to take positions on a wide variety of issues due to the country's election to the United Nations Security Council for a third time as a non-permanent member for the period 2019–20. Ramaphosa's approach to the vexed question of South African membership of the International Criminal Court (ICC) will also be a key foreign-policy decision. In October 2016, Zuma announced that South Africa would withdraw from the ICC following the controversy over his decision in 2015 to allow Sudanese President Omar al-Bashir to leave South Africa after he visited Johannesburg for an African Union (AU) summit. By refusing to arrest Bashir, the Zuma administration defied a domestic court order mandating Bashir's detention in compliance with an ICC indictment for war crimes. Not only did South Africa then pledge its own withdrawal but it also sought – ultimately unsuccessfully – to galvanise a wider African exodus from the ICC. The High Court of South Africa blocked South Africa's own proposed departure from the ICC in February 2017, ruling that the planned withdrawal was unconstitutional as parliamentary approval had not been sought and gained for such a move. Before Ramaphosa's accession, it was understood that the government had accepted this ruling but was still intent on withdrawing from the ICC and planned to introduce legislation in the National Assembly to effect that preference. Given Ramaphosa and Sisulu's project to restore South Africa's standing in global politics, the new president is likely to attempt to reform the ICC from within, rather than positioning South Africa as an outlier and spoiler in the field of international justice. However, this assumes that the president has sufficient political strength to carry his party with him on the issue.

Economic diplomacy

The maxim that foreign policy begins at home will be central to Ramaphosa's thinking about international relations. He understands that the overriding purpose of South African foreign policy at this point is to help facilitate domestic socio-economic transformation and address chronic deficits in housing, education and healthcare as well as alarming levels of unemployment, poverty and inequality. To achieve this, the country's diplomatic endeavours will have a pronounced economic thrust and foreign policy is likely to become less stridently anti-Western, with a pragmatic emphasis on trade expansion and the creation of a climate favourable for foreign direct investment (FDI). In this more technocratic era, efforts will be directed towards accelerating the current levels of economic growth, which at 1–1.5% are inadequate. This points to a more universalist foreign policy making the most of global opportunities, a broadening of perspectives rather than exclusive reliance upon Zuma's dogmatic fixation with the BRICS forum which has yet to deliver impressive, tangible economic benefits for the country. Ramaphosa will likely view BRICS in a more pluralist context as one of several important economic relationships instead of being the beginning and end of South African foreign policy.

A foreign policy largely driven by domestic economic considerations will make serious demands of DIRCO and the wider diplomatic service. DIRCO will have to position itself at the centre of a web of complex relationships to coordinate the international economic activities of government departments, as well as improving links with the business sector and liaising with civil society, the academy and foreign-policy think tanks. Stimulating trade expansion, investment and tourism will require a highly professional diplomatic corps which is closely attuned to global and regional political and economic trends and able to act as an ambassador for 'brand South Africa'. However, at present 80% of ambassadors and those in senior positions in South Africa's external missions are political appointees and only 20% are career diplomats (this ratio distribution is the opposite of most states), highlighting the extent to which ANC cronyism has prevailed over developing talented, experienced career diplomats, who find their career options restricted and are leaving the profession, taking institutional memory and expertise with them. Ramaphosa and his foreign minister will have to tackle this issue directly if they want DIRCO and the foreign service to become effective instruments of economic diplomacy, but reforming these institutions will involve confronting vested interests and an established culture of patronage within the ANC itself.

Engagement with the African continent

Given the implications of a troubled continent for South Africa's own well-being – limited economic opportunity, refugee and migrant flows, and reduced inward investment – Africa will continue to be one of the principal preoccupations of South African foreign policy under Ramaphosa. However, Ramaphosa will have to be sensitive to the need to engage Africa without compromising his domestic agenda. He inherits a generally troubled relationship with the continent, despite Zuma's attempts to play to the gallery on the ICC issue. South Africa continues to generate resentment in Africa because of its political and economic weight, imbalances in its trading relationships, the perceived aggressive expansionism of its companies, the presumption that it 'represents' Africa in multilateral bodies and persistent xenophobic violence against the citizens of other African states in South Africa itself.

Yet South Africa must play a key role in conversations around several continental issues: the proposed African free-trade area (which Ramaphosa has committed South Africa to joining); Agenda 2063 (the

African Union's strategic framework for the socio-economic development of the continent over the next 50 years); and equipping the AU to meet security challenges more effectively. South African (and Nigerian) involvement will also be crucial in the promotion of good governance and moving joint initiatives on energy, infrastructure and the environment from aspiration to implementation. Ramaphosa is likely to continue promoting the African cause within BRICS, as was evident at the tenth BRICS summit in Johannesburg in July 2018, and South Africa's membership of the UN Security Council in 2019–20 will afford similar opportunities to speak for Africa, although, as noted above, that may generate as much hostility as gratitude from other African states.

Crises in individual states will continue to test South Africa, particularly in Burundi, the Democratic Republic of the Congo, Swaziland and Zimbabwe. Ramaphosa has registered an early success by engineering a rapprochement with Rwanda, after the relationship had nosedived under Zuma largely due to Rwanda's extra-territorial attacks on dissidents. Additionally, Ramaphosa has played a significant role in stabilising Madagascar's politics by encouraging the central protagonists in that country's crisis to resolve their differences with elections. These successes augur well for Ramaphosa's ability to repair and enhance the relationship with Nigeria, which both parties have allowed to wither over the last decade. Over that time the two have viewed each other suspiciously, differing over a range of issues including the behaviour of South African companies in Nigeria, xenophobic attacks in South Africa, Nigerian resentment at South African membership of BRICS and the G20, and the continuing manoeuvring over a permanent African seat in a reformed UN Security Council. Progress on continent-wide issues will be impossible if South Africa and Nigeria remain at loggerheads, and that pivotal relationship will be the focus for Ramaphosa's diplomatic skills.

Equally, it will be difficult if not impossible for South Africa to play a leadership role in its own sub-region – still less on the wider continent – if it is unable or unwilling to allocate more resources to the South African National Defence Force (SANDF). The defence budget as a percentage of GDP has been in sharp decline since 1994, standing at a mere 0.98% of GDP in 2018 and scheduled to fall further to 0.97% of GDP in 2019 (compared with 4.4% of GDP in the late-apartheid era and 1.5% of GDP in 2004). Despite the lengthy lament on the condition of the SANDF provided by the 2014 Defence Review – which bluntly stated that the military was incapable of performing its core functions without a substantial increase in its budget – the situation has continued to deteriorate with severe cuts in funding. General Solly Shoke, the head of SANDF, has said that SANDF is 'bleeding' while 'doing [its] level best' to fulfil its mandate. In May 2018, Vice-Admiral Mosuwa Hlongwane, the head of the navy, suggested that the force is now at a crossroads 'where its very existence is threatened' as it struggles to carry out its primary tasks of maritime defence and counter-piracy. The ongoing cuts in the defence budget from 50.6bn rand (US$3.5bn) in 2018 to R47.9bn (US$3.3bn) in 2019 will have a detrimental impact on the full spectrum of SANDF activities, from the safeguarding of the country's borders to participation in African peacekeeping operations. The South African Department of Defence's Annual Performance Plan, released in June 2018, highlighted that the current situation was unsustainable:

> The persistent disconnect between the government's defence expenditure and the resources allocated to defence has eroded the capability to the point where the Defence Force will be unable to fulfil its defence commitments. The SANDF therefore cannot even support the current modest level of ambition. South Africa's defence ambition and defence capacity are clearly at odds with one another, further warning of the need to invest in its military if South Africa is to arrest its declining influence in Africa.

The problem for advocates of higher defence spending is that the arguments for an increase in resources, although compelling, are fundamentally out of step with the prevailing political mood in the country. Such arguments are largely confined to the ministry and SANDF itself and struggle to resonate more widely or find significant constituencies of support. Given South Africa's chronic problems of poverty, inequality and mass unemployment, the defence budget has inevitably failed to establish itself as a deserving or worthy cause. Consequently, the likelihood of reversing the current trajectory is extremely remote, as other departments (such as health, housing, education and social welfare) have a much stronger claim to state funding.

Ramaphosa has made a positive impact by his determination to confront issues which his predecessor, who was almost incapable of taking a lead on policy, allowed to fester for too long. In the arena of defence, this should mean a scaling down of SANDF missions and tasks to fit the existing budget and ending the dangerous self-deception that SANDF can do more with less. However, his government must also be prepared to face the unpalatable consequence of that choice: namely, a diminution of South Africa's standing in Africa and the wider international community, where it has long been identified as the African state best equipped to provide the leadership and heavy lifting required in the field of continental peace and security.

Challenges ahead

Ramaphosa must weave these disparate narratives into a coherent whole while remaining sensitive to the tensions likely to arise as these goals are pursued simultaneously. Even a skilled diplomat such as Ramaphosa will have great difficulty in recapturing the spirit of Mandela and promoting human rights and democracy without antagonising and encroaching upon the interests of other authoritarian African states. Similarly, if Ramaphosa, like his predecessors, is committed to solidarity with fellow liberation parties – in Angola (the MPLA), Mozambique (Frelimo), Namibia (SWAPO), Tanzania (the CCM) and Zimbabwe (ZANU–PF) – such solidarity will immediately dilute any commitment to values and rights, given the record of bureaucratic authoritarianism (and in some cases egregious violence) of the parties concerned. A commitment to human rights and democracy may also collide with the desire to maximise South African interests within BRICS. The emphasis on economic diplomacy and expansion of global trade and investment will not always square easily with ethically based approaches.

One of the principal barriers to a restructured foreign policy may be the ANC itself. The ANC's foreign-policy documents and resolutions from the Mbeki era onward reveal entrenched dogma and often 'read like a Bolshevist tirade against the imperialist West', in the words of academic and former South African diplomat Gerrit Olivier. The leftist Tripartite Alliance of the ANC, the Congress of South African Trade Unions (COSATU) and the South African Communist Party (SACP) – core parts of the support base that helped elevate Ramaphosa to the leadership – may look aghast at a business-oriented policy committed to removing all barriers to investment when they seek a more intervention-ist, state-driven development model. To them, Ramaphosa's approach may recall Thabo Mbeki's supposedly neoliberal Growth, Employment and Redistribution (GEAR) strategy, which the SACP and COSATU both resisted vehemently. However, policies favoured by the left are likely to deter the investment Ramaphosa craves and invite further downgrades to South Africa's credit rating or prevent it re-emerging from the junk status to which it has already been consigned by Standard & Poor's and Fitch. For example, the ANC's explicit commitment to land expro-priation without compensation – which Ramaphosa has now pledged to deliver through a constitutional amendment – is likely to be toxic to investors concerned with property rights.

Finally, the character of the ANC normally ensures that lowest-common-denominator politics prevails at the expense of clear policies and dynamic leadership across the policy spectrum. Ramaphosa is also hindered in this regard by his relatively narrow leadership victory in December 2017, which left several internal opponents in place and com-promised his authority. The fact that 2019 is an election year also carries with it the risk of the ANC making short-term populist gestures and announcements which may undermine some of the long-term pragmatic features of Ramaphosa's economic diplomacy. Again, the commitment to land expropriation without compensation is highly problematic in this regard.

Ramaphosa has made a promising start to his presidency at home and abroad, improving the political atmosphere and committing to a culture of accountability which aims to correct the entrenched problems inherited from the Zuma era. However, Ramaphosa is seeking to reconstruct South African foreign policy in the most exacting of international landscapes, and is likely to be buffeted by global forces beyond his control (such as US President Donald Trump's trade wars and disruption of the post-war international order) while being unable to guarantee that his own deeply divided party will support his moves. While there may be great confidence in Ramaphosa personally, both inside and outside the country, that is not synonymous with a wider confidence in South Africa or the ANC.

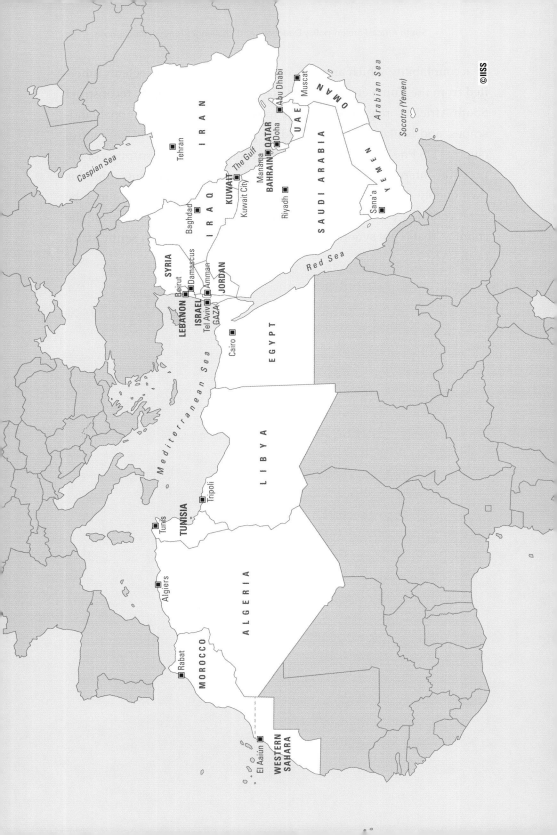

Chapter 7

Middle East and North Africa

2017–18 Review

The explosive combination of regional competition, state fragility and authoritarian consolidation that has characterised Middle East geopolitics in the past 15 years has shown no sign of abating. The dislocation of the regional order – prompted by the United States' 2003 invasion of Iraq and aggravated by the political and security tremors of the Arab uprisings of 2011 – has made regional powers simultaneously more anxious and more ambitious. The ensuing power play has come at great cost, yet as of 2018, it remains inconclusive.

The struggle to shape this volatile regional landscape and to adjust to changing global politics has remained the main determinant of the behaviour of its leading powers. Turkey, Israel, Iran, Egypt, Saudi Arabia, the United Arab Emirates and Iraq are each involved in direct or proxy military operations and engaged in delicate diplomacy in their immediate neighbourhood at a time of US disarray and Russian opportunism. The resulting lines of fractures, tactical alignments and hedging strategies have been dizzying, and the focus on defeating transnational threats (such as the Islamic State, also known as ISIS or ISIL) has produced little geopolitical carry-over effect. Indeed, no new order has yet emerged from the ruins of Mosul in Iraq, Aleppo and Raqqa in Syria,

Cirze in Turkey, Benghazi in Libya, Taizz and Hudaydah in Yemen, Arish in the Sinai Peninsula or Gaza.

Just as they pursue costly military engagements and high-wire diplomacy, however, each of these powers face serious challenges at home that drain attention and resources and, at times, support from their geopolitical ventures. Enduring sources of domestic weakness – from economic underperformance to challenges to central authority – stand in the way of elite ambitions. As a result, each regional power is arguably overextended and faces potential backlash, both internally and externally.

Turkish power has regressed as a result of regional setbacks, tense relations with traditional Western allies, myriad security challenges and authoritarian consolidation by President Recep Tayyip Erdogan. The wars in neighbouring Iraq and Syria have challenged Turkish security by reviving Kurdish dreams of autonomy and compelled Ankara to scale down its once-ambitious regional agenda in order to focus on containing Kurdish aspirations. Abandoning conciliatory approaches, Turkey has conducted a brutal counter-insurgency campaign at home. The Turkish security forces began to make forays into northern Iraq in 2017, with the Kurdistan Workers' Party (PKK) stronghold in Mount Qandil as the ultimate target. Turkey intervened in Syria in 2016 and then in early 2018 to neutralise Kurdish ambitions, seizing a large area along its southwestern border and becoming a de facto occupying power.

Russia acquiesced to Turkey's actions as Moscow sought to reorient Turkish policy towards accepting the survival of Syrian President Bashar al-Assad, but Turkey's hostility towards the Kurds conflicted with US policy, which relied on Kurdish groups to defeat ISIS. Relations with the US are tense over deep differences regarding US support for Kurdish militias in Syria and Ankara's developing defence relations with Russia. In general, the estrangement between Turkey and its traditional Western allies appears profound and potentially irreversible. Erdogan's authoritarianism and bullying tactics have alienated Western leaders and jeopardised Turkish accession talks to the European Union.

This upheaval in Turkish foreign policy is occurring alongside Erdogan's consolidation of power. In recent years, he has proceeded to reshape the Turkish political system, giving the presidency vast executive powers and purging the military, bureaucracy, media and business community of real and alleged critics. While exhibiting signs of weakness – notably in his management of the economy and accusations of corruption and nepotism – Erdogan has sought and obtained electoral mandates, culminating in his June 2018 first-round victory during the presidential elections, despite a concerted challenge from the urban-based nationalist opposition. However, deep political and social divides over Erdogan's brand of Islamic authoritarianism remain potent; combined with a deteriorating economy, they suggest a bumpy trajectory for the country.

Since 2011, Israel has shown great scepticism about political changes in the Arab world, seeing the resulting disorder as benefiting Iran's proxy-building strategy; as weakening traditionally pliant Arab neighbours; and as distracting the US. Faced with massive instability and uncertainty along its borders in recent years, Israel has therefore opted for a strategy of containment and limited military engagement to shape proximate areas. It has prioritised the development of military options to meet the perceived Iranian threat and established transactional relations with willing Arab governments, such as Egypt. Israeli pragmatism has taken several forms: regular engagement with Russia (now considered the de facto arbiter of Syria's future) and acceptance of the Assad regime; support for the Egyptian regime and covert strikes in support of its campaign against jihadi groups in the Sinai; and quiet hopes for a convergence of interests with key Arab states over Iran. Indeed, since 2016 Israel has conducted more numerous, deeper and bigger attacks against Iranian targets in Syria, with a view to pre-emptively destroying Iran's expanding military networks and denying Iran a two-front war option.

This strategy and Iran's determination to build a presence throughout Syria, including in its southern region, have created the conditions for enduring, small-scale conflict that could escalate into a region-wide war. Iranian and Syrian responses to Israeli attacks have included the downing of an aircraft and the dispatching of a drone over the Golan Heights, which was promptly shot down by the Israel Defense Forces.

For its part, Israel has extensively bombed major air bases inside Syria that it suspects of harbouring Iranian troops and allies and weapons caches. The size of the bombings and Israel's growing acknowledgement of its responsibility pointed to Israel's desire for military dominance and total freedom of manoeuvre over Syrian territory.

Despite this tense atmosphere, Israeli Prime Minister Benjamin Netanyahu has displayed confidence stemming primarily from a strong alignment with the administration of US President Donald Trump. In May 2018, Trump announced the US withdrawal from the Joint Comprehensive Plan of Action (JCPOA) nuclear deal with Iran, reversing an Obama diplomatic achievement that Netanyahu had fiercely resisted. The latter had actively lobbied for this withdrawal despite opposition from senior Israeli military and intelligence officials, and had provided public endorsement for the move a few months before by revealing the capture of a considerable cache of Iranian documents that Iran had allegedly concealed to secretly restart its nuclear programme. The potential for a direct Israeli–Iranian confrontation rose as a result.

Netanyahu obtained another highly symbolic win from Trump: in May, the US formally relocated its embassy to Jerusalem despite a decades-long policy that conditioned such a move on an Israeli–Palestinian peace. The highly choreographed transfer was met with international criticism and Arab condemnation. Compounding this was the rumoured content of a peace plan developed by Jared Kushner, Trump's son-in-law, that denied Palestinian control of east Jerusalem and return of refugees, and kept illegal settlements in the West Bank under Israeli authority. This fed Palestinian anger, notably in Gaza, where deteriorating living conditions, Palestinian factionalism and Israeli intransigence led to massive protests along the fence with Israel. These protests were met with disproportionate Israeli fire that caused hundreds of casualties and ignited international outcry. Even then, the Palestinian Authority was not able to capitalise politically: its ailing leadership faced a legitimacy crisis, and its rivalry with Hamas debilitated Palestinian politics.

Domestically, the judicial and political travails of Netanyahu continued, with allegations of corruption and divisions inside his cabinet eroding his standing. However, no political opponent emerged as a credible alternative. Indeed, the Israeli electorate continued to veer to the right, with polls showing Netanyahu's Likud party likely to win the 2019 elections.

Domestic security and regime consolidation remained the primary focus of the regime of Egyptian President Abdel Fattah Al-Sisi. The tightening of the political space and the punishment of dissent were described as the most severe since the 1960s. The March 2018 presidential election served to illustrate Sisi's political dominance as well as his paranoia. The regime prevented credible candidates from running, including a former army chief and a former prime minister, both of whom were strongarmed and detained, as well as a popular leftist lawyer. Sisi won around 97% of the votes, with turnout approaching 40%.

The inner workings of the Sisi regime proved obscure. Over the year, senior military and security figures, including the defence minister and the intelligence chief, were removed from office, exposing rifts within the ruling elite. However, the swiftness of these moves and the lack of pushback also indicated that Sisi remained firmly at the helm, as did the increasing presence of military officials in the bureaucracy and the economy. This dire political context affected adversely the economic situation and compelled Egypt to implement an IMF reform programme (combined with a US$12-billion loan) that imposed unpopular austerity measures and cuts to state subsidies.

Having largely neutralised the jihadi and Islamist challenges in the mainland through intense repression, the government nevertheless struggled to end the ISIS insurgency in the Sinai Peninsula. The fighting showed no sign of abating, with a couple hundred military casualties and thousands of civilian and combatant casualties per year. The military-first strategy of the government only fuelled local resentment over weak services and bad economic prospects. The revelation that Israel had conducted covert strikes against ISIS targets in the Sinai province was humiliating for the government, which quickly denounced it as a fabrication.

Internationally, Egypt continued its flirtation with Russia, hoping that Moscow's assertive role would deliver political and economic returns. The two countries shared common views on the future of Syria and Libya, and Russia relished the attention of the erstwhile ultimate American partner in the Middle East. Yet Egypt's domestic weakness proved a significant brake on its regional standing. In neighbouring Libya, Egypt supported a military strongman, Khalifa Haftar, against the United Nations-recognised government in the name of fighting Islamism, but Haftar seemed unable to make decisive gains and rally enough support.

Further illustration was the government's slow realisation of and reaction to the building of a massive dam on the Blue Nile River by Ethiopia. The US$4bn hydroelectric Grand Renaissance Dam, set to open by the end of 2018, will have immense implications for Egypt's water supply and the viability of its agriculture and its cities. A political crisis quickly escalated, with Egypt facing Ethiopia and Sudan from a weak position. Talk of war circulated, including the possible destruction of the dam by the Egyptian Air Force, but diplomatic and technical talks between the three countries were launched instead.

The ambitious modernisation agenda of Crown Prince Mohammed bin Salman, whose spectacular rise has transformed the governance structure of the Saudi kingdom, made headlines throughout the year. Domestically, Mohammed bin Salman pursued parallel tracks that alternately reinforced and undermined each other. Economic modernisation proceeded apace alongside announcements of major projects and social-liberalisation moves, but there were also spectacular crackdowns on rivals and businessmen. The detention of hundreds of senior princes, businessmen and bureaucrats at the Ritz-Carlton in Riyadh in November 2017 testified to Mohammed bin Salman's simultaneous desire to combat corruption and debilitate any opposition or dissent to his rule. Likewise, the authorisation given to women to drive cars was accompanied by a crackdown on activists who had championed this move in previous decades, forming a clear statement that progress was solely the ruler's prerogative. This delicate game of balancing between competing priorities illustrated the fragility of the modernisation programme. The sense that Saudi Arabia was finally moving ahead after decades of somnolence was tempered by the brutal manner in which Mohammed bin Salman consolidated power and questions about the viability and sustainability of his vision.

On the economic front, and despite active courting of domestic and international audiences, Mohammed bin Salman's reforms did not pay off immediately. The economy was in recession in 2017; efforts to encourage Saudi employment in the private sector mostly failed; and the Ritz episode, which was presented as essential to reform the economy, dissuaded many foreign investors who worried about the risks and costs of business in the kingdom. In June 2017, the government was forced to reverse benefit cuts and salary freezes to end discontent. The IPO of Saudi Aramco, a central element of the reform programme, was delayed over the lower-than-expected valuation of the company and the difficulty in meeting transparency and disclosure standards.

Saudi Arabia was similarly energetic abroad, but the returns were elusive. The ostensible alignment between Trump and Mohammed bin Salman, which culminated in the US president's theatrical visit to Riyadh in May 2017, emboldened Saudi foreign policy. The Saudi kingdom sought to assert its Arab primacy. It adopted an uncompromising line on Iran and welcomed the US withdrawal from the JCPOA nuclear deal, pledging to extend political and practical support to US efforts to isolate Tehran. In a surprising show of diplomatic flexibility (directed at countering Iranian influence in Baghdad), Riyadh courted Iraqi political elites it had shunned since 2003, including the Shia radical cleric Moqtada al-Sadr.

On other regional issues, mutual expectations were harder to meet: Saudi efforts to convince the US to isolate and punish Qatar failed, and the US struggled to enrol a reluctant Saudi Arabia in the stabilisation of eastern Syria. The potential for mutual disappointment remained high, compelling Saudi Arabia to continue diversifying its relationships. Mohammed bin Salman accordingly courted Russia, China and other Asian powers, for both economic and geopolitical reasons.

Just as Saudi Arabia attracted positive headlines for its internal reforms, its image was tarnished by rash decisions. In November,

Mohammed bin Salman detained Lebanese Prime Minister Saad Hariri and forced him to resign, a move that was widely condemned and ultimately backfired, as Hariri subsequently revoked his resignation, boosted by a wave of popular support in Lebanon. The Saudi focus on isolating Qatar failed to gather international support and was seen by Saudi Arabia's closest Western and Asian allies as petty, vindictive and counterproductive. The disastrous war in Yemen continued to bring financial and reputational costs as the struggles of the Saudi coalition and the stubborn resistance of the Houthi insurgency emphasised the gap between Saudi aspirations and performance.

Iraq illustrated again the gap between expectations and the difficult politics of divided countries. The victory against ISIS in Mosul in 2017 boosted both Iraqi nationalism and the standing of Iraqi Prime Minister Haider al-Abadi, and presaged more consensual, appeased governance. Outreach to regional powers, including Turkey and the Gulf states, was meant to bring Iraq back into the regional order.

By mid-2018, however, Iraq had entered a new phase of political dysfunction and expressions of popular discontent that threatened the fragile gains of the previous year. The Kurds rushed to organise a referendum on independence in September 2017, despite the advice of friendly governments and neighbouring countries. A swift military move by Iraqi government forces and Iranian-backed militias set Kurdish ambitions back as the Kurds lost control over the disputed city of Kirkuk and its oilfields, as well as territory in western Iraq. The defeat led to intra-Kurdish acrimony and a general sense of drift and hopelessness within the Kurdish community, which felt that its contribution to the fight against ISIS and its alliance with the West had not been rewarded with tangible political benefits.

The Iraqi elections of May delivered surprising results. A coalition headed by the cleric Sadr came first, followed by a coalition of extremist Shia militia commanders beholden to Iran. Abadi, the favourite of Western and Arab states, placed third, followed by several other smaller slates. Sadr emerged as a kingmaker, but the tight distribution of seats made for hard and dizzying bargaining between the various parties, a process made worse by accusations of fraud that led to calls for a full recount of the ballots. The country seemed headed toward a political settlement that rewarded all factions with government seats at the expense of coherent reform and governance agendas.

Such uncertainty inevitably undermined the confidence of foreign governments and companies interested in the reconstruction and development of Iraq, compounding an economic crisis driven by low oil prices and enduring corruption and bad governance. Some foreign-investment and development plans were agreed at a conference in Kuwait held ahead of the elections but were subsequently put on hold, even as an unprecedented electricity, agricultural and water crisis hit the country.

Re-establishing the authority of the state after the defeat of ISIS proved difficult. The demining and reconstruction of Mosul, once seen as essential, lagged behind because of a lack of funding and government indifference. In parallel, the debate over the future of the Shia militias that had contributed to the defeat of ISIS remained unsettled. These militias, which had been recognised by the state, extended their influence inside the bureaucracy and territorial control in important areas around Baghdad, the northwest and along the border with Syria, even joining the fight against ISIS inside Syrian territory. Political dysfunction in Baghdad and the success of the militias' electoral slate ensured that their fate would not be addressed imminently.

Middle East: Drivers of Strategic Change

- The US withdrawal from the 2015 nuclear deal with Iran and the imposition of new sanctions on Tehran have raised uncertainty in the troubled Middle East, and anchored the US in partnerships with Israel and Saudi Arabia to counter Iran.

- Saudi Arabia is pursuing a process of modernisation under Crown Prince Muhammad bin Salman, but the sweeping social and economic reforms and their autocratic nature may encounter internal resistance and upset fragile balances. In parallel, Saudi Arabia is facing costly setbacks on the regional front, notably over its intervention in Yemen.

- Violence in Syria remains high even as the mainstream rebellion withers away. President Bashar al-Assad has reasserted his control over most of the country, aided by Russia and Iran, but the shape of post-war Syria will be determined by ongoing intense regional brinksmanship and questions about the regime's ability to stabilise and rebuild the country.

- Iraq's politics have remained in flux. While the security forces managed to reduce the territorial hold of the Islamic State (also known as ISIS or ISIL) and Kurdish independence aspirations were crushed, dysfunction and competition in Baghdad generated a fragmented political landscape. The 2018 elections produced no clear victor, leading to intense political jockeying just as popular discontent over bad governance and corruption erupted.

- States in North Africa continue to focus on short-term crises rather than developing long-term strategic plans, leaving the region vulnerable to future shocks.

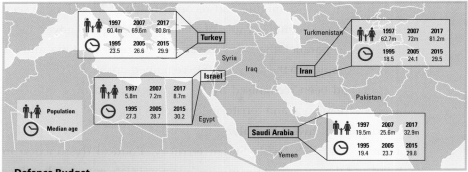

Defence Budget
(US$, constant 2010 prices)

	2008	2013	2018
Israel	$16.14bn	$16.73bn	$15.65bn
Saudi Arabia	$37.76bn	$56.44bn	$77.24bn
Turkey	$10.03bn	$10.98bn	$14.07bn
Iran	$10.59bn	$17.02bn	$18.89bn

'Vision 2030' – Crown Prince Muhammad bin Salman's ambitious reform plan – is intended to modernise and diversify Saudi Arabia's economy

GDP per capita, Purchasing Power Parity (International $, constant 2011 prices)

Country	GDP
1997	
Israel	$24,760
Saudi Arabia	$43,838
Turkey	$13,776
Iran	$12,698
2007	
Israel	$28,744
Turkey	$17,901
Saudi Arabia	$45,130
Iran	$17,338
2017	
Israel	$33,132
Saudi Arabia	$49,045
Turkey	$25,129
Iran	$19,082

Sources: IISS; UN Department of Economic and Social Affairs (Population Division, 2017); World Bank

Muhammad bin Salman and the Remaking of Saudi Arabia

The emergence of Crown Prince Muhammad bin Salman Al Saud on the world stage has changed the domestic and international profile of Saudi Arabia. Many of the old constraints, domestic and foreign, appear to have weakened or dissolved. In its crown prince, Saudi Arabia has a young leader with the energy and powers to pursue ambitious domestic and foreign policies.

Muhammad bin Salman has already begun to challenge some of the conventions on which modern Saudi Arabia has rested. At a dazzling launch in October 2017 in the capital, Riyadh, the crown prince promoted a new city, NEOM, which will include tourist facilities reminiscent of Dubai and involve economic cooperation with Egypt, Jordan and Israel. Muhammad bin Salman actively promoted tourism to Saudi Arabia, casting aside the uneasiness that the Al Saud family have previously evinced towards it. He made high-profile overtures towards Christians and other religious minorities, and on a trip to Cairo in March 2018 he became the first Saudi royal to pay an official visit to St Mark's Coptic Cathedral. While there, he issued a joint statement with Coptic Pope Tawadros II that called for moderation and tolerance. (Photographs of the event that appeared in the Saudi media even showed Christian religious symbols.) At home, the crown prince took a huge step by permitting women to drive. It was not an isolated gesture: promoting women in the workplace is central to 'Saudi Vision 2030', Muhammad bin Salman's plan to transform the economy. In April, he lifted the ban on cinemas and public performances of music.

Social liberalisation, however, has been accompanied by a concentration of political power and notably less tolerance for internal opposition or dissent. Shortly before granting women the right to drive in June 2018, the authorities arrested Lujain al-Hathloul, a high-profile female activist. The message was clear: the country is undergoing reform, not revolution.

Externally, too, Saudi Arabia has struck a different posture under the decisive direction of the crown prince. It has cast aside the Gulf

Cooperation Council (GCC) by choosing to isolate Qatar as punishment for Doha's support for the Muslim Brotherhood and openness to dealing with Tehran. American pleas for a rapprochement between its Gulf allies have fallen on deaf ears in Riyadh. Saudi Arabia has joined with the United Arab Emirates to intervene militarily and at scale in the civil war in Yemen.

Saudi Vision 2030 and the capacity for change

Saudi Vision 2030 is a plan for a new economy that will be entrepreneurial rather than patrimonial, with strong financial and other services and value-added manufacturing. It foresees an open economy, attractive to foreign direct investment (FDI) and with a fundamentally new approach to wealth creation. Rather than simply owning assets, the vision is for Saudi citizens to become creators of wealth, but to achieve this will require a transformed workforce. This transformation is a core element of Saudi Vision 2030, which mandates higher rates of participation, greater skills and more flexibility among the working population. This will certainly require major changes in education, but it will also involve deeper cultural shifts, such as cuts to social services, which are likely to upset existing politico-social arrangements. Muhammad bin Salman has already taken steps to curb Saudi Arabia's exceptionally generous welfare system. Utilities are no longer provided free of charge, and from January 2018 the country introduced value-added tax (VAT) on a range of goods at a rate of 5%. These measures were unthinkable just a few years earlier, and mark not just the beginning of overdue economic reform, but also potentially a change in the relationship between Saudis and their state, from patronage to one based on economic contribution.

The reforms introduced up to mid-2018 amount to the greatest challenge to Saudi Arabia's austere social model since King Faisal bin Abdulaziz Al Saud's modernisation drive in the 1970s. Thus far there has been no public opposition from religious figures within the establishment or by cultural conservatives. Members of the royal family who have protested against paying taxes may represent a limited constituency. That may change as the effect of reforms becomes apparent in

Najd, the conservative central region of the country, although any opposition will have to take into account the widespread support for the new measures, especially among the young.

The absence of opposition may be partly because Muhammad bin Salman has introduced measures to offset the impact of spending cuts. For instance, alongside the introduction of utilities charges, he awarded a pay rise to public-sector workers and announced plans to distribute wealth to middle- and lower-income groups through a 'Citizen's Account'. Compensating measures have not, to date, arrested the reform momentum but the dynamic between the two is worth watching closely. The crown prince may, by seeking to placate conservatives, be stoking resentment on both sides.

Preserving the sense of a contract between the state and its people will be important for social cohesion and the success of the modernisation programme. The crown prince will be expected, through direct intervention, to lessen the inequalities that liberalisation will generate. However, his reconfiguration of the state and economic model will make this more difficult, because the traditional solution – providing public-sector jobs – will be greatly reduced. Thus other ways of redistributing wealth, short of the periodic gouging of the rich, must be developed and institutionalised. But that will require skills (such as tax collection) in areas in which Saudi Arabia is not adept.

A related question centres on the role of the Al Saud family in a state that still bears their name. Although the primacy of the family remains unquestioned, it no longer seems viable for royals and insiders to treat the country as their private estate. Muhammad bin Salman struck a blow for reform in November 2017 by including prominent royals in the mass arrest and internment in the Ritz-Carlton hotel in Riyadh of super-rich Saudis suspected of corruption. The operation was conducted with a precision and efficiency which suggested it had long been in the planning, and the fact that no details were leaked is a mark of the loyalty that the crown price commands. The arrests can be interpreted as a signal of his determination to fight corruption without fear or favour, although whether the episode amounts to a reset of the royals' relations with the state or a settling of scores remains to be seen. One thing, however, is certain: the spectre of corruption will not have been banished by one night of arrests. Opportunities for Saudi royals and their coteries to benefit unfairly from their position will abound as Saudi Vision 2030 is realised. The funds which Muhammad bin Salman theatrically reappropriated from those held at the Ritz-Carlton were generated by a system as much as by individuals – a system, ironically, that was established during an earlier bout of nation building. There is as yet no sign that the crown prince's commitment to economic liberalisation will impinge on the commercial activity of the royal family. He has been criticised in the Western media for his personal wealth and the government contracts held by his commercial concerns. Royal involvement in the private sector is unlikely to cease: their patronage and wealth are integral to the running of the economy, but the excesses of earlier generations are likely, at least for a while, to have been tempered.

Amid many doubts about the prospects for the achievement of Saudi Vision 2030, two stand out. The first centres on whether it is possible to build a modern economy on Saudi Arabia's existing legal and social structures. A digital economy requires openness to innovation and an educated and flexible workforce, as well as a very different financial system to the one that Saudi Arabia currently has. Despite the ambitions of Saudi Vision 2030, these changes will not easily be accommodated within the sharia-based legal and social system. The participation of women in the workforce has been limited, and there are plenty of unproductive men too. As the number of migrant workers falls, making better use of native labour will become a more pressing issue. The key challenges are to increase productivity, diversity and inclusion. There is an assumption at the heart of Saudi Vision 2030, that everything it entails is compatible with Saudi identity. This rests on the conviction that the original Saudi identity was of a 'tolerant, moderate Islam open to the world'. The crown price has promoted this position at home and abroad. It remains to be seen whether his vision and Saudi values as practised are compatible.

The second concerns whether emerging political arrangements are conducive to engineering an economic transformation. Muhammad bin Salman has concentrated power, eliminated checks on his rule and sidelined rivals, in particular the deposed crown prince Muhammad bin Nayef Al Saud. He has also brooked less internal dissent than previous Saudi rulers. Western states kept their reservations private in the first half of 2018, although by the middle of the year disquiet among them was rising. Yet the crown prince showed no sign of heeding the counsel of friendly nations or backing down. A gathering authoritarian trend across the Middle East, including in Turkey, and a US administration less insistent on promoting human rights than its predecessor, created a permissive environment for this tougher approach.

Concentrating power in the court of the crown prince (and the two key committees he controls) and eliminating checks and balances has enabled the government to take decisive measures directed at large-scale reform. Yet the scale of the transformation required, plus the importance of maintaining a brisk tempo in decision-making and implementation, raises the question as to whether there is sufficient executive and administrative capacity. Many important decisions are referred to the crown prince and his closest advisers, which may potentially create a bottleneck. This is the kind of bureaucratic inefficiency which creates the conditions for corruption.

The requirement to decentralise decision-making and empower technocrats will rise as the reform programme is implemented, but progress in reforming decision-making itself has been slow. Indeed, there is little indication that Muhammad bin Salman regards the devolution of power as an enabler of reform. On the contrary, he seems to prefer to maintain direct control.

Regional muscle-flexing

Saudi policy in the Arab and Islamic world has largely been defined by a commitment to contain and confront Iran and other regional challengers. Personal relations between leaders in the Persian Gulf, and the convictions of those key players, have been instrumental in strengthening policy. There is a close alignment in the views of Muhammad bin Salman, the UAE ruler Muhammad bin Zayed Al Nahyan, the King of

Bahrain Hamad bin Isa Al Khalifa and Egypt's President Abdel Fattah Al-Sisi concerning the threat that Iran poses to the region – and the ways in which that threat should be countered. Although from the Saudi perspective, Iran does not pose a direct military threat to the territorial integrity of the kingdom, Tehran does have a track record of attempting to develop subversive influence inside the country, especially in Saudi Arabia's Eastern Province.

Similarly, the Gulf rulers have taken a tough line against the Muslim Brotherhood and their sponsors, most notably Qatar. Saudi Arabia and the UAE have led the way in isolating Qatar and intervening in Yemen's civil war. In the process, they have reduced the relevance of the GCC and downgraded the importance of acting in concert with more moderate states such as Kuwait and Oman. Theirs is a binary approach, with an adversarial focus and a greater inclination to act decisively and, if necessary, without the US.

Yet while Saudi Arabia has succeeded in demonstrating resolve and can claim some success with regard to Yemen and Qatar, elsewhere it has suffered defeats. The crown price summoned Lebanese Prime Minister Saad Hariri to Riyadh and pressed him to resign, probably because of Hariri's political association with Hizbullah, which is notably anti-Saudi. However, the gambit failed: Saudi Arabia's Western partners did not support the move and both Hariri and Hizbullah were buoyed by a wave of patriotic indignation within Lebanon. At the elections in May 2018, Hariri was returned as Lebanon's prime minister while Hizbullah won a record number of parliamentary seats. The episode underscored the perils of extending the norms of Saudi power overseas, as well as the ability of Iran and its partners to punish and exploit mistakes.

This was not the only setback for Saudi Arabia's regional policy. In Syria, the reinvigorated Assad regime, supported by the coalition of Iran, Russia and Turkey, seems poised to reduce Saudi and Emirati influence in the country to negligible proportions. This is an historic setback for Riyadh, which wielded influence in Syria even when Assad's father was in power. In Iraq too, Iran has outmanoeuvred Saudi Arabia by building its influence through militias (such as the Popular Mobilisation

Units) that have dislodged the Islamic State, also known as ISIS or ISIL. Even the intervention in Yemen has fallen short of expectations. Despite notching up military gains, Saudi Arabia and the UAE have been unable to halt missile attacks by the Houthis into Saudi Arabia, some of which have even reached the capital. Given Saudi Arabia's ability to intercept the majority of missiles, such attacks do not pose a significant military threat, but symbolically, it matters a lot. Overall, Saudi Arabia has yet to develop the techniques and alliances that can successfully contain Iranian projection through proxies. Nevertheless, the axis between Saudi Arabia, the UAE and Egypt has strengthened as a result of the multi-theatre confrontation with Iran. Within the Arab world, the weight of those three states combined is considerable and they have the means to impose their will on their Gulf neighbours, as the Qatar episode has shown. Saudi Arabia and the UAE formed a joint defence and economic cooperation committee in December 2017, which gave formal expression to an existing partnership based on congruent security agendas that are not limited to Yemen alone.

With youth and popularity on his side, Muhammad bin Salman will continue to push hard to realise his vision. If he is successful, Saudi Arabia's leadership role in the Gulf and the Arab world will be secured for another generation and the Saudis will have an economic model which will potentially survive the demise of hydrocarbons. If he fails, Saudi Arabia could relapse into conservatism, with the management of its current model falling into obsolescence. Somewhere in between the two lies the most likely outcome. Young Saudis will demand and help create a more outward-looking society but many of the traditional power centres and privileges will remain, and the prestige projects may well be deferred or scaled back.

A consequence for Muhammad bin Salman of even moderate success – and of the absence of any challenge or accountability – will be a rising confidence of the crown prince on the international stage, which will play directly into the confrontation with Iran. Further afield, there is a risk that he may misjudge his reaction to the inevitable criticisms of elements of the Saudi legal system and security apparatus, which are still highly contentious, even among his allies. (The stormy dispute with Canada in July–August 2018 over the detention of a Saudi activist is a case in point.) But Muhammad bin Salman has so far done well in maintaining a broad coalition of support in the Middle East and the West, and in developing a new persona for Saudi rulers overseas. The potential dividends for his country and the region are huge. The risks are worth it, but neither his adversaries nor events will give him the luxury of a clear run. Resilience, poise and consistency will matter as much as energy and decisiveness.

Iran and the JCPOA

Iran will face a critical choice in late 2018 and 2019 in terms of its strategic alignment, as the US withdrawal from the 2015 nuclear deal leads to the imposition of US primary and secondary sanctions that threaten to remove nearly all of the economic benefits promised to Iran in exchange for halting its nuclear activities. The loss of trading ties with European firms is hurting the Iranian political project of rapprochement with European countries, despite the strong rhetorical opposition of EU governments to the US decision. Iran may then turn to China, Russia, India and Turkey for economic and political support. All of these states resent US unilateralism, but Iran's revolutionary zeal has proven to be a barrier to strong relations in the past, and this may be the case once more. Ultimately, domestic politics will drive Tehran's approach to nuclear affairs. At a minimum, this could involve the resumption of enrichment activities if the benefits of the 2015 nuclear deal are no longer available.

US withdrawal

On 8 May 2017, US President Donald Trump made good on his earlier threats to withdraw from the 2015 Iran nuclear deal, known as the Joint Comprehensive Plan of Action (JCPOA). Rather than effectuating the 'soft withdrawal' that some observers had expected – that is, the re-imposition of pre-deal nuclear sanctions without rigorous enforcement

– he issued orders to 're-impose sanctions lifted or waived in connection with the JCPOA as expeditiously as possible', or no later than 180 days. The US Department of State and the White House subsequently clarified it was a clean withdrawal. The United States, no longer being a party, would not employ the sanctions snap-back provisions of the JCPOA in the event of a claimed Iran violation. Trump's decision was a material breach of the agreement, which has no withdrawal clause. Whether the JCPOA can survive without the US is open to considerable doubt.

Throughout his campaign and in the early months of his administration, Trump harshly condemned the JCPOA, calling it the 'worst deal ever', but he did not take the first step to walk away until October 2017, when he refused under US law to certify Iranian compliance. On 12 January 2018, he issued an ultimatum, demanding that European partners – France, Germany and the UK (the E3) – work to 'fix the deal's disastrous flaws' on pain of US withdrawal. Specifically, the president demanded three major changes to the agreement: more robust inspections with immediate access to any requested site, including military ones; elimination of the so-called 'sunset clauses' so that limits on Iran's nuclear programme would continue indefinitely; and firm restrictions on ballistic-missile development. Although the E3 were opposed to renegotiating the JCPOA, they sought to address Trump's concerns in working-level negotiations with the US State Department. According to participants, the parties were only a few words away from reaching an agreement to maintain it.

As the 12 May deadline approached, French President Emmanuel Macron and German Chancellor Angela Merkel visited Washington to try to convince Trump to accept the fixes under discussion and remain in the nuclear deal. Their efforts were in vain. After meeting Trump, Macron said that the US president 'will get rid of this deal on his own, for domestic reasons', as in fact he did. Fulfilling his campaign pledge, Trump decided to re-impose all nuclear-related penalties, including secondary sanctions on foreign firms. Going beyond the letter of the pre-JCPOA measures, John Bolton, the US national security advisor, indicated that it was 'possible' for European businesses to be sanctioned for interacting with Iran, and Richard Grenell, the US ambassador to Germany, tweeted that 'German companies doing business in Iran should wind down operations immediately'.

EU leaders have three main reasons to seek to save the deal. Firstly, the JCPOA is regarded in Brussels as the European Union's crowning foreign-policy achievement and reflective of the principles that shape its identity: the rule of international law, multilateralism, non-proliferation and the primacy of diplomacy in resolving international disputes. Secondly, the EU has significant economic and commercial stakes in a viable nuclear deal. It has become one of Iran's main trading partners, with EU exports to Iran valued at over €10.8 billion (US$12.7bn) and EU imports from Iran at over €10.1bn (US$11.9bn) in 2017. In addition, Iran has significant energy resources that Europe, an energy-deficit continent, needs. Thirdly, Brussels assesses that the deal is working to inhibit Iran's acquisition of nuclear-weapons capability, and that it therefore strengthens regional and European security. From Europe's standpoint, a nuclear Iran would further destabilise the Middle East, exacerbating the existing refugee crisis and increasing the potential for an arms race between key regional actors and a pitched Sunni–Shi'ite strategic confrontation.

Furthermore, European leaders see themselves as having gone out on a limb to address Trump's concerns. They feel both betrayed and deeply worried about the global consequences of the United States' withdrawal. Donald Tusk, the European Council president, tweeted that Trump's decision to withdraw would be met with a 'united European approach', and condemned the 'capricious assertiveness of the American administration'. News outlets across Europe characterised the decision as destructive to the transatlantic alliance and as an assault on international cooperation. A *Der Spiegel* editorial concluded that 'the trans-Atlantic relationship has been seriously damaged'.

Perhaps most notably, Merkel said that Europe could no longer rely on the US, but instead 'must take its destiny in its own hands'. Faced with the stark choice of either bending to the United States' will to preserve the transatlantic relationship's security and market advantages or exercising an independent foreign and security policy, the EU and major European powers seemed inclined to the latter.

In theory, the JCPOA could be salvaged through various mechanisms, such as passing legislation that protects EU member countries' businesses and implementing practical pathways for providing alternative financial-transaction channels that would win continued compliance from Iran. On 16 May, the EU decided on a nine-point economic plan to keep the JCPOA in place. This plan includes assurances for oil and gas industries, sources of international financial support and the protection of EU companies engaging with Iran from US sanctions through amended blocking regulations, which make it illegal for European firms to comply with any foreign sanctions. But the EU's leverage is limited by the huge disparity between the EU–Iran trade balance of €682 million (US$806m) and the EU–US trade balance of €120bn (US$141bn). The majority of EU firms have already abandoned business with Iran in order to avoid the risk of facing US secondary sanctions. In 2017, Total planned a nearly US$1bn investment in Iran, but decided to terminate the project soon after Trump's announcement. Other major European companies, such as Allianz and Maersk, have made similar announcements. By mid-2018, the US administration continued to insist that European companies would not be granted waivers.

An economic pivot to Asia?

To offset the impact of US sanctions, Tehran is likely to explore the potential of closer economic ties with Russia and the larger Asian economies. The EU and the major US allies South Korea and Japan will probably find it hard to resist US demands for an appreciable cut in imports of Iranian oil, but other states will be more receptive to Iranian business or drive a hard bargain for toeing the US line. China and India, for instance, are Iran's two largest oil customers – both may accommodate the US by finding new suppliers, but this could require that the US agrees to concessions on other sensitive bilateral issues. On the contrary, Turkey, Iran's fourth-largest customer, will resist US pressure to switch suppliers, and Russia likewise will baulk at any US efforts to interfere with its commercial ties to third states. Indeed, Moscow and Beijing may well use the United States' abandonment of the JCPOA as an opportunity to step up their roles as great powers, particularly in the Middle East. It is plausible that these two players could bring together both allies and non-allies of the US to defy the sanctions regime if the US administration seeks to challenge their regional power in their spheres of influence.

Iran prioritised economic ties with Asia in the period immediately before the JCPOA when it was under tough Western sanctions. Although there were downsides to this orientation, Tehran is set once again to pivot towards Asia in order to sustain its economy. Since the Islamic Revolution in 1979, the motto of Iranian foreign policy has been 'Neither East, nor West, but the Islamic Republic', yet Iran has mostly been more eastward-facing than westward-facing, especially since the 2000s when China became the leading trading partner of Iran, replacing EU countries. As the US and its allies sought to contain Iran, Tehran looked to Asia and – putting aside its historic rivalry with Russia – included Moscow in its Asian Triangle policy (*mosallas asiai*). This is supported by the Supreme Leader in particular. The Iranian search for bilateral partnerships with China, Russia and India is part of a broader project to integrate the country into Asian regional organisations such as the Shanghai Cooperation Organisation (SCO) and the Association of Southeast Asian Nations (ASEAN). This Iranian strategy was partly successful: Iran was able to secure observer status in the SCO in 2005 and to sign a friendship treaty with ASEAN in 2018.

However, the increasingly strident rhetoric from Iran and its ascendant conservatives establishes an obstacle to deeper relations. Tehran's anti-Americanism does not sit easily with the more pragmatic approach evident in Beijing, New Delhi or even Moscow. For Moscow, the main priority in dealing with Iran will be stability in their common neighbourhood, stretching from Syria to the Caspian Sea and Central Asia. For New Delhi, the priorities are bilateral energy cooperation and the construction of the Chabahar port in Iran. For China too, the energy trade looms large and the opportunity has grown to integrate Iran in the Belt and Road Initiative. All three will also view deeper ties to Iran as leverage in their negotiations with the US.

Iranian analysts perceive that China shares Iran's opposition to Western imperialism and the 'US hegemonic order'. However, there is disquiet in Iran over aspects of their country's relationship with China, motivated in part by competing economic interests and Beijing's repression of the Muslim Uighur population in the western province of Xinjiang in China. Tehran is convinced that China is opposed to US military action against Iran, as well as efforts to sanction the regime. However, Beijing is also against Iran becoming a nuclear-weapons state and would suffer considerable damage if Tehran responded to US sanctions by seeking to disrupt tanker traffic in the Strait of Hormuz, a key shipping choke point between the Gulf of Oman and the Persian Gulf. Iranian President Hassan Rouhani has signalled that disruption to shipping is an option, while the commander of Iran's Revolutionary Guards threatened to 'make the enemy understand that either everyone can use the Strait of Hormuz or no one'. With almost 17m barrels passing through the strait per day (the equivalent of 35% of all seaborne oil exports), any attempt to block tankers could cause a sharp increase in oil prices. The effect would be exacerbated by market concerns around the current thinness of spare capacity, notably in Saudi Arabia after Riyadh's agreement to raise output.

Iran's relationship with Russia is a complex one. Because of the asymmetry in power – Russia is a global player and P5 member, whereas Iran is a regional power – Iranian policymakers insist that an alliance or equal strategic partnership is scarcely possible. The two states have often competed for influence in their common neighbourhood and, as energy exporters, are potential rivals in the European market, which Russia relies on deeply. Russia's longstanding refusal to join OPEC has also been a source of tension. However, the two states have shared economic and geopolitical interests that can form the basis for cooperation. They have made common cause in supporting the Assad government in Syria and pushing for peace talks. In September 2016, Moscow offered support for Iran's return to the international oil market and it has since been more cooperative in its dealings with OPEC. For Iranian reformists, this highlights the unreliability of Russia; conservatives acknowledge this but prioritise closer ties as a way to deflect US pressure on Tehran.

India and Iran share a common interest in Afghanistan and the realisation of the Chabahar port project. However, the recent improvement of India's bilateral relationships with the US and Israel has put a limit on the deepening of ties between Tehran and New Delhi. New Delhi still cooperates with Tehran to check Pakistani influence in Afghanistan, and India regards Iran as a potential strategic partner.

Tehran's strategic calculus

The Iranian government is at a critical juncture both domestically and internationally. The JCPOA has been Rouhani's signature foreign-policy achievement. He ran both of his presidential-election campaigns in 2013 and 2017 promising economic improvements through sanctions relief. Thus, the vitality of his presidency as well as his political legacy is substantially dependent on how he manages this crisis. As a first step, the Rouhani government exercised strategic patience in refraining from withdrawing from the deal. Instead, it indicated that it would pursue its grievances through the legal framework of the JCPOA. Iran is also negotiating with the remaining parties (now typically labelled the P4+1 – United Nations Security Council permanent members China, France, Russia and the UK, plus Germany) to explore guarantees to secure Iran's interests. On 13 May, Rouhani announced that 'if the remaining five countries continue to abide by the agreement, Iran will remain in the deal'.

However, Iran is unlikely to uphold the JCPOA merely to maintain the moral high ground without economic and geopolitical gains. Following the United States' withdrawal from the deal, hard-line factions in parliament and the military establishment have been increasingly vocal in criticising Rouhani's government for its continuing compliance. (Supreme Leader Ayatollah Ali Khamenei himself publicly said that his own approval of the JCPOA in 2015 was a political mistake.) Complaints based on economic factors – in particular, the need for hard currency – are also likely to escalate if the remaining parties to the JCPOA are unable to mitigate secondary US sanctions. Unless the EU and other trading partners impose blocking regulations, shipping and insurance could pose major complications to implementation.

If Asian states can deliver substantive economic benefits to Iran, and if they are keen to uphold the JCPOA, there is some chance that Iran might not withdraw from the nuclear deal or declare it null and void. However, in the face of US primary and secondary sanctions, designed to trigger systemic change in Iran or a return to the negotiating table (for a tougher, wider-ranging agreement on US terms), Iran will most likely be inclined to resume nuclear-enrichment activities that are currently prohibited under the JCPOA. At the same time, even if it withdraws from the deal, Tehran may judge actual advancement of its nuclear capability as strategically imprudent.

Possible measures occupy a broad spectrum, and those actually taken would depend on whether Iran prioritises caution or provocation. If the latter, in addition to resuming enrichment activities, Tehran could limit International Atomic Energy Agency inspections. There are obvious risks involved in pursuing the more destabilising path, as it could antagonise the Europeans as well as provoking the Americans, but Iran's calculus might very well tilt in that direction in order to sustain the government's domestic position.

The worst-case scenario would be one in which the withdrawal of the US, coupled with the failure of the international community to salvage the deal, creates a groundswell of militant desperation in Iran in favour of emulating North Korea. This would involve Iran withdrawing from the Nuclear Non-Proliferation Treaty and accelerating its nuclear and ballistic-missile programmes with an eye to building significant hedging capabilities, or even a deliverable bomb. The rationale for such a course would be to strengthen Iran's bargaining position vis-à-vis both the US and regional actors such as Israel and Saudi Arabia. Yet it rests on an assumption that there would be no military action against the Islamic Republic of Iran (which could potentially lead to regime change) before the nuclear project was complete. Considering the animus repeatedly demonstrated by the Trump administration towards Tehran, that seems an unsafe assumption.

Yemen: The Broken Country

The conflict in Yemen shows no signs of ending. There is broad international consensus that there is no military solution to the conflict, but the warring parties themselves disagree. None of the primary actors – Saudi Arabia, the United Arab Emirates, the Yemeni government or the Houthis – have suffered enough to make them willing to embrace the difficult choices and inevitable compromises that come with an agreement. War remains easier than peace. Nor have the two primary external actors – the United States and Iran – shown a willingness to apply the sort of sustained pressure that might force the parties towards an agreement in spite of themselves. Instead, the various sides remain far apart, the fighting continues and three successive US special envoys have been unable to do anything to bring the fighting to a close. Civilians have borne the brunt of the continuing conflict: in April 2018, United Nations Secretary-General António Guterres described the situation in Yemen as the 'world's worst humanitarian crisis', stating that approximately three-quarters of the population needed humanitarian assistance and protection.

Entrenched conflict

Despite an initial offensive in early 2015 that reached as far south as Aden, the Houthis have been pushed back towards the northern highlands. They continue to control the port city of Hudaydah, where much of Yemen's aid, food and medicine enters the country. (The Houthis receive approximately a quarter of their income from taxing these supplies as the goods pass through Hudaydah.) Hudaydah is also the target of a coalition offensive (which was paused on 1 July 2018), and as such is the focal point of the UN special envoy Martin Griffiths's proposed peace talks, which are due to start in Geneva on 6 September 2018.

Unlike in 2016 and 2017, when the military conflict was essentially at a stalemate, the Houthis lost some territory in 2018. None of these losses, however, have been significant, being mostly outlying districts along the Red Sea coast, small areas in Nihm east of Sana'a and some territory in Sadah along the border with Saudi Arabia. Perhaps the most significant shift of 2017–18 was the collapse of the Houthi–Saleh alliance in December 2017. The alliance, which had always been one of convenience, first showed signs of strain in August when a key Saleh aide was killed in a shoot-out with Houthis in Sana'a. The final break came in early December when Saleh announced that he was ending the alliance with the Houthis. A brief but brutal battle ensued around three Saleh strongholds in Sana'a: on 4 December, Ali Abdullah Saleh was killed by the Houthis, while two of his sons, a nephew and a grandson were taken into Houthi custody. (Saleh's eldest son, Ahmed – who has been sanctioned by the UN Security Council – remains under informal house arrest in the UAE, as he has been since 2015.) What was left of Saleh's military network – about 3,000 men – is currently under the command of one of Saleh's nephews, Tariq Muhammed Abdullah Saleh, who is participating in the battle for Hudaydah against the Houthis.

Yet despite the loss of territory and the collapse of their alliance with Saleh, the Houthis continue to believe that they are in the stronger position when it comes to peace negotiations, which makes them less likely to make the compromises necessary for an agreement. The Houthis still control Sana'a and much of Yemen's more populous north. Nearly three and a half years of continuous airstrikes have been unable to dislodge them. When it comes to the military campaign against the Houthis, the Saudis only have three options: they can continue carrying out airstrikes and hope for a different result; they can withdraw completely, forgo a peace deal and let the Houthis declare themselves the victor; or they can insert ground troops for what would likely be a long and bloody guerrilla war with no guarantee of success. None of these options are attractive.

The Houthis believe that they only have to wait for Saudi Arabia to tire of the war and withdraw. Although this war started in mid-2014 with the Houthis' march on Sana'a and the slow-motion *coup d'état* that forced Yemeni President Abd Rabbo Mansour Hadi to flee the country in early 2015, the Houthis have been fighting almost continually for much longer. From 2004–10, the Houthis fought six successive wars against Yemen's central government. During that time the movement proved resilient despite losing its first two leaders, Hussein al-Houthi and his father, Badr al-Din al-Houthi: Hussein was killed by Yemeni government troops in 2004 and Badr al-Din was killed in a suicide attack carried out by al-Qaeda in the Arabian Peninsula (AQAP) in 2010. Should Abdulmalik al-Houthi – the current leader of the Houthis and younger brother of Hussein and son of Badr al-Din – be killed or die, the movement would be unlikely to fracture significantly.

In some ways, the Houthis' current strength is itself a result of the Saudi-led coalition's airstrikes, many of which have killed civilians. The Houthis currently control more territory than they could hope to represent or successfully administer under any sort of an inclusive framework. The coalition's bombing campaign gives the Houthis a ready-made excuse for deficiencies in governing, as they can blame shortages of food, fuel, medicine and even inefficient or non-existent government services on the Saudi airstrikes.

From the civilian perspective, Yemen is broken. The country has split into a handful of quasi-autonomous regions fought over by several different armed groups. Its financial system has fractured: there are now two central banks, one in Sana'a controlled by the Houthis and one in Aden controlled by Hadi's government, but neither functions at full capacity. There is some food on the shelves in northern areas but, increasingly, little money with which to buy it. Civil servants are paid infrequently or not at all, and more and more families are subsisting on less and less. The World Food Programme estimates that 18 million Yemenis are food insecure, and 8.4m of those severely so. Cholera has made a comeback, with multiple outbreaks since October 2016. The Yemeni riyal continues to fall against the US dollar, losing approximately 40% of its value between

January 2017 and January 2018 despite a US$2-billion injection by Saudi Arabia into the Central Bank in Aden. Fuel is in short supply. There are often long lines at petrol stations and customers pay an electricity premium for refrigerated bottled water. Desperate families are resorting to extreme measures, including the sale of young girls as child brides. Yemen's infrastructure, never strong to begin with, has been destroyed and will take years to rebuild.

The bulk of the costs of the war in Yemen has been borne by the civilian population. The political leadership on all sides – the Houthis, Saudi Arabia, and the UAE – has largely remained unscathed. This means that, as unpopular as the war may be internationally, there is little pressure on any of these three entities to make the difficult choices inherent in any peace agreement. Unless this situation changes, the war is likely to continue.

Two roads to peace

The current framework for a peace agreement – UN Security Council Resolution 2216 – is unworkable. The situation on the ground has changed dramatically since Resolution 2216 was implemented in April 2015. Among other things, Resolution 2216 demands that the Houthis withdraw from all areas seized during the conflict, relinquish their arms and cease all activities exclusively within the authority of the legitimate government of Yemen. This is unlikely to happen, and certainly will not take place in the unilateral manner demanded by the resolution.

There are, however, two potential roads to a peace agreement in Yemen. The first would require the parties themselves – the Emiratis, the Houthis, the Saudis and the Yemeni government – to negotiate in good faith and be willing to make the difficult choices and compromises that are necessary for an agreement. The second option that could lead to an agreement is concentrated and sustained international pressure on the various actors. A less likely scenario is that a clean and decisive military victory by the coalition in Hudaydah would give Saudi Arabia a face-saving victory that would allow it to negotiate an exit from the war. In such a scenario, however, it is unclear whether the Houthis could or even would negotiate from such a position of weakness when they would be completely landlocked and without a functioning airport. It is more likely that the Houthis would resume fighting to regain territory and a stronger negotiating position.

There are several challenges to the first option of a negotiated peace between the parties, but the main one is the lack of political imperative or will to compromise. The Houthis are willing to meet for peace talks, but they want to be treated and dealt with as equals to the Yemeni, Saudi and Emirati governments. What they want to avoid is losing diplomatically what they have gained militarily. As mentioned above, the Houthi political leadership has been largely insulated from the shortages associated with this war. Targeted UN sanctions on Houthi leader Abdulmalik al-Houthi, his brother Abd al-Khaliq al-Houthi and Abdullah al-Hakim (a key Houthi military commander) have had little impact, given that the sanctions consist of a travel ban and an asset freeze – top Houthi leaders rarely travel abroad and have no international assets or accounts to freeze. Indeed, there is evidence to suggest that top Houthi commanders are actually making money on this war through a lucrative black-market trade. With a handful of exceptions – Saleh al-Sammad, the president of the Houthi Supreme Political Council, was killed in April 2018 – few top Houthi leaders have been killed.

In much the same way that the Houthi's top leadership has not paid a political price for this war, neither has the Saudi leadership. Economically, of course, the war has been expensive, costing by some estimates nearly US$100bn. Diplomatically, the kingdom's image abroad has been tarnished by the war and in particular the frequent reports of civilian casualties. Crucially, however, the conflict has not cost Crown Prince Muhammad bin Salman domestically. Saudi casualties remain low and Houthi ballistic-missile launches into Saudi Arabia are a frequent reminder of the threat from Yemen.

The UAE, which does not share a border with Yemen and is less ideologically inclined than Saudi Arabia, is likely to experience war weariness before either Saudi Arabia or the Houthis. The UAE, unlike Saudi Arabia, has significant troops on the ground in Yemen, although many of these are expatriate forces. However, in July, the UAE announced that it was extending compulsory military service from 12 months to 16 months for all males. The UAE also has different goals in Yemen than Saudi Arabia, which make any sort of unilateral withdrawal unlikely.

In the absence of political willingness from the players themselves to negotiate and agree on a final peace settlement, the second road to a peace settlement is sustained international pressure. For the Saudi-led coalition, this pressure would come from the US and United Kingdom, although US pressure is by far the most significant. The US provides intelligence, logistical and material support to the coalition, including mid-air refuelling. Crucially, the US says it does not track which coalition planes it refuels or what bombing runs they carry out, in part because it does not want to be considered party to the conflict in Yemen and does not want to be implicated in mistaken strikes that kill civilians. However, the 2018 National Defense Authorization Act requires that the US either certify that Saudi Arabia and the UAE are meeting humanitarian obligations in Yemen or give them a national-security waiver, which has to be submitted to the US Congress as an unclassified document. The US is involved in armed conflict against AQAP and the Islamic State, also known as ISIS or ISIL, in Yemen, but when it comes to the Houthis, the US position is that it is only supporting its Saudi and UAE allies.

Under US President Donald Trump, the US has appeared reluctant to apply the sort of pressure that would force Saudi Arabia and the UAE to negotiate in good faith. Saudi Arabia was Trump's first foreign visit in May 2017. The US remained neutral in the Saudi–Canada Twitter feud over human rights in August 2018 (which escalated into Saudi economic sanctions against Canada), while the Trump administration has also withdrawn from the Joint Comprehensive Plan of Action (JCPOA) nuclear deal and reinstated sanctions against Iran.

Iran is the only country that has significant influence with the Houthi side. Iran has suggested that it would be willing to play a constructive role in bringing the Houthis to the negotiating table, in part because Iran wants a seat when the terms are discussed. Indeed, while getting the warring parties to agree on a solution in Yemen may be difficult, Yemen might, conversely, be the low-hanging fruit in the Saudi–Iran regional conflict. Iran has relatively little invested in Yemen and may be willing to show some flexibility. Iran is also eager to split the US and Europe on what is left of the JCPOA nuclear deal, and it may be willing to agree to cease sending ballistic missiles to the Houthis in return for a pledge from the Saudis to cease airstrikes and to show EU countries that it has peaceful intentions.

Neither of these options – peace negotiated directly or brought about through external pressure – appears likely in the current political climate. However, there are a number of steps that might be taken if the Houthis and the Saudi-led coalition determine that a peace deal is in their best interests. To begin with, it may be possible to persuade the Houthis to withdraw from Hudaydah in exchange for Saudi's re-opening of the airport in Sana'a, which the Houthis have long sought. This could be a good first step that would de-escalate the situation in Hudaydah and give each side a win.

The Houthis categorically reject the idea of disarmament (one of the key aims of the UN special envoy's negotiations) but there may be room for negotiation on transitional arms control, which would allow for a gradual building of trust between the two sides. One hypothetical scenario might involve the Saudi-led coalition ceasing airstrikes while the Houthis would agree to stop launching missiles at the kingdom. According to the terms of a transitional arms-control agreement, the Houthis would put their heavy and medium weapons under lock and key, but would keep the key. This would give them the ability to quickly rearm should they feel threatened. Part of any peace deal will also likely include a proposal to lift sanctions on Abdulmalik al-Houthi, Abd al-Khaliq al-Houthi and Abdullah al-Hakim in exchange for the dissolution of the Houthi Supreme Political Council, which would pave the way for a national reconciliation or a caretaker government.

Tensions within the coalition

Saudi Arabia and the UAE, the two main countries in the Saudi-led coalition, are united at the executive level, where the crown prince of

Saudi Arabia, Muhammad bin Salman, and the crown prince of Abu Dhabi, Muhammed bin Zayed Al Nahyan, maintain a close relationship. On the ground in Yemen, however, their policies, approaches and long-term goals have diverged significantly since they entered the war on 26 March 2015.

Saudi Arabia is predominantly concerned with preventing the rise of an Iranian proxy, along the lines of Hizbullah, on its southern border. Ideally, Saudi Arabia would like to see the Houthis defeated, driven from Sana'a and dependent on the central government in Sana'a. However, as that appears unlikely, Saudi Arabia wants the Houthis as weak as possible, landlocked and unable to receive Iranian ballistic missiles.

By contrast, the UAE appears less concerned with the future configuration of Yemen – whether that is partition, federalism or some other solution – than it is with maintaining its own network of influence with the country. Saudi Arabia is providing money to local allies on the ground, but the UAE is going a step further by establishing, funding, training and equipping a network of proxy forces. This process began in early 2016 with the formation of the Hadrami Elite Forces (HEF) to take back the port city of Mukalla in Hadhramaut governorate from AQAP. That offensive was successful, although AQAP withdrew from the city (reportedly after striking a deal with the UAE) rather than fight. The HEF, however, were not disbanded and now number between 3,000 and 4,000 troops, whose salaries are paid by the UAE. The UAE also established the Shabwani Elite Forces (SEF) and the Security Belt Forces (SBF, also known as Hizam) along the same lines as the HEF in 2016. The SEF and SBF are active in Abyan, Aden and Lahij. The SEF number approximately 3,000–4,000 troops, and the Security Belt Forces are estimated at 10,000–15,000. The UAE has also conducted joint raids with US forces against AQAP targets, which builds on its counter-terrorism experience in Afghanistan and continues to cement its partnership with the US. Over the past few years, the UAE has established military bases and is operating ports along the Red Sea corridor in the Horn of Africa.

Post-peace fighting

Even if a peace deal is reached between the Saudi-led coalition and the Houthis, it is unlikely to end the fighting in Yemen. The country is too divided and hosts numerous armed groups which can act as spoilers whenever they disagree with a particular decision. Indeed, what is often described as the war in Yemen is in reality three separate wars. There is the US-led war against AQAP and ISIS in Yemen, in which the UAE plays an active role. There is a local and multi-sided civil war between the Houthis, Yemeni government forces, an increasingly vocal southern secessionist movement, UAE proxy forces, Salafi militias and tribal militias. Finally, there is a regional conflict that pits Saudi Arabia, the UAE and its coalition against the Houthis and their Iranian backers.

It is unlikely that any one peace agreement would be able to end all of these three overlapping conflicts. Any peace agreement would probably end only the regional war, leading to the withdrawal of Saudi and UAE troops while the fighting in Yemen continues. The UN special envoy has already said that the future of the south would not be part of the forthcoming negotiations, but would be discussed separately as part of a future national dialogue. However, Yemen has been through this scenario before, with poor results. There is no longer a single Yemen. There are multiple Yemens, and no single individual or group is capable of reuniting them into a coherent whole.

The Maghreb's Strategic Myopia

From Morocco in the west to Libya in the east and Algeria and Tunisia in between, the Maghreb countries are uniformly focused on the near term and the tactical, not the long term and the strategic. Why this is the case varies from one country to the next, but North Africa's collective myopia leaves the countries in the region vulnerable to unexpected shocks that could be acutely destabilising. In Morocco, while the institution of the monarchy is strong, the king himself has lost interest in being

Morocco's monarch, but has also absolved himself of any responsibility in reforming the monarchy so that it is more in line with contemporary political norms. Algeria is stuck with a sclerotic system, drawing from the same depleting source of legitimacy for the last 60 years and unable to formulate a new narrative that would give meaning to the country and its leadership. Tunisia too is preoccupied with the present, grappling with the ongoing aftershocks of the immediate past as it tries to figure out what the 2011 revolution really meant and how much change it should introduce and at what cost to stability. Lastly, Libya is at war with itself. Its two or three governments are backed by sundry militias for whom the chaotic status quo is profitable and for whom political stability and governance would mean a loss of power and money. In all of these countries, the needs of the present overwhelm the political leadership's ability to think about – let alone implement policies for – the future. While Rabat, Algiers, Tunis and Tripoli obsess about today and tomorrow, there are dynamics that will undoubtedly impact them over the longer term, dynamics which the Maghreb countries ignore at their peril.

Morocco

It has often been said that King Mohammed VI is the king who never wanted to be king. Or rather, he would have preferred to have been king of a different kind of monarchy. When Mohammed VI ascended the throne in 1999, he was hailed as 'the King of the Poor'. He was uncomfortable with the notion of an absolute monarchy, deeming it out of step with contemporary forms of government, and he quietly harboured a vision of transforming Morocco into a constitutional monarchy where the royal family played a role similar to that in Spain or the United Kingdom.

Now, nearly two decades later, Mohammed VI has abandoned his vision of diminishing the palace's role as the country's primary governing institution and devolving more political power to Morocco's popularly elected parliament. Faced with the power of the palace to preserve itself, the idealistic king has grown cynical and dejected. After all, the monarchy is not just the king. It is an institution with members of the royal family, courtiers, active investments that benefit from an uneven playing field and vast landholdings throughout the country. Dismantling the monarchy would have jeopardised more interests than just the king's and, consequently, the king faced institutional opposition.

However, in giving up on his notion of a constitutional monarchy, Mohammed VI did not revert back to the role of a more authoritarian absolute monarch that was embodied by his father, Hassan II. Instead, he has almost entirely receded from the corridors of political power in Rabat. For the most part, he has delegated responsibility for running the country to a cohort of oligarchs and only infrequently steps in as the final arbiter in more protracted political disputes that periodically arise, such as the 2017 government-formation crisis during which the king ultimately compelled the Islamist Party for Justice and Development to oust its secretary-general.

In early 2018, Mohammed VI was completely absent from the political scene in Morocco for more than 50 days. He spent his time in Paris and at his chateau in the French countryside. The extensive time he spends outside of Morocco has prompted populist grumblings on social media and, in a remarkable development, everyday Moroccans have started to murmur about the king. Criticising the king and the monarchy is against the law in Morocco, which only underscores how dissatisfied Moroccans have to be to speak ill of their sovereign.

Some within the royal palace do have a vision for Morocco, but that vision is tactical and focuses narrowly on their own personal interests and potential financial gain rather than on a strategic outlook for the country. The palace is dominated by wealthy courtiers-cum-advisers and ministers – it is thought that the king's minister of agriculture, the billionaire industrial magnate Aziz Akhannouch, and the king's childhood friend Fouad Ali El Himma make most decisions on the king's behalf.

If Morocco were to be said to have a vision, it would be oriented exclusively toward the south, first to the disputed territory of Western Sahara and then further into Africa. Again, this is less a strategic vision than a near-term tactical approach. Morocco would like to bring the long-running dispute over Western Sahara to a close, to which end it has reached out to other African countries to rally their support for Morocco's sovereignty claims. Morocco was able to rejoin the African Union (AU) in 2017, which was considered a major milestone in trying to advance broader international recognition of its sovereignty over the disputed territory (which Rabat calls Southern Morocco). However, such recognition would not dramatically alter Morocco's strategic position in the region or its relations with North American and European allies because (except in rare instances) Morocco already has de facto sovereignty over the territory. Even so, major obstacles remain, such as AU and Algerian support for Western Saharan residents who have been displaced in refugee camps in southern Algeria for nearly three decades.

Morocco's lack of a far-sighted strategic vision could cost it dearly. There is a growing unease in Morocco as the gap between the rich and poor widens. The royal court and its hangers-on are capturing more and more of the state while Moroccans in the cities and the countryside alike are being neglected. Protests and riots, such as those that occurred at Al Hoceima, Jerada, and Sidi Boualem, are evidence of a more endemic problem that risks escalating if left unaddressed. In addition, Morocco suffers from a latent terrorism threat which is exacerbated by Morocco's increasing economic disparities. For potential jihadists, of which there seem to be many based on the number of arrests and disrupted plots, the injustice illustrated by the differences between the very rich and the very poor is a call to action. The king, however, does not recognise it as such, firstly because he is so frequently out of the country, and secondly because he sees Morocco's wealthy citizens as proof of the country's success. Morocco avoided the Arab Spring in 2011 because conditions were not yet ripe and Mohammed VI was able to respond rapidly, but conditions have changed and the cosmetic political reforms of 2011 would likely no longer be sufficient.

Algeria

Although he can no longer walk or talk, Abdelaziz Bouteflika has been Algeria's president since 1999 – the same year that Mohammed VI became king. Although the constitution initially limited him to two five-year terms, Bouteflika has amended the constitution to allow him a third and fourth term and he is in the process of preparing for a fifth. Bouteflika's supporters say that although he is physically weak, he is still mentally agile and that he is fully apprised of what is taking place in Algeria and around it. His detractors say that the sole reason that Bouteflika is still president despite being incapacitated is that Algeria's political elite has not been able to decide upon a successor. In the meantime, the frail, immobile 82-year-old is the symbol of stability in Algeria.

Algeria's political elite – the oligarchs, the high-ranking military officers, the heads of political blocs, labour bosses – know that Bouteflika cannot go on forever. Even if he were to win a fifth term in 2019, at some point the elite will have to choose a successor. In the meantime, though, Algeria's bureaucracy and political elite are consumed with speculation about what happens when Bouteflika dies. With all effort devoted to ensuring that nothing goes wrong as Algeria transitions to the post-Bouteflika era, Algeria does not have the capacity to engage in strategic thinking about the region, about its relations with Europe or about building bridges to other parts of Africa.

Algeria does not lack for strategic challenges. The country faces a youth bulge and high levels of unemployment and underemployment among its university graduates (as attested to by the six-month-long medical-students' strike in 2017 and the first half of 2018). Historically, Algeria's approach to social unrest emanating from frustrated youth and elsewhere across the population was to buy the peace, using revenue from the sale of oil and gas to pay for social services to keep popular discontent in check. However, Algeria's oil and gas revenue is declining at the same time that its population is increasing, straining its conventional approach to dealing with social unrest, and yet the state has not explored any alternatives. Algeria has no meaningful plans to address the country's educational deficits, increase employment or diversify the economy away from oil and gas dependency. All Algeria can hope for is that the price of peace becomes cheaper or that oil prices rebound.

Algeria is also especially vulnerable to being marginalised by Europe. Europe is Algeria's primary trading partner for both imports and exports.

Algeria receives more than US$350 million a year in remittances from Europe (0.02% of Algeria's GDP in 2016), and Algerians with financial means travel to Europe for everything from education to healthcare and leisure activities. However, given its preoccupation with the presidential succession, Algiers does not have a long-term plan to engage with Europe. To the contrary, it frequently instigates fights with the European Union over seemingly minor issues. For example, Algiers reprimanded the EU ambassador to Algeria for comments made by a former journalist of Algerian origin while inside the EU headquarters in Brussels that Algiers regarded as derogatory toward Algeria. However, the Algerian reaction was more of a fit of pique rather than part of a broader policy approach to EU–Algeria relations.

Algeria's lack of strategic vision is especially worrying to outside observers. Algeria is by far the largest country in North Africa: were it to destabilise, the consequences for the region and for Europe could be perilous. An enormous swathe of territory would open up to already prolific jihadi groups in the Sahara, and it is possible that Algerian jihadists would revive their European networks in order to carry out attacks on the continent.

Tunisia

Algeria's Bouteflika is old, but Tunisian President Beji Caid Essebsi is even older. Essebsi was 88 years old when he became Tunisia's second post-revolution president in 2014, and will be 92 years old by the end of 2018. Despite Essebsi's advanced age, however, the question for Tunisia is not what comes next, but how Tunisia can regain its footing from the unexpected political transition in 2011. Tunisia's capacity for political conversation is absorbed by domestic political considerations about the near term.

In the first years after the 2011 Jasmine Revolution, Tunisia was justifiably focused on its immediate future. It needed to figure out how to stitch Tunisia back together again after the deliberately divisive policies of ousted president Zine-el-Abidine Ben Ali. Tunisia needed to determine how to reconcile with the country's past and how to accommodate (or not) members of the previous venal and kleptocratic government. Simultaneous to these debates that cut to the core of what Tunisia was and could be, the country was also grappling with an unprecedented terrorist threat arising from al-Qaeda and Islamic State (also known as ISIS or ISIL) affiliates alike.

From this emerged Essebsi, an experienced political hand who represented safety and stability, which may have just been a euphemism for the old and the familiar. However, seven years after the revolution, Tunisia's leadership is still preoccupied with consolidating its power and not focused on Tunisia's regional role or its relations with its neighbours. Essebsi himself is spending considerable time and effort to position his son Hafedh Caid Essebsi to succeed him.

Tunisia, though, has very real problems that require long-term strategic approaches and not just quick fixes. Like the rest of North Africa, Tunisia faces a youth bulge and unemployment. Dissatisfaction is especially acute in Tunisia's marginal communities, both in the far south and in the west along the border with Algeria. The government has tried to address these communities' grievances by creating employment opportunities and by initiating infrastructure projects. The employment opportunities, however, are not economically sustainable, while the infrastructure projects generally break ground with much pomp, fanfare and goodwill but are rarely seen through to completion. The IMF has warned that Tunisia needs to implement tough reforms or it will face economic ruin, but the government in Tunis is too brittle to heed the IMF's advice and is itself afraid of inciting a second revolution. As a consequence, the government does nothing – neither addressing marginal communities' concerns in a sustainable way nor reforming the economy in a way that will safeguard Tunisia's future. Meanwhile, the country is preparing for presidential elections in 2019. It is expected that Hafedh Caid Essebsi will be a candidate and could possibly inherit the office from his father.

Libya
Libya lacks an effective government, is riven by powerful militias-cum-organised-crime cartels and has been embroiled in an intensifying civil

war over the last four years. The civil war itself seems to be handicapped by the warring parties' lack of strategic vision and their obsession with their zero-sum approach. As a consequence, Libya is fully preoccupied with fluid day-to-day developments, with attempts at strategic planning frequently blindsided by a new development or crisis.

One of the fundamental problems afflicting Libya is its lack of governance. Libyan Prime Minister Fayez al-Sarraj, the head of the UN-backed Government of National Accord (GNA), is unable to project power uniformly throughout Tripoli, Libya's capital, let alone elsewhere in the country. Libya is also suffering from the debilitating slippage between organised crime, armed militias and political figures. Armed militias are increasingly involved in organised crime and form allegiances with political actors who can represent their interests in Libya's different political institutions. These groups have become so entrenched that they are benefiting from the status quo and have very little interest in seeing law and order reimposed. Without law and order, any strategic planning is impossible.

In the east of the country, Sarraj's rule is being challenged by the House of Representatives (HoR), Libya's rump legislature that does not recognise Sarraj's legitimacy. The HoR is allied with the Libyan National Army (LNA) led by Field Marshal Khalifa Haftar. Haftar is intent on defeating his enemies in the east of the country, primarily in Benghazi and Derna, and then launching a campaign to move westward toward Misrata and then Tripoli itself. Although Haftar has said that he is willing to entertain a role in the GNA, he will not accept anything less than head of Libya's armed forces, which many fear he would use as a stepping stone towards a coup. As a result, they are strongly opposed to his inclusion in any national unity government.

Libya also faces a severe threat of terrorism. Although ISIS was ousted from its stronghold in Sirte in 2016, it is gradually reconstituting itself and it will likely regain the capability to attack key institutions and critical infrastructure throughout the country, including in the capital and the all-important Sirte oil basin. Lastly, Libya has become a transit point for sub-Saharan African migrants trying to reach Europe. The scale of human trafficking in Libya and the number of migrants dying off the Libyan coast has become a humanitarian crisis and has complicated Libya's diplomatic relations with Europe, quickly making Libya a pariah country.

The only institution in Libya that functions both as it should and at a national level is the National Oil Corporation (NOC), but even the NOC's ability to maintain operations throughout the country and plan for the future is regularly challenged by terrorist organisations such as ISIS; violent non-state actors such as the rogue Petroleum Facilities Guard leader Ibrahim Jadhran; or other coalitions of Libyan militias, such as Haftar's LNA, that are fighting for power. NOC Chairman Mustafa Sanalla has repeatedly said that Libya could produce up to 2m barrels per day (b/d), but he has been unable to implement any plans that would get Libya to those levels and the production remains stagnant, vacillating between 500,000 b/d and 1m b/d.

In short, Libya is lurching from one domestic crisis to the next and is struggling to devise a viable path towards domestic political stability. This leaves no time and no inclination for longer-term strategic thinking. The question is not how Libya would like to position itself vis-à-vis its neighbours on both the southern and northern shores of the Mediterranean over the next three to five years, but whether there will be a Libya in the next three to five years. Haftar's threat in July 2018 to market oil from terminals under his control and without the involvement of the National Oil Corporation in Tripoli was the first real indication that Libya could be heading toward permanent fracture and not just state failure. Although Haftar ultimately acquiesced, the potential for Libya to split in two remains. Alternatively, Libya could disintegrate into fiefdoms controlled by militias-cum-organised-crime cartels.

In sum, the Maghreb's vision problem is a leadership problem. Morocco has an absentee king, Algeria an absentee president. Tunisia's own president is preoccupied with orchestrating a handover to his son, and Libya's leaders are at war with one another. In the absence of leadership, political elites are jockeying for immediate influence and are not engaged with planning for their countries' futures.

The risk is that even as the Maghreb countries drift leaderless, powerful dynamics are stirring – economic stagnation, dissatisfied youth, strained relations with Europe and an ever-present threat of terrorism – that may jeopardise their stability, such as it is. The problem is compounded by the fact that there are no easy solutions to the Maghreb's leadership deficit. King Mohammed VI's son, Moulay Hassan, is only 15 years old and would not be able to rule for another three years. In Algeria, no one knows who Bouteflika's successor will be. In Tunisia, Essebsi's apparent plans to transfer power to his son would leave Tunisia's leadership without any popular legitimacy. In Libya, there is no leader currently capable of uniting the country, and neither is one likely to emerge. From a strategic perspective, North Africa is very much in danger.

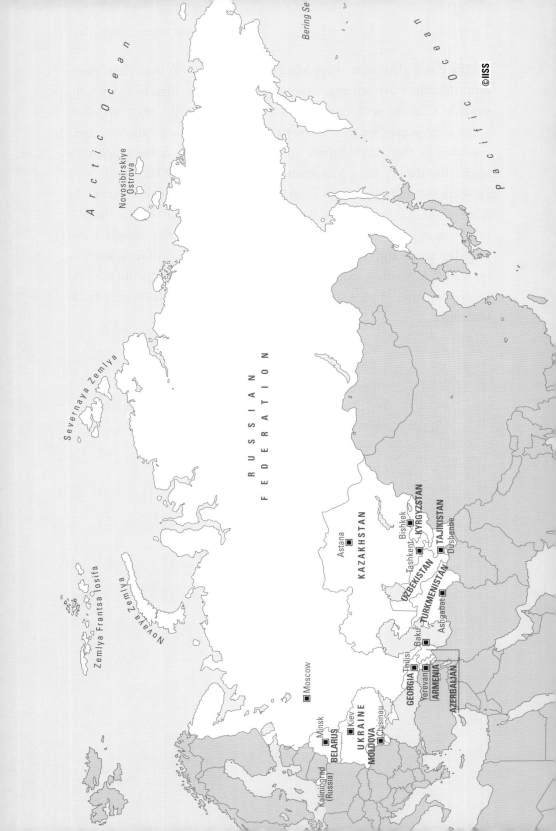

Chapter 8

Russia and Eurasia

2017–18 Review

The structural crisis in Russia's relations with the West showed few signs of easing in 2017–18, and remained the key determinant of Russia's foreign policy. The ongoing trade war between Russia and the West continued to push Russia in the direction of a mobilisation economy, with a strong emphasis on import substitution, state control of strategic industries and increasingly ambitious efforts to develop a parallel financial and trade architecture outside the dollar system. During *Zapad 2017* – a major military exercise in western Russia – Moscow continued the practice of role-playing a conflict with a coalition of NATO members backed by the US over Belarus, although the scale of the exercises, which involved around 40,000 servicemen, was more modest than some observers had anticipated.

US President Donald Trump continued to make the case for re-engagement with the Kremlin, calling in June 2018 for Russia to be readmitted to the G8. However, bilateral relations remained highly adversarial. The position of much of the US establishment has been hardened by the Special Counsel investigation into Russian interference in the 2016 US presidential election. In August 2017, Trump reluctantly signed the Countering America's Adversaries Through

Sanctions Act, which wrote existing sectoral sanctions on Russia into law (making them very difficult to rescind) and opening the way for further sanctions on the defence and energy sectors, including Russian export-pipeline projects. Russian Prime Minister Dmitry Medvedev responded that the bill had ended any hope of an improvement in US–Russia relations, and the Kremlin subsequently ordered a sharp reduction in the number of US diplomatic personnel in Russia. In April 2018, the US Treasury placed far-reaching sanctions on the assets of 17 senior Russian officials and several leading Russian businessmen, temporarily halting the operations of Rusal, the second-largest aluminium producer in the world. In August, US senators introduced a new sanctions bill, which if adopted could place restrictions on investing in new Russian sovereign debt. This would mark a further escalation of US sanctions policy.

The crisis in Russia's relations with the West deepened further in March 2018, after the UK government accused the Russian authorities of poisoning Sergei Skripal, a former Russian military-intelligence officer, and his daughter, Yulia, in the British city of Salisbury using the nerve agent Novichok. The gravity of the attack prompted a strong show of solidarity from Western states, many of which joined the United Kingdom in expelling Russian diplomats. The motivation for Russia's actions – effectively a chemical attack by Russia on a NATO member – remains unclear. The attack came just prior to Russia's presidential elections – a time when the Russian establishment is assumed to be focused on maintaining stability. The UK's position, evidently supported by its allies, was that the attack was either directly sponsored by the state or the result of gross negligence on the part of the Russian authorities to enable a non-state actor to obtain the agent.

The attack fits within the Kremlin's broader framing of its relations with the West as an ongoing and highly antagonistic geopolitical struggle fought across many dimensions. Given its relative economic weakness, the Russian establishment has resorted to asymmetric and unconventional means to respond to Western pressure. As with the cyber attack on the US Democratic Party, the Russian leadership has flatly rejected

UK allegations of complicity, limiting the potential for dialogue. At the same time, the linkage between Russian actions and US sanctions has also become blurred and the preconditions for an easing of sanctions are unclear. There thus seems little prospect that Russia and the West can escape the logic of confrontation in the near future.

Nevertheless, the Trump presidency has presented new diplomatic openings for Moscow. In mid-July 2018, a long-awaited bilateral summit between Trump and Putin took place in Helsinki. For Moscow, this was a welcome acknowledgement that the diplomatic isolation imposed by the Obama administration had effectively ended. However, the summit brought no immediate progress on key areas of contention, including the conflicts in Ukraine and the US withdrawal from the Iran deal. The Russian Ministry of Defence subsequently briefed that it was ready to start negotiations with the US on extension of the new Strategic Nuclear Arms Reduction Treaty beyond 2021, but it is unclear if Trump will be willing to engage with Russian concerns over developments in US conventional capacity, and the implications for Russia's strategic deterrent. The White House's expanding trade war with China over the past year may give new impetus to Russia's pivot towards Asia, and in particular for Russian energy giant Gazprom to further expand gas exports. Despite warm bilateral ties, Russia has struggled to deepen its economic and financial ties with China. In May 2018, a US$9 billion deal to sell a stake in Rosneft to China's CEFC China Energy collapsed.

Putin also sought to use the Helsinki summit to re-engage the US over Syria by positioning Russia as the only actor able to engage with Syria and Iran over Israel's security concerns. Russia was at the centre of intensive diplomacy in the first half of 2018 over the status of forces in the territory bordering the Israeli-occupied Golan Heights. Russia's Syria policy continued to adhere to three main principles: unambiguous support for the government in Damascus; a relatively small military footprint (military analysts at IHS Jane's estimate the cost of the conflict at US$4 million a day, which the Russian budget can easily absorb); and a policy of engaging with all external powers involved in the conflict. As a result, the Kremlin has drawn diplomatic dividends from the intractability of the conflict, establishing itself as a mutually acceptable middleman between all the external powers.

The Kremlin has also had modest success in pushing forward proposals for a political resolution of the crisis. Conflict management has broadly advanced according to the blueprint set out by Moscow through the creation of de-escalation zones, the fourth of which, around the opposition-controlled Syrian city of Idlib, was agreed with Turkey and Iran at a meeting in Astana, the Kazakh capital, in September 2017. In December 2017, Putin made a surprise visit to the Russian-controlled Hmeimim air base in Latakia province, where he announced that 'the conditions for a political solution under the auspices of the United Nations have been created', and ordered the withdrawal of Russian forces. This was not the first time Putin had announced such a withdrawal, with no appreciable impact on troop numbers. Nevertheless, it signalled Moscow's confidence that the conflict has entered a new stage in which negotiations could move forward over a political deal involving greater dialogue on reconstruction, humanitarian aid and constitutional reform. During a visit to the southern Russian city of Sochi in May 2018, Russia finally secured President Bashar al-Assad's agreement to form a committee to rewrite Syria's constitution.

The establishment of the de-escalation zones has in fact led to an increase in Russia's military footprint in the country. Having largely fought the campaign from the air in support of the Syrian government and Iranian infantry, Moscow has expanded its use of military police to maintain order in the de-escalation zones. In late July 2017, Russian Minister of Defence Sergei Shoigu confirmed that four battalions of military police, largely recruited from Chechnya and Ingushetia, had been deployed in Syria. This marks the first time the military police, which were established in 2011, have been used abroad. In October 2017, the Collective Security Treaty Organisation (CSTO) conducted a training operation for a peacekeeping deployment in Syria. In November, the head of the Russian-led military bloc said that it was ready to deploy peacekeepers to the country. If realised, this would be a significant precedent for the organisation, although the other member states –

Kazakhstan, Kyrgyzstan, Belarus and Armenia – have yet to publicly endorse the plan. Russia's ground deployments are nevertheless likely to remain modest, and the Kremlin has not made a serious attempt to improve governance in the de-escalation zones.

Russia's expanded interests in the Middle East may have encouraged the Kremlin to give greater attention to stabilising its southern flank. To this end, in June 2018 the Russian government approved a draft convention on the legal status of the Caspian Sea with the four other littoral states. Under the agreement, military vessels of non-littoral states will be forbidden from accessing Caspian waters, entrenching Russia's dominance of the sea. During the Syria conflict, Russia has experimented with power projection from the Caspian, firing rockets at targets in Syria from its Caspian fleet. Agreement on the sea's legal status could in theory enable the construction of a trans-Caspian pipeline to carry gas from Turkmenistan to Azerbaijan and on to Turkey and Europe through the Southern Gas Corridor. However, Russian media reports suggest that other littoral states will retain the right to assess the environmental impact of pipeline plans, giving Russia a mechanism to delay and potentially veto any future projects. In any case, the financial obstacles to the realisation of such a project remain formidable, and extensive investment would also be required into Turkmenistan's gas sector. The Kremlin appears to be willing to accept the highly contingent risk to Gazprom's exports for the sake of greater stability on its borders.

The Kremlin has also adopted a more innovative diplomatic approach to the conflict in eastern Ukraine over the past year. The basic contours of this conflict were set following the signing of the Minsk II accord in February 2015. This ended a period of high-intensity fighting but has so far failed to lead to a political settlement. The line of contact remains heavily militarised and there are almost daily violations of the peace agreement involving both gunfire and artillery. Efforts to renew the ceasefire, the most recent one agreed on 1 July, have broken down within days. According to the Organisation for Security and Cooperation in Europe (OSCE) Special Monitoring Mission to Ukraine, more than 160 people were killed in the first seven months of 2018. More than 10,000 people have died since the conflict began in April 2014.

In September 2017, Vladimir Putin unexpectedly put forward a draft Security Council resolution for the deployment of an international UN peacekeeping mission to Donbas. Russia has proposed a narrow mandate for the mission to protect the OSCE monitoring mission along the line of contact. In early 2018, a counter-proposal commissioned by the Ukrainian government proposed a UN force of around 20,000 to be deployed across the Donbas region and along the international border with Russia. Proposals for a UN force were discussed at foreign-minister level by the Normandy Four (Ukraine, Russia, France and Germany) in June 2018. The mandate dispute is unlikely to be resolved as it reproduces the fundamental disagreement over the sequencing of the Minsk peace deal. Ukraine insists the political process to reintegrate the Donbas cannot begin until it has control of its border, while Russia first seeks constitutional reform to embed pro-Russian forces in Ukraine's political system.

The Russian démarche is nevertheless significant. This was the first time in the post-Soviet period that Russia has proposed the deployment of an international UN peacekeeping force in a neighbouring country. It also indicates that Russia is still seeking a political resolution to the conflict, although its current terms remain unacceptable to the Ukrainian side. Putin's meeting with Trump in Helsinki in July 2018 provided further evidence that Russia is seeking a political route out of the impasse. Following the summit, Western and Russian media reported that Putin had proposed to the US president that a referendum be held on the status of Donbas.

Domestically, Ukraine continued to make limited but uneven progress on domestic reform under heavy pressure from outside sponsors. The economy continued to stage a weak recovery from the severe recession of 2014–16, although the country's macroeconomic foundations remain weak. The IMF has dispersed only US$9bn of a US$17.5bn financing package that is due to expire in March 2019. It has delayed release of the fifth tranche of the package, originally due in July 2017, because of slow progress on reform, and in particular the establishment of an anti-corruption court. The law to establish the court was finally adopted in June 2018, but had to be amended in July in response to IMF concerns. Polling suggests that Petro Poroshenko is unlikely to be re-elected as president, with former prime minister Yulia Tymoshenko consistently topping the polls. Her election would be likely to lead to a continuation of the existing oligarchic system of governance.

The Ukrainian government achieved several foreign-policy successes over the past year. In December 2017, the US government confirmed the direct supply of lethal-defence hardware to Ukraine for the first time, including anti-tank *Javelin* missiles. The supplies make no meaningful difference to the military balance but will have calmed concerns in Kiev that the Trump administration could seek to reach an accommodation with Russia on the Donbas conflict over the heads of the Ukrainian government. At the Arbitration Institute of the Stockholm Chamber of Commerce, a long-standing dispute over the 2009 gas contract between Ukraine's Naftogaz and Russia's Gazprom was decided largely in the Ukrainians' favour. The Trump administration has also set itself against the expansion of the Nord Stream II gas pipeline, threatening to impose sanctions on Western firms involved in the project. Construction of the pipeline, which would significantly reduce Gazprom's reliance on transit through Ukraine, has been delayed. At the same time, Gazprom's gas sales to Europe reached record levels in 2018. This has put Naftogaz in a stronger position to conclude a new transit agreement with Gazprom from 2019, when the current ten-year deal expires. However, Gazprom's reluctance to accept the judgments of the Stockholm arbitration suggests that the negotiations will be fraught. Given the broader crisis in bilateral relations, there is a risk of brinkmanship or a breakdown in talks, leading to an energy-supply crisis in early 2019.

Elsewhere in Eurasia, the most dramatic geopolitical development took place in Armenia in April–May, where a popular uprising led to the overthrow of the government. Towards the end of his second and final presidential term, Serzh Sargsyan had sought to maintain his grip on power through constitutional reform to transfer substantial powers to the prime minister's office. His decision to take up the prime ministership in April, in defiance of earlier promises, provoked mass street protests. After clinging to power for a week, Sargsyan stepped down – a rare case of a Eurasian leader bowing to popular pressure – allowing for a peaceful transition of power to a movement led by the opposition leader Nikol Pashinyan. In contrast to the 2014 Maidan Revolution in Ukraine, Russia quickly accepted the legitimacy of the new government, and Putin received Pashinyan in Sochi in mid-May. The new prime minister, for his part, reaffirmed Armenia's commitment to close military and economic ties with Russia. However, bilateral relations may yet become strained by the arrest of Yuri Khachaturov, the Armenian head of the CSTO, as part of a new investigation into the violent crackdown on protesters following the presidential election in March 2008.

Russia and Eurasia: Drivers of Strategic Change

- Western economic sanctions are prompting Russia's government to push the economy towards a mobilisation model, with a strong emphasis on import substitution, state control of strategic industries and efforts to build a financial and trade architecture beyond the reach of the United States.

- Russia's political elite views itself as locked into an antagonistic struggle with the West across many dimensions; it seeks to offset the power imbalance by using asymmetric and unconventional responses on its periphery and deep within Western states.

- Russia is positioning itself as the indispensable power in the resolution of the Syrian conflict, given its ties to Damascus, Iran, Turkey and Israel. Its military footprint in Syria has increased somewhat.

- Ukraine's economy has stabilised after years of recession but its reform progress has been halting. The oligarchic political system, which seemed mortally imperilled in 2014, has proven resilient, but popular sympathy for Russia has largely evaporated since the annexation of Crimea and the start of the conflict in Donbas.

- Extra-constitutional change in Armenia has highlighted the brittle nature of some governments in the former Soviet Union, but in Yerevan's case the power shift is unlikely to have geopolitical ramifications as the country remains closely tied to Russia militarily and economically.

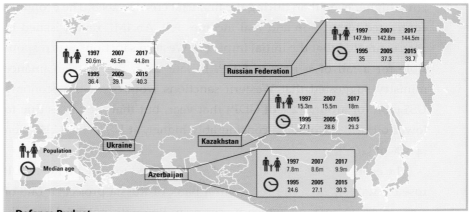

Russian Federation

	1997	2007	2017
	147.9m	142.8m	144.5m
	1995	2005	2015
	35	37.3	38.7

Ukraine

	1997	2007	2017
	50.6m	46.5m	44.8m
	1995	2005	2015
	36.4	39.1	40.3

Kazakhstan

	1997	2007	2017
	15.3m	15.5m	18m
	1995	2005	2015
	27.1	28.6	29.3

Azerbaijan

	1997	2007	2017
	7.8m	8.6m	9.9m
	1995	2005	2015
	24.6	27.1	30.3

Population
Median age

Defence Budget
(US$, constant 2010 prices)

	2008	2013	2018
Azerbaijan	$1.50bn	$1.48bn	$2.04bn
Kazakhstan	$1.35bn	$1.71bn	$1.78bn
Russian Federation	$39.92bn	$52.33bn	$55.46bn
Ukraine	$1.89bn	$1.93bn	$3.49bn

A soldier walks past the national flags of the Shanghai Cooperation Organisation member states during the *Peace Mission 2018* joint counter-terrorism exercises

GDP per capita, Purchasing Power Parity (International $, constant 2011 prices)

Country	GDP
1997	
Azerbaijan	$3,488
Kazakhstan	$8,732
Russian Federation	$12,564
Ukraine	$4,497
2007	
Azerbaijan	$13,243
Kazakhstan	$18,885
Russian Federation	$22,799
Ukraine	$8,497
2017	
Azerbaijan	$15,847
Kazakhstan	$24,056
Russian Federation	$24,766
Ukraine	$7,894

Sources: IISS; UN Department of Economic and Social Affairs (Population Division, 2017); World Bank

Russia's Sanctioned Economy and Putin

Russia's economy has endured considerable turbulence since 2014, when a combination of a sharp drop in the price of oil and other Russian export commodities and the effect of Western sanctions (imposed because of Russia's annexation of Crimea and role in the conflict in eastern Ukraine) had a severe impact. The rouble collapsed, losing around 40% of its value against the dollar over the course of 2014; inflation almost doubled from 6.5% year-on-year in 2013 to 11.4% in 2014; and capital flight spiked from US$61 billion in 2013 to US$151.5bn in 2014, higher even than during the financial crisis in 2008. The economy contracted in 2015–16 and real incomes fell. An IMF report issued in 2015 estimated that the initial impact of Western sanctions was responsible for a fall of 1–1.5% in GDP. In late 2014, the Russian finance ministry suggested that Western sanctions would cost the economy US$40bn (or around 2% of GDP) that year, but that the losses due to lower oil prices would be considerably higher, at US$90bn–US$100bn (4–5% of GDP).

The economy has since stabilised and returned to growth. Real GDP rose by 1.5% in 2017 and the Central Bank of Russia projects a rate of 1.5% to 2% in 2018–20, which it sees as in line with potential growth. However, growth remains weak for an economy at Russia's stage of development, particularly in the context of a robust global economic performance. This weakness is due in large part to other factors beyond sanctions. Growth had already slowed to 1.3% in 2013 before sanctions were imposed, reflecting the end of the commodities super-cycle and structural weaknesses in the Russian economy.

A key reason for Russia's persistent relative economic underperformance has been lacklustre investment (both domestic and foreign), which is discouraged by the weak rule of law. Gross fixed investment has been in the range of 21–22% of GDP for most of the past decade. This compares to rates typically of around 25–30% (or even higher) for fast-growing Asian emerging economies. In 2015, Russia's ratio of fixed investment to GDP slipped further to 20.7%.

Western sanctions have deterred foreign investment, in part because of the uncertainty and reputational risks for Western firms. Data from the Central Bank of Russia indicates that net foreign direct investment (FDI) inflows collapsed from US$69bn in 2013 to US$22bn in 2014 and just US$7bn in 2015, before recovering somewhat to US$33bn in 2016 and US$28bn in 2017. The decline was mainly due to European countries, which traditionally have been Russia's main source of FDI. Russian hopes that investment from other sources – primarily Asia – would compensate have not been realised. Apart from a spike in 2016 due to the part-privatisation of Rosneft (for US$11bn to a Singapore-registered investment vehicle), net FDI inflows from Asia have continued barely to exceed US$2bn annually.

Another factor in Russia's prolonged economic underperformance has been the weakness of competition, which import-substitution programmes and protectionist measures in response to Western sanctions will only exacerbate. Russia's attempts to develop the Eurasian Economic Union (EEU) as a Russian-dominated economic bloc to rival the EU do not appear in practice to amount to very much in economic terms.

The sectoral impact of sanctions

Sanctions by the US and its allies focused on three sectors of the economy: defence, finance and energy. In the defence industry, Ukraine cut all ties to Russia in the wake of the annexation of Crimea, breaking supply chains that had been built over decades. The US prohibited the sale of military and dual-use components to Russia, and the EU adopted similar measures. Western sanctions denied Russia some important platforms, such as the *Mistral*-class amphibious assault ship and Italian armoured vehicles. Perhaps more importantly, the loss of access to Western-made components affected many of Russia's defence enterprises. The country's shipbuilding programme, for example, suffered delays because of its inability to import Ukrainian engines. Other planned procurements had to be delayed or the size of orders reduced.

The Russian policy response was multifaceted. A government commission was established to promote self-sufficiency. The state dramatically increased credits and guarantees to the defence industry, and increased the size of the defence order. Funds were allocated not only to purchase equipment, but also to retool manufacturing capacity. To ensure that weapons could be procured while industry retooled, there was a significant push to import components from Asia as a substitute for Western states.

Although some of the initial targets for greater self-sufficiency have been revised, definite progress has been made. Special financial vehicles have been created to fund sanctioned defence enterprises, and more and more commercial data is being made secret to frustrate the enforcement of sanctions. The result of all these measures is a defence industry that may lack the sophistication of its Western counterparts, but is less reliant on Western inputs and still able to meet the needs of the armed forces.

Financial-sector sanctions had the greatest initial impact, restricting access to Western capital markets for named Russian companies and individuals. (Russia's dependence on Western capital markets since the 1990s has rendered the economy particularly vulnerable to this measure.) Russia's five largest banks – accounting for nearly 60% of the sector by assets – were effectively shut off from Western financial markets from mid-2014 onwards, necessitating a succession of government bailouts totalling 1 trillion roubles (US$16.5bn) in December 2014. The long-standing weaknesses of the Russian banking sector also played a key role in the crisis, as did the decline in oil prices and the fall in the rouble, both of which put pressure on borrowers. However, sanctions were also an important factor.

Although the sector has broadly stabilised, sanctions are contributing to ongoing difficulties. Three more major banks had to be bailed out by the government in 2017 and foreign financing remains limited, contributing to the continued weakness of investment in the economy. According to data from the Bank for International Settlements (BIS), the total lending of foreign banks to Russia was US$122bn at the beginning of 2018, down by more than half since the beginning of 2014.

Beyond the successful launch of a domestic payment system (Karta Mir) to rival Visa and Mastercard, there has been little progress on developing ways to allow the economy to detach itself from the international financial system in order to boost resilience to any future deepening of sanctions. International sovereign-bond issues, for instance, continue to rely on the global eurobond market.

The third sector targeted by the EU and US was the energy sector, which is the backbone of Russia's economy. In July 2014, restrictions were placed on the export or sale of technology for use in deep-water exploration, Arctic exploration or unconventional (shale) production. A further prohibition on oil-sector services for these projects followed soon afterwards, although it is notable that the sanctions did not seek to harm current oil and gas production.

Russia's energy sector showed few ill effects. Investment remained robust and Russian oil companies were able to deploy advanced technology to boost the productivity of existing wells. Oil production has been increasing steadily, reaching a 30-year high of 10.98 million barrels per day (b/d) in 2017, while gas production also hit a record level of 650bn cubic metres. Russia has also been able to progress with important new gas pipelines to Germany and China, both due for completion in 2019. These new pipelines will, respectively, diversify its supply routes to Western Europe and allow it to access the Chinese market, although Russia's need for a good strategic relationship with China in light of poor relations with the West helped the Chinese to drive a hard bargain on pricing in the 30-year supply deal worth US$400bn struck in May 2014.

However, the sanctions were designed to slowly strangle the energy sector's growth potential, rather than to trigger a short-term crisis. A key question for the Russian oil and gas industry remains what will happen in the longer term as Soviet-era fields run dry. The deals with Western oil majors to develop deposits in the Arctic and to unlock the country's shale potential were made with an eye on sustaining oil production at above 10m b/d to 2030 and beyond. Russia's 'Energy Strategy of the Russian Federation until 2035', for instance, forecast that oil production in Eastern Siberia and the Russian Far East would reach 20% of the total by 2035, compared with just 3% in 2008. Sanctions have largely ended cooperation with Western firms on Arctic, deep-water and shale-oil projects.

The main exceptions have been for liquefied natural gas (LNG), which is not directly sanctioned. The US$27bn Yamal project – Russia's giant LNG plant on the Yamal Peninsula in the Arctic Circle – came into operation in late 2017, benefiting from US$12bn in Chinese funding and from continued participation by France's energy company Total. (Total has also taken a 10% stake in another Arctic LNG project, the US$25bn LNG 2.) ExxonMobil, meanwhile, is going ahead with a US$15bn LNG project in the Russian Far East in collaboration with Rosneft (although new US sanctions might yet force it to reconsider). Such projects boost Russia's ambition to catch up with leading global LNG producers.

However, the restrictions on the oil sector matter more. Oil is a much bigger exporter earner, and tax generator, than gas for Russia. Combined, the two contribute roughly one-third of federal tax receipts, but four-fifths of that total is attributable to taxes on the extraction and export of oil and oil products. A 2018 analysis of the likely impact of sanctions on the oil sector by Tatiana Mitrova and her colleagues at the Skolkovo School of Management's Energy Centre forecast that oil output would rise from 550m tonnes in 2016 to 580m tonnes in 2020, but that sanctions-related delays in the development of new deposits would result in output falling to 540m tonnes in 2025 and 480m tonnes in 2030. The study also cautioned that further sanctions, coupled with tighter enforcement, would result in deeper production cuts, to 505m tonnes in 2025 and 245m tonnes in 2030. The difference in the forecasts for 2030 amounts to just over 1m b/d.

In April 2018, the US imposed further sanctions on Russia as punishment for its alleged interference in elections in the US and certain European states. The sanctions were targeted at 24 individuals and 14 companies, completely excluding them from the dollar financial system – a move that made it difficult for those sanctioned to continue operating internationally. Oleg Deripaska, for instance, was forced to cede ownership of Rusal. The measures had a pronounced impact on the rouble and Russian stocks – the rouble fell 10% against the dollar and the RTS index lost 12% in just a few days after the announcement of the sanctions.

Further US sanctions are pending in response to Russia's alleged use of the military-grade nerve agent Novichok in the UK in March. The US State Department announced targeted new measures in August (including on exports of technologies with military applications) and threatened broader measures (including a non-food trade embargo). The US Congress is also considering whether to prohibit dealings with Russian state-owned banks and purchases of new Russian sovereign-debt issuances. However, it is unclear which of these measures will pass. The US Treasury Department warned in February 2018 that sanctioning Russian sovereign debt would risk triggering broader financial instability.

The spectre of stagnation

The Russian economy is more resilient than it was in 2014: foreign-currency debt has fallen considerably; public debt is very low (only 13% of GDP at end-2017); the shift to a free-float for the rouble provides an important shock absorber; and still-large foreign-exchange reserves (at US\$457bn in June 2018, close to their level before sanctions were first imposed) continue to give the government scope to offset the impact of sanctions as needed. Most importantly, the oil price has rebounded markedly since mid-2017.

However, the imposition of sanctions and the authorities' policy response have compounded Russia's problems of weak investment and competition, and will hinder economic modernisation. The growth model that served Russian President Vladimir Putin so well in the 2000s had reached the point of near-exhaustion even before oil prices fell in 2014, and few economists predict GDP growth will exceed a modest 2% in the coming years. This compares poorly with the high single-digit growth rates posted during Putin's first two presidential terms from 2000–08.

Already, the signs of strain on the Russian population are apparent. Real incomes did not fall during the deep but brief 2009 recession. However, the doubling of the rouble's exchange rate to the dollar between mid-2014 and the end of 2015 drove inflation, and real incomes have fallen considerably since 2014. Household consumption started to recover in 2017, but was still only at the level of 2012. Some 19.3m Russians (13.2% of the population) lived below the poverty line in 2017, up from 16m in 2014. An estimated four out of ten families cannot always afford food. Strong growth in payday loans and credit-card debt suggest that households are still struggling to make ends meet.

Putin has consistently been a fiscal conservative, wary of running sizeable government deficits and being in hock to foreign lenders. Thus when the economy suffered a downturn in 2014 and sanctions hit the energy, finance and defence sectors, Putin responded by bailing out the banks and boosting funding for the defence sector, but to offset these spending increases, he cut the budgets for education and healthcare. Although the government has avoided triggering mass protests, social unrest has increased. There were 409 labour protests in 2015 – representing a 40% jump from the previous record high in 2014 – due to layoffs, wage cuts and salary arrears, as well as the imposition of new taxes and charges. The number of protests annually has subsequently stabilised at around this new level. Protests on local issues such as social services, housing, transport and employment have also risen steeply since 2014, according to a report in November 2017 by former finance minister Alexei Kudrin's Committee on Civil Initiatives. Few if any of these protests are reported on the federal television channels from which most of the population get their news and, in contrast to 2011–12, most of them are located far from Moscow and St Petersburg.

In July 2018, Levada-Center (Russia's foremost polling agency) reported that 41% of respondents thought protests over economic challenges were likely and 28% said they would be willing to participate; the corresponding numbers in the March 2018 survey had been 17% and 8%. This indicates that while Russians seem able to accept a certain amount of economic hardship in return for stability and security, their tolerance is not limitless.

By mid-2018, increased discontent even affected Putin's popularity rating. In January 2014, before the Ukraine crisis, 65% of respondents approved of his performance and 34% disapproved. By mid-2014 his approval rating was in the mid-80s and it remained there to the end of 2017. Even as recently as April 2018, 82% approved of his performance and just 17% disapproved. Yet in July, his approval rating fell to 67% and 32% of respondents disapproved of his performance, appearing to signal that the 'Crimea effect' had dissipated.

The proximate cause of Putin's poll decline was government proposals to reform pensions and increase the rate of value-added tax from 18% to 20%. The planned changes would progressively raise the pension age from 60 to 65 for men and from 55 to 63 for women. They have proven hugely unpopular (which would be the case anywhere, but it was especially controversial because life expectancy for men in Russia is just 66 years). Thousands have protested across the country, and the changes were probably behind a sudden sharp swing in responses to polling firm Levada-Center's monthly question on whether the country is moving in the right direction – positive responses slumped from 56% in May 2018 to 46% in June, and negative responses jumped from 27% to 42%, with only a slight rebound in July.

Policy responses

Past experience would suggest that the Kremlin will probably delay or dilute the pension changes, although there are also signs that the regime is readying itself to crush protests if necessary. The formation of a 350,000-strong National Guard in 2016 under the leadership of Putin's former bodyguard Viktor Zolotov was partly a response to the perceived threat of a popular uprising.

Putin is aware of the continuing impact of the 2015–16 recession on the population. Before and after his re-election as president in March 2018, he promised to boost social spending and create millions of well-paid, high-tech jobs. (He made similar pledges regarding jobs around the time of the 2012 election as well.) However, his unwillingness to raise budgetary spending (financed either through borrowing or tax rises) or to undertake structural reforms to improve the business environment have made it all but impossible for these electoral pledges to become policy.

The relatively gloomy economic picture and multiple signs of popular discontent have prompted some analysts to speculate that the Kremlin might seek to provoke a crisis in Europe or elsewhere to distract the population. They point to the surge in the authorities' popularity after the annexation of Crimea and the subsequent decision to intervene decisively in Syria's civil war as examples of Putin's propensity to engage in population-distracting adventurism.

However, only the Crimea case properly captured the popular imagination in Russia, and Crimea should be considered *sui generis* because of the peninsula's role in Russian history, its majority Russian population, the presence of the Russian Black Sea Fleet and the particular circumstances in which it was gifted to Ukraine by Nikita Khrushchev in the 1950s. The Syria intervention, by contrast, made little difference to the poll rating of the authorities, and the same is true of Russia's intervention in eastern Ukraine. Both these ongoing conflicts barely touch on the Russian public consciousness (and Putin has been careful to ensure this remains the case by using private military contractors and, in the case of Syria, relying mainly on airpower). In other words, neither conflict serves a domestic purpose such as bolstering support for the authorities.

Indeed, now that socio-economic concerns are coming to the fore, the Kremlin's foreign-policy choices are beginning to cause irritation. According to Levada-Center's polling, in March 2016 some 22% of respondents supported Putin's foreign policy and regarded it as a 'plus', but by July 2018, only 16% of respondents felt the same way.

Russia is potentially a threat to some NATO states and has shown a willingness to project force in the Middle East. Yet the trigger for such actions has not been the domestic socio-economic situation. It is worth recalling that the 2008 military intervention in Georgia occurred at a time when Russia was posting GDP growth of around 8%, the oil price was over US$100 per barrel and real incomes were rising steadily. Russia's use of force since 2008 has been directed to achieve limited political objectives; it had the ability to escalate in eastern Ukraine in 2014 and 2015, but chose not to do so (perhaps in part because of the deterrent impact of Western sanctions, which were strengthened greatly after a Malaysia Airlines plane was shot down over eastern Ukraine on 17 July 2014).

Conversely, it is difficult to imagine that a return to vigorous economic growth would lead to a fundamental change in the Kremlin's world view. Indeed, the imposition of sanctions in 2014 and their expansion thereafter has reinforced a perception that Western states (principally the US) are hostile towards Russia and seek to contain it, weaken it and, if possible, change the government. This perception certainly has an effect on Russia's external behaviour. Vladislav Surkov, a long-serving Putin adviser with literary inclinations, wrote in April 2018 that Russia's four-century effort to integrate with the West came to an end with the Ukraine crisis and that the country now faced '100 years of solitude'; this would not amount to isolation, he added, but it would mean the country was more inward-looking and focused on the East.

Sanctions have supported this shift. They have put into reverse a 25-year process of integrating Russia with Western economies. Russian companies have delisted from Western exchanges, Western credits to Russian corporations have contracted and trade has been reduced by sanctions. Russian policy has taken a turn towards statism and opacity, with efforts under way to de-offshore and de-dollarise the economy. Between April and May 2018, Russia reduced its holdings of US government securities from US\$96bn to US\$15bn. These may be the first steps towards refashioning the economy in ways that will reduce dependence on the West. With its attendant economic costs and political benefits for the Kremlin, this would be a strategically significant development.

Russia's Influence in the Former Soviet Space

There has long been a consensus among the Russian leadership that the post-Soviet region is, in the words of then-president Dmitry Medvedev in 2008, an area of 'privileged interests'. Russia's determination to dominate the post-Soviet space is motivated above all by deep-seated security concerns and a desire to maintain stability on its borders. The advance of Euro-Atlantic institutions to Russia's borders is seen not simply as a challenge to regional influence, but also as an existential threat. In 2015, Nikolai Patrushev, the head of the Russian security council, summed up the Russian view of the revolution in Ukraine: 'Through events in Ukraine the Americans are trying to draw the Russian Federation into an inter-state military conflict, overthrow our government and ultimately break up our country.'

Russia's framing of the region has developed in response to its changing relations with the West. As relations have evolved from potential partnership to open confrontation, Russia has increasingly positioned itself in opposition to the West – not just as a major power in the international system, but as the centre of a civilisational alternative. The Kremlin has sought to establish a distinctive political, normative and economic community in the post-Soviet space, built around a Russian core. This is framed both as a Russia-centric community – the 'Russian world' – and as a formal bloc within the framework of the Eurasian Economic Union (EEU), which is intended to function as a counterpoint to the European Union.

Despite talk of the return of 'global Russia', and notwithstanding the annexation of Crimea, Moscow's policy in its immediate neighbourhood remains fundamentally defensive in nature and reliant on coercive measures. Russia's efforts to develop new models of post-Soviet integration deserve serious attention but face significant strategic challenges. The effectiveness of the EEU is undermined by weak institutions in the member states and Russia's lack of economic dynamism. While Russia seeks to dominate its immediate neighbourhood, it is likely to play a subordinate role to China in the evolution of the international economic system. This poses a long-term challenge to its efforts to shape regional norms.

Russia, the West and the 'common neighbourhood'

The annexation of Crimea in 2014 and military intervention in eastern Ukraine achieved Russia's tactical objectives of securing military assets on the Crimean Peninsula and preventing the consolidation of the Ukrainian state along overtly pro-Western lines. However, Russia's military intervention was also emblematic of the broader strategic failure of Russia's policy towards post-Soviet states in the 'common neighbourhood' with the EU (Armenia, Azerbaijan, Belarus, Georgia, Moldova and Ukraine): in much of this region, Russia now depends heavily on coercive measures to retain influence. In the absence of softer forms of influence, Russia has instrumentalised unresolved territorial conflicts in the post-Soviet space to maintain control. It has provided strong political and material support to the breakaway territories of Transdniestria, South Ossetia and Abkhazia. Russia has also supplied large volumes of arms to both Armenia and Azerbaijan, despite the significant risk of a return to open conflict over the contested territory of Nagorno-Karabakh, which would have devastating consequences for the region. While the Azerbaijani elite have been careful to maintain cordial relations with Moscow, mutual trust is low given Russia's extensive security guarantees to Armenia.

The situation is similar in Ukraine, where as a result of the Donbas conflict Russia has forfeited almost all other mechanisms for maintaining geopolitical leverage. The Ukrainian government has sought to unpick its energy and economic relationship with Russia. Mutual trade embargoes have led to the de-integration of the countries' industrial and defence sectors. Russia has also suffered a series of setbacks in its energy relations with Ukraine, which have traditionally been an important instrument to corrupt and influence the Ukrainian elite. Following a series of major increases in domestic energy prices, Naftogaz, the state-owned Ukrainian gas distributor, has eliminated its chronic losses. From 2015, Naftogaz stopped buying gas directly from Russia's Gazprom, replacing these supplies with 'reverse flows' from Poland and Slovakia.

Russia's preferred resolution of the conflict is the reintegration of the breakaway regions into a loose federal or confederate Ukrainian state. This would effectively institutionalise Russian influence over Ukraine's politics, enabling it to block further integration with NATO or the EU.

This scenario would largely be realised by full implementation of the Minsk II agreement signed by Ukraine in 2015 following a sharp escalation in Russia's military activity. However, constitutional reform to give special status to the breakaway regions is unacceptable to the majority of Ukraine's society and political elite.

The Russian leadership has grounds to hope that the disruption caused to the transatlantic alliance by US President Donald Trump's 'America First' doctrine could create new openings to reassert its influence in Eastern Europe. Trump has consistently advocated an improvement in ties with Russia and has expressed understanding for Russia's annexation of Crimea. He does not appear to acknowledge any US security or economic interests in the region and appears inclined, either implicitly or explicitly, to accept the reality of Russian hegemony in the post-Soviet space. Trump has regularly questioned the value of NATO, and views the EU – and Germany in particular – as at best a competitor and at worst an adversary of the United States.

There is also a significant risk that the EU's engagement with the post-Soviet space will lose momentum. Since 2013, the EU has concluded Association Agreements and far-reaching free-trade deals with Georgia, Moldova and Ukraine. In the long term, these agreements have the potential to fundamentally reorient the economies of these states towards the EU. However, the crisis in transatlantic relations and major internal challenges have removed almost all prospect of further enlargement of the EU to include any post-Soviet states. Without the possibility of EU membership to act as a policy anchor, elites will continue to resist the EU's external governance, and progress on reform and normative convergence will be slow or entirely absent.

In recent years, both Moldova and Georgia have shown signs of a limited political realignment with Russia. Several months after Moldova concluded its Association Agreement with the EU in 2014, a US$1-billion fraud (accounting by some measures for up to 13% of Moldovan GDP) led to the collapse of the country's banking system and a major political crisis. Popular anger at widespread corruption led to the election of a pro-Russian candidate, Igor Dodon, to the largely ceremonial presidency in

2016. He negotiated observer status for Moldova in the EEU and pledged to restore relations with Russia. Russia's relations with Georgia have also improved markedly since Mikheil Saakashvili's United National Movement (ENM) was replaced in 2012 by Georgian Dream, whose patron, the billionaire Bidzina Ivanishvili, has long-standing business ties with Russia. Georgian Dream has nevertheless maintained the country's commitment to transatlantic integration, a stance it reiterated in the Georgia–NATO Commission Declaration at the NATO summit in Brussels in July 2018.

Western engagement with Ukraine has also encountered challenges. The IMF has repeatedly delayed dispersal of the fifth tranche of the Extended Fund Facility (which was originally due to be paid in July 2017) to Ukraine because of lack of progress on structural reforms, and in particular the adoption of a new anti-corruption law (the law was finally adopted in June 2018, and amended under heavy pressure from Ukraine's external sponsors in July). For the broader population, the most obvious benefits of EU integration – visa-free travel – have been achieved; any further economic or political dividends will be incremental at best. There is a significant risk that Ukraine and Moldova have entered a new uneasy equilibrium characterised by weak institutions and low growth.

The sense of strategic drift in the EU and Eastern Europe has given new impetus to Russian diplomacy. In September 2017, Russia put forward a United Nations Security Council draft resolution on the deployment of armed peacekeepers to the Donbas region, the first such mission that Russia has supported in the former Soviet states since the end of the Soviet Union in 1991. The proposal was subsequently discussed at a meeting of the Normandy Four (France, Germany, Russia and Ukraine) in June 2018. Ukraine has not rejected the possibility of a UN mission, but there are fundamental disagreements over the potential mandate. Ukraine has called for the force to be deployed across the Donbas region, including the Ukraine–Russia border. Russia insists that the force should be deployed only on the line of contact between Ukrainian and separatist forces to maintain peace and protect the Organisation for Security and Cooperation in Europe (OSCE) monitoring mission. The divergent proposals effectively reproduce the stalemate over the sequencing and implementation of the Minsk II agreement – Ukraine insists that no steps can be taken towards holding local elections in Donbas in accordance with the agreement until it has re-established control of its international border.

Given the crisis in the transatlantic alliance, it is possible that Russia may also revive proposals for an overhaul of Europe's security architecture. This was last raised by then-president Dmitry Medvedev in 2008, who proposed a new debate on European security and a new all-European security treaty (which would also involve Russia, while diminishing the role of NATO and the US). While the plans were vaguely formulated, they reflected Russia's view that NATO and EU expansion creates new dividing lines that threaten Russia's interests and undermines collective security.

Recent developments appear to support Moscow's contention, regularly repeated in Russian official documents, that the US-led order is in crisis and fundamental shifts are taking place in the international system. However, it remains unclear whether this will evolve in Russia's favour. US policy is running in divergent directions. While Trump as president appears committed to a closer relationship with Russia and a hands-off approach with regards to Ukraine, evidence that Russian intelligence services interfered in the US elections has hardened attitudes towards Russia across much of the US establishment. In late 2017, the Trump administration approved the supply of lethal weaponry to Ukraine, a move his predecessor had consistently refused to make. In April 2018, the US Treasury adopted sanctions against major Russian businessmen and companies.

More broadly, the Kremlin faces the structural challenge that society and elites in post-Soviet states tend to construct notions of statehood and sovereignty in opposition to the former imperial hegemon. Even in Belarus (the country most politically, economically and strategically integrated with Russia), the leadership has undertaken a soft nationalisation project, promoting a culturally distinct Belarusian identity while seeking to diversify international ties and deepen relations with the EU. These processes have been accelerated by the conflict in Ukraine.

The Ukraine crisis also underlined clear deficiencies in Russian officials' understanding of social and political processes in countries that are of paramount concern to the leadership. The Maidan Revolution and overthrow of then Ukrainian president Victor Yanukovych came as a shock to the Russian leadership. Despite the importance of the region, Russian officials' approach to the post-Soviet space is often characterised by complacency. As senior government officials share a common language and cultural codes, little effort is made to study the local language or engage with non-Russian-language history or sources. Russia's soft-power overtures in the post-Soviet space have often appeared crude or counterproductive, focused on mobilising limited constituencies around imperial or Soviet nostalgia, often alienating the broader public. Russian policy is focused on the influencing and suborning of incumbents within informal elite networks – in the case of Ukraine, focused around the gas trade. This elite-focused approach means Russian policymakers are liable to discount broader social developments in the countries concerned. This in turn makes the Russian leadership more inclined to see political protest in post-Soviet states as the product of Western interference, rather than the product of internal factors.

Central Asia and the Caspian

In contrast to Russia's interactions with the West in the post-Soviet region, Russia and China have successfully managed their interaction in Central Asia to minimise the risk of conflict. Both countries have a strong interest in maintaining a positive bilateral relationship; Central Asia represents a strategic hinterland for both powers and ensuring stability in the region allows both states to address more pressing strategic challenges.

Whereas the Russian leadership has resorted to military coercion to push back against EU and NATO enlargement, in the Caspian and Central Asia it has prioritised conflict prevention. In June 2018, the Russian government approved a draft convention to settle the long-running dispute over the legal status of the Caspian Sea, with the leaders of the five littoral states (Azerbaijan, Iran, Kazakhstan, Russia and Turkmenistan) signing the document on 12 August 2018. The agreement permits the signatories to construct pipelines on the seabed on a bilateral basis – by signing the deal, Russia may have given up its veto over the future development of the region's energy resources. This presents a potential long-run risk to the business model of Russia's Gazprom, although the obstacles to realising such a project remain substantial. Set against this, the draft agreement provides legal guarantees that non-littoral states will not be permitted to deploy naval units, consolidating Russia's military dominance in the Caspian. Russia's increased engagement in the Middle East may also have incentivised the leadership to clarify the Caspian's legal status. The Kremlin has recently experimented with projecting military power from the Caspian, firing rockets from the Caspian fleet at targets in Syria. Overall, the agreement shows that Russian diplomacy is more accommodating to the interests of rival powers in areas where the US has limited interests.

The nature of the Central Asian regimes means that, unlike in Europe and the Caucasus, political transition has tended not to be geopoliticised. In all the states except the Kyrgyz Republic, national democratic movements have been completely marginalised by authoritarian governments. These regimes broadly share a common normative and security agenda with Russia and China, one that is focused on the prioritisation of state and regime stability. Despite the weak institutional and constitutional order and the highly personalised nature of the regimes, Central Asian elites have devised a range of strategies to maintain the existing system during transitions of power. This was illustrated after the death in 2016 of Islam Karimov, who had led Uzbekistan since before independence. His successor, Shavkat Mirziyoyev, came to power in an extra-constitutional manner, but as part of an elite compact. Since coming to power Mirziyoyev has made limited moves to re-engage with Uzbekistan's neighbours and liberalise the economy, but the essential nature of the regime remains unchanged.

Nevertheless, China's rising economic and political clout represents a long-term challenge to Russia's influence in the region. The expansion of

China's economic footprint in Central Asia over the past ten years has been striking. It is estimated that Chinese companies now control around 30% of Kazakhstan's oil production, while China is now in effect the sole consumer of Turkmen gas and the primary destination for Uzbek gas. Given the increasing antagonism between China and the US, the value to China of a secure energy supply from its western hinterland is only likely to increase. Chinese state banks are now the largest creditors of Kyrgyzstan and Tajikistan, the poorest and economically weakest states in the region. Central Asia is also a key element of China's Belt and Road Initiative (BRI), which is aimed at improving regional connectivity and creating new markets for the industrialisation of China's western provinces.

The key issue for the region is the extent to which China will seek to buttress its expanding investment in Central Asia with enhanced institutional or security engagement. A significant development in this context was the establishment in January of two international courts in China that will handle disputes arising in the BRI, an indication that China is seeking to exercise governance and shape the rules in which its investments operate. Given China's growing economic interests in Central Asia, an increased political and security presence in the region appears likely. In August 2016, a suicide-bomb attack on the Chinese Embassy in Bishkek, the Kyrgyz capital, underlined the potential for spillover of security concerns from Xinjiang province. China is gradually expanding its defence cooperation with Central Asian states. It has established strategic partnerships with all five countries and increased military aid and defence sales, although these remain relatively modest. In 2016, China announced a Quadrilateral Cooperation and Coordination Mechanism with Afghanistan, Pakistan and Tajikistan to engage in sharing intelligence and building anti-terrorist capabilities. (Notably, this was the first Chinese security initiative in Central Asia that did not include Russia.) In the same year, China and Tajikistan held their first bilateral military drills, conducting anti-terrorist exercises on the border with Afghanistan.

To date, Chinese security and institutional engagement with Central Asia has remained relatively thin. Russia remains the dominant military partner for Central Asian states through the Collective Security Treaty

Organisation (CSTO), which does not include China. Crucially, China has also been careful to engage with the region in a way that minimises friction with Moscow. China has been willing to mitigate tensions with Russia by negotiating on trade issues with the EEU as a whole, conferring legitimacy on the bloc and effectively acknowledging Russia's position as a regional norm-setter. The EEU – established in 2015 and comprising Armenia, Belarus, Kazakhstan, Kyrgyzstan and Russia – is one of the key vehicles for the integration of the post-Soviet space, with Russia at the centre. The bloc is explicitly modelled on the EU, and seeks ultimately to establish single markets for labour, capital, goods and services.

In May 2018, the EEU and China signed an agreement on trade facilitation. A free-trade deal is a long way off and may prove impossible to conclude given strong domestic support for protectionist policies in Russia. Nevertheless, China's approach contrasts markedly with that of the EU, which has refused to negotiate with the EEU over a possible free-trade agreement, presenting Ukraine with a stark choice between the two integration projects.

The future of the Eurasian Economic Union

From its inception, analysts have been sceptical of the EEU's long-term prospects as a developmental project. Russia's weak economic dynamics means that it is poorly placed to act as a driver of regional growth. The official consensus within Russia is that without structural reform – for which there is little domestic support – Russia's potential growth rate is no more than 2%. (Economic growth has averaged just 1% annually over the past decade, leading Alexei Kudrin, a leading economic adviser and former finance minister, to talk of a 'lost decade'.) Russia's share of global GDP is therefore set to decline in the medium term. As a World Bank report noted shortly before the launch of the EEU, Russia is already 'over-weighted' in terms of trade with other EEU members, suggesting that higher growth rates could be achieved through expanding trade ties with economies outside the post-Soviet space. The EEU's prospects as an effective single market are also undermined by the weak institutional environment in all the member states. The coherence of the union was undermined even before its official launch, when Russia imposed restrictions on food imports on a unilateral basis in 2014 in response to Western sectoral sanctions.

The EEU is best understood not as a developmental project but as an attempt to establish semi-porous boundaries to member states' engagement with third countries and competing economic blocs, in particular the EU. While the institutional design of the EEU is modelled on the EU, this is the wrong yardstick with which to measure its success. Russia has indicated that it will tolerate, and indeed has itself contributed to, significant divergence from single-market principles. From the start, Russia was willing to allow members states to carve out exceptions and concessions to secure their accession to the bloc.

The case of Armenia's membership of the EEU is indicative. Under strong Russian pressure, Armenia abandoned plans in 2013 to sign a free-trade agreement with the EU in favour of joining the EEU. Within the EEU, however, Armenia was permitted to retain preferential rates on a range of EU products, and in 2017 was able to sign a Comprehensive and Enhanced Partnership Agreement with the EU which set a framework for the liberalisation of bilateral trade and incorporated elements of the Association Agreement which Armenia was forced to abandon in 2013.

The primary function of the EEU is therefore to enforce *informal* rather than formal rules of the game, to maintain elites within existing cross-border networks and limit their room for geopolitical manoeuvre. Armenia's membership of the EEU may help to explain Russia's sanguine response to major protests in April and May 2018, which swept Nikol Pashinyan, a genuine opposition figure from outside the established political elite, into power. Serzh Sargsyan, the head of the ruling Republican Party of Armenia, was forced to abandon his attempt to retain power by moving from the prime minister's office after his second presidential term ended in April 2018. The Armenian revolution had some commonalities with the Maidan Revolution in Ukraine in 2014 that prompted Russia to annex Crimea. In this case, however, there was little prospect that Armenia's government would seek a geopolitical realignment. In contrast to Ukraine in 2014, the Kremlin stayed on the sidelines while the revolution unfolded. Pashinyan had previously criticised Sargsyan's decision to abandon the Association Agreement in favour of membership of the EEU. Once in power, however, he was quick to emphasise that he would not seek to pull Armenia out of the bloc.

The EEU project thus embodies an underlying tension between Russia's approach to the international system and the post-Soviet region. On a global level, the Russian leadership believes that the international system is undergoing a period of dramatic disruption, characterised by the decline of US influence and the emergence of new centres of power. Russia's regional policy, however, is primarily conservative; it is aimed at retaining existing channels of influence and constraining the evolution of the political and economic systems of the member states.

Following the annexation of Crimea and intervention in Syria, Russia is widely regarded as an assertive and potentially revisionist power. But across much of the post-Soviet region, Russia's strategic interests are under pressure. The current limit of Russia's capabilities is to act as a geopolitical spoiler, maintaining a belt of weak, non-aligned states and unresolved territorial disputes. In Central Asia, Russia and China have to date succeeded in maintaining a cooperative relationship and avoiding normative conflict. This is likely to become more difficult to sustain as China's economic influence continues to grow. In response to the conflict with the West, Russia has sought to expand its economic ties with China and to engage with the BRI, but despite enthusiastic rhetoric from both sides, the BRI has yielded few investment opportunities for Russia. Moreover, the BRI implicitly places Russia in a subordinate position vis-à-vis China as another recipient country for Chinese investment alongside the Central Asian states. This framing is at odds with the Russian vision of a new international order jointly shaped by Russia and China.

Central Asia: An Emerging Regional Order?

At a summit on 12 August 2018, the Caspian littoral states signed an agreement that resolved their decades-long differences over the legal status of the Caspian and how its waters and seabed could be used. The agreement opened the way for Turkmenistan, after years of obstruction by Russia and Iran, to address the possibility of building a gas pipeline to Europe via the Caspian, South Caucasus and Turkey. More generally, the summit was an indication of the increasing political connections and concord among the states in the centre of the Eurasian landmass, a process that has been largely driven by the Shanghai Cooperation Organisation (SCO).

The SCO has changed enormously since it was established in 2001. After the fall of the Soviet Union in 1991, newly independent Central Asian states – with the exception of assiduously neutral Turkmenistan – were keen to establish a new regional order. China, Russia, Kazakhstan, Kyrgyzstan and Tajikistan formed the Shanghai Five grouping in 1996, which led to the establishment of the SCO five years later, with Uzbekistan as an additional member. Initially, the SCO aimed mainly to address border security and Uighur separatism. (Both issues were legacies of Sino-Soviet disputes in Central Asia originating in the 1960s, when the Soviet Union amassed troops along the Xinjiang frontier separating western China from Central Asia and implicitly threatened to induce Uighurs and other Muslims to revolt to hold Beijing in check.) The SCO has subsequently expanded both in terms of size and remit. India and Pakistan became members in 2017, which resulted in the eight members of the SCO accounting for 80% of Eurasia's landmass, 43% of the world's population and a quarter of the world's GDP. The SCO is the largest regional organisation in the world in terms of geographical coverage and population.

From its initial narrow focus on border security and terrorism, the SCO has become the main vehicle for building and expanding Central Asia as a coherent political entity. It now addresses security, cultural and economic cooperation across the region in league with ten associate members and dialogue partners. Russia and China set the agenda, exercising different strengths. Russia takes the lead on political–military affairs, communications and culture, and also has far greater experience in multilateral affairs. China leads on economic development, investment and infrastructure. International pressures may help reinforce the bonds between the two leading powers in the SCO. Although Moscow aspired to a closer relationship with China after the deterioration of its relationship with the West over the annexation of Crimea in 2014, Beijing was unwilling to alienate the United States and preferred a less committed, although still friendly, partnership. Trump's accession to the US presidency, however, has made Beijing less sensitive and cautious in this regard.

Security cooperation

Regional security was the SCO's original mission and remains the group's primary goal. SCO members are concerned that forces of international jihadism may be infiltrating the region and are worried that Islamism could become an alternative to the prevailing secular political order. Afghanistan serves as a warning that Central Asia and its borderlands to the south are susceptible to serious instability, which individually the Central Asian states may not be able to contain. The region has produced a large contingent of fighters for Islamic State, also known as ISIS or ISIL, some of whom have found their way into Afghanistan. Stability in Afghanistan is therefore a key concern: in October 2017, an SCO–Afghanistan Contact Group was formed in Moscow, and held a second meeting in Beijing in May 2018. Apart from the secretariat in Beijing, the SCO's only permanent operational structure is the Regional Anti-Terrorist Centre (RATS) in Tashkent, the capital of Uzbekistan. RATS's location at the heart of Central Asia and in the vicinity of Afghanistan reflects both the importance of RATS in the SCO and the seriousness with which the terrorist threat in the region is understood. In May 2018, Pakistan hosted its first meeting of SCO RATS legal experts and advisers from the eight member states to discuss regional terrorist threats and possible measures to address them. China also has its own challenge of the ethnic Uighur minority in its Xinjiang autonomous territory, where grievances increasingly tilt towards violent extremism.

At the SCO summit in June 2018 in Astana, the capital of Kazakhstan, Chinese President Xi Jinping reiterated the SCO's focus on countering transnational threats, emphasising the need to combat the 'three evil forces' of 'terrorism, separatism and extremism', while tackling drug trafficking and cyber crime were also cited as security issues. The summit adopted several key security documents, such as the 'Programme for Cooperation in Counter-terrorism, Separatism and Extremism for 2019–2020', and approved the 'Anti-Drug Strategy for 2018–2023' and an action plan to support it. The SCO leaders' 'Appeal to Young People' proposal – which outlined youth employment and education programmes designed to prevent young people from becoming involved with extremist groups – was also adopted at the summit.

Defence cooperation is developing. China and Tajikistan formally agreed on intelligence-sharing in September 2017, while in April 2018 India and Pakistan attended the SCO Defence Ministers' Meeting for the first time. Joint military exercises are among the most tangible outcomes of SCO proceedings in terms of defence cooperation. Biennial 'peace missions' pose scenarios involving counter-terrorism operations and employ heavy firepower, such as air-to-air missiles. In the simulated operations, troops pursue terrorists, repel counter-attacks and take down terrorist networks, testing combat readiness and military cooperation. Given that China has little inter-operability experience with foreign militaries, Russia typically takes the lead. Russia holds cultural and linguistic advantages – many Central Asian officers were trained in Russia, and even more have some proficiency in Russian – but efforts have been made to integrate China and the new South Asian members into SCO exercises. *Peace Mission 2018* will be held in Russia's Chebarkulsky training ground in the Urals region in August 2018, and will involve China, India and Pakistan operating together for the first time. There are also more limited exercises organised by RATS to tackle particular issues such as anti-narcotics operations and disaster relief. Two joint cyber-security exercises were also conducted in 2015 and 2017, and China would like more.

Economic cooperation

One of the most marked changes in the activity of the SCO concerns the increasing level of economic cooperation between the members. The SCO views socio-economic development as a means to greater stability, reflecting a shared understanding between the members that fuller employment and improved social welfare will reduce the grounds for internal strife and the appeal of radicalised movements. The SCO has a long-term goal of establishing a free-trade zone (an idea strongly supported by China) and an immediate goal of creating an enabling environment for trade and investment. At the 18th meeting of the SCO heads of state in June 2018 in Qingdao, China, Xi launched proposals for a targeted credit line worth 30 billion yuan (US$4.7bn) and said that the SCO should work to reduce dollar dependency.

These are very ambitious and perhaps unrealistic goals. However, progress has already been made in the more defined area of energy investment and infrastructure. In December 2009, Line A of the 3,666-kilometre Central Asia–China gas pipeline – which runs from the Turkmenistan–Uzbekistan border to Horgos, China, and cost US$7.3bn – became operational. (China is the main consumer of Turkmenistan's gas.) In 2013, China agreed with Kyrgyzstan, Tajikistan and Uzbekistan to build the Line D pipeline, which is expected to increase Turkmenistan's gas-export capacity to China from 55bn cubic metres per year to 85bn cubic metres per year. After a number of delays, work resumed on the 410-km Tajikistan section of the pipeline early this year, with substantial completion projected for 2020.

Although Turkmenistan is not a member of the SCO, it has a potentially important role to play in the region as an energy supplier. Turkmenistan's gas is important for the development of energy-poor Pakistan and India's western regions, to be delivered via the Turkmenistan–Afghanistan–Pakistan–India (TAPI) pipeline, which is currently under development. This project, which binds India and Pakistan in a common cause, may help to expand and unify the region.

China's commercial stake in Central Asia is modest. In 2015, only 0.8% of China's US$2.3 trillion in exports went to the five Central Asian countries. Still, Beijing is anxious to narrow the developmental inequalities between its poorer western regions bordering Central Asia and the richer eastern ones. Integrating those poorer regions into Central Asian economies through the Belt and Road Initiative (BRI) could be a partial solution. In 2014, Beijing adopted three plans to remedy uneven regional development in China. One idea was to render the China–Pakistan corridor to Gwadar port an outlet for landlocked Xinjiang, which is located several thousand kilometres away from China's coastal ports. The planned corridor has been projected to receive US$46bn (later increased to US$62bn) in investments and credit lines.

The BRI, however, covers an area much larger than that of the SCO member states, given that it seeks to expand maritime routes and land infrastructure which will connect China with Asia, Africa and Europe. One of the aspects most relevant to the SCO is the China–Mongolia–Russia corridor, which bypasses Central Asia and includes the Trans-Siberian railway. The corridor also features a passage crossing directly from China into Russia. This route services China's east coast and facilitates its land trade with Europe. It is about 13,000 km long, and at present takes around 16 days to travel. A China-led consortium won a US$375-million contract in 2015 to build a 770-km high-speed train line between Moscow and Kazan in Russia that would significantly reduce the travel time. The New Eurasian Land Bridge – which consists of a set of railways from central China (Wuhan, Chongqing and Chengdu) to Europe via Kazakhstan, Russia and Belarus – helps satisfy transportation requirements from inner China. Northern railway connections to Europe are already in place. The signing of the Eurasian Economic Union (EEU) by Kazakhstan, Russia and Belarus was a major breakthrough for trade between China and the European Union, reducing delays and costs.

The China–Central Asia–Western Asia corridor follows the old Silk Road through Central Asia, Iran and Turkey to Europe. The first Silk Road train, carrying cargo from China to Iran, arrived in Tehran in February 2016 as the post-sanctions era enabled cooperation between China and Iran to begin. However, the route involves crossing Kyrgyzstan, Uzbekistan and Turkmenistan – countries known for poor connectivity, inadequate transport infrastructure, border delays and burdensome customs procedures. In addition, US withdrawal from the nuclear deal with Iran and the re-imposition of sanctions has raised further challenges. The alternative trans-Caspian route through Central Asia to Turkey, which bypasses Russia and Iran, is underdeveloped. High costs of the Caspian crossing between Azerbaijan and ports in Kazakhstan and Turkmenistan, inadequate containerisation and irregular ferry schedules due to weather conditions mean that the route compares unfavourably with the others in terms of speed and cost. At best, it can complement the routes through Russia but cannot compete with them.

A community of interests?

Given the challenges facing the China–Central Asia–Western Asia corridor, Russian concerns that the BRI might displace Russia from Central Asia seem exaggerated. Moscow was resentful when China first built a gas pipeline to Turkmenistan, although Russia's own decision in 2009 to set aside its gas-purchase contract with Turkmenistan was instrumental in that development. Since then, Russian policy has raised few objections. It helps that China has been solicitous of Russian concerns and that since 2014 Xi and Russian President Vladimir Putin have come into closer alignment. The expansion of trade in the region will be beneficial for both states. In May 2018, the EEU and China signed a cooperation agreement in Astana, and Russia and China are preparing an agreement on Eurasian Economic Partnership to align the BRI with EEU trade, investment and infrastructure plans that will be open to all SCO members. In security terms, meanwhile, the SCO is a complement to the 25-year-old Collective Security Treaty Organisation (CSTO) in Central Asia. Russia commands the only standing regional military force – the CSTO Collective Rapid Reaction Force – in which China does not participate.

While Russia and China have largely dictated the overall direction of the SCO, Central Asian states have drawn tangible benefits in the security and economic fields. For these states, it is more advantageous to have both of their giant neighbours in the organisation, rather than just one; the inclusion of India will possibly give them greater opportunity to work alongside and manoeuvre around more powerful states. The SCO has made considerable progress in meaningfully integrating the Central Asian states – which are members of few regional organisations outside of the former Soviet space and have often been treated as junior partners – into the international system. Within the SCO they are treated as formally equal through such mechanisms as the rotating secretary-generalship of the organisation, currently held by Rashid Alimov of Tajikistan. Participation in the SCO enables member states to host SCO summits and channel their officials into other positions in multilateral organisations, and thus affords them a more prominent international platform and profile. They are also associated with an organisation that is on the rise.

In that regard, the SCO has received a further boost since Shavkat Mirziyoyev became president of Uzbekistan in 2016. Under his long-serving predecessor, Islam Karimov, Uzbekistan was an awkward neigh-bour that opposed regional initiatives and sought to bully its smaller neighbours by politicising energy supplies. This approach was encapsu-lated at the Central Asia Summit in April 2009, when Karimov refused to discuss water-management issues with Kyrgyzstan and Tajikistan. Under Mirziyoyev, Uzbekistan has become a more open and cooperative partner in Central Asia, ending its objections to its neighbours' hydro-power projects, restoring full energy supplies, increasing transport links and showing a willingness to consider defence cooperation.

The Eurasian way

The SCO is not a dense or highly integrated organisation in the manner of the EU, although it is worth noting that Europe's signature institution is a global outlier. Even prominent regional organisations beyond Europe have limited ambitions and are built on intergovernmental rather than supranational principles. Accordingly, expectations as to what the SCO can deliver should remain modest.

SCO members have readily aligned with the 'Shanghai spirit' of 'mutual trust, mutual respect, equality, respect for diverse civiliza-tions and pursuit of shared development'. At the same time, the values that bind the SCO together are centred around national sovereignty, territorial integrity, social stability and an opposition to liberal interventionism. The idea is to show that there is a different way of doing things than the way established by the West. The EU, for instance, holds aspiring members to tight benchmarks, while the SCO offers a flexible range of options other than eventual membership, such as observer status (Afghanistan, Belarus, Iran and Mongolia) or 'dialogue partner' status (Armenia, Azerbaijan, Cambodia, Nepal, Sri Lanka and Turkey). Additional countries, including Bangladesh, Egypt, Israel, the Maldives, Qatar, Syria and Ukraine, have expressed an interest in becoming observers or partners.

In the belief, based on the SCO's perception of the EU's experience, that more obligations can bring more problems, the SCO is following a light blueprint and is loath to advance an institutional agenda that might limit national sovereignty. Within the SCO, efforts are focused on strengthening political and diplomatic capacity to relieve tensions on SCO external borders, resolve disputes within Central Asia, help stabilise Afghanistan and ameliorate discord between India and Pakistan.

The SCO leadership has not forced its members and associates to choose between 'Western' or 'Eastern' options; they can maintain independent foreign policies if they wish to do so, and some do. Most have ties with the West, and some – for instance, those forged by India and Turkey – are more robust than others. Among SCO-affiliated countries, only Iran could be characterised as an isolated state in dire need of friends.

The membership's ability to meet in a forum where the West does not play a key role is important, but the SCO's coolness towards the West should not be overestimated. Reformist as opposed to revisionist, the organisation does not want to change existing international rules radically, but rather aspires to adapt them to the changing international environment while broadly upholding existing norms. Widening membership and association arrangements have consolidated general regional support. Criticism of the US has been measured, and the SCO has pragmatically expanded its links with broadly established international bodies such as BRICS and UNESCO.

Potential challenges

As organisations expand, new challenges can emerge. The SCO has succeeded in managing latent friction between China and Russia in their common neighbourhood, despite China's economic rise in Central Asia, but the inclusion of rivals India and Pakistan may create difficulties for the organisation. The SCO does not aspire to manage tensions between New Delhi and Islamabad – which is prudent, given India's strong historical preference for handling its problems with Pakistan on a bilateral basis – but merely to ensure that those bilateral tensions do not disrupt the organisation. In that endeavour, the prospects seem reasonable. The two states have been observers for several years without difficulty, while attendance at SCO summits has afforded them an opportunity to meet at times of tension.

A more severe threat to the SCO would be a rupture in relations between Russia and China. China has become a driving force behind the SCO in the last few years. It was the power that ensured India and Pakistan joined the organisation. At the outset, it was content with the modest agenda of the organisation and the fact that it bore the name Shanghai. Now, however, Beijing has a strong reason to be interested in the SCO, namely that it can be a vehicle to promote the BRI across an important swathe of territory, advancing China's interests without conflict. The SCO is not a resilient structure and it could disintegrate rapidly if its two principal founder members fall out. Russia harbours a lingering concern over China's emergence as a global power and some in Moscow are concerned that this could include Chinese encroachment into Central Asia that might ultimately result in the displacement of Russia from the region. To date, these concerns – which have been given greater focus by the BRI – have been eased by a solicitous Chinese leadership, which has been at pains to reassure Russia and stress their mutual economic interest. However, China is now selling arms to Turkmenistan, to Moscow's irritation. More broadly, it is possible that China's expanding economic and commercial presence in Ukraine, Belarus and Europe (at Russia's expense) will shock Moscow into a reassessment. Whether the BRI will be developed in ways that do not undercut Russia's aspirations for infrastructure development in Central Asia, the South Caucasus, the western members of the Commonwealth of Independent States (Belarus, Moldova and Ukraine) and southeastern Europe remains to be seen.

Tensions between China and India in the SCO context might also trouble the organisation. Both powers have striven since mid-2017 to focus on areas of common agreement, yet their agendas beyond the bilateral relationship carry the risk of clashing interests. India wishes to build its profile in Central Asia but China has stolen a march on it. Greater Chinese purchases of Turkmenistan's gas, for instance, might put into doubt the viability of the TAPI pipeline project which is dear to India. Afghanistan, an SCO observer that might one day become a member, is an obvious point of potential tension between China and India. New Delhi is not a party to the principal efforts to forge a peace agreement between the government of Afghanistan and the Taliban, which puts it at a disadvantage to China and Pakistan. China wants Afghanistan to be stable, partly to ensure the peace in Xinjiang, but also because it wishes to dominate the extraction of minerals (such as rare-earth elements) from Afghanistan. China is now funding an Afghan military base in Badakhshan province, mainly to protect its projects in Pakistan, but this might constitute a pull factor for Chinese military involvement beyond its borders. Increased Chinese influence in Afghanistan, particularly beyond the economic sphere, is unlikely to sit well with Indian interests.

A final concern centres on the risk that Russia and China will seek to use the organisation as a platform for openly challenging the West. As noted, the SCO has not obliged its members to forswear ties to Western states. However, Moscow has shown irritation at Kazakhstan's recent decisions to open its ports to the US for the purpose of sustaining the military mission in Afghanistan and to introduce visa-free travel for US citizens visiting Kazakhstan. Moreover, China and Russia both disagree with multiple aspects of the US-engineered international order; the size and heft of the expanded SCO might encourage Putin and Xi to use the organisation in support of their aspirations to remake parts of the global order and check US influence. This would not be welcomed by several other SCO members, including the Central Asian states and likely India, which has drawn closer to the US over the last decade. The SCO has been a vehicle for Central Asian states to build their global profile and slowly to become more networked; they have little wish to participate in a bloc contest.

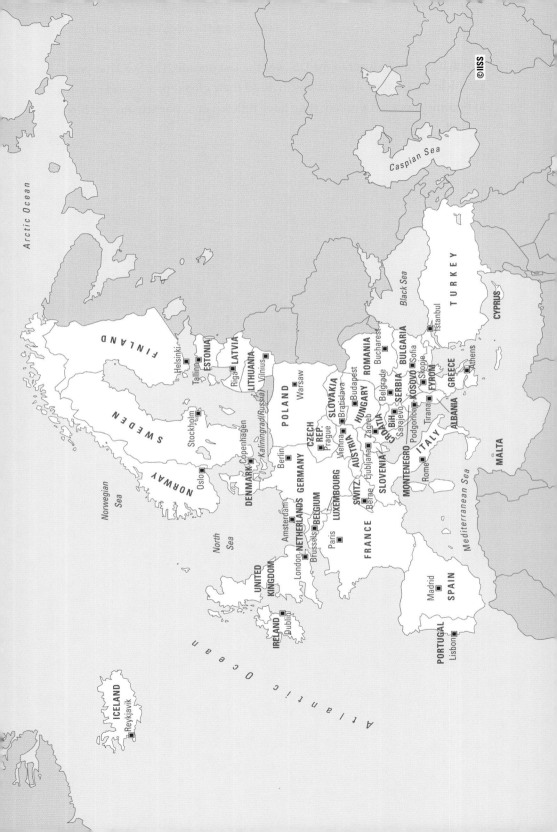

Chapter 9

Europe

2017–18 Review

A decade on from the global financial crisis, Europe's economy is recovering and the eurozone has established firewalls that have managed to prevent the break-up of the single-currency area, if not address its structural shortcomings. However, as economic recovery has taken hold in Europe, boosting employment and giving governments some fiscal space to ease up on austerity policies, popular resentment towards established political parties has continued to grow, fuelled by the effects of globalisation (including immigration and job displacement) and a perceived increase in inequality as a result of the policies adopted since the global crisis. Elections held in several major European Union countries during the 12 months to June 2018 have seen an increase in political fragmentation, complicating the formation of governments, weakening pro-European governments (as in the case of Germany) or bringing to power anti-establishment eurosceptic parties (as in Italy). In the United Kingdom, the government has teetered on the brink of a crisis since the June 2017 snap election, and negotiations with the EU regarding the UK's withdrawal from the bloc (Brexit) are entering their most difficult phase. More broadly, populist parties and leaders have exacerbated divisions within the bloc, particularly over immigration policies, despite a sharp fall in the number of arrivals from a peak in October 2015.

Recent events in Europe indicate that this trend of political upheaval and economic uncertainty is likely to continue and possibly get worse, especially if the economic recovery falters as the global business cycle draws to a close and global trade tensions rise. At the same time, the Bank of England and the European Central Bank (ECB) are under pressure to reverse a decade of ultra-loose monetary policy so that policymakers will have the tools to respond to the next economic downturn. However, this could potentially bring forward the downturn or even exacerbate it.

Elections will dominate the political agenda in Europe in 2019. Established pro-European parties will struggle to stem the rising tide of support for populists and nationalists at the European Parliament elections in May 2019, while Belgium, Denmark, Greece, Poland and Portugal will also hold parliamentary elections in 2019. Immigration will be high on the agenda in Belgium and Denmark, which have well-established far-right parties. The election in Greece is due in September 2019 but could be called earlier once the country exits its third bailout programme in August 2018 because of the weakness of the coalition government of Prime Minister Alexis Tsipras, which has been sapped by years of austerity and unpopular reforms. A comfortable lead in opinion polls for New Democracy suggests that the pro-European conservative party will win the next election in Greece, but greater political fragmentation is likely to complicate the formation of a government. With the nationalist, socially conservative government likely to remain in power in Poland, tensions with the EU are likely to continue over Poland's refusal to take its allocation of refugees and the erosion of the independence of the judiciary and of press freedom. Portugal appears to be the outlier of the countries in this group. Euroscepticism has not been a growing trend, perhaps because the Socialist government led by Prime Minister António Costa has eschewed the austerity policies that the EU sought to impose and the economy has recovered much better than expected.

With the Brexit deadline of 29 March 2019 fast approaching, negotiations between the EU and the United Kingdom have entered a critical stage. Even though there is already agreement on large parts of the draft withdrawal agreement and the terms of the transition period until the end of 2020, the risk of both failing to agree a deal and the collapse of the UK government has risen. The Conservative Party minority government led by Prime Minister Theresa May is weak, divided on Brexit between Leavers and Remainers and dependent on support from the Northern Irish Democratic Unionist Party in Parliament. It is therefore unclear whether May can obtain Parliament's approval of her Chequers plan announced in June 2018, which proposes to establish a common rulebook for goods to avoid customs and regulatory checks. On the other side of the negotiating table, the bloc of 27 EU members has remained unified, despite UK government efforts to persuade individual member states to soften their positions. The chief EU negotiator, Michel Barnier, had until recently shown few signs of flexibility, particularly over the issue of the border between Northern Ireland and the Republic of Ireland, but he has indicated since June 2018 a desire to depoliticise the issue, which could take some pressure off May.

A 'no deal' scenario is unlikely because it would be in neither side's interests, but given the state of flux in UK politics and the EU's fear that concessions would embolden populists across the bloc, it cannot be ruled out. It would have serious political and economic consequences for both the UK and the EU. Besides the hit the British economy would suffer as a result of disruption to trade and investment ties, a no-deal scenario could further destabilise the political system. A no-deal scenario would also damage the EU economically, although the damage would be greater for those member states with closer trade and investment ties to the UK. According to IMF research, the member states most affected would be (in order) Ireland, the Netherlands, Denmark and Belgium.

Since Emmanuel Macron's victory in the French presidential election in May 2017, France has been one of the few bright spots on the European political horizon. Macron has made steady progress on his domestic-reform agenda, which includes liberalising the labour market; overhauling the provision of public services; and introducing a more flexible social-welfare system and tighter immigration policy. Opposition in parliament is weak and divided and Macron has a comfortable majority in the National Assembly comprising his centrist Republic on the Move (LRM) party and the smaller Democratic Movement (MoDem). Given the resistance of the powerful railway unions, the passage of legislation to reform the state railway company SNCF in June 2018 represents a significant achievement ahead of Europe-wide rail-transport liberalisation. This success will embolden Macron to press ahead with the next wave of reforms, which include further labour-market reform related to training and apprenticeships as well as an overhaul of France's generous social-welfare system. However, Macron's ambition for France to play a greater role on the international stage has had mixed results. This is in part because of the French president's tendency to overreach (such as by trying to play the role of mediator in the conflict in Syria where there are already too many international actors with conflicting agendas), but also because of conflicting agendas with some of France's EU partners (for example, with Italy in Libya), as well as the EU's limited effectiveness in the foreign-policy sphere.

Hope that Macron and German Chancellor Angela Merkel would focus on enhancing the Franco-German relationship after the German federal elections in September 2017 and forge ahead with much-needed EU reform has yet to be fulfilled. Merkel won a fourth and probably last term as chancellor, but her government has been significantly weakened. It took several rounds of talks after the vote before she managed to form another grand coalition with the much-weakened Social Democratic Party (SPD) in March 2018. The election also saw a further rise in support for the far-right Alternative for Germany (AfD), which finished third with 12.6% of the votes, becoming the first far-right party to be represented in the national parliament in more than 50 years and Germany's largest opposition party following the formation of the government with the SPD. AfD's presence in parliament has already started to put pressure on the government over immigration policy, fuelling sharp divisions between Merkel's centre-right Christian Democratic Union (CDU) and its smaller Bavarian sister party, the Christian Social Union (CSU). In June 2018, Merkel was forced to seek a tougher EU stance on the issue to avert a split with the CSU, but refused to agree to demands from the CSU Minister of the Interior Horst Seehofer to give German border police powers to turn away refugees registered in other EU countries.

This inherent weakness of the Merkel government, as well as staunch opposition in creditor countries (led by Germany) to risk-sharing or fiscal transfers in the single-currency area, make Macron's ambitious plans to reform the eurozone unfeasible. However, the reforms – which include plans to establish a European Monetary Fund (EMF) to provide a backstop to the banking union and provide financing to member states affected by an asymmetric shock, as well as creating a eurozone economy and finance minister who would oversee the fund – are likely to remain on the EU agenda, if only to counter eurosceptic criticism within the bloc.

Italy is the eurozone's third-largest economy; it has high government debt at over 130% of GDP; its banks are burdened with high levels of non-performing loans; and its economic recovery is fragile. None of the three main political blocs contesting the parliamentary election in March 2018 obtained a majority of seats in parliament, but the anti-establishment Five Star Movement (M5S) and the far-right anti-immigration Northern League (LN) emerged as the clear winners and formed a government headed by the little-known and unelected Giuseppe Conte on 1 June 2018. Although both parties backed away from hardline eurosceptic positions during the election campaign, Matteo Salvini, the leader of the LN and de facto leader of the government, has continued to call into question Italy's commitment to European integration, especially with his uncompromising stance on immigration, and is resisting the imposition by the EU of further fiscal tightening.

Salvini's hardline rhetoric on immigration appears to align him with Hungarian Prime Minister Viktor Orbán and the conservative Austrian Chancellor Sebastian Kurz, who has called for an 'axis of the willing' against illegal immigration comprising Austria, Germany and Italy. Besides fuelling domestic fear of migrants and sending a message to voters that he is looking after Italy's national interests in Europe, Salvini wants to see greater EU burden-sharing to deal with rising numbers of migrants embarking on the perilous journey across the Mediterranean

Sea from North Africa to Europe. It is unlikely that either Orbán or Kurz, who formed a government alliance with the far-right Freedom Party after his win in the October 2017 election, will offer to contribute 'on a voluntary basis', as agreed at the European Council meeting on 28–29 June, to establish 'controlled centres' for migrants in member states other than the front-line countries such as Italy, Greece, Spain and Malta.

On the economic front, the combined electoral promises of tax cuts championed by the LN and increased social spending favoured by the M5S could, if implemented, push Italy's budget deficit as high as 6–7% of GDP, more than double the EU's 3% ceiling. Fearing another sell-off of Italian assets on the financial markets, the country's Minister of the Economy and Finance Giovanni Tria insists that the fiscal targets agreed with the EU will be adhered to in the 2019 budget. However, like Conte, he is unelected and has no political base.

Spain was plunged into a profound political crisis by an illegal referendum and unilateral declaration of independence by the separatist government in the Spanish region of Catalonia in October 2017. The move prompted the national government to assume direct control of the region and call a snap regional election in December. The separatists retained their majority in the Catalan parliament, which elected a hardline secessionist as president of the region in May 2018, leaving the crisis unresolved. On 1 June a corruption-related censure motion in parliament brought down the national government led by then-prime minister Mariano Rajoy of the conservative People's Party (PP). Rajoy has been replaced by Pedro Sánchez, the leader of the centre-left Spanish Socialist Workers' Party (PSOE), who tabled the motion. Supported on the motion by a heterogeneous alliance of opposition parties and small regional nationalist parties, Sánchez leads a fragile minority government that is unlikely to survive until the end of the parliamentary term in mid-2020. The government will be unable to pass legislation in most policy areas because of its lack of a majority, but Sánchez appears set on reducing tensions with the Catalan regional government – direct rule was lifted in June 2018 – with a view to granting greater autonomy but not secession.

The EU's external relations with its two largest neighbours, Russia and Turkey, have remained strained. In response to a nerve-agent attack on a former Russian intelligence officer in the UK in March 2018, the EU presented a united front with the UK as scores of Russian diplomats were expelled across the bloc. EU sanctions imposed on Russia following the Russian annexation of Crimea in 2014 have also remained in place and were rolled over in mid-June 2018 for another 12 months, despite earlier calls from Italy's new, more Russia-friendly populist government for sanctions to be lifted.

Compared with the first half of 2017, when Turkish President Recep Tayyip Erdogan accused several EU governments of Nazi practices during his government's presidential-reform referendum campaign, tensions between the EU and Turkey eased somewhat in the 12 months to June 2018. The main exception has been the revival of historical tensions with Greece, largely over the Greek courts' refusal to extradite Turkish military officers who fled to Greece on the night of the attempted coup on 15 July 2016. Since March 2018, Turkey has been holding two Greek border guards who strayed into Turkey during a night-time patrol. With both governments using nationalist rhetoric in the foreign-policy sphere for domestic consumption, the issue has re-ignited long-standing territorial disputes, notably over the Aegean island Imia/Kardak, which brought the two countries close to war in 1996.

Neither Turkey nor the EU appear willing to take action to improve relations, and this is unlikely to change in the short term at least. However, despite repeated Turkish threats that it would open its gates to allow a flood of refugees to reach Europe's borders, Turkey has continued to implement the Turkey–EU joint action plan aimed at stopping the flow of irregular migration via Turkey to Europe, a plan which has been in place since March 2016. Given how divisive the migrant issue has become in Europe, the EU is unlikely to take any action against Turkey that would jeopardise the deal.

For the most part, Turkey has directed its anti-Western rhetoric at the United States over a series of disputes ranging from US backing for Syrian Kurdish groups that are affiliated with Turkey's Kurdistan

Workers' Party (PKK) to Turkey's refusal to release an American pastor jailed on flimsy charges of being a supporter of the so-called Gulen Movement, which the Turkish government believes carried out the attempted military coup in July 2016. These tensions have weighed heavily on the Turkish economy, especially as they have been combined with tightening global liquidity and shortcomings in Turkey's economic policymaking under the executive presidential system of government that came into effect following Erdogan's victory in the presidential election on 4 June 2018. The Turkish lira has been in freefall since April 2018, raising the risk of a full-blown balance-of-payments crisis in the country, which could have negative contagion effects on other emerging-market currencies and European economies with large exposures to Turkey, especially in the banking sector.

Enlargement fatigue – as well as the difficult challenges of negotiating Brexit and trying to reform the bloc to prevent rising populism from undermining its fragile cohesion – has weakened the Union's role as a beacon of stability in the unstable but strategically important Western Balkans comprising Albania, Bosnia-Herzegovina, Kosovo, Macedonia, Montenegro and Serbia. Amid statements of 'unequivocal support for the European perspective of the Western Balkans', in February 2018 the European Commission published a strategy document that insisted that accession countries must strengthen the rule of law, judicial independence and fundamental rights if the EU's enlargement policy is to be part of its larger strategy to strengthen the Union.

Further enlargement to Serbia and Montenegro is not envisaged before 2025, and could be pushed back further, given the divisions among the 27 member states over proposed EU reforms. The EU hopes that the initial breakthrough in the long-standing name dispute between Greece and the Former Yugoslav Republic of Macedonia (FYROM) in June 2018 will be followed by progress in the dispute between Serbia and Kosovo. However, the Macedonia name dispute is far from resolved, given strong public and political opposition in both countries to the agreement to rename FYROM as Northern Macedonia. The agreement must be ratified by the parliaments of both countries and put to a referendum in Macedonia later in 2018. The EU's decision not to open accession negotiations with Macedonia and Albania until mid-2019, after the May European Parliament elections, was hardly encouraging.

Arguments about the virtues of stronger European ties with China also reached a peak in 2018. The distaste of US President Donald Trump for alliance politics and deepening cracks in the transatlantic foundation prompted some European observers to float the proposition that China might be a more reliable partner in upholding parts of the global rules-based order. China, in turn, did its part to be seen in Europe as an 'anchor of stability' and partner of choice on questions of global governance. Beijing pursued a charm offensive that entailed the exchange of market-access lists – a major milestone in bilateral treaty investment negotiations between the EU and China – support for the Iran nuclear deal, a joint statement with the EU on climate change and the release of Liu Xia (the widow of the late Nobel Laureate Lui Xiaobo), who has subsequently left China for Germany.

However, 2018 was also a year during which fundamental frictions in relations between Europe and China persisted and even became exacerbated. The political hardening in China that followed the 13th National People's Congress in March 2018 and Beijing's more confident export of its economic and political model have prompted concerns in European capitals that Europe may be headed for fundamental systemic competition with China in the years ahead. China's shopping tour in Europe's high-tech industry and its investments in critical infrastructure spurred decisive steps towards the adoption of a European investment-screening mechanism, while more visible Chinese Communist Party political influencing and interference activities in Europe met with growing scrutiny. Meanwhile, Europe has been more outspoken about its concerns regarding the flagship foreign-policy project of China's President Xi Jinping, the Belt and Road Initiative. Specifically, China's related sub-regional diplomacy cooperation with 16 Central and Eastern European countries, the so-called 16+1 initiative, has generated harsh criticism of Beijing's divide-and-rule tactics and raised questions about China's continued interest in European stability and integration.

Europe: Drivers of Strategic Change

▨ The United Kingdom's decision to leave the European Union (Brexit) continues to dominate the political agenda in the bloc, with a 'no-deal' scenario likely to have serious political and economic consequences for both the UK and the EU.

▨ France is undergoing a wave of reform, driven by President Emmanuel Macron's overhaul of the labour market and public services, which has the potential to redefine the power of the unions and rein in state spending on benefits.

▨ China's influence in Europe is increasing through its acquisition of strategic infrastructure and participation in the '16+1' platform, which is designed to foster improved understanding between 16 Eastern European countries and Beijing.

▨ European states are increasing defence spending and collaborating more closely on reducing reliance on the United States. While European states are attempting to save NATO, they are also insuring themselves against its demise through new European Union defence initiatives such as the Permanent Structured Cooperation framework.

▨ The persistent populist presence in European politics – most notably in Austria, Germany and Italy – has impacted the framing of political discourse in many states, potentially representing the start of a coherent, sustained challenge to post-war consensus policies.

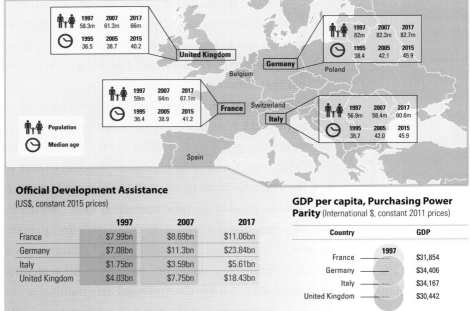

Official Development Assistance
(US$, constant 2015 prices)

	1997	2007	2017
France	$7.99bn	$8.69bn	$11.06bn
Germany	$7.08bn	$11.3bn	$23.84bn
Italy	$1.75bn	$3.59bn	$5.61bn
United Kingdom	$4.03bn	$7.75bn	$18.43bn

Defence Budget
(US$, constant 2010 prices)

	2008	2013	2018
France	$54.51bn	$50.79bn	$55.82bn
Germany	$39.89bn	$42.32bn	$45.14bn
Italy	$31.01bn	$24.19bn	$24.48bn
United Kingdom	$68.69bn	$55.33bn	*

*no data available

GDP per capita, Purchasing Power Parity (International $, constant 2011 prices)

Country	GDP
1997	
France	$31,854
Germany	$34,406
Italy	$34,167
United Kingdom	$30,442
2007	
France	$37,755
Germany	$40,474
Italy	$38,612
United Kingdom	$38,384
2017	
France	$38,606
Germany	$45,229
Italy	$35,220
United Kingdom	$39,753

Sources: IISS; OECD; UN Department of Economic and Social Affairs (Population Division, 2017); World Bank

Europe's Changing Perceptions of China

As Europe is forced to re-evaluate its global strategic alignments in light of fundamental changes in the transatlantic partnership, European governments are also in the process of recalibrating their relationship with China. The way the relationship between Europe and China will evolve in 2019 will therefore have a significant impact on the way Europe will see and approach China for some time to come and also yield some important insights into how China sees Europe. While Europe is set to pursue a more autonomous strategic role on the global plane in the future and thereby to follow long-standing calls by Beijing to that effect, it remains doubtful that this new role will result in more ambitious cooperation with China in 2019 and beyond.

No fundamental convergence in economic policies

At the European Union–China Summit in July 2018, both sides committed themselves to exploring joint proposals for global trade governance reform and to taking meaningful steps towards addressing the reciprocity challenge in investment relations. In a global context, US President Donald Trump's administration also offered a point of agreement between the two sides with regard to trade. Europe and China were equally alarmed by the United States' exploitation of loopholes that allow World Trade Organisation (WTO) members to impose tariffs in times of national emergency. Both sides are also profoundly worried by Washington's refusal to appoint or reappoint any member of the WTO Appellate Body, which could result in the collapse of the WTO dispute-settlement system by late 2019.

However, agreement on the flawed nature of the Trump administration's approach to global trade is where Europe–China commonalities by and large end. Despite the launch of an EU–China working group on WTO reform in July 2018, an approximation of European and Chinese visions for strengthening the rules-based trade order is unlikely to materialise over the course of 2019. The EU shares US concerns about China's persistent failure to abide by the letter and spirit of WTO principles, as a result of which Chinese state-owned enterprises and opaque subsidies for Chinese industries no longer only produce large-scale distortions on domestic but also increasingly on global markets, with Chinese state-owned enterprises, for example, swallowing more competitive and innovative global rivals at the expense of the welfare of global consumers. However, unlike the Trump administration, which has embarked on a trade war with China that might tear down the WTO in the process, European leaders prefer reforming the WTO as the weapon of choice in dealing with China's illiberal economic policy. While appearing more benign at first sight, the European course of action might turn out to be as challenging to China and its interests as a protracted trade war with the US.

The EU will push for three principal elements of WTO reform in 2019. Firstly, the EU will propose new procedures for assessing state distortions to markets – a measure first and foremost targeted at China's state-led approach to economic governance. Secondly, the EU will propose measures to widen the scope of definitions of public bodies engaged in state distortion and banned subsidies, as the current regime fails to provide WTO members with sufficient legal leverage to call out illiberal and ultimately unfair economic behaviour by a wide range of Chinese state-affiliated bodies. Finally, given the frequent inability of WTO members to prove the existence and extent of Chinese illiberal economic practices in the face of opaque business ownership and financing structures, the EU will call for lowering the burden of proof for state distortions and banned subsidies. While these reform proposals might even win the support of the US administration, it seems hard to conceive that they would also be welcomed by China. In June 2018, Beijing issued a White Paper on China and the WTO that underscored the Chinese government's strong preference to maintain the status quo of global trade governance and the WTO. Notwithstanding promises made to the EU that it would support WTO reform, Beijing will have little interest in undertaking any ambitious commitments for WTO modernisation or the negotiation of progressive plurilateral arrangements that could eventually result in the redefinition of appropriate roles for the state and state subsidies in WTO economies. Accordingly, over the course of 2019, Chinese concessions to Europe on bolstering the existing global trading system are unlikely to go beyond selective – and mostly cosmetic – trade-liberalisation steps, similar to the reduction of tariffs on cars from 25% to 15% announced in May 2018, none of which will help to substantially address European concerns.

Similarly, mounting European concerns about a persistent lack of reciprocity in investment relations with China are not likely to subside over the course of 2019. More forceful European calls for greater reciprocity in investment relations with China in 2018 have been driven by a dramatic reversal of capital-flow dynamics between Europe and China, with Chinese foreign direct investment (FDI) in the EU surpassing EU FDI in China by a factor of three in 2017. Three developments in particular have contributed to the changing dynamics in Europe–China investment relations. Firstly, the outward-facing elements of Beijing's ambitious 'Made in China 2025' industrial policies have driven Chinese companies to embark on a high-tech-industry shopping tour in Europe, raising concerns about the technological hollowing out of Europe's industrial base. Secondly, Chinese President Xi Jinping's vision for a China-built global energy network has encouraged Chinese state-owned enterprises to step up their efforts to acquire or build energy infrastructure in Europe, prompting security concerns regarding the transfer of ownership of critical infrastructure to Beijing. Finally, while European economies are among the most open destinations for FDI in the world, significant market-access barriers remain a very present reality for European investors in China.

Since 2014, high-ranking Chinese officials had repeatedly made pledges to reduce market-entry restrictions and post-market entry discrimination against foreign investors. However, in 2018 Beijing presented concrete market-access improvement measures that were aimed at meeting with favourable responses in Europe. In spring 2018, Beijing released a new and more limited set of so-called 'negative lists' (which stipulate those Chinese industries that remain either partially or completely off-limits to foreigners), raising hopes that China could start gradually to open up sectors of significant interest to European investors, such as aviation, finance or insurance. Beijing's decision to abolish joint-ownership requirements in the automobile sector were also widely seen as an important concession to Europe. Finally, the exchange of market-access offers at the July 2018 EU–China summit has been another potentially important milestone in progressing towards greater reciprocity.

However, with overall progress on market-oriented reforms in China having been slow or even partially reversed during the tenure of Xi, significant doubts persist about the sincerity of China's interest in enabling FDI from Europe and other countries. Indeed, long-established patterns of ring-fencing (or only selectively opening up) industrial sectors that are deemed either essential to China's future global economic power or critical to maintaining the power of the Chinese Communist Party (CCP) – such as media and communications – will die hard and certainly not in 2019. Moreover, as China opens up new sectors to foreign investors on paper, European companies might simply experience a further increase in the application of post-market access barriers, which are already omnipresent. Significantly, almost half of participants in a June 2018 business-confidence survey by the European Chamber of Commerce in China said that they expected regulatory obstacles in China to increase in the years ahead.

While market-access barriers will remain a major concern for European decision-makers in 2019, Beijing will doubtlessly become more vocal in its criticism of increased European scrutiny of Chinese investments. The new EU investment-screening mechanism – which could see its first applications in 2019 – has already met with staunch criticism from Beijing, and further frictions will emerge as additional measures are implemented at the national level. Hence, over the course of 2018, major European economies, such as France, Germany and the United Kingdom, have engaged in a process of lowering the screening threshold for foreign investment in firms (i.e., the percentage a buyer seeks to amass in a firm's shareholdings at which the government can intervene and block an investment), or engaged in revising rules related to the 'golden' shares governments hold, which give them special voting rights and the ability to block potential takeovers. Other European countries have tabled fresh legislation on creating investment-screening mechanisms, as has been the case in the Netherlands for the telecommunications sector. Many European countries have also sought to widen the scope of security concerns on the basis of which they can screen foreign investments. In 2019, some European countries might even contemplate 'net benefit test' legislation for foreign investments, which would allow for incorporating economic considerations in the screening of investments, such as the effect of a given investment on overall national economic performance as well as technological development, product innovation and product variety. Calls for more targeted European industrial policies that could help to compete more effectively with China on core technological developments might also become more prominent in Brussels as the UK exits the EU, leaving France and Germany with greater leeway to push for pan-European efforts in this space.

As China seeks major investments in energy infrastructure, the European debate about the risk of technological hollowing-out through Chinese investments will be complemented more prominently again by arguments about the security risks associated with Chinese investments in critical infrastructure. Specifically, 2019 will mark the start of a more high-profile debate across Europe on whether Chinese companies should be awarded contracts to build 5G mobile networks. Many European governments will draw conclusions from the failure of a body set up by the UK's technical-intelligence and cyber agency GCHQ and made up of information and communications technology (ICT) experts to scrutinise the software and hardware installed by the Chinese telecoms company Huawei in UK broadband and mobile infrastructure equipment. In July 2018, London issued a report which concluded that after four years in operation, the body provided 'only limited assurance' that Huawei software and hardware posed no threat to national security. Next to the debate on technological entanglement with China in the realm of 5G, several European countries will also revisit collaboration schemes with China on emerging technology domains such as big-data

China's Growing Influence in Europe; Europe's Struggle to Access China

China has become an increasingly influential presence in Europe as it seeks to expand the reach of its Belt and Road Initiative (BRI) through investment in key infrastructure (such as the Greek port of Piraeus) and by financing (and often building) ambitious infrastructure projects in Eastern Europe, such as the Montenegro–Serbia motorway.

However, Chinese influence is more pervasive. Beijing engages in tactics to help boost the visibility of Chinese ideology and to influence intellectual and political discourse on the continent. The 16+1 platform, inaugurated in 2012, has enabled China to engage directly with 16 Eastern European countries with the stated aim of intensifying and expanding cooperation, outside the strictures of the European Union. By contrast, European countries still face significant hurdles in accessing the Chinese market.

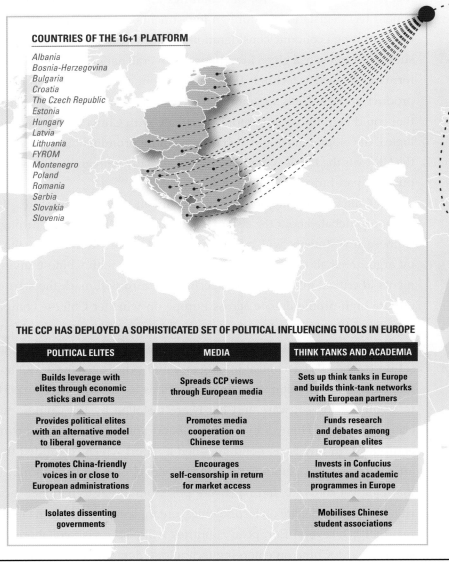

COUNTRIES OF THE 16+1 PLATFORM

Albania
Bosnia-Herzegovina
Bulgaria
Croatia
The Czech Republic
Estonia
Hungary
Latvia
Lithuania
FYROM
Montenegro
Poland
Romania
Serbia
Slovakia
Slovenia

THE CCP HAS DEPLOYED A SOPHISTICATED SET OF POLITICAL INFLUENCING TOOLS IN EUROPE

POLITICAL ELITES	MEDIA	THINK TANKS AND ACADEMIA
Builds leverage with elites through economic sticks and carrots	Spreads CCP views through European media	Sets up think tanks in Europe and builds think-tank networks with European partners
Provides political elites with an alternative model to liberal governance	Promotes media cooperation on Chinese terms	Funds research and debates among European elites
Promotes China-friendly voices in or close to European administrations	Encourages self-censorship in return for market access	Invests in Confucius Institutes and academic programmes in Europe
Isolates dissenting governments		Mobilises Chinese student associations

Sources: *Bloomberg, European Commission; European Chamber of Commerce in China, Forbes, Global Public Policy Institute, MERICS, Rhodium Group*

THE PRINCIPAL DIRECTION OF EU–CHINA INVESTMENT FLOWS HAS REVERSED IN JUST A FEW YEARS

€ (billion)

—— Value of Chinese FDI transactions in EU

—— Value of EU FDI transactions in China

35.9
29.7
7.5 6.9

2000 2001 2002 2003 2004 2005 2006 2007 2008 2009 2010 2011 2012 2013 2014 2015 2016 2017

EUROPEAN BUSINESSES FACE SIGNIFICANT POST-MARKET ACCESS BARRIERS IN CHINA

BARRIERS RELATED TO THE APPLICATION OF LAWS AND REGULATIONS

- Discriminatory application of anti-monopoly and competition laws and regulations
- Discriminatory application of environmental, labour and tax laws and regulations

- Restrictive administrative practices as well as licensing and approval processes
- Tightened visa and work-permit requirements that hinder foreign hiring

BARRIERS RELATED TO INTELLECTUAL PROPERTY

- Joint-venture partner demands for technology transfer
- Failure to prosecute intellectual-property-right infringements

- Exclusion from standard-setting procedures

BARRIERS RELATED TO CYBERSPACE

- Internet restrictions that hinder access to information and hamper data exchange and collaboration with headquarters and other partners outside China
- Mandatory use of expensive and insecure government-approved VPN providers

- Data-localisation requirements that threaten data security
- Hardware security certification requirements that hinder the import of foreign ICT equipment

BARRIERS RELATED TO INNOVATION, BUSINESS AND FINANCING SUPPORT

- Exclusion from national-innovation and industrial-policy schemes
- Exclusion from state-backed grants, loans, subsidies and below-market-value land-acquisition schemes
- Exclusion from access to financing through local stock exchanges
- Exclusion from public-procurement schemes

applications and artificial intelligence, where Chinese companies have significant capability, but standard-setting and privacy concerns will create a growing headache for European governments.

New avenues for China's influencing in Europe

In 2018, political-influencing activities by the CCP met with growing scrutiny across Europe, with various governments conducting reviews of these activities and contemplating possible counter-strategies. Political influencing has become an increasingly prominent feature of China's engagement in European countries for some time, having the potential to be more consequential in the medium to long term than Russian activities. Rather than engaging in Moscow-style short-term disruption techniques, which are geared to fostering public distrust in liberal and democratic values at specific points in time, the CCP aims to build lasting influence in Europe to help popularise the Chinese model of illiberal, authoritarian political governance with uncontested powers for the regime, extensive population control and state capitalism over time.

Despite greater European pushback against Chinese influencing activities, it would be premature to assume that the CCP will scale back its efforts in 2019 and beyond. Beijing's efforts to exert political influence in Europe and other parts of the world have deep roots in domestic CCP practices of dealing with opposition. Indeed, political-influencing efforts pursued abroad first and foremost serve the existential function of underpinning regime stability, silencing voices that are critical of the CCP and Chinese policies, such as Beijing's treatment of individual freedoms or minorities. At the same time, they help the CCP to secure third-party legitimisation of and support for critical foreign-policy XZprojects and positions, such as its global infrastructure foreign policy the Belt and Road Initiative (BRI), or territorial claims in the South China Sea. However, stepping up influencing activities in the rest of the world, the CCP also seems increasingly convinced that its approach to political and economic governance is not only highly competitive, but ultimately even superior to that of liberal democracies.

CCP influencing efforts in Europe are set to broaden in terms of targets and geography in 2019. In recent years, the CCP has pursued a broad range of influencing activities, including economic carrot-and-stick tactics, exploiting ideological proximities among European political elites and making targeted investments into think tanks and universities, with Central European countries often being a prime target. Going forward, the CCP will put even greater emphasis on engaging European populist parties, seasoned politicians and business representatives as well as on expanding its footprint in European media. While Western European concerns about the 16+1 format have resulted in a preoccupation of media and political analysts with Chinese influencing activities in Central and Eastern Europe, China's activities have been no less virulent in Western Europe. As more evidence on the CCP's activities in Western Europe come to light, the distinction between Chinese influencing activities in Central and Western Europe will become increasingly less prominent.

While the CCP has a long track record of engaging European political parties from across the political spectrum, it became clear in 2018 that Beijing's rhetoric is most likely to fall on fertile ground among populist movements across Europe. In Germany, Chinese diplomats and journalists have stepped up their influencing efforts with members of parliament of the far-right Alternative for Germany political party, some of whom have praised China's political and economic governance approach as a model for Germany. In the same vein, senior representatives of Italy's populist government have expressed admiration for the Chinese model. In June 2018, Under Secretary of State for Economic Development Michele Geraci, who has close ties with the Northern League (LN), published an op-ed on the widely read blog of Beppe Grillo, the leader of the Five Star Movement, which called for Chinese solutions to the most pressing Italian problems, from budget deficits to migration. Notably, Geraci's 11-point proposal for greater engagement with China also included cooperation and exchange of information with China on matters of public security.

In 2019, the CCP may also intensify efforts to cultivate individuals close to political decision-making processes. A growing number of former top-level politicians from Western Europe are on China's payroll and expected to popularise Beijing's policies. In the most high-profile case, in December 2017 the former British prime minister David Cameron became the head of a US$1-billion infrastructure investment fund supporting the BRI. Similar roles have also been accepted by former prime ministers and ministers from France, Germany and Italy. The CCP has also sought to incentivise boardroom-level decision-makers from major European companies such as ABB and Siemens to lend their support to China's BRI, with such support being a prerequisite for becoming an 'attractive' Western partner for Chinese investors and contractors in the realisation of BRI projects in third markets outside Europe where the bulk of BRI commercial activity plays out. As BRI has increasingly met with headwinds, it will be even more important for Beijing to make sure that senior European company executives will publicly echo Chinese BRI marketing language.

In another attempt to gain greater influence over the way in which Europe sees China and its policies, the CCP will also step up efforts to take over media outlets in Europe. A late 2017 bid by the state-owned enterprise CEFC China Energy to buy Central European Media Enterprises – a media conglomerate with significant market share in six Central European EU member states – failed to result in a swift takeover due to governance issues within CEFC but was indicative of Beijing's aspirations. At the same time, China seeks to expand the footprint of Chinese state-owned media in Europe. A milestone in this respect might be the 2019 UK launch of a European hub of the China Global Television Network (CGTN) – the principal Chinese state broadcaster – in the UK, which is expected to employ up to 300 more producers and journalists. The US arm of CGTN has already been criticised for an unwillingness to portray China and the Chinese government in a negative light, while suppressing or demonising anti-CCP voices.

As China expands and recalibrates its influencing efforts in Europe in 2019, European countries will need to take more serious steps to promote transparency and public awareness. Within the existing legal frameworks, this will first and foremost require greater funding of investigative journalism, think tanks and academia. At the same time, European governments will need to live up to the challenge of defining what constitutes illegitimate efforts of political influence by the CCP and others, and also consider follow-up legislation to counter such efforts more effectively. European decision-makers will doubtlessly look to Australia, which has been exposed to Chinese influencing activities to a much greater extent and for a longer period of time than Europe and passed innovative legislation in June 2018 to counter foreign interference and influence.

The future of Beijing's Europe policy

In the run-up to the 2016 UK referendum on EU membership, high-ranking Chinese officials repeatedly voiced concern about the prospect of a British EU exit, and even Xi expressed discontent with the idea of Britain leaving the EU. Beijing's intervention constituted an unusual departure from standard Chinese diplomatic practice. It was seen as a strong indication that Beijing remains committed to its traditional support for a united Europe, which offers a huge and integrated market for Chinese goods and services and – at least potentially – constitutes one influential pole in the multipolar world order the CCP would like to see emerge. However, over the past two years, Beijing's BRI infrastructure foreign policy and the related 16+1 format – which was established in 2012 and comprises China, 11 EU member states and five Western Balkan countries – have increasingly called into question China's long-term interest in European stability and integration and hence the nature of Beijing's Europe policy.

China's BRI has already started to create fiscal instability on Europe's periphery and hardly aligns with what has been identified by the EU as sound rules and standards related to building large-scale infrastructure – not to mention European connectivity priorities. The Bar–Boljare motorway in Montenegro, which will be built by Chinese contractors with an €809-million (US$944m) loan from the Chinese Export–Import Bank, illustrates the point rather well. The IMF has found that, without construction of the highway, Montenegro's debt would have declined to 59% of GDP, rather than rising to 78% of GDP in 2019, warning that the construction of the highway would come at the expense of debt sustainability. The European Commission has noted a growing lack of appreciation for EU rules on public procurement and state aid, environmental-impact assessments and sound cost–benefit analyses. Brussels is also concerned that the significant resources invested in the project will create 'other important transport bottlenecks and high maintenance needs'.

Next to raising concerns about the fiscal stability of countries in the European neighbourhood, China's BRI has also increasingly posed a challenge to the integrity of the EU's single market and the rules that come with it. In February 2017, the European Commission opened a formal investigation into what is meant to become the flagship BRI construction project in the EU, namely a €2.45bn (US$2.89bn) high-speed rail link between Belgrade and Budapest. At the time, Brussels not only expressed doubts about the financial viability of the rail link but also suggested that the project failed to comply with EU public-procurement rules, given that Budapest had not issued a call for public tender normally required for projects of this magnitude. An official call for tender for the project was issued at the Budapest 16+1 summit in November 2017, but the timeline for the tender process was remarkably short, suggesting that one of the tenderers might have had an inside track. Indeed, Budapest made it clear behind closed doors to EU officials that it expected Chinese companies to win the contract. As tender bidders and the winner may not be made public before the end of 2018, the Hungarian part of the Belgrade–Budapest rail link might become an important indicator in 2019 as to whether China is serious in its response to European concerns about the adherence to international procurement, labour and environmental standards.

In the face of mounting European criticism of its infrastructure foreign policy, China undertook several steps over the course of 2018 to win greater European support for BRI. These include first and foremost promises to be more responsive to European connectivity priorities identified by the EU and its member states and Chinese policy banks partnering up with the European Bank for Reconstruction and Development and European development agencies to strengthen respect for due-diligence principles and relevant standards in the implementation of BRI projects in Europe and its immediate neighbourhood. The first trials of Chinese policy banks cooperating with European partners in 2019 will also be important test cases for establishing whether co-financing arrangements can produce outcomes whereby European companies get a chance of winning BRI-related contracts in third countries on purely technical grounds where political support by companies for the BRI plays no role.

However, 2019 will be a critical year not only for how the EU perceives the economic effects and governance of the BRI, but also for how the BRI will be seen in the 16+1 region. China has increasingly fallen into a capability-expectations gap in the region. Many of the infrastructure and investment projects promised to the European states have been significantly delayed or not materialised at all, leading to a more sober outlook by a growing number of 16+1 countries. Significantly, in what was a clear snub for Beijing, at the Sofia 16+1 summit in July 2018, Poland as the biggest European 16+1 economy was only represented by Deputy Prime Minister Jaroslaw Gowin, with Prime Minister Mateusz Morawiecki giving preference to attending a pilgrimage gathering at home.

Despite meagre economic outputs, the 16+1 format has provided China with greater political influence in Central Europe, exacerbating existing tendencies towards greater fragmentation in Europe. Significantly, Beijing does not seem to regret the divisive political effects of 16+1, with several senior Chinese political analysts openly admitting that the point of the format was to find a new way of shaping EU politics in the face of a perceived lack of EU responsiveness to Chinese interests and concerns. Not surprisingly, China has remained unimpressed by calls from Berlin, Brussels and Paris to tone down its 16+1 activities, and has even sought an intensification and broader institutionalisation of interactions within the format. It also welcomed ideas by Austria and Greece to seek promotion from being 16+1 observers to becoming full members. China's successful efforts to bring the Sofia 16+1 summit forward by almost half a year to have it only a few days before the July EU–China summit left EU officials rather irritated and even made some of the EU members of 16+1 feel uncomfortable.

China has also not given up on the idea of establishing sub-regional formats with both Northern and Southern European countries, and it seems set to court Westminster more actively after Brexit, potentially in a way not conducive to pan-European interests. All of this could indicate a more permanent shift in China's European policy as part of which influence within Europe trumps the desire for European cohesion. China's sub-regional activities in Europe will therefore remain an important space to watch in 2019 and a bone of contention in Europe–China relations. Both the EU and NATO will launch policies to counter the growing economic and political influence of China in the European periphery, with the former starting to implement its own connectivity strategy released in October 2018 and the latter revisiting what can be done within the framework of NATO partnership mechanisms.

Indeed, in 2019, changing dynamics in Beijing's Europe policy might also become more visible in the context of NATO. Hence, Beijing took a range of steps over the course of 2018 to bolster the profile of an enlarged Shanghai Cooperation Organisation (SCO) and no longer seems averse to the idea of the SCO being in limited strategic competition with transatlantic security cooperation. Arguably, this shows most clearly in the context of Sino-Turkish relations. Over the past three years, Turkish President Recep Tayyip Erdogan has on various occasions publicly toyed with the idea of SCO membership. Given that relations with the EU and the US are unlikely to become any easier in 2019 and that, following his latest re-election in 2018, Erdogan has openly threatened NATO allies that Turkey has 'alternatives', Ankara may revisit the idea of stepping up cooperation with the SCO. Beijing has already expressed support for any potential Turkish membership aspirations, although Turkish membership of the SCO would hardly be reconcilable with NATO obligations. While Turkey's full-blown turn from NATO to SCO membership will remain an unlikely prospect for some time to come, the episode underscores that Europe needs to rethink its current global strategic alignments – and that it needs to be realistic about the prospects of greater cooperation with China.

NATO at 70

In April 2019, NATO will celebrate its 70th anniversary, presumably in the form of a summit meeting of NATO heads of state and government. Ever since the end of the Cold War, a chorus of commentators has suggested that NATO was destined to search for new roles to justify its continued existence after the demise of the Soviet Union and the Warsaw Pact. Most of these observers would probably now agree that NATO turned out to be rather good at identifying new tasks and evolving with the international security environment, of which it is a key component. As the *New York Times* editorial board argued on the eve of the July 2018 NATO summit in Brussels, NATO 'remains the most successful military alliance in history, the anchor of an American-led and American-financed peace that fostered Western prosperity and prevented new world wars. No one has proposed anything credible to improve upon it.' The opening paragraph of the 2018 Brussels summit declaration states that NATO allies 'will continue to stand together and act together, on the basis of solidarity, shared purpose, and fair burden-sharing'.

And yet on the eve of its 70th anniversary NATO finds itself in the uncomfortable position of having to contend with both external and internal challenges. Proceedings around the Brussels summit created an odd sense that NATO existed in two parallel worlds. In the first, NATO as an organisation was busy implementing yet another transformation, designed to address challenges such as a resurgent Russia on its eastern flank and continued regional instability on its southern borders. The summit declaration issued on 11 July speaks to the progress achieved and outlines the steps ahead in a systematic way. In the second, however, NATO as an alliance of governments looked chaotic and in danger of ripping itself apart from the inside. US President Donald

Trump declared behind closed doors in Brussels that if European allies did not commit to spending more on defence, the US 'might do its own thing'. This created a crisis moment that could only be contained (not solved) through an emergency meeting of NATO leaders hastily convened by NATO Secretary-General Jens Stoltenberg. Turkish Foreign Minister Mevlüt Cavusoglu declared on the margins of the summit that NATO allies had refused to provide his country with adequate defences and that Turkey therefore had to buy advanced air-defence equipment from Russia, which in turn contributed to the US Congress looking into measures that would block the transfer of F-35 fighter aircraft to Turkey. Contrary to the summit declaration, solidarity, shared purpose and fair burden-sharing were in scarce supply.

The three ages of NATO

In a 2016 speech at the Harvard Kennedy School, Stoltenberg spoke of 'the three ages of NATO'. The first age, according to Stoltenberg, covered collective defence in the Cold War setting, while the second age covered the 1990s and 2000s, decades that were characterised by overseas military crisis management and cooperative security. Stoltenberg puts the beginning of the third age as 2014, when Russia annexed Crimea. The main feature of this new age, according to Stoltenberg, is that NATO 'must do both collective defence and manage crisis and promote stability beyond our borders', thus combining the tasks of the previous two periods. While Stoltenberg is being slightly reductionist with regards to the division of NATO's priorities – NATO's 2010 strategic concept defines collective defence, crisis management and cooperative security as the three core tasks, so the thought that NATO might have to do more than one thing is not new – his analysis captures the wider movement and institutional development.

The first age of NATO, which can now appear somewhat rose-tinted in hindsight, experienced moments that brought a still-young organisation close to the brink. From the late 1950s onwards, France's role in the Alliance became more complicated. Then-president Charles de Gaulle tried in 1958 to convince the US and the United Kingdom that Paris should be allotted an equal political co-leadership role in NATO. When the idea of a triangle of leaders was rebuffed, French defence policy turned national, pursuing an independent nuclear deterrent and withdrawing from NATO's integrated command structure (to which it only returned in 2009). When the US and the Soviet Union directly discussed important arms-control measures in the 1970s, European NATO member states worried that their interests would be forgotten. The answer to European concerns came in form of the 1979 double-track decision to link the offer of limitations on medium-range and intermediate-range missiles to the threat that more medium-range missiles would be deployed by NATO in Europe in case of disagreement.

In the 1990s and 2000s, NATO turned itself into an organisation that managed security problems of relevance to its members, although these problems never reached the level of existential threat. The three core elements of NATO policy in that period were an enlargement process designed to extend stability and encourage democratic transitions in Central and Eastern Europe; international crisis-management operations 'out of area'; and the offer of strategic partnership with Russia. Each of these policies was controversial at the time and triggered heated debates within NATO. The enlargement of NATO to Central and Eastern Europe, based on Article 10 of the North Atlantic Treaty, was widely judged a success, with new allies joining in 1999, 2004 and 2009, bringing the total of NATO member states at the time to 28. However, enlargement subsequently seems to have run out of steam: although Montenegro joined in 2017 and the Former Yugoslav Republic of Macedonia (FYROM) looks likely to become the 30th member following the resolution of its dispute with Greece in June 2018 (FYROM agreed to change its name to Republic of North Macedonia), neither will contribute much to the Alliance militarily. Bosnia-Herzegovina, Georgia and Ukraine have all stated their ambition to join, but their path to membership remains unclear. Recurring speculations that Finland and Sweden – already cooperating closely with NATO in many ways, including on operations – might at some point ask to join the Alliance have yet to be substantiated by formal policy.

Military operations overseas have often resulted in crisis for the Alliance. The air campaign over Kosovo in 1999 led several allies to conclude that coalition war fighting was to be avoided because of the attendant political friction and the negative effect this friction had on military effectiveness. It furthermore exposed European dependencies on US military assets. Operations in Afghanistan from 2002 saw more than a decade of competing explanations and justifications of what NATO members were trying to achieve, with caveats imposed by troop contributors and the resulting division of operational risk putting strain on the Alliance. The lengthy and inconclusive engagement in Afghanistan (which is still ongoing, albeit on a lower scale and with different roles) in particular put a damper on NATO member states' appetite for interventions.

However, Russia's war against Georgia in 2008 made NATO strategists worried about the Alliance's capability portfolio. Focused on power projection for crisis-management purposes, NATO's capabilities might not be robust enough for contingencies that amounted to collective defence. However, the issue was papered over at NATO's 60th-anniversary summit in 2009. The Strasbourg–Kehl summit declaration suggested that

> NATO's ongoing transformation will strengthen the Alliance's ability to confront existing and emerging 21st century security threats, including by ensuring the provision of fully prepared and deployable forces able to conduct the full range of military operations and missions on and beyond its territory, on its periphery and at strategic distance.

The assumption seemed to be that power projection for collective defence was ultimately not that different from power projection for crisis-management operations. There was no serious consideration during the second age of NATO that collective defence in Europe would anytime soon require the ability to exercise, move, deploy and operate combined arms formations at corps level and above in a contested military environment. As a result, NATO lost the corresponding muscle memory.

Ukraine 2014: the trigger for action

Russia's illegal annexation of Crimea in 2014 and its direct and indirect support for an armed insurgency in eastern Ukraine was the external shock that finally triggered NATO into action. Hopes that NATO–Russia relations could be reset after the 2008 Georgia–Russia summer war were revealed as misplaced: Russia under President Vladimir Putin was a strategic rival which continued to consider NATO as the enemy. In 2014 and 2015, several NATO member governments (in particular the Baltic countries and Poland) argued that NATO's deterrence had become brittle. Supported by a range of think-tank reports and table-top war games, they argued Russia could easily achieve a conventional-force overmatch, limited in time and geographic extent, that would put their security at risk. The overmatch would effectively mean that, should Russia decide to occupy part of NATO territory in the Baltics, NATO forces could not prevent it from doing so.

While the scenario of Russian offensive action was deemed unlikely by most NATO member governments, it was nevertheless considered plausible. Deterrence by denial – discouraging an attack by convincing the enemy that his attack will be defeated – did not look credible in this scenario, but even more worrying was the fear of some decision-makers that if NATO allies were presented with a fait accompli in the form of a Russian land grab in the Baltics, the Alliance would not muster the cohesion and resolve to fight Russia to get its territory back. Deterrence by punishment was certainly still possible and militarily credible, but looked politically questionable at best. However, if such a provocation were to go unanswered, NATO would be finished as an alliance – a prospect that in itself might prove tempting to Russia.

NATO began to address this problem at the September 2014 Wales NATO summit, where it agreed a set of measures which focused on reassuring the affected allies through increased exercises and rotational deployments and by providing rapid-response elements as well as politically binding commitments to increase defence spending. However, NATO leaders in 2014 did not focus to the same extent on the problem that Russia had built up anti-access/area-denial capabilities (such as air defence, advanced radars, anti-ship missiles, coastal artillery and cruise missiles), including in Kaliningrad, that would make the Baltic region a very contested environment in which to operate. NATO would not be able to reinforce its exposed allies unopposed. Other allies also suggested that NATO's response did not provide satisfying answers to the very different security challenges that the Alliance faced on its southern flank, such as regional instability across the Mediterranean driven by the conflicts in Iraq and Syria, and the broader issues of migration and terrorism. Accordingly, the NATO summit in Warsaw in 2016 stressed the need for heavy and high-end forces to underpin deterrence in Eastern Europe and to ensure that a large follow-on force would reinforce a limited forward presence and the rapid-response elements stationed in the region. Even before the meeting, NATO had started to speak of a '360-degree approach' which would take all adversaries and all strategic directions into account, thus providing a policy label for the idea that a balance among member states' differing threat perceptions had to be found.

The discussions at the summits in Wales and Warsaw represented a systematic attempt by NATO to work through the problems arising from an evolving security environment. To a degree, the transformation agenda set in motion after 2014 even revitalised NATO. NATO did what it always did when the world around it changed: it tried to change with it. NATO kept up the pace at the 11–12 July 2018 summit in Brussels. Based on US suggestions, a new readiness initiative was agreed committing NATO member states collectively to have 30 battalions, 30 air squadrons and 30 naval combat vessels ready to use in 30 days. Known as the 'four thirties', this goal is meant to be achieved by 2020. At Brussels, NATO also agreed measures to improve military mobility and defined a new enablement plan for the Supreme Allied Commander Europe (SACEUR) which would look at the administrative challenges of moving military personnel and assets across countries. The NATO Command Structure (NCS) was adjusted with the creation of a Cyber Operations Centre as well as two new commands: a Joint Force Command dealing with transatlantic lines of communication to be based in Norfolk, Virginia and a Joint Support and Enabling Command to be based in Germany. Both commands will strengthen logistics capacity and support military mobility and mean that the NCS will grow again in terms of personnel (by about 1,200) after severe post-Cold War cuts. Regarding its southern flank, NATO launched a training and capacity-building mission in Iraq and agreed to conduct more exercises focused on southern-flank scenarios and contingencies. In general, NATO leaders confirmed their intention to provide the means to anticipate and respond to crises in the south; conduct expeditionary operations; and enhance NATO's ability to project stability to its southern neighbourhood by means of partnership and capacity building.

Internal challenges

NATO actions since 2014 underline the resilience of the Alliance in the face of changing external threats. The organisation itself has enough bureaucratic capacity to design, propose and drive forward initiatives. NATO governments continue to see value in the Alliance and invest in implementation. NATO is indeed in search of a role in the light of changing circumstances – some commentators suggest this means that NATO has become obsolete, but the majority of governments appear to see the adaptation as a transactional approach to safeguarding their almost 70-year-old investment and not as an attempt to prop up a failing organisation.

This picture of healthy progress is incomplete, however, without also looking at the political sclerosis that has beset NATO from within. Throughout its history, NATO has always had to address structural challenges concerning both US commitment to European security and European commitment to the idea that the financial and military burden should be more evenly spread between the two sides of the Atlantic. The challenges are fundamental because if they are mismanaged they threaten the unity and cohesion of NATO from within and hence expose the actual centre of gravity of the organisation, leaving it vulnerable to attack.

The reality on the European side is that the 25 years of NATO's second age saw a massive reduction in European defence expenditure in terms of GDP, with a consequent reduction in military capability. Whereas in 1990 West Germany alone would have been able to field 215 regular combat battalions, in 2016 – at the beginning of NATO's third age – France, Germany, Italy, the United Kingdom and US European Command combined would have been able to field no more than about 190. The reasons for this development are simple: European governments interpreted the end of bloc confrontation and the changes in the international system associated with it as a net gain in security. While the risks that continued were diffuse and confusing, in the 1990s and 2000s they seemed manageable with a smaller defence outlay. More defence cuts were ushered in when the 2008 financial and economic crisis reduced the fiscal strength of NATO governments.

Europe reaped the so-called 'peace dividend' and politically prioritised macroeconomic concerns over defence until the situation in Ukraine in 2014 made it clear that defence could no longer be relegated to a subsidiary concern. In 2014–15 European governments began to reinvest in defence. Governments have begun to spend more money again in three key areas: on spare parts, maintenance, training and logistics in order to improve military readiness; on a modernisation drive to replace or at least upgrade ageing equipment and close existing capability shortfalls across all military domains; and to review force structures, possibly expanding the number of active service personnel or build up reserve elements. With European NATO governments spending a collective total of about US$240 billion on defence in 2017, plans are in place to extend spending increases well into the 2020s. This upward trajectory, rebuilding some of what was lost, for the time being nevertheless falls short of NATO ambitions and does not yet relieve the US from some of its burden in the Euro-Atlantic realm – it is simply not yet enough.

While the spending issue is usually the headline-grabbing aspect, the European pillar in NATO has other problems as well. One of them is the increasing nationalism and authoritarianism of Turkey under President Recep Tayyip Erdogan. Recent constitutional changes in Turkey concentrate power in the presidency, further restricting the available expertise in security and defence policymaking. The failed coup attempt of 15 July 2016 led to a major shake-up of the Turkish Armed Forces (TAF) which had implications for its domestic and international role, including in NATO. By September 2016, the number of serving officers in the three armed services had fallen by 10%, with the largest decline affecting the upper echelons due to detentions and suspensions following the coup attempt. While the purge at times appeared heavy-handed, it is unlikely to have cleared the TAF of all coup sympathisers, thus leaving two potentially significant strains on morale and cohesion in the force. At the political level, the failed coup has already exacerbated existing strains in Turkey's relations with its NATO allies. Ankara insists that Fethullah Gülen – who has been living in exile in the US since 1999 – was to blame for the coup attempt, but Washington has refused to extradite Gülen because of a lack of evidence. Turkey's decision to treat its engagement in the Syria crisis from a counter-insurgency standpoint aimed at containing or reversing any gains made by militias linked to the Kurdistan Workers' Party (PKK) led to clashes with local armed groups sponsored by the US to fight the Assad regime. Growing Turkish links with Russia and Iran further strained the Turkish–US bilateral relationship as it created suspicions in Washington that Ankara was rethinking its Western stance as a NATO ally. A very public confirmation came in the form of an op-ed penned by Erdogan for the *New York Times* on 10 August 2018 in which the Turkish president suggested that, unless the US reversed its position of 'unilateralism and disrespect' vis-à-vis Turkey, he would 'start looking for new friends and allies'.

Turkish relations with another important ally, Germany, also hit a low point between 2016 and 2018. German leaders grew increasingly worried by the fact that Erdogan and his party's representatives were aggressively campaigning in Germany in order to canvass votes from the Turkish population, often on an anti-Western platform. (About 1.5 million Turkish citizens live in Germany out of a total of just under 3m people of Turkish origin in the country.) The spats escalated, leading to Turkish restrictions on visits from German parliamentarians to German troops deployed in Turkey on NATO and other international missions, which ultimately led Germany to move some military assets and personnel from the Incirlik air base in Turkey to a base in Jordan.

Closer integration of Ukraine into Euro-Atlantic security structures is a declared aim of NATO but this has run into problems in the shape of Hungary, which has tried to obstruct interaction between NATO and Ukraine. Hungary objects to a Ukrainian education bill passed in 2017 that restricts education for ethnic minorities in their mother tongue, legislation that impacts Hungarians who live in the Transcarpathian region of Ukraine. Hungary blocked meetings of the NATO–Ukraine Commission in the run-up to NATO's 2018 summit and even suggested that it might try to prevent Ukrainian President Petro Poroshenko from attending the event, only lifting its objections at the last minute. Overall, there are clear signs among European allies that burden-sharing, solidarity and shared values are all under pressure.

Outside Europe, the commitment of the US to NATO has been a key issue. With an eye to countering rising Chinese influence in the Indo-Pacific region, the Obama administration sought to rebalance its security responsibilities, but found this to be more difficult than expected, in part because security challenges in Europe re-emerged and North Africa and the Middle East were once again afflicted by regional instability, resulting in the increased movement of foreign fighters, terrorists and migrants from the region. Sustaining a multi-region security presence – the ambition that drives the size of the US defence budget – has not become any easier for Washington. European allies traditionally react nervously to any signs from the US that might foreshadow disengagement from the European theatre. Of course, the US presence in Europe has evolved. In 1989, the US had 326,000 troops deployed to US European Command equipped with some 5,000 main battle tanks, 1,600 pieces of artillery and 639 fighter and ground-attack aircraft. Today those numbers are a fraction of what they were in NATO's first age.

However, what propelled European worries about the US commitment to NATO into a new orbit in 2017–18 were not primarily these numbers – in fact, since 2014 the US has begun to reinforce its presence in Europe, albeit in a moderate way. Rather, it is the policy of Trump, summarised by the 'America First' slogan, which has created a strong belief among Europeans that the US administration does not value alliances. Europeans point to the US withdrawal from the Paris climate accord, the decision to pull out of the nuclear agreement with Iran and a growing lists of trade disputes with the US as evidence that Trump is set to undermine the international order, including NATO. In the run-up to the 2018 NATO summit, Trump told a US audience, 'I'm gonna tell NATO: "You gotta start paying your bills. The United States is not gonna take care of everything."'

Trump supporters argue Europeans should not overinterpret Donald Trump's words in relation to the policies his administration adopts. For example, despite criticism of European defence-spending levels, the Trump administration has actually increased funding for the European Deterrence Initiative (a US programme to help fund activities of the US European Command in response to a changing security environment in Europe). In reality, some observers argue, 'America First' would lead to stronger US leadership of the Western camp. However, even if one were to give credence to this position, it is hard to see how Trump's leadership would be driven by effective multilateralism rather than unilateralism and expectations of followership vis-à-vis allies. Disagreements between the US and its European allies about what elements of the international order are worth preserving therefore seem unavoidable. It seems simply not feasible for a US administration consistently to adopt policies that contradict the publicly expressed position of the US commander-in-chief. Secondly, if Trump's statements are simply a negotiating tactic or an artificial means of producing drama as part of the proceedings (to then provide relief in the form of yet more public statements downplaying the previous disagreements), they are bound to fail in the long run, despite some possible short-term gains. Trump's tactics undermine trust and the ability to engage in meaningful repeated interaction over time, and hence the very essence and idea of what NATO is about. While Trump seems to interpret multilateralism as one long set of isolated win–lose decisions, most other allies look to balance their political gains and losses over time.

NATO is extremely resilient when it comes to external challenges. When undermined from within, on the other hand, NATO has few instruments available other than the diplomatic peer pressure among allies not to stray from what are deemed to be the boundaries of mutually acceptable behaviour. On the road to NATO's 70th anniversary, Stoltenberg has the unenviable task of making sure that the adaption agenda stays on track while also minimising fallout from political disagreements. In his 2016 Harvard speech he said

> the world has changed and NATO evolves. This is the way we have kept our nations safe for almost 70 years but while NATO evolves, it also stands true to its founding principles, that united in common cause and common values, we are stronger together than we ever could be apart.

The signs that this statement no longer represents undisputed common sense are mounting. Europeans are reinvesting in the EU's capacity as a security and defence actor, in part because not all of them are convinced that the US will be a reliable ally. A process aiming to increase European strategic autonomy, while costly and drawn out, could ultimately be upgraded to address the question of how to guarantee the defence of Europe without the US. The third age might yet prove to be NATO's most challenging one.

Europe: Time for a Strategic Makeover?

Europe's respite from strategic thinking in the years that followed the end of the Cold War has been brought to an unceremonious end by recent developments within and beyond the continent's borders. In the years that lie ahead, the interactions of Europe and the European Union with the world of grand strategy, security and defence need to become considerably more serious and substantive. Albeit born out of necessity and adversity, the first signs of a more credible, revived and refashioned

European engagement in defence and security concerns might now be emerging.

Europe in crisis

Europe's crises have come thick and fast since the eurozone debt crisis began in 2009. While some have been more successfully managed than others, none have been fully resolved. The crises in cohesion, credibility and policy creativity were quickly accompanied by a crisis of populism, the consequences of which continue to be keenly felt. The 2019 European election will see Eurosceptic parties enter the European Parliament in sufficient numbers to make their impact felt on one of the EU's central institutions. The migration crisis may have peaked in numerical terms in 2016 with the filing of almost 1.3 million applications for internal protection within the EU, but the political costs of the challenge continue to mount, as witnessed in the evident weakening to German Chancellor Angela Merkel's authority in her fourth term in office. Concerns over managing migration now appear an unshakeable feature of the domestic political debate in many European states. According to the UN Refugee Agency, each day in 2017 saw an average of 44,000 new refugees – while 85% of these continue to be hosted by developing countries, the attractions of Europe and the pressures this will bring for the continent are clear. However, the crisis surrounding migration came not so much in the numbers as in the politics between member states regarding the management and distribution of the refugees, most obviously with regard to the rift between states on the front lines of the refugee crisis, such as Italy, and those arguing for their right to continue largely unaffected, such as Hungary and Poland. Meanwhile, the United Kingdom's decision to exit the EU (Brexit) poses a serious strategic challenge to the remaining 27 EU member states, whose handling of this development will shape the future of their continent.

The continent has been also forced to confront the realities of what Russia has become under the leadership of President Vladimir Putin, re-elected to office for a fourth presidential term in March 2018. Under Putin, Russia has redrawn Europe's borders by force and conducted targeted assassinations on the continent, including the March 2018 attempted assassination of a former Russian spy using a nerve agent that later inadvertently resulted in the death of a UK citizen. The country also stands accused of directly aiding the killing of nearly 300 civilians when a Malaysian passenger plane was shot down in eastern Ukraine, with its subsequent veto of a UN-proposed international tribunal to investigate the tragedy doing nothing to support its claims of innocence.

Moscow has an increasingly impressive track record in political interference overseas, including in Europe. Even as it denies breaking the Intermediate-Range Nuclear Forces (INF) Treaty, Moscow blames the US for pushing Russia into a new arms race, which also has consequences for European defence. In short, the 'Modernisation Partnership' launched by the EU and Russia in June 2010 has completely failed to influence the behaviour of Moscow. Europe is also witnessing the rise of strongman politics and the implications this has for global order elsewhere, from President Recep Tayyip Erdogan's aspirational autocracy in Turkey to President Xi Jinping's assertive authoritarianism in China. Some 40 years on from former Chinese leader Deng Xiaoping's momentous 'Reform and Opening Up' policy, Xi's China is doing a better job at reshaping Europe than Europe is at reshaping China.

However, perhaps most consequential of all for Europe's potential strategic revival is the crisis in transatlantic relations. With US President Donald Trump in the White House, the EU finds itself confronted with a president not just ambivalent about European integration but willing even to misrepresent this most powerful symbol of post-war reconciliation as a project 'set up to take advantage of the US'. Any hopes that the system around Trump could moderate his most worrying instincts were swept aside in a few brutal months in early 2018. Heavy European lobbying could not forestall the United States' announcement in May 2018 of its unilateral withdrawal from the Joint Comprehensive Plan of Action (JCPOA) with Iran regarding its nuclear ambitions. The US approach to reimposing sanctions on Iran also has potentially wider consequences: the United States' rejection of EU requests for sanctions exemptions for European companies operating in Iran risks motivating the EU to join other rival powers to the US in exploring the development of independent financial channels and payment systems that would reduce US dominance of the global financial system.

Trump's imposition of tariffs on European steel and aluminium was soon followed by the public display of Western strategic dissonance at the G7 in Quebec, including Trump's subsequent retraction of US support for the joint statement agreed there. Then came the barely concealed tensions of the NATO summit in Brussels in July, including the president's verbal assaults on Germany as 'totally controlled by Russia'. Year-on-year increases in the US budget for the Pentagon's European Deterrence Initiative (EDI; originally the European Reassurance Initiative) are all too easily lost in this noise. While the authorised budget for the US Department of Defense for its EDI was US$3.4 billion for 2017, the requested budgets for FY2018 and FY2019 were US$4.8bn and US$6.5bn respectively.

Renewed European interest in defence

At the 2014 NATO summit in Wales, European NATO member states pledged to reach the benchmark of 2% of GDP spending on defence within a decade, galvanised by the evident threat posed by Putin's Russia. The European approach to defence spending – which had been defined by cuts even before the onset of the financial crisis in 2008 – finally began to turn around. Notwithstanding the majority of member states that continued to struggle with the 2% target, by 2017 Europe had become the fastest-growing region in real-terms defence spending in the world. By 2018, however, other galvanising forces were renewing European interests in effective security and defence. As fears rose that US military retrenchment from Europe would someday follow the United States' political and diplomatic retrenchment, so European conversations around the NATO 2% benchmark became as informed by doubts over the future dependability of the transatlantic alliance as by the growing list of geopolitical threats and complications emanating from more expected corners of the world. While the demands by US President Trump for European states, at a minimum, to meet their NATO obligations for defence spending represented a continuum of US policy, they were usually pursued by less diplomatic, and at times more erratic, means. To more than a few Europeans, the 'dim if not dismal' future for NATO that then-US defense secretary Robert Gates had warned about in 2011 should European states fail to address spending shortages now appeared to loom large.

Of course, there have been other drivers behind renewed European interests in security and defence beyond presidents Putin and Trump and the prospect of Brexit. For example, even as concerns to manage migrant flows to and within the continent threatened to destabilise the EU from within, these pressures also contributed to pushing defence and security concerns back up European and EU agendas. The necessity of improving both Europe's external defences and its internal security were further reinforced by ongoing concerns over returning foreign fighters and the threat of jihadi terrorism. During 2017, Western Europe experienced at least 20 attacks in eight countries, with the UK the target of four deadly attacks in six months alone.

The need for Europe to strengthen both its defence capabilities and its operational capacities has become an accepted part of the mainstream political narrative not just beyond Europe but finally also within it. In 2017, the EU Rome declaration – which celebrated the 60th anniversary of the Union – pledged to strengthen security and defence, while in early 2018, the EU Commission announced budgetary plans that they trumpeted as amounting to a 22-fold increase in defence spending for the 2021–27 budgetary cycle compared with the 2014–20 budget cycle. In addition to the €27.5bn (US$32.2bn) allocated to defence and security, a European Peace Facility, financed by an off-budget fund to a ceiling of €10.5bn (US$12.3bn), will, among other activities, give the EU greater flexibility in financing peace-support activities and capacity building in the security sectors of partner countries around the world.

A slew of security and defence initiatives, with their associated acronyms, have been announced within EU structures. Any discussion of EU defence tends to be notably heavy on acronyms, reflecting at least in part the EU's ongoing tendency to create new frameworks where old ones have failed, and arguably leaving the reasons why these old initiatives might have failed unaddressed. In the relatively early days of these new initiatives, much of their purported progress has inevitably been confined to relatively comfortable discussions of process design. More time will be needed for the extent of member states' commitments to the full implementation of these assorted processes – and therefore the results they can deliver – to become clear. There are, however, four such initiatives (three led by the EU, one by a member state) whose development is worth paying particular attention to in the coming years.

In December 2017, the EU launched Permanent Structured Cooperation (PESCO), permitting member states that are willing and able to deepen defence cooperation to do so under the EU framework. The activation of PESCO – provided for in the 2009 Lisbon Treaty but never used – has at least the theoretical potential to prove something of a turning point, although this initiative still has a long way to go to prove itself to the degree that its establishment in December 2017 might fairly be described as the 'historic day for European defence' claimed by EU High Representative for Foreign Affairs and Security Policy/Vice-President Federica Mogherini. Certainly PESCO is doomed to disappoint if it focuses, as currently appears likely, on softer defence capabilities at the expense of delivering much-needed high-end capabilities. For example, one of the most popular projects among the first batch of 17 projects formally adopted in March 2018 concerns the development of a European Union Training Mission Competence Centre. This project is led by Germany and supported by Austria, Belgium, Cyprus, the Czech Republic, France, Ireland, Italy, Luxembourg, the Netherlands, Romania, Spain and Sweden. Nevertheless, the contribution to high-end capabilities that could be made by the full implementation even of the first 17 projects initially identified under PESCO is not to be disparaged. Italy is, for example, leading a project (supported by Greece and Slovakia) to build a prototype inter-operable European armoured infantry fighting vehicle/amphibious assault vehicle/light armoured vehicle. Furthermore, the development of PESCO is also interesting for the opening that its activation potentially provides for Germany to increase its defence engagement. Higher defence spending channelled through commitments under PESCO can at least be styled, in particular to a left of centre traditionally unenthusiastic about such engagements, as measures that promote 'more Europe', in a way that is not possible with unilateral or minilateral spending. If Berlin can follow through on its initial enthusiasm for this cooperation, then there are potential positive consequences for German defence capabilities, for the EU and for European defence cooperation, at least with regard to capability development.

A trial run of the EU's new Coordinated Annual Review of Defence (CARD) has also been under way since May 2017. CARD's objective is 'to develop a more structured way to deliver identified capabilities based on greater transparency, political visibility, and commitment from Member States'. The initiative is undoubtedly welcome – greater synchronisation in national-defence planning cycles and capability-development practices has an obvious contribution to make to Europe's quest for strategic seriousness. The results of the first trial run will be presented in autumn 2018 in preparation for full implementation of CARD on a voluntary basis from autumn 2019.

The European Defence Fund (EDF) – already under way but fully funded from the start of the EU's next budget cycle in 2021 – is intended to provide a comprehensive funding mechanism from research to the collaborative development of new defence capabilities. Set to be able to provide up to €13bn (US$15.2bn) in funding through the duration of the EU's next budgetary cycle from 2021–27, the EDF establishes the EU as the fourth-biggest defence-research and -technology investor in Europe (after France, the UK and Germany).

However, integrating these three key new EU processes with one another and with pre-existing processes under the EU and NATO umbrellas will be critical. CARD, for example, is supposed to analyse the implementation of priorities identified in the European Defence Agency's Capability Development Plan (CDP). The conclusions of CARD should then, in turn, inform the launch of new collaborative European projects, whether under PESCO, the European Defence Agency or in other bilateral or multilateral frameworks, some of which will be partly funded by the EDF. CARD will also have to be carefully integrated with NATO's Defence Policy Planning Process.

National interests persist

It will not be easy for the assorted actors and institutions involved – the EU Commission, the European Defence Agency and the EU member states – to escape the usual turf wars on decision-making, not least as the European Commission starts to establish itself as more of an influence on European security and defence planning, at least with regard to capabilities development.

Perhaps the most interesting of the increasing number of associations between European military forces taking place beyond the auspices of the EU under bilateral and multilateral arrangements is the initiative, championed by French President Emmanuel Macron, to develop a joint military intervention force. In June 2018, eight European states joined France in signing the initial 'Letter of Intent concerning the development of the European Intervention Initiative' (EII). Where PESCO appears set to focus largely on capabilities, the EII is more focused on operations. The inclusion in this initiative of a Brexit-bound UK as well as Denmark (an EU member state that has opted out of the Union's Common Security and Defence Policy) highlights the initiative's more flexible pragmatic focus on building active collaboration between some of the continent's forces most interested in security stabilisation.

However, Paris refused Berlin's persistent requests to develop this initiative directly under the PESCO framework, concerned in part that the inclusive nature in which PESCO appears, under German auspices, to be being fashioned (at least with regard to the EU), is likely to constrict PESCO's ambition and effectiveness. This decision to establish the EII between a group of 'willing and able' countries outside of the PESCO framework is likely to confuse the prospects for a similar effort that has been launched as one of the initial 17 projects under PESCO. There is a clear potential for overlap between the EII and the promised creation of an EU Force Crisis Response Operation Core, aimed at building up a list of deployable and inter-operable force components ready to deploy upon the decision to launch an EU operation.

In short, European efforts to engage more seriously on issues of defence and security may be improving, but redundancies and duplications of effort will not be easily limited. Europe's sovereign member states will continue to pursue their national interests and agendas in parallel to and beyond broader EU-related efforts. Despite the increasing role of the European Commission, EU member states will continue to take centre stage in the development of more effective European defences in the immediate future. The revised Elysée Treaty, due by the end of 2018, will confirm new ambitions for improving Franco-German bilateral defence cooperation. France will continue to lead the way for Europe in Africa, and increasingly in Asia. As it departs the EU, the UK will seek to build up stronger bilateral and minilateral ties with the continent, spurred on by the clear shortfall in its own military budgets. This includes renewing efforts with France under the 2010 Lancaster House Agreement, still the continent's most ambitious bilateral military partnership, and one that expanded bilateral cooperation in fields from capabilities to industry and from operations to intelligence. However, the UK will also want to find ways to continue to support collaboration on defence technology with other European member states, most notably Germany, which the UK specifically cited as an 'essential partner' in its Strategic Defence and Security Review in November 2015.

Joint minilateral efforts will remain very much in vogue. In addition to French-led efforts on the EII, NATO's Framework Nations Concept includes the UK-led Joint Expeditionary Force (focused on high-intensity operations); Italian leadership on joint stabilisation operations; and German efforts on Joint Force Protection (coordinating the development of capabilities as well as large multinational formations).

Escaping old realities?

Even with new initiatives, old constraining realities remain in place. Concerns of sovereignty and differences of strategic culture and ambition will continue to constrict the effectiveness and impact of European defensive capabilities and ambitions. At least some of the strategic make-over on which the EU and its member states appear to have embarked will end in failure. Issues over political will that have prevented the deployment of EU battlegroups – the multinational military units that have been operational since 2007 – will not disappear overnight, while the Common Security and Defence Policy missions will likely remain largely underwhelming in their mandate and ambition.

However, the pressures of events and the requirements to bolster both European resilience and resources of crisis management are perhaps finally forcing member states to find better ways to work around these old problems. As the activation of PESCO indicates, there is a growing recognition in Europe that coalitions of the willing are necessary for achieving effect. The EU and its member states appear to have decided that delivering on defence and security is more important than the former belief that unity is best preserved by acting only unanimously. That will have consequences for the future shape and nature of the EU, but it will also have consequences for European defence.

In the immediate years ahead, there are perhaps two key variables that are both directly related to security and defence and within European control. The first will be the EU's management of the Brexit process and the strategic nous its member states are collectively able to demonstrate in instructing their representative institutions towards an outcome that ensures that the UK remains a close security and defence partner. This is likely to have to involve some fundamental reimagining of the nature of the EU's relations and associations with third parties. Certainly, any potential defence and security benefits from the key initiatives discussed above would be dramatically overshadowed by a badly handled Brexit, given that the UK currently provides approximately 21% of EU defence spending and around 40% of the continent's total defence research and development spending. The second key variable is the development of the domestic discussions within Germany on the greater role this country now has to play in European defence and security. Even before it reaches NATO's 2% target, in the years ahead Germany is set to become Europe's largest military spender. How the German government chooses to invest in capabilities (and how it chooses to deploy them) will play a key part in the writing of both Europe's and the EU's strategic future.

There will be challenges to come that could yet derail these plans from other angles. One irony is that just as the EU is showing some early signs of starting to get its act together on security and defence, forces elsewhere could yet be mounting to tear it apart. The EU's future integrity is far from secure, with the Union under threat from populism and the pressures of managing migration, even as it continues to face efforts to divide and rule emanating from Moscow, Beijing and even now at times from Washington. Around the world, structural shifts are under way – could the makings of a structural shift, albeit of a different kind, now be in progress in Europe?

Although Europe's poor track record at turning strategic pretensions into reality makes it risky to be optimistic about its future efforts, the first signs could be emerging of a Europe that is crafting a response that at least aspires to be both structural and strategic. In the years ahead, it should not be beyond our imagination that Europe could yet realise at least some of its aspirations with regard to the reworking of its hard-power profile and presence.

MEXICO

Havana

THE BAHAMAS

CUBA

DOMINICAN
REPUBLIC

Mexico City

BELIZE

JAMAICA HAITI

Santo Domingo

Belmopan

Kingston

Port-au-
Prince

GUATEMALA

Tegucigalpa

Guatemala City

HONDURAS

EL SALVADOR

NICARAGUA

San Salvador

COSTA RICA

TRINIDAD & TOBAGO

Managua

Panama
City

Caracas

Georgetown

San José

PANAMA

Paramaribo

VENEZUELA

Cayenne

Bogotá

FRENCH GUYANA

Quito

COLOMBIA

GUYANA

SURINAME

ECUADOR

PERU

B R A Z I L

Lima

Brasília

La Paz

BOLIVIA

PARAGUAY

Asunción

CHILE

Santiago

URUGUAY

Buenos Aires

Montevideo

ARGENTINA

Atlantic Ocean

Pacific Ocean

Falkland Islands (UK)

South Georgia (UK)

©IISS

Chapter 10

Latin America

2017–18 Review

The year to mid-2018 in Latin America was marked by shifting relations with the US; risks presented by US President Donald Trump's war on trade; intensifying popular discontent with ineffective and corrupt governments; a worsening political and economic crisis in Venezuela; and disruptions to the Colombian peace process.

More than 18 months after taking office, the Trump administration still had not articulated a comprehensive policy towards Latin America, instead placing it under an overall umbrella doctrine of 'America First'. In this context, the administration has focused on trade protectionism and immigration – hallmarks of Trump's populist/nationalist platform. These have both short- and long-term implications for Latin America and are reshaping relations between the US and the region. The short-term impact is evident in a strong renewed emphasis on border security (in July 2018, Trump threatened to shut down the US government if Congress failed to provide more funds for a border wall); a crackdown on immigration (leading to the controversial policy of separating migrant children from their parents, which the courts forced the administration to reverse); a reduction in development aid to the region; a partial reversal of the previous Obama administration's rapprochement with Cuba;

the imposition of tariffs on steel and aluminium (affecting Mexico and Brazil); and the stringent demands being made by the US during talks to renegotiate the North American Free Trade Agreement (NAFTA) with Mexico and Canada.

Trump's hostile approach towards NAFTA in particular and Mexico in general since the start of his administration put the future of the trade agreement in jeopardy and risked profoundly harming relations with what has until now been a close US ally. NAFTA has been the centrepiece of US–Mexico economic ties since it came into effect in 1994. Despite this, Trump has made tough demands on Mexico and threatened to withdraw from the accord. After some compromises, Mexico accepted the Trump administration's changes (such as stricter local content requirements for the auto industry) in August 2018, in order to avoid a collapse of the trade agreement. However, the fate of a three-way NAFTA still hung in the balance, as Canada had not signed on to the modifications. Canada opposes strongly, for example, a provision that eliminates a dispute-settlement mechanism, and calls for changes to its dairy subsidies. Whether NAFTA survives as a three-nation accord, or as a bilateral deal with Mexico alone (and it is not certain that the US Congress would ratify a bilateral treaty), damage will have been done to the US–Mexico relationship.

In the longer term, Trump's nationalist stance and 'Make America Great Again' agenda also risks eroding cooperation between the US and Mexico and other Latin American countries in a range of other areas, such as drug trafficking, the fight against organised crime, terrorism, illicit financial flows, disaster preparedness and environmental issues. In addition, Trump's approach will further fuel a trend already under way in Latin America: the drive to diversify trade and economic relations away from dependency on the US. This trend has to a large extent benefited China, which has made inroads in Latin America since the turn of the millennium and has become a significant rival to the US for economic and geopolitical influence in the region. In that period, China has vastly expanded trade with the region, investing in infrastructure projects, locking in long-term access to natural resources (such as oil, metals and soybeans) and bailing out governments with tens of billions of dollars in loans. Although the US is still the largest trading partner for Latin America and the Caribbean as a whole, China is the second, and since 2015 has been the largest partner for South America, which exports mostly commodities. In some cases, such as that of Ecuador and Venezuela, China is also now the largest foreign creditor. According to the Boston University Global Development Policy Center, trade between China and Latin America and the Caribbean reached an estimated US$244bn in 2017, more than doubling the level achieved a decade earlier, and nearly halfway to the goal stated in 2014 by Chinese President Xi Jinping to raise bilateral trade with the region to US$500bn by 2024.

Besides its growing diplomatic, financial and commercial ties to the region, China is beginning to play a bigger role militarily as well. It sells some military equipment to governments in the region (notably Venezuela and Bolivia) and has hosted military officials from the region in Beijing. The China Satellite Launch and Tracking Control General, a division of the armed forces that directs China's space projects, has quietly built a US$50-million satellite-and-space mission-control centre in Argentina's Patagonia region. (The centre began operations in March of 2018.) With the Trump administration further alienating governments in Latin America with its harsh immigration and trade policies, China's influence in the region is likely to continue to grow.

Internally, Latin America has seen a shift in popular sentiment towards democratic institutions and, in some cases, a fundamental political realignment. Throughout the region, popular anger over corruption, impunity and rising crime has intensified. This has led to an erosion of support for traditional political parties and a loss of confidence in institutions and in democracy itself. According to a report released in August 2017 by the Latin American Public Opinion Project (LAPOP), a research institute housed at Vanderbilt University, support for democracy in the hemisphere has dropped significantly from 66.4% in 2014 to 57.8% in 2016–17. (Support for democracy peaked at 69.8% in 2008). Similarly, according to Latinobarómetro, an annual public-opinion survey which covers 18 countries in Latin America, public support for democracy has declined from 61% in 2010 to 53% in 2017.

The LAPOP survey revealed an even sharper fall in faith in elections. In 2016–17, only 39.1% of respondents said that they trusted elections in their countries. Confidence in the judiciary is also faltering. In some countries, a significant share (38–40%) of respondents voiced support for military coups, evidently seeing the armed forces as an alternative to corrupt and ineffectual politicians and political parties. Support for coups was highest in Jamaica, followed by Peru, Guatemala and Mexico.

Corruption was the major story of the region in 2017. Investigations into corruption continued to engulf Brazil's political class, exposing malfeasance among politicians and several of the country's largest companies, mainly entailing kickbacks in return for government contracts and other political favours. The investigation into the corrupt practices of the Brazilian construction giant Odebrecht continued to spread around the region last year, leading to the resignation of then Peruvian president Pedro Pablo Kuczynski and the forced removal from office of Ecuadorean vice-president Jorge Glas. Investigations of possible bribes received by politicians from Odebrecht continue in Peru, Colombia, Panama and the Dominican Republic.

In this environment, electorates in many countries have pushed out traditionally dominant political parties, opting in some cases for anti-establishment, anti-corruption and populist politicians. This was exemplified by the landslide victory of the left-wing candidate Andrés Manuel López Obrador in Mexico's general election in July 2018. López Obrador's party, the National Regeneration Movement (Morena), which was only founded in 2013, is now the dominant party in both houses of Mexico's Congress, while the Institutional Revolutionary Party (PRI), the political powerhouse which has controlled politics for most of the last 90 or so years, is in much-diminished third position. Of the nine states that had elections for governor, Morena won five, making these its first-ever wins for governorships; it also won control of the capital, Mexico City.

Similar developments are evident in Brazil, where allegations of misconduct led to the impeachment of then-president Dilma Rousseff in 2016; the conviction and imprisonment of some 100 politicians and businessmen; and the imprisonment in April 2018 of the former (and still popular) president Luiz Inácio Lula de Silva (Lula). The front-runner in the polls is Jair Bolsonaro, a far-right-wing congressional deputy. A retired military officer, Bolsonaro has long expressed a preference for dictatorship and promises strong leadership; to implement law and order; and to change the way politics is traditionally done in Brazil. Meanwhile, *Operação Lava Jato* (*Operation Car Wash*) – the massive investigation into corruption, kickbacks and illegal campaign financing – continues, threatening to take down more of the political and business elite.

While a trend that leads to cleaning up corruption and ending impunity is positive, there are potential downsides. Anti-corruption drives (such as *Operation Car Wash*) foment greater political polarisation and uncertainty, and the accompanying rise of outsider politicians puts at risk the shift in recent years away from populism and towards a more fiscally responsible, pro-globalisation stance that governments in Argentina, Peru, Colombia, Chile, Mexico and Brazil had been adopting.

Cuba remains the only fully authoritarian and one-party state in the region, and the only one that still espouses nearly complete state control of the economy. However, the death of Fidel Castro in November 2016 began the process of Cuba's transition to a new generation of leaders. Raúl Castro (aged 86) stepped down from the presidency in April 2018 and was replaced by Miguel Díaz-Canel (aged 58). There have also been economic changes: under Raúl Castro, Cuba expanded the role for a nascent private sector, and in July 2018 the National Assembly approved a new constitution that explicitly recognises private property and foreign investment as legitimate elements of Cuba's economic model. The new constitution also uses the term 'socialist rule of law' rather than 'communism' for the first time in describing its system. In addition, the new constitution seeks to decentralise political power, creating the position of prime minister and imposing term and age limits for top leadership positions. There have been no attempts to introduce more democratic practices, however, nor does the current round of economic liberalisation (which has been limited and heavily controlled from the top) suggest a shift to capitalism any time soon. Nonetheless, the new constitution and economic reforms could potentially present opportunities for broader political and economic change over time.

Cuba's influence in the Latin American region, meanwhile, has been much diminished in recent decades, since its economy suffered deeply from the demise of the Soviet Union in 1991 and more recently from the collapse of the economy of Venezuela, Cuba's latest benefactor. Nonetheless, Cuba remains a powerful symbol of self-determination and retains the support of and solid diplomatic relations with most countries in the region. With regard to the US, prospects for warmer relations have evaporated under Trump, who in November 2017 partly reversed the détente with Cuba introduced by former president Barack Obama, by tightening restrictions on travel to and business with the island. In March 2018 Trump reduced the size of the staff at the US Embassy in Havana.

The political and economic crisis in Venezuela – once one of Latin America's wealthiest and most democratically stable countries – presents one of the biggest challenges for the Latin American region. The country's woes have deepened significantly since 2017, marked by a heavily rigged election in May 2018 in which President Nicolás Maduro was elected to a second term; a collapse of the economy; soaring prices; rampant crime; and widespread hunger. According to IMF projections in July 2018, inflation in Venezuela could reach one million per cent in 2018, and the economy will contract by 18%. If the prediction holds, the economy will have shrunk by 50% over the last five years, one of the most severe economic collapses in the world in the last six decades, according Alejandro Werner, the head of the IMF's Western Hemisphere Department.

Escaping massive food and medicine shortages, rising crime and an increasingly repressive government, Venezuelans have abandoned the country en masse. More than 1m refugees fled to Colombia alone between mid-2017 and mid-2018, according to the International Federation of Red Cross and Red Crescent Societies. Others have left for elsewhere in

Latin America, the US and Europe. This is fuelling crime and presenting major fiscal, security and humanitarian challenges for neighbouring countries, which lack the necessary response capabilities. With economic mismanagement continuing, the critical oil industry in severe straits and Maduro's insistence that the country's woes are caused by an economic war being waged against it by the US, there is little sign of a turnaround in Venezuela in the near term. The economic and security spillover effects to other states in the region look set to persist.

Colombia's five-decade-long civil conflict with FARC was nominally brought to a close with the signing of a peace accord in 2016 and the group's demobilisation and transformation into a political party in late 2017, constituting a historic achievement for the outgoing administration of then-president Juan Manuel Santos that earned Santos a Nobel Peace Prize. However, uncertainty over the peace accords, which continue to be opposed by segments of Colombia's population, has heightened since the election to the presidency in June 2018 of Iván Duque. The new president's party, the right-wing Democratic Centre (CD), has been the most vocal opponent to the peace agreement. The Duque government, albeit unable to legally completely reverse the peace process, has promised to pursue changes to the accords, in line with his campaign promises. Some of the changes pertain to the Special Jurisdiction for Peace (JEP), a legal body created to try those accused of crimes related to the conflict. Duque and his supporters believe the tribunal will be too lenient with ex-FARC combatants. Furthermore, there is a risk that Duque will slow the implementation of other provisions under the agreement, including peacebuilding projects designed to integrate former guerrillas into civilian life and plans to invest in rural areas where FARC was previously active. Lack of government investment and interest in such initiatives could push more former guerrillas back into armed action.

There have been other obstacles and risks to peace in Colombia. A smaller armed group, the National Liberation Army (ELN), remains active, attacking primarily oil-related infrastructure and engaging in kidnappings, but Duque is unlikely to resume peace talks with the

ELN initiated by his predecessor. Some FARC combatants have also refused to demobilise, instead joining dissident groups that remain active in illicit activities. Duque will have to balance bringing about some modifications to the peace agreements with the improvement in security that he promised during his campaign, while avoiding a derailment of the demobilisation process. Until the peace process is more firmly entrenched, Colombia's socio-economic potential will not be realised.

Latin America: Drivers of Strategic Change

- The Trump administration's approach to Mexico, NAFTA and Latin America in general has damaged relations and risks eroding cooperation in tackling organised crime, drug trafficking and climate change.
- US policies have increased geopolitical opportunities for China in Latin America; the world's most populous country has already become a leading trade partner and creditor for many states in Latin America and it is building, slowly but surely, a stronger political and military profile.
- Corruption scandals across Latin America continue to disrupt the political order. Established parties have been usurped, and while public anger might lead to cleaner government through stronger oversight and judicial sanction, it might also tarnish faith in democracy and give greater scope for populist or authoritarian forms of government.
- Cuba has embarked on a generational change in leadership, which seems likely to support modest political and economic liberalisation. However, a reversion by the US to more hostile policies towards Cuba may act as a brake on this process.
- Venezuela's economic, political and humanitarian crisis shows no signs of easing or coming to an end. The negative economic and security effects on neighbouring countries are likely to worsen.

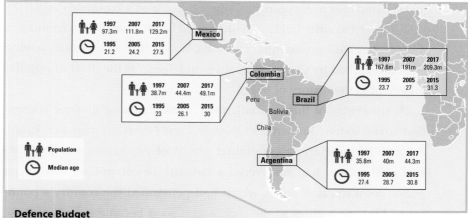

Defence Budget
(US$, constant 2010 prices)

	2008	2013	2018
Argentina	$3.55bn	$4.16bn	$4.21bn
Brazil	$28.26bn	$30.67bn	$33.73bn
Colombia	$10.52bn	$12.43bn	$12.82bn
Mexico	$3bn	$5.36bn	$5.85bn

An oil well operated by Venezuela's state-owned oil company PDVSA in Morichal, Venezuela

GDP per capita, Purchasing Power Parity (International $, constant 2011 prices)

Country	GDP
1997	
Argentina	$15,479
Brazil	$11,335
Colombia	$8,634
Mexico	$14,460
2007	
Argentina	$17,901
Brazil	$13,268
Colombia	$10,307
Mexico	$16,372
2017	
Argentina	$18,934
Brazil	$14,103
Colombia	$13,255
Mexico	$17,336

Sources: IISS; UN Department of Economic and Social Affairs (Population Division, 2017); World Bank

Brazil's *Operation Car Wash* and the Anti-corruption Wave

On 1 January 2011, Brazil's most powerful politicians waved at the crowd gathered outside of Planalto, the presidential palace in Brasília. To the left, Luiz Inácio Lula da Silva (popularly known as Lula) was ending his second term as president with an approval rating of 80%. In the centre was Dilma Rousseff, his hand-picked successor who had just become the country's first female president. To the right stood Michel Temer, Rousseff's vice-president from a centrist party, whose support had secured four more years for Lula and Rousseff's Workers' Party (PT). Fast-forward to 2018: Lula is in jail, banned by the courts from running in the October 2018 presidential elections; Rousseff is out of office, having been impeached by Congress in 2016; and Temer is the most unpopular president in the history of Brazil.

At the centre of this dramatic turn of events was a massive corruption investigation known as *Operação Lava Jato* (*Operation Car Wash*). An activist judiciary, a committed group of journalists and a mobilised civil society had uncovered a network of corruption, overpriced public contracts and bribes which had penetrated the country's political and business elites to the core, and it soon became clear that these corruption networks extended beyond Brazil. Once unleashed, citizen indignation about corruption and mismanagement spread throughout Latin America, as did judicial investigations (some related to the Brazilian case, some not). In nearly every country in Latin America, corruption is now at the centre of the political debate. Historically, the region has been known for its lack of transparency (most Latin American and Caribbean countries consistently score below the world average in Transparency International's Corruption Perceptions Index) and has had its share of corruption scandals. However, the regional fallout from *Operation Car Wash* has been unprecedented in terms of the scale of the corruption schemes uncovered, the number of politicians involved, the activism of judiciary systems in some countries and the level of public pressure in favour of prosecuting corrupt officials and businessmen. This anti-corruption wave is already having major consequences for political institutions and democratic governance in Latin America. It remains to be seen if the uncovering of corruption will strengthen the rule of law in Latin America or permanently erode citizens' trust in democratic institutions, fuelling a new era of anti-establishment populism that weakens the very checks and balances that are required for uprooting corruption in the long term.

Brazilian political dysfunction and scandals under Lula

The Brazilian political system is highly fragmented: political parties are weak and frequently (and abruptly) change their ideological orientation depending on what is politically convenient. Moreover, evangelical churches, the rural sector and other organisations have created their own parties to promote their particular interests, siding with parties of the left or the right to gain access to patronage networks. Outside of the most established parties – Lula's PT and the Social Democratic Party (PSDB) – and a few others, party labels mean nothing, and merely function as platforms to boost the careers of their leaders. In the 2014 elections, for instance, the lower house of Congress was split among 25 different parties, a world record. As a result, presidents from the PT and PSDB have created loose coalitions of many parties, joined together only by promises of government jobs and ministries for their leaders. For example, Dilma Rousseff's first cabinet included 37 minister-level officials, of which her own party held only 16 positions.

This highly volatile political environment has created a powerful incentive structure for corrupt practices to fester. Since Brazil's transition to democracy in 1985, almost every government has been accused of promoting or benefiting from corruption. In 1992, then-president Fernando Collor de Mello was impeached by Congress under allegations of influence-peddling, corruption and handing out government jobs for political support. The next major scandal erupted in 2005, when the Lula administration was accused of managing a complex system of monthly payments to lawmakers to ensure their support in Congress. The case was known as *Mensalão* (monthly allowance). Several leaders from Lula's PT and top public officials in his government were arrested and convicted, but Lula himself avoided prosecution. During that time the Brazilian economy was booming and the president was highly popular, both domestically and abroad. Despite the scandal, Lula was re-elected in 2006 with 60% of the vote in the second round against the candidate from the PSDB.

Things started to change once Rousseff – Lula's former chief of staff – became president in 2011. While she drew praise at the beginning of her term for her anti-corruption stance, which included sacking several ministers after they were accused of mismanagement, it soon became clear that Rousseff lacked Lula's charisma and political skill. That became a liability once the economy began to unravel: Brazil's GDP grew by only 0.5% in 2014 before entering the worst recession of its history in 2015 and 2016. She won re-election in 2014 by 3.2 percentage points, the narrowest margin in the country's history. Known for her inflexibility, the president was unable to maintain her coalition as her popularity began to wane sharply during her second term.

Petrobras and *Operation Car Wash*

In early 2014, a judicial investigation into a money-laundering scheme gradually uncovered a massive network of corruption centred around Petrobras, the Brazilian state-controlled oil company and the country's largest corporation. Prosecutors started looking into Petrobras after obtaining evidence while raiding a currency-exchange office located within a car wash in Brasilia. It was the starting point of the largest corruption investigation in Brazil's (and Latin America's) history: *Operation Car Wash*.

Unlike the *Mensalão* scandal, this time prosecutors did not relent in their investigation, aided by the scale of the allegations and the political weakness of the government. The middle classes, which had grown substantially during the economic boom, demanded accountability and expressed their anger against the political class by protesting in the streets. Under constant judicial pressure, several politicians and business leaders signed guilty pleas and began sharing information with judges and prosecutors to reduce their sentences. This allowed the judiciary to uncover a massive corrupt network by which Brazil's largest corporations overcharged Petrobras for construction and service work. The extra money was shared between officials from Petrobras and their partners and used to pay bribes to dozens of politicians in Brazil and other countries to secure contracts and influence. It is estimated that US$2 billion was misappropriated in this way.

With her popularity in single digits and the economy in free fall, Rousseff lost control of the streets and Congress: as tourists and athletes arrived in Brazil to attend the Rio 2016 Olympics, thousands of Brazilians were protesting in the country's main cities against corruption and economic stagnation. Unable to prove that the president had been personally involved in the Petrobras scheme, lawmakers instead impeached her for massaging public accounts by temporarily transferring funds from state banks to the national treasury, an illegal practice that had been common for decades. At the time of Rousseff's impeachment proceedings, almost two-thirds of the 594 members of Congress had been convicted or were under investigation for corruption. In August 2016, Rousseff was removed from office and vice-president Temer – who had switched to the opposition months before – replaced her as the president of Brazil.

Rousseff's removal did nothing to quell citizen indignation and judicial investigations. Several members of Temer's cabinet had to resign after prosecutors linked them to *Operation Car Wash* and other scandals. Temer himself remains under investigation – phone conversations were leaked in which he allegedly discusses bribes – but is being protected by Congress, which has refused to lift the president's judicial protection. Temer's approval rating is almost non-existent at only 4%. Meanwhile, *Operation Car Wash* continues to involve politicians of all parties. In April 2018, the Supreme Court ordered Aécio Neves – the PSDB leader who lost against Dilma Rousseff in 2014 – to be prosecuted for corruption. One month later, the previously untouchable Lula was sent to prison, accused of receiving an apartment as payment from Petrobras's contractors.

Odebrecht and the anti-corruption wave in Latin America

Brazilian prosecutors soon discovered that the network of illegal payments established by Petrobras and other major Brazilian corporations included politicians in other Latin American countries (and some African ones, such as Angola and Mozambique.) The Odebrecht corporation – Brazil's major infrastructure contractor – was identified as the most active in paying bribes throughout Latin America. In July 2015, Marcelo Odebrecht (head of the company that bears his family's name) agreed to cooperate with *Operation Car Wash* prosecutors in exchange for a reduced sentence. His information precipitated a wave of new allegations which had massive political consequences in many countries in addition to Brazil. In some countries – notably Guatemala and other Central American nations – previously dormant judicial systems responded to citizen indignation by accelerating corruption investigations. The strength of civil society proved a key factor: connected by social media, anti-corruption groups were able to organise protests, target their campaigns against corrupt politicians and pressure the media and the judiciary to take allegations seriously. The Petrobras and Odebrecht scandals might have served as triggers, but anti-corruption efforts in the region quickly included other cases.

The anti-corruption wave struck Guatemala first. In early 2015, the International Commission against Impunity in Guatemala (CICIG) – a United Nations-backed body created to support the country's judiciary – began uncovering evidence of corruption in the customs office that implicated then-president Otto Pérez Molina and his vice-president Roxana Baldetti. Amid unprecedented public demonstrations, by September 2015 both had been forced to resign and were in jail awaiting trial. Chile is one of the least corrupt countries in Latin America according to Transparency International, but in early 2015 the Chilean press revealed dubious land deals by a company owned by President Michelle Bachelet's daughter-in-law, tarnishing the president's image. Allegations of improper relations between large corporations and public officials caused uproar and affected politicians of the centre-right and centre-left. In early 2017, Peruvian prosecutors opened an investigation against former president Alejandro Toledo, who was accused of having received US$20 million in bribes from Odebrecht. (Toledo fled to the United States and remains a fugitive.) In March 2018, Peru's embattled incumbent president Pedro Pablo Kuczynski resigned as Congress was getting ready to impeach him after new evidence suggested that he had received payments from Odebrecht during his tenure as Toledo's finance minister.

Inevitably, corruption became a main issue in Latin America's political debates. In Ecuador, President Lenín Moreno supported the prosecution and imprisonment of his vice-president Jorge Glas in late 2017 under charges of receiving bribes from Odebrecht during a previous stint as minister of strategic sectors. Glas was a protégé of former president Rafael Correa, who accused Moreno of using the scandal for political gain. In Colombia, imprisoned Odebrecht managers confessed to having made illegal payments in 2014 to the presidential campaigns of Juan Manuel Santos (the incumbent who won re-election) and his main opponent, Oscar Zuluaga, an ally of former president Alvaro Uribe. Some of Uribe's former ministers were also charged with taking bribes. In Argentina, Odebrecht claims to have paid US$35m in bribes in exchange for public contracts between 2007 and 2015. Although the Argentine judiciary has launched investigations into Julio de Vido (the infrastructure minister at the time) and he is in jail awaiting trial for other cases, to date there have been no convictions in Argentina related to this scandal.

Mexico is a peculiar case: there is evidence linking public officials to the Odebrecht scheme but the courts have been remarkably slow in their investigations. This did not stop the investigations of civil society and the press, which uncovered numerous corruption cases under the administration of Enrique Peña Nieto, including a house worth US$7m given by a public-works contractor to Peña Nieto's wife. Citizen indignation over these scandals boosted anti-corruption candidate Andrés Manuel López Obrador, who won the presidency with 53% of the vote in July 2018 and will succeed the unpopular Peña Nieto. Finally, the former representative of Odebrecht in Venezuela confessed to having paid over

US$35m in bribes to the government of Nicolás Maduro in exchange for public-works contracts (80% of which were never finished). Not surprisingly, given the total control Maduro exerts over the judiciary, there were no investigations.

Implications for democratic governance and the economy

The current anti-corruption wave in Latin America is unprecedented in at least three ways: firstly, because of the geographical scope of the scandals, which have affected most countries in the region; secondly, because of the sheer number of former and incumbent public officials from all levels of government who are under investigation or in jail; and thirdly, because polls confirm that corruption has risen to the top of citizen concerns. However, the current situation is perhaps more reflective of changing attitudes rather than a dramatic rise in corrupt practices. As millions of Latin Americans left poverty during the economic boom of the early 2000s, they also became more demanding of their governments. For decades, most Latin Americans tolerated corrupt politicians as long as they delivered in terms of economic growth and social policies. Even during previous times of economic downturn (as in the late 1990s), anti-corruption movements were short-lived, only took place in a few countries and were usually unable to push judicial systems into seriously investigating corruption allegations, especially when they involved incumbent presidents or ministers.

The new lack of tolerance towards corruption may mark a major breakthrough for Latin American democracies. The transition to democracy which began in the 1980s resulted in most countries in the region (with some exceptions, such as Venezuela) putting an end to authoritarianism, military coups and political violence. However, democratic institutions and the rule of law – including judicial independence, functioning checks and balances, and transparency and accountability mechanisms – remain weak in many countries. If sustained, citizens' new-found concern about corruption could provide the necessary political incentives to reinforce these institutions. There is evidence of this already happening: even before the scandals broke, civil society successfully lobbied for

access-to-information laws to ensure the public availability of government data and official documents. In recent years, some countries have
increased the mandatory minimum sentences for corruption and created
special commissions to issue recommendations on how to better fight corruption and mismanagement. Non-governmental organisations devoted
to investigating corruption have been established across Latin America
(some extremely competent, others less so). Finally, a new generation
of judicial officers – of which *Operation Car Wash* judge Sérgio Moro is
the best example – are not afraid to take on their countries' most powerful politicians and cultivate relations with the press and civil society to
defend their investigations against pressures from political elites.

On the other hand, there are reasons to be less optimistic. As proven
all over the world, anti-establishment sentiments can open the way for
political outsiders with little capacity or willingness to strengthen the
rule of law. In Guatemala, for instance, former comedian Jimmy Morales
won the presidency on an anti-corruption platform, only to turn against
the CICIG when the international body began investigating corruption
allegations against his family and ministers. In Brazil, with Lula in jail
and unable to compete in the October 2018 presidential elections, the race
is being led by Jair Bolsonaro, a former military officer and extreme-right
candidate who praises the country's military dictatorship (including its
human-rights violations) and has made grotesque remarks about black
people, women and sexual minorities.

Anti-corruption proceedings have also exacerbated political polarisation in many countries, straining democratic processes. For example, PT
supporters in Brazil think that the impeachment of Rousseff by Congress
in 2014 was a 'coup' and accuse judges of jailing Lula based on fabricated
evidence in order to exclude him from returning to the presidency. It
does not help that most of the lawmakers who impeached Rousseff are
themselves under investigation for corruption; that Lula was running
again for the presidency in October 2018 and was ahead in opinion polls
at the time of his arrest; and that Michel Temer will remain president
until January 2019, despite the mounting evidence against him and his
closest political associates. As the Brazilian case shows, the new-found

celebrity of judges and prosecutors such as Moro is a double-edged sword: it increases their influence but also tarnishes their claim to be impartial. Protracted citizen distrust and political turmoil have also made it harder for governments to rule effectively as well as impacting economic growth. There is a regional tendency to cast doubt on the credibility of all public officials, regardless of their background and actual probity. In a tense political environment, political negotiations and compromises – which are necessary elements in democratic governance – are viewed with suspicion, which may paralyse the government's machinery.

The economic impact of the anti-corruption campaign has been twofold. The first impact was direct: Brazilian corporations involved in the corruption networks brought to light by *Operation Car Wash* had contracts all over Latin America, most of which have been cancelled or suspended. The second type of impact has been indirect, and perhaps broader: with political instability and numerous changes in legislation in many Latin American countries, some of the region's largest corporations (whether involved in corruption cases or not) are keeping their distance from government-backed projects and reducing their investment in infrastructure, construction and other sectors that are critical for long-term economic growth. Once again, the political and economic aspects of *Operation Car Wash* are closely tied: Latin American and extra-regional companies will start investing again if they sense that governments are capable of implementing regulatory frameworks and dealing with corruption scandals. However, it may take time for the effectiveness of such changes to become apparent: while almost all countries in Latin America have changed regulations and laws on public procurement and transparency after the scandals, most of these changes have not been fully implemented yet and the region is notable for the weakness of enforcement mechanisms. In Peru, for instance, the government banned companies under investigation from participating in public works, only to backtrack when most infrastructure projects became paralysed. It will take time for Latin American countries to get regulations right and to ensure that these laws are actually implemented and enforced.

What now?

One of the most significant changes this wave has brought is an unprecedented level of collaboration between judiciaries and anti-corruption bodies in different Latin American countries. This cooperation allowed prosecutors and judges to share information, gather evidence and put together the multiple pieces of Latin America's massive corruption schemes. The role of the US Department of Justice has also been significant as most of the suspected corporations are registered in the US or participate in the New York Stock Exchange. In early 2018, for example, Petrobras agreed to pay US$2.95bn to settle a class-action corruption lawsuit in the US. Besides Petrobras, one of the most important cases is JBS, the world's largest meat-processing company, which is also accused of paying bribes to politicians in Brazil. In May 2017, JBS agreed to pay US$3.2bn to settle a legal case in Brazil, and it is being sued by US investors as well.

However, regional cooperation and internationally backed bodies cannot replace strong and independent domestic institutions. The funding of the CICIG is under threat, while the Mission to Support the Fight against Corruption and Impunity in Honduras (MACCIH) – created in 2016 and backed by the Organisation of American States – has been plagued by lack of interest in the region, resistance from the local government and internal dysfunction. The political outlook for the region once again highlights the crucial need for robust institutions to emerge from the scandal. A Bolsonaro victory (although still unlikely) in the October 2018 presidential elections in Brazil would only deepen the erosion of Brazilian institutions. During his successful campaign for the Mexican presidency, López Obrador pledged to tackle corruption in the country but was ambiguous about what specific reforms he would pursue – his effectiveness at delivering on this promise will be a key indicator of whether there is genuine political desire for reform. Either way, it is not enough to have honest politicians; strong institutions are needed to make these efforts sustainable.

Latin America's long-overdue campaign against corruption will have lasting consequences. If channelled through democratic institutions, the political and social forces behind Latin America's anti-corruption wave may result in stronger and more independent judiciaries, actual enforcement of existing anti-corruption regulations and increased accountability at all levels of government. These are difficult processes that take time, even under the most optimistic scenarios. If Latin America manages to clean up its governments and private sectors without succumbing to anti-democratic forces, then the current painful period of intense scrutiny and uncertainty will be worth it.

China and Latin America: From Boom to Maturity

Relations between China and Latin America and the Caribbean (LAC) took off in the early years of the twenty-first century, driven by the rapid increase in exports to China. LAC experienced what was known as the 'commodity boom' as Chinese demand for raw materials improved the terms of trade and fuelled a period of economic growth. In addition, China provided billions of dollars in loans to LAC governments, mostly for infrastructure and energy projects carried out by Chinese corporations. However, Chinese growth rates declined sharply in 2012, putting an end to the boom and sending most of LAC into a period of economic stagnation from which it still has not fully recovered. China's growing role in LAC has also generated concern in the United States about the emergence of a competitor in its traditional zone of influence.

Economic engagement

The new era in China–LAC relations began after Beijing launched its 'going-out' policy in 1999. Under this framework, the Chinese government encouraged its state-owned and private companies to expand overseas in order to achieve three goals: firstly, to secure the raw materials needed to sustain high-speed growth and urbanisation within China; secondly, to streamline and reform Chinese corporations by forcing them to compete in the global economy; and thirdly, to conquer new markets for China's manufacturing exports.

LAC, a relatively stable region with vast natural resources and significant consumer markets, was ideal for the new policy. To support the economic effort, the Chinese government boosted its diplomatic presence in LAC, including visits to the region by presidents Jiang Zemin in 2001 and Hu Jintao in 2004. Chinese overtures had an almost immediate impact on trade with LAC, which grew by more than 200% between 2006 and 2016. In less than a decade, China became the first- or second-largest trading partner of most LAC countries, and the second largest for the region as a whole after the US. According to the United Nations Economic Commission for Latin America and the Caribbean (ECLAC), trade with China represented 1% of LAC's exports and 2% of LAC's imports in the year 2000. By 2014, China's share had increased to 9% and 16% respectively.

China's demand for oil, iron, copper, soybeans and other commodities lifted international prices and led to a period of fast growth for most LAC economies, especially South American raw-material exporters. Real GDP for commodity exporters in LAC grew by 4.5% per annum on average between 2003 and 2012, up from 2.3% per annum on average between 1990 and 2002. This economic expansion was much welcomed in a region that had been hit hard by a 'lost decade' for growth in the 1980s and the high social costs of macroeconomic adjustment in the 1990s. Sustained trade with China also allowed these countries to overcome the 2008 global crisis: LAC GDP grew by almost 4% that year and fell by 1.8% in 2009, only to rebound in 2010 by a robust 5.8%. Growth, together with targeted social policies, also had positive effects on LAC's socio-economic landscape: according to the IMF, poverty in LAC decreased from 27% to 12% and inequality dropped by 11% between 2000 and 2014, at the height of the China-induced commodity boom.

At the same time, the growing presence of Chinese manufactured goods (of increasing complexity and technological content) put pressure on LAC industries as relatively cheap Chinese industrial goods competed with those of LAC companies in their own countries and pushed local companies out of their traditional markets in the region and in the US. Although Brazilian and Argentinian manufacturers were affected, these countries still benefited from China's imports of raw materials. In contrast, Mexico and Central America did not enjoy a 'China boom', as Chinese goods competed with their industrial exports to the US market. Booming trade with China has therefore deepened LAC's dependence on commodity exports, exposing the region to sudden shifts in terms of trade and tying it to the performance of the Chinese economy. LAC exports to China are much more concentrated in commodities than LAC's overall sales: between 2011 and 2016, for instance, raw materials represented 87% of regional exports to China, but only 52% of LAC's total exports to the world.

The challenges of imbalanced trade patterns became clear in 2012. From that year on, the Chinese economy entered what was termed the 'new normal' period, with Chinese GDP growth rates falling to around 7% a year, a steep decline from the 10% annual rates of previous decades. The Chinese authorities amended their development plan to place more emphasis on domestic consumption as an engine for growth, instead of depending on exports and foreign direct investment. China's new normal reduced international prices of commodities (between 2011 and 2016 energy prices fell by 70%, metals by 50% and agricultural commodities by 35%) and moderated demand in the Asian giant for LAC exports. This brought a sudden end to LAC's commodity boom, causing many countries in the region to fall into a recession. The Brazilian economy – LAC's largest – contracted by 3.8% in 2014 and by 3.6% the following year, representing the worst recession in the country's history. More broadly, economic stagnation threatens to reverse recent social improvements in LAC as the millions who entered the middle classes during the boom period risk falling back into poverty.

'Going-out' policy becomes the Belt and Road Initiative?
China's economic engagement in LAC under the going-out policy is not limited to trade. Since 2005, Chinese development banks have disbursed nearly US$150 billion in loans to LAC, mostly devoted to infrastructure and energy projects. This is more than the World Bank, IMF and Inter-American Development Bank (IADB) have spent in the region in that

period, combined. These loans are usually conditional on recipient governments hiring Chinese companies to build the projects in line with the going-out policy goal of promoting Chinese corporations abroad. Nearly half of the projects took place in Venezuela, followed by Brazil, Argentina and Ecuador, although not all announced initiatives have come to fruition. Several China-funded mega-projects (such as the planned railway between Brazil and Peru) have been on hold for years, while others (such as the Nicaragua Canal) appear to have been cancelled. But throughout LAC, Chinese funds have been used to improve oil production, renew decrepit railways and build hydroelectric power plants. In addition, the People's Bank of China (China's central bank) has signed currency-swap agreements with its counterparts in Argentina, Brazil and Chile to reinforce financial cooperation and promote the use of the renminbi as an international reserve currency.

Besides trade and finance, the third main instrument of Chinese economic engagement under the going-out policy in LAC is investment. Although they are not as prominent as their American and European counterparts, Chinese state-owned and private corporations have expanded their operations in LAC countries, both by acquiring local companies and through greenfield investments. Following the general goals of China's overtures to the region, most of this investment goes into infrastructure, energy and extractive industries. For instance, Chinese corporations control most of Brazil's electric grid and have a strong presence in Peru's mining sector. In recent times, however, other types of Chinese corporations have made inroads in LAC as well, including car manufacturer Chery (which built a production plant in Brazil) and telecoms giant Huawei. Chinese commercial banks – including ICBC, the largest bank in the world – are also opening branches in LAC to provide financial services.

China's engagement with LAC took on a new dimension in 2013 when Xi Jinping took office as president of China and launched a more assertive foreign policy that was aimed at increasing China's global influence abroad as part of a national rejuvenation programme dubbed 'China Dream'. Xi visited the region in 2014 and 2016, with Premier

Latin America's Trade with China

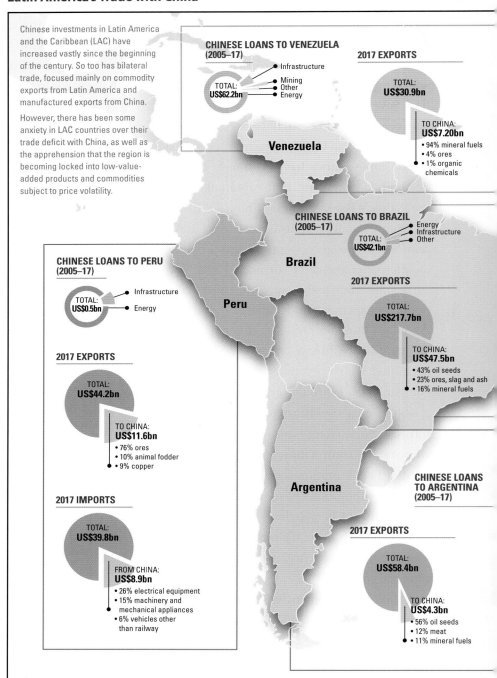

Chinese investments in Latin America and the Caribbean (LAC) have increased vastly since the beginning of the century. So too has bilateral trade, focused mainly on commodity exports from Latin America and manufactured exports from China.

However, there has been some anxiety in LAC countries over their trade deficit with China, as well as the apprehension that the region is becoming locked into low-value-added products and commodities subject to price volatility.

CHINESE LOANS TO VENEZUELA
(2005–17)
TOTAL: US$62.2bn
- Infrastructure
- Mining
- Other
- Energy

2017 EXPORTS
TOTAL: US$30.9bn
TO CHINA: US$7.20bn
- 94% mineral fuels
- 4% ores
- 1% organic chemicals

Venezuela

CHINESE LOANS TO BRAZIL
(2005–17)
TOTAL: US$42.1bn
- Energy
- Infrastructure
- Other

Brazil

2017 EXPORTS
TOTAL: US$217.7bn
TO CHINA: US$47.5bn
- 43% oil seeds
- 23% ores, slag and ash
- 16% mineral fuels

CHINESE LOANS TO PERU
(2005–17)
TOTAL: US$0.5bn
- Infrastructure
- Energy

Peru

2017 EXPORTS
TOTAL: US$44.2bn
TO CHINA: US$11.6bn
- 76% ores
- 10% animal fodder
- 9% copper

2017 IMPORTS
TOTAL: US$39.8bn
FROM CHINA: US$8.9bn
- 26% electrical equipment
- 15% machinery and mechanical appliances
- 6% vehicles other than railway

Argentina

CHINESE LOANS TO ARGENTINA
(2005–17)

2017 EXPORTS
TOTAL: US$58.4bn
TO CHINA: US$4.3bn
- 56% oil seeds
- 12% meat
- 11% mineral fuels

Sources: *Atlantic Council-OECD, Inter-American Dialogue*

LATIN AMERICA AND CARIBBEAN TRADE WITH CHINA

2017 IMPORTS

TOTAL:
US$10.1bn

FROM CHINA:
US$1.8bn
- 22% machinery and mechanical appliances
- 11% electrical equipment
- 10% iron and steel

US$ (thousands)

- Imports from China
- Exports to China

200,000,000

150,000,000

100,000,000

50,000,000

0

2001 2002 2003 2004 2005 2006 2007 2008 2009 2010 2011 2012 2013 2014 2015 2016 2017

LATIN AMERICAN AND CARIBBEAN IMPORTS/EXPORTS FROM/TO CHINA

2017 IMPORTS

TOTAL:
US$150.8bn

FROM CHINA:
US$27.3bn
- 32% electrical equipment
- 15% machinery and mechanical appliances
- 8% organic chemicals

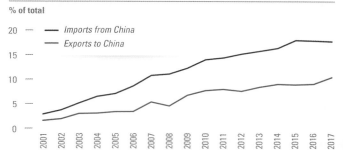

% of total

— Imports from China
— Exports to China

20

15

10

5

0

2001 2002 2003 2004 2005 2006 2007 2008 2009 2010 2011 2012 2013 2014 2015 2016 2017

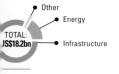

- Other
- Energy
- Infrastructure

TOTAL:
US$18.2bn

ANNUAL CHINESE FOREIGN DIRECT INVESTMENT IN LATIN AMERICA

2017 IMPORTS

TOTAL:
US$66.9bn

FROM CHINA:
US$12.3bn
- 32% electrical equipment
- 20% machinery and mechanical appliances
- 6% organic chemicals

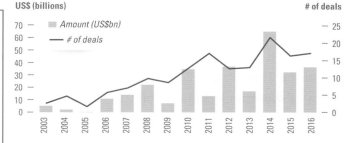

US$ (billions)   # of deals

70   Amount (US$bn)   25
60   — # of deals   20
50   15
40
30   10
20   5
10
0   0

2003 2004 2005 2006 2007 2008 2009 2010 2011 2012 2013 2014 2015 2016

CHINESE FDI IN US$BN (2003–2016)

Venezuela	Argentina	Peru	Brazil
2	5	18	61

of the State Council Li Keqiang visiting in 2015. In January 2018, the Chinese authorities formally invited LAC to participate in the Belt and Road Initiative (BRI) – a grand plan of massive infrastructure projects funded by China – despite the region being nowhere near Eurasia, the original geographical area of the project. Some China-funded infrastructure projects in LAC have already been rebranded to make them part of the BRI, including a railway that will run parallel to the canal in Panama, with more expected to come. China has also sought to institutionalise its relationship with LAC countries through the Community of Latin American and Caribbean states (CELAC), a group created in 2010. Xi promised an era of renewed cooperation at the China–CELAC forum held in Brasilia in July 2014, citing targets of US$250bn in Chinese investment in LAC and US$500bn in bilateral trade by 2024. Brazil is a founding member of the Asian Infrastructure Investment Bank and the BRICS's New Development Bank (both based in China and dedicated to funding infrastructure projects), and other LAC countries are expected to join soon.

Challenge to US influence in LAC

China's rapid and sustained rise in LAC poses an unprecedented challenge to US influence in the region. While the US administration under Barack Obama warned about the imbalances of growing LAC–China relations, it also attempted to counter Beijing's increasing influence in the region with more US engagement. These efforts included the negotiation of the Trans-Pacific Partnership (a large-scale trade agreement covering 12 countries including Chile, Colombia and Mexico); a thaw with Cuba after years of a policy of isolation that was much derided in LAC; and an assistance package to some Central American countries.

However, the Trump administration has taken a markedly different approach, stepping up the rhetoric against China's role in LAC while dismantling most of Obama's initiatives to restore US standing in its neighbourhood. Ahead of a tour of LAC in early 2018, then US secretary of state Rex Tillerson said that China was 'using economic statecraft to pull the region into its orbit', while US Under Secretary for

International Affairs David Malpass warned that China's offer to assist with development 'often involves trading short-term gains for long-term dependency'. The US government has also criticised China for its role in sustaining the regime of Nicolás Maduro in Venezuela. In February 2018, Malpass said that 'China has been by far Venezuela's largest lender supporting poor governance'. Chinese development banks have provided over US$60bn in loans to Venezuela since 2005, mostly to sustain Venezuela's crumbling oil sector. The majority of these loans are commodity-backed, which means that Venezuela will repay them with oil shipments to China. Despite an economic and social collapse that has reached catastrophic proportions, along with US sanctions and increasing pressure in LAC against Maduro's authoritarianism, ties with China and Russia have allowed the Venezuelan regime to stay afloat.

The more forthright US tone regarding China's involvement in the region was read by some LAC countries as a demand to choose between Beijing and Washington, a choice which LAC countries refuse to make. An ascending China has increased the space of manoeuvre for the region, and for the first time in more than a century, LAC has an opportunity to reduce its dependence on the US. The US and multilaterals such as the IMF and the World Bank were for decades the only options for LAC countries under financial strain or looking for infrastructure funds. By contrast, funds from China come with almost no conditionality (no transparency measures, oversight, etc.) and tend to be approved more quickly. A US policy based on anti-Chinese rhetoric combined with isolationism will be self-defeating, and will open new opportunities for Beijing to extend its influence in LAC.

China will not be able to replace Washington's military, economic and geopolitical clout in LAC, but it is not trying to. Military cooperation between China and LAC is relatively small outside of Venezuela, and Beijing – recognising LAC as a US zone of influence – is very careful to avoid antagonising Washington. The non-economic goals of Chinese policy in LAC are so far limited to increasing its soft power (by presenting itself as a partner for regional development) and promoting the 'One China' policy against Taiwan: ten of the 19 countries that still recognise

Taipei as the legitimate representative of China are in LAC. Panama switched diplomatic recognition to Beijing in 2017, and the Dominican Republic followed suit in 2018. Although there is no official confirmation, it is believed that many other LAC nations have already privately expressed their desire to switch recognition to the Chinese government. Beijing, however, prefers to pace these announcements so that they have maximum impact in international media and over the Taiwanese government. Decades ago, Taiwan could compete with Beijing in trade opportunities and handouts to its diplomatic allies. With China on its way to being the world's largest economy, the costs of not recognising Beijing are getting higher, highlighting the extent to which economic interests lie at the heart of LAC political realignment. The ambition of BRICS to reshape the global system has subsided (at least for now), especially in Brazil given its economic and political crisis, but LAC countries are more than willing to join Chinese initiatives such as the Asian Infrastructure Investment Bank and the BRI if they provide more financing opportunities. Such moves are pragmatic and have little to do with the recipient country's geopolitical ambitions.

Ultimately, despite the sterner US rhetoric and Xi's new initiatives, China's goals in LAC remain mostly economic in nature, just as they were when China's going-out policy was announced in 1999. China's involvement in Venezuela, for example, had more to do with economic interests than ideological affinity. Given Venezuela's increasing isolation and imploding economy, Beijing saw an opportunity to secure access to one of the world's largest reserves of oil – the fact that it was also propping up an anti-US regime in Caracas was a welcome by-product – but the deal itself did not prove a clear win for China. The corruption and mismanagement of the Venezuelan government and state-owned oil company PDVSA meant that Chinese loans were not used to optimise oil production, with Venezuelan oil production plummeting from more than 2.4 million barrels per day (b/d) in 2008 to fewer than 1.5m b/d ten years later. In a tacit acknowledgement of what had become a failed investment, in 2017 Chinese banks stopped all loans to Venezuela and refused to extend the grace period of previous disbursements.

Challenges ahead

The first challenge to LAC–China relations is LAC demands for a more balanced trade relationship in contrast to the prevailing North–South pattern of manufactured goods being exchanged for commodities. Beijing is aware that tension surrounding the current trade model is hurting its image in the region and is looking to address it without jeopardising its economic goals in LAC. In 2014, for instance, Xi Jinping announced a new framework for LAC–China cooperation in which traditional topics such as agriculture and energy were joined by new areas, including manufacturing, innovation and information technologies. To date, China's tariff and non-tariff trade measures have favoured imports of basic raw materials from LAC, blocking more elaborate goods, but that position is beginning to change. In line with China's new emphasis on domestic consumption, the Chinese Ministry of Commerce has made it easier for LAC products such as beef, wine and soybean oil to enter the Chinese market. This opening could become even more accentuated if the trade war with Washington becomes permanent, creating an opening for LAC countries to replace US agro-industry in the Chinese market by exporting more value-added goods based on commodities.

The second area of concern for LAC is the environmental and regulatory impact of Chinese activities in the region. Increased agricultural production to meet Chinese demand has accelerated deforestation in Brazil and other countries, while projects for massive Chinese-funded roads and hydroelectric dams negatively affect natural and indigenous reserves in the Amazon River basin, generating protests from local communities. In Argentina, the construction of two hydropower dams financed by China in Patagonia has been delayed and suspended several times due to environmental concerns. In Colombia, a China-backed fund managed by the IADB is financing the construction of the Ituango Dam, which will become the largest in the country. The Ituango Dam has been marred by environmental conflicts and a near overflow in May 2018 which threatened thousands of people living in its vicinity. Chinese mining corporations operating in Colombia, Ecuador and Peru (among other countries) are accused of poisoning the soil and water supplies and not consulting local populations before starting new projects. It is important to note, however, that different Chinese actors in LAC have particular interests that are not always aligned: while Chinese diplomatic officials stationed in LAC want to address local concerns to preserve their long-term goals in the region, corporations are increasingly driven by short-term profits and prioritise revenue over pleasing domestic populations. That said, pressure from Beijing and a desire to secure their projects in LAC have led companies to adapt to local demands: mining corporations in Peru, for example, have hired local lawyers and public-relations firms to improve their rapport with indigenous and environmental organisations and are working with the Peruvian government to comply with environmental regulations. Ongoing changes to China's development model include a new emphasis on sustainability. Under this framework, Chinese corporations are boosting their investment in green-energy projects in LAC, including solar plants in Chile and Argentina.

The third challenge involves addressing the impact of China on issues of governance and corruption in LAC. In contrast to US and European corporations and multilateral organisations such as the World Bank and the IADB, Chinese actors have few internal transparency requirements and prefer government-to-government agreements. These agreements are usually negotiated in secret and without public bidding, which creates opportunities for corruption and overpriced projects, although Chinese companies have begun adapting to local conditions and have been successful in winning contracts for public works through open processes in Chile, Argentina and other countries.

LAC has still to come up with a common strategy to negotiate changes with Beijing and develop regional value chains that can foster innovation and diversify regional exports to China. So far, LAC countries have been relatively passive in their talks with China, happy to receive funds and investments from Beijing without articulating their own goals. Politicians and governments of all ideological stripes recognise the enormous potential of ties with China: centrist governments in Argentina and Brazil took over in 2015 and 2016 respectively and changed very little regarding relations with Beijing compared to their centre-left predecessors. Even in Peru, where the environmental impact of Chinese activities is perhaps clearer, there is little political appetite to pick a fight with China. In all of LAC, the assessment of relations with China remains positive: political opponents might criticise a particular project, but so far that has not turned into a broad denunciation of relations with Beijing. However, where change is desired, evidence suggests that strong regulatory environments and capable state bureaucracies can shape the terms under which Chinese corporations act in the region. The example of how Peru was able to work with Chinese mining corporations to improve relations with local communities is encouraging and could be replicated in other countries.

Rebalancing the relationship with China will largely depend on Latin Americans themselves – achieving a new status quo will involve LAC countries pooling their resources to gain economies of scale and, ultimately, deciding what they want from China. Given the volatile political and economic situation in the region, this coordinated effort is unlikely to materialise in the near future.

Venezuela: Staring into the Abyss

Venezuela's socio-economic implosion has reached critical proportions. The economy plunged by more than 35% between 2013 and 2017; inflation in 2018 will reach 1,000,000% according to the IMF; there are chronic shortages of basic goods, medicines and food, and a dramatic rise in malnutrition; previously eradicated diseases have come back; and murder rates have shot up (Caracas, the country's capital, is one of the most dangerous cities in the world). Hundreds of thousands flee every year looking for opportunities in other countries, especially Colombia. Amid this destruction, the dictatorial rule of Nicolás Maduro seems as solid as ever, thanks to an alliance with the country's armed forces; the repression (through violence if necessary) of most expressions of dissent;

the division and weakness of the opposition; and the firm support of at least 25% of the country's population. Condemnation from nearly all Latin American countries and targeted sanctions by the United States and the European Union against top regime officials have not dented their resolve to remain in power at all costs.

Venezuela's decline appears even starker in the context of the country's extraordinary resources and recent history: Venezuela holds the world's largest proven oil reserves and was a consolidated democracy in the 1960s, decades before the rest of Latin America. However, Venezuelan political elites subsequently ossified and ignored social inequality and grievances. This opened the way for the emergence of Hugo Chávez – the late founder of the revolutionary regime Maduro now presides over – in the late 1990s. Chávez promised to address the demands of the poor, and in exchange got popular support to dismantle all checks on his power. In the end, Venezuelans saw their hopes trampled on: they gave away their democracy and got nothing in return but disaster. Amid the global challenges facing liberal democracy, Venezuela is a stark warning: there is nothing irreversible about the democratic institutions most countries in the West take for granted, and political systems ignore unaddressed social grievances at their own peril. In the past few years, pundits, diplomats and journalists have said many times that Venezuela is at a 'breaking point', but the country's collapse seems to have no end in sight.

The rise of Hugo Chávez

After the end of a military dictatorship in the late 1950s, Venezuela's two traditional parties – Democratic Action (AD) on the centre-left and the Social Christian Party (COPEI) on the centre-right – signed a power-sharing agreement in 1958 that set the basis for a robust democracy. Because of rising oil revenues, the Venezuelan economy boomed in the 1960s and 1970s, resulting in standards of living that were among the highest in Latin America. This system, however, was incapable of dealing with the economic and social crisis that followed the collapse of oil prices in the late 1970s and 1980s. Corruption festered, inequality and poverty rose, and the traditional elites were perceived as aloof and insensitive to social problems. An attempt to raise fuel prices in 1989 to reduce the public deficit led to the *Caracazo*, a series of riots, protests and violent clashes in the capital that lasted for days.

In this context, Lieutenant-Colonel Hugo Chávez led a group of nationalistic military officials who tried to topple the democratic government in 1992. The coup attempt failed, but Chávez became a symbol of the prevailing demand for change. After his release from prison in 1994, Chávez entered politics and was elected president in 1998 in a landslide against the joint AD–COPEI candidate. The old regime was dead.

After taking office in 1999, Chávez drafted a new constitution that 'refounded' the country, changing its name to the Bolivarian Republic of Venezuela, after independence hero Simón Bolívar (whom Chávez had adopted as a symbol). The new constitution strengthened the powers of the presidency, centralised the state and drastically reformed the judiciary, allowing Chávez to pack the courts with his followers. It also recognised new social rights and increased the government's capacity to intervene in the economy. Despite the opposition of the AD, COPEI and several new parties, Venezuelans massively endorsed the new constitution in a referendum. This would become a defining trend of Chávez's rule: the gradual erosion of democratic norms and institutions through electoral means and with majoritarian approval. In 2000, Chávez was elected again (this time under the new, 'Bolivarian' constitution) with more than 60% of the vote.

Polarisation and radicalisation

While Chávez was a charismatic leader and a shrewd political strategist, he was also lucky. He came to power just as international oil prices began to rise again, from US$12 per barrel in 1998 to more than US$130 per barrel in 2008. Chávez used the massive inflow of revenue to fund new government programmes: social services improved, poverty and unemployment went down, education and health expanded and housing programmes bloomed. For the millions of Venezuelans who had felt neglected and invisible under the old regime, Chávez became a hero (and remains so to this day, more than five years after his death).

Initially, Chávez presented himself as a moderate and respected private property, while strengthening the government's role in the oil sector and the economy in general. While elections under Chávez were relatively free and transparent, Venezuelan politics entered a tragic cycle of polarisation, in which the opposition saw Chávez's every move as an attempt to consolidate a dictatorship, and Chávez accused opposition parties of wanting to dismantle his social policies and return to the old status quo, which served him as a pretext to concentrate his power even more. By focusing solely on defending institutions, opposition forces underestimated the strength of Chávez's mandate and his popularity, and ignored the fact that democracy was secondary to social welfare for many Venezuelans who felt left out by the old regime.

The radicalisation of the opposition allowed Chávez to amass even more power. In 2002, he thwarted an attempted coup that tried to install Pedro Carmona, a top businessman, as de facto president. (The coup had the not-so-tacit support of opposition forces and the US government.) The coup reinforced Chávez's democratic credentials and allowed him to purge the armed forces, ensuring their loyalty. A year later, Chávez broke a months-long strike of PDVSA managers and workers and took full control of the oil company, turning it into the main financer of his social policies. Finally, in 2004, Chávez won a recall referendum requested by the opposition with almost 60% of the vote. All opposition parties boycotted the parliamentary elections in 2005, citing the lack of guarantees. It was a fatal mistake: Chávez's coalition won control of all the seats in Congress, granting him almost absolute power.

After these events, Chávez's rule turned sharply towards a Cuban-inspired authoritarian model. In 2005, he announced Venezuela's entry into 'twenty-first-century socialism' and moved decisively against the private sector and all independent actors that could threaten his power: the state took full control of the oil sector (expelling foreign companies), the country's largest industries in all sectors were nationalised and media outlets critical of Chávez were stripped of their licenses or force-fully sold to government allies. Chávez also increased his control over the judiciary and other state institutions (such as the electoral council) and strengthened his alliance with the armed forces through significant arms purchases and by appointing top military officers to the administration and nationalised companies. Displays of public affection and loyalty towards Chávez among his followers reached totalitarian dimensions.

At the same time, Chávez held grandiose ambitions of regional leadership and sought to curtail US influence in Latin America. As he became more radicalised, Chávez strengthened his alliance with the Castros in Cuba – the island provided doctors and technicians for social programmes in Venezuela (and, allegedly, spies and military advisers) in exchange for cheap oil. This initiative turned into ALBA (Bolivarian Alliance for Latin America), a regional bloc of Venezuela, Cuba and left-wing governments in Bolivia, Ecuador and Nicaragua, among others. In 2005, Chávez created Petrocaribe, a programme through which Venezuela began to send subsidised oil shipments to ALBA members and other Central American and Caribbean nations. Chávez built good relationships with centre-left presidents Luiz Inácio Lula da Silva of Brazil and Néstor and Cristina Kirchner of Argentina. While neither country joined ALBA or endorsed Chávez's most outlandish anti-American conspiracies, they expressed their solidarity with Chávez and with his attempt to promote a more autonomous and statist path for Latin America.

Outside of Latin America, Chávez oriented Venezuela's foreign policy towards China, Iran and Russia, with Washington's hardline stance against Venezuela under the Bush administration helping Chávez to present himself as the leader of Latin American resistance to US imperialism. Venezuela also signed military-cooperation agreements with Russia (including joint exercises in the Caribbean and arms purchases) and became the largest recipient of Chinese loans in Latin America: from 2005 to 2017, Beijing disbursed more than US$60 billion in Venezuela, mostly for oil-related projects which Caracas would repay with oil shipments.

Despite mounting evidence of government mismanagement and growing insecurity, as well as increasing goods shortages and inflation, Chávez continued to benefit from rising oil prices (and foreign debt) and in 2006 he was re-elected with 63% of the vote. One year later he urged all members of his coalition to join a new (and highly centralised) United Socialist Party of Venezuela. Then, however, came an unexpected defeat, Chávez's first and only: in 2007 Venezuelan voters narrowly rejected a proposed constitutional amendment that would have allowed Chávez to remove term limits and be re-elected indefinitely as president. In 2009, however, Chávez tried again, mobilised all state resources in his favour, instilled fear in beneficiaries of social programmes and won a second constitutional referendum with 54% of support to enable his indefinite re-election.

The era of Nicolás Maduro

Hugo Chávez did not live to see the full extent of the ruin his model brought to Venezuela. He won re-election in October 2012 with 55% of the vote while receiving medical treatment in Cuba. Shortly after his election victory, a cancer-stricken Chávez named vice-president and foreign minister Nicolás Maduro (a staunch *Chavista* with scant charisma and no political base of his own) as his successor. In March 2013, Chávez died and Maduro took office as president of Venezuela. A month later, Maduro was elected president in his own right by a margin of only 1.5 percentage points against the joint-opposition candidate, amid claims of widespread irregularities. With the economy in ruins and oil prices falling since 2012, Maduro could not afford Chávez's spending largesse and drastically reduced imports to preserve foreign currency, deepening scarcity and food shortages. In December 2015, *Chavismo* – the left-wing political ideology associated with Chávez – suffered its most resounding electoral defeat since 1998 as opposition forces won a two-thirds majority in the National Assembly, Venezuela's parliament.

Most Venezuelans had hoped that the parliamentary elections of 2015 would mark the restoration of democracy, but instead the elections signalled the transition of *Chavismo* towards a full dictatorship. The pro-government courts and the electoral council stripped the opposition-controlled National Assembly of nearly all its powers and quelled an attempt to hold a recall referendum against the president in 2016 (which he was certain to lose). The opposition turned to the streets in 2017 and held massive protests, but the security forces responded with violence and dozens were killed. The final nail in the coffin of Venezuelan democracy came in August 2017, when an all-*Chavista* Constituent Assembly (an illegal body whose members had been selected through an indirect system to ensure government control) effectively replaced the democratic National Assembly. The Constituent Assembly also removed chief prosecutor Luisa Ortega, a dissident *Chavista* who was investigating human-rights violations committed against opposition protesters. She was forced to flee to Colombia, claiming that she feared the Maduro government would 'deprive me of my life'.

Meanwhile, numerous attempts to promote a dialogue between the government and the opposition – some brokered by the Catholic Church and others by a group of former presidents of Latin America and Spain – collapsed due to a lack of trust between the parties and the increasing authoritarianism of the government (along with its refusal to accept foreign aid to alleviate the deepening humanitarian crisis). At the same time, the regime became increasingly isolated on the world stage. In Latin America, new governments in Brazil, Argentina and other nations began raising their voices against Maduro's blatant authoritarianism. Luis Almagro, the secretary-general of the Organisation of American States (OAS), became a leading regional voice for the restoration of democracy and the respect of basic human rights. Caracas, however, had enough regional backing (in no small part due to its subsidised oil shipments through Petrocaribe, which had been reduced but not eliminated) to avoid a full condemnation at the OAS. The Obama administration acted carefully to prevent Maduro from claiming to be a victim of a US-led conspiracy, but established sanctions on top members of the regime who had been charged with violations of human rights or had ties to drug trafficking.

Maduro took advantage of the opposition's disarray and internal divisions to call for early presidential elections in May 2018. With most opposition forces banned and their leaders in prison or prohibited from running, the opposition coalition MUD (Democratic Unity Roundtable) refused to participate. With the elections marred by irregularities and lacking basic guarantees, Maduro claimed victory. As in other authoritarian regimes, elections in Venezuela have become a charade with no consequences for the country's political life.

A lack of good options

In August 2017, US President Donald Trump publicly stated that he was considering an armed invasion of Venezuela to topple Maduro. The announcement shocked Latin American governments and even members of Trump's administration, who knew that it would provide Maduro with political ammunition for his crackdown on dissent. While Trump appears to have been persuaded that a military attack would be counterproductive and would lack regional support, his outrageous proposition highlighted the lack of good options to deal with Venezuela's implosion.

There are four key reasons why Maduro's grip on the country looks likely to persist in the near future. Firstly, *Chavismo* has a monopoly on violence within Venezuela due to its alliance with the armed forces: military officers occupy key positions within the administration, have taken over most nationalised companies and control the black market of smuggled goods and drugs. The regime's turn towards criminal activities started under Chávez but intensified after his death, as the economic situation deteriorated even further. In May 2018, Maduro crushed a plot to overthrow him and arrested dozens of officials, which further weakened the group of dissidents within the armed forces.

Secondly, differences inside the regime seem to have subsided. Unlike Chávez, Maduro is not an unquestionable leader, but part of a collective leadership structure that includes all *Chavista* factions (some pragmatic, others radicalised). One of the most powerful factions is led by hardliner Diosdado Cabello, a former military official charged with corruption and drug trafficking in the US, who presides over the Constituent Assembly. As *Chavismo* has evolved into a massive criminal organisation, top regime leaders such as Cabello know that they risk jail or worse if they lose power, which is a powerful incentive to back Maduro.

Thirdly, Maduro's rule is relatively strong because he maintains the support of at least 25% of the population: some due to ideological affinity or loyalty to Chávez, others because they fear losing government handouts if Maduro is ousted and because they do not trust the weak opposition. In addition, more than one million Venezuelans have emigrated since 2015, reducing the number of active opponents of the regime within the country. With widespread shortages of food and other basic goods, people spend most of their time ensuring their survival, which leaves little time to organise an effective opposition.

Finally, there is little indication of an imminent collapse of the dictatorship because of the weakness of its opponents. After its recent setbacks, the MUD (created in 2008 to coordinate all opposition parties) has practically ceased to exist – the AD left the opposition coalition in 2018. The opposition lacks clear leadership and strategic direction: some moderates attempt to connect with those Venezuelans (nearly 50% of the population) who remember Chávez fondly even if they disapprove of Maduro, while others take a much more confrontational approach and talk of a 'restoration' of the old democracy.

The international community has also proven ineffective in designing a coherent policy of isolation and pressure against Venezuela. Only recently have most Latin American countries come together in denouncing Maduro's authoritarianism through a regional grouping known as the Lima Group. However, their impact remains limited and Venezuela still has enough allies in the region to block major sanctions at the OAS. The US and some European countries have imposed sanctions on top regime leaders, and Washington has drastically restricted financial transactions with Venezuelan government actors including the PDVSA, although Washington and Europe have both avoided wider sanctions that might increase the suffering of the Venezuelan people. The US, for instance, remains the largest buyer of Venezuelan oil, although the Trump administration has considered sanctioning these purchases.

That said, the regime is far from being invulnerable. Although oil prices have recovered slightly since mid-2015, Venezuela's production has fallen sharply due to years of mismanagement and lack of investment: the country produced about 2.5m barrels of oil per day in 2015, but fewer than 1.5m per day in 2018 (it could fall to fewer than 1m in 2019).

With oil revenues decreasing every year, the government has come close to defaulting on its debt many times in the past few years, and so has the PDVSA. Even traditional lenders such as China are less willing to continue bankrolling Maduro. If the regime runs out of cash to maintain its alliance with the military and pay government employees, the situation could spiral out of control. Even if the regime collapses due to an insurrection within the military or infighting within *Chavismo*, it would take many years (or decades) for Venezuela to restore its economy and its society. The country has become a hotbed for smuggling and drug trafficking, and armed groups loyal to *Chavismo* will continue to operate regardless of who is in power. Given that there is no functioning economy outside of the deteriorated oil industry, a non-*Chavista* government would have no resources to rebuild crumbling infrastructure or provide basic public services.

In a context of economic ruin and social polarisation, a restored Venezuelan democracy would be fragile – robust, long-lasting and well-planned international support could mean the difference between stability and chaos. Urgent humanitarian assistance (food, medicine and other basic supplies) should be made available as soon as Maduro (or a subsequent government) requests it. In the longer term, if the regime falls, the country will require its own multibillion-dollar Marshall Plan, one that exceeds the capacity of even the IMF or the World Bank and which would need a highly capable government bureaucracy, which Venezuela now lacks. Ultimately, Venezuela's future after *Chavismo* will depend on domestic leadership. As foreign actors prepare for a post-Maduro scenario, they must also urge the opposition to come together and connect with disenchanted *Chavistas* whose support will be critical for the success of an eventual transition. The skills and resources of the Venezuelan diaspora will be crucial to rebuild the country, but émigrés must be ready to listen to those who stayed behind and experienced the worst of the country's crisis. Venezuelans have endured years of unprecedented hardships; only they can bring their country back from the abyss.

©IISS

Atlantic Ocean

NEWFOUNDLAND

QUEBEC

PRINCE EDWARD ISL.
NOVA SCOTIA
NEW BRUNSWICK
MAINE
VERMONT
NEW HAMPSHIRE
MASSACHUSETTS
RHODE ISLAND
CONNECTICUT
NEW JERSEY
DELAWARE
MARYLAND

Ottawa

ONTARIO

NEW YORK
PENNSYLVANIA

Washington DC
WEST VIRGINIA
VIRGINIA
NORTH CAROLINA
SOUTH CAROLINA

MICHIGAN

OHIO

KENTUCKY
TENNESSEE

FLORIDA

GEORGIA
ALABAMA

WISCONSIN

ILLINOIS
INDIANA

MISSOURI
ARKANSAS
MISSISSIPPI
LOUISIANA

MANITOBA

MINNESOTA

IOWA

NUNAVUT

SASKATCHEWAN

NORTH DAKOTA

SOUTH DAKOTA

NEBRASKA

KANSAS

OKLAHOMA

TEXAS

C A N A D A

U N I T E D   S T A T E S

NORTHWEST TERRITORIES

ALBERTA

MONTANA

WYOMING

COLORADO

NEW MEXICO

IDAHO

UTAH

ARIZONA

NEVADA

BRITISH COLUMBIA

WASHINGTON

OREGON

CALIFORNIA

YUKON TERRITORY

Alaska (United States)

P a c i f i c   O c e a n

Chapter 11

North America

2017–18 Review

In the year to mid-2018, US President Donald Trump made good on several of his election-campaign promises. He placed tariffs against China and Europe and initiated the renegotiation of the North American Free Trade Agreement (NAFTA) with Mexico and Canada; he withdrew from an international agreement that curbed Iran's nuclear programme; and he moved the US embassy in Israel to Jerusalem. Throughout 2017, the president responded in ever-more hawkish tones to the development of nuclear weapons and missiles by the Democratic People's Republic of Korea (DPRK). Trump went so far as to threaten the total destruction of the DPRK in his first address to the UN General Assembly in September 2017. Yet in mid-2018 he held a summit meeting with North Korean leader Kim Jong-un that Trump claimed represented a breakthrough in relations between the two powers. Most of these decisions put the United States at odds with its allies in Europe and Asia, as well as neighbouring Canada. The tensions within the Western camp were particularly evident at the G7 summit in Quebec in mid-2018.

Domestically, Trump's Republican Party succeeded in pushing through Congress the most significant reform of the US tax code in 20 years. This promised to further stoke an already vigorous US recovery, underpinned by further deregulation. Yet despite a boom in wages and employment, the president's approval rating barely exceeded 40% during the year. He failed to repeal his predecessor's healthcare reform and backed away from a pledge that Mexico would pay for a wall to secure the US southern border. The investigation into Russian interference in the 2016 election, under former FBI director Robert Mueller, levelled charges against some members of the Trump campaign to the fury of the president, who regarded the probe as a 'witch-hunt' and repeatedly threatened to shut it down. Eighteen months into his term, Trump showed little sign of adopting a more conventional approach to government. He remained disinclined to be bound by a formal process and was willing to undertake dramatic shifts in position with little warning in pursuit of victories he could readily publicise.

US domestic policies

In his victorious election campaign, Trump offered voters a package of policies that had not been put forward by either of the main parties before. He challenged the orthodoxies of promoting free trade and liberal values that had enjoyed bipartisan support for decades, while promising tax cuts, infrastructure renewal and strong defence – without compensating measures to curb the fiscal deficit. He also proposed a much tougher approach to illegal immigration and the protection of US borders.

One of the new administration's first major legislative initiatives was an effort to repeal the Affordable Care Act (ACA), which was the signature healthcare reform by the previous president, Barack Obama. The ACA was intended to reduce sharply the number of Americans without health insurance, which stood at approximately 45 million. It brought that number down by half, but in some US states insurers quit the market and premiums rose, in particular for those whose earnings were slightly too high to qualify for subsidies. The worst impacts were felt in the less populous states and fell on the self-employed. In Oklahoma, the cost of a benchmark plan for a family of four rose from US$7,500 in

2014 to US$18,500 in 2017. Nationally the rise was less vertiginous, but still dramatic.

Trump had pledged to scrap the ACA early in his term. However, by mid-2017 the effort to replace it was struggling in the Senate. The Congressional Budget Office (CBO) forecast that the new bill would result in 22m people losing health insurance. Unable to pass the bill, the White House sought a straight repeal that, according to the CBO, would have resulted in 32m people losing insurance. It too failed to command a majority.

This was a serious setback for the Trump administration, and it called into question the ability of the president and his staff – few of whom had experience of Washington – to work with Congress in order to pass legislation. Some observers wondered whether it portended difficulties for tax reform, the next legislative priority, where the administration and congressional Republicans were interested in cutting rates to stimulate the economy.

The last major reform of the US tax system had taken place in 1986, when then-president Ronald Reagan had cut rates sharply. It was a bipartisan endeavour that was revenue-neutral, as the cuts in headline rates were balanced by the scrapping of many allowances. Trump was determined to cut corporate taxes from 35% to 20% or lower. A first draft, issued in late September 2017, proposed cutting the top personal rate from 39.5% to 35%, while increasing the bottom rate from 10% to 12%. It also proposed to abolish the deductions for state-and-local taxes, the benefits of which fall disproportionately to Americans earning over US$100,000 per year and which are regarded by Republicans as rewarding high-taxing Democrat states. The bill passed in December delivered temporary cuts to individual tax rates and permanent cuts for corporations (for the latter, the rate was cut from 35% to 21%), as well as ending the unusual practice of taxing global earnings on repatriation to the US. This was an important legislative victory for the White House, although it favoured business over individuals and was forecast to increase borrowing by US$1 trillion over a decade. As a result, the US is expected henceforth to run federal budget deficits of around 5% of GDP, which is markedly higher than in the previous decade, mainly because of the rising cost of mandatory spending including on social security and healthcare.

Trump's focus on immigration was central to his advance through the ranks of Republican presidential aspirants to secure the nomination. He argued that the US was failing to control its borders; that the country was overwhelmed with illegal immigrants, to the detriment of the prosperity and security of citizens; and that it was essential to build a wall on the border with Mexico and to deport undocumented migrants in large numbers. In a country with strong popular support for gun ownership, high rates of incarceration and border security – and a sense that the federal government failed to take the last of these seriously – the appeal to perceptions of insecurity was powerful, and critics' characterisation of this as racism proved counterproductive. Trump's stance mobilised Republicans as well as working-class whites who had traditionally supported the Democratic Party; in the process he exposed a yawning divide between the political elite and millions of Americans. Polling after the election showed that 63% of Trump voters (and 42% of those who voted for Hillary Clinton) felt that those born outside the country were not fully American. Over the preceding four decades, the number of foreign-born people in the US population had increased sharply, from 4.7% in 1970 to 7.9% in 1990 and 12.9% in 2010. It stood at 13.5% in 2016. This fuelled status anxiety – a fear of losing one's position in society – on the part of working-class whites, especially those in the industrial northeast and Midwest, who had suffered from de-industrialisation and perceived that immigrants, women and minorities had received favourable treatment from the Democrats. Urban African Americans likewise evinced status anxiety in response to the arrival of Asian and Hispanic immigrants.

The US had experienced politically turbulent periods of high immigration before. In 1850 only 9.7% of the US population was foreign-born. Immigration rose swiftly in the next few decades, including the arrival of large numbers of Chinese, changing the ethnic mix in California and other states. Populist pressure led to a law in 1875 that barred Chinese women from immigrating to the US and in 1882 the Chinese Exclusion

Act prohibited the immigration of all Chinese labourers. Immigration remained a potent issue, however, until the 1924 Immigration Act that placed a cap on immigration and distributed visas according to the nationality mix of the US in 1890. It completely excluded immigrants from Asia. Among the wave of immigrants who entered the US between 1890 and 1930, one-quarter were not naturalised. As a result of the immigration cap adopted in 1924, the number of US residents born outside the country fell to 8.8% in 1940 and 6.9% in 1950.

Immigration from Latin America and Asia rose after the national-origins quota was abolished in 1965. In 1960, 75% of immigrants were European. In 2018, 89% were non-European. In addition to this change in the ethnic mix, levels of legal and illegal immigration have risen, and immigrants have moved to new areas. When Trump took office, there were 11m undocumented immigrants in the country. In September 2017, the president announced that he would cancel another of his predecessor's initiatives, Deferred Action for Childhood Arrivals (DACA), which gave residency and work permits to approximately 700,000 of the 1.8m residents who entered the US illegally as children. In his first state of the union speech, Trump proposed a path to citizenship for all 1.8m, provided that it was accompanied by funding to build barriers on the frontier with Mexico, more officers for Immigration and Customs Enforcement (ICE), the elimination of the Diversity Visa (which seeks to broaden the pool of countries providing immigrants to the US) and a restriction on so-called 'chain migration', by which one immigrant is joined by family members.

There was little prospect of any legislative solution for the 9m other undocumented migrants in the country; the notion of an amnesty for people who had broken US law when entering the country was anathema to Republicans, who feared it would also encourage further immigration. However, in the absence of a sizeable increase in the number of ICE enforcement officers, there was also little prospect of mass deportations. Arrests for immigration violations in the first nine months of 2017 were 42% higher than in the same period in 2016 as ICE cast its net wider. In May 2018, controversy arose over the separation of immigrant children from their parents at the US border. Amnesty International called on the US to halt the practice, which Trump blamed on the Democrats – although his own officials confirmed in March and April that the policy was a new one intended to deter a customary seasonal surge in immigration. In late June, the practice was suspended, although some children remained in the US without their parents.

The president was more easily able to reduce the number of refugees admitted to the US. He cut the annual quota to 45,000, which was the lowest level in 30 years, and compiled a list of 11 countries from which no refugees would be admitted. As a result of tighter security vetting, it was projected that the US was on course to admit just 23,000 refugees in the year ending 30 September 2018. There were only 44 admissions from Syria in the first half of the 2018 fiscal year. In the same period, only 17% of admitted refugees were Muslim, compared with 41% between 2013 and 2017.

Trump's claims of deft economic management were ostensibly supported by the economy's performance. GDP growth exceeded 3% year-on-year in the second and third quarters and, despite the Federal Reserve tightening monetary policy, the government's pro-cyclical fiscal policy promised to further stoke the economy and stock market. Perhaps the most notable improvements were seen in the labour market. Unemployment fell from 4.8% at the start of his presidency to 3.8% in May 2018, which marked an 18-year low, with vacancies exceeding the number of unemployed workers. This raised the possibility that, contrary to the accepted wisdom of economists, working-age adults who had dropped out of the labour force in the preceding years might actually return. At the start of Trump's presidency, just 89% of males aged 25–54 were in the labour force – the lowest level in US history.

As the labour market tightened, wages rose. In January 2018, hourly wages were 2.9% higher than one year earlier, marking the fastest increase since 2009. Moreover, wage growth was strongest among those towards the bottom of the income-distribution scale. Over 2017, the bottom quartile of earners experienced 5% wage growth, while the top quartile enjoyed a 2.5% increase and the median 3.2%.

The extent to which Trump could claim the credit for these improvements was debatable. The recovery had started under his predecessor and had been girded by rising global growth, although Trump's deregulation drive and tax cuts also likely contributed to the accelerating economy. Yet although the president did claim credit for the miracle economy, his approval rating (perhaps surprisingly) was low by historical standards. Trump took office with an approval rating of 45%, according to Gallup weekly polling; for most of the time since it has hovered in the 37–42% range. Trump's presidency further galvanised his opponents and civil-society groups. Underlining the country's polarisation, his approval rating among Republicans was 89%.

Foreign policy

After 18 months in office, the administration's foreign policy displayed a lack of coherence. The appointment of a new secretary of state and national security advisor in spring 2018 narrowed the ideological gap between the president and his key officials, but Trump's fixation on a few campaign pledges and his determination to score victories rendered policy disjointed and unpredictable. It did not help that many important posts remained unfilled. There are 1,200 posts that require Senate confirmation: by mid-2017, after six months in office, Trump had submitted 210 names and had just 49 confirmed. At the same point in his presidency, George W. Bush had submitted 315 names and had 80 confirmed, while Barack Obama had submitted 369 names and had 203 confirmed. The gaps were particularly apparent at the State Department, where only two of 26 posts were filled, and the Defense Department, where five of the 18 posts were filled. By March 2018, when then-secretary of state Rex Tillerson was dismissed by a presidential tweet, several undersecretary posts at the State Department were unfilled and 40% of all Senate-confirmable positions there lacked a nominee. In December, Trump told a TV interviewer that the vacancies were an irrelevance because he was the only official who mattered.

In his first speech to the UN General Assembly, Trump mocked North Korean leader Kim Jong-un for pursuing a nuclear-weapons capability and asserted that, if the US or an ally was attacked by Pyongyang, 'we will have no choice but to totally destroy North Korea'. No US president had ever used such language at the UN. Trump was also highly critical of the Joint Comprehensive Plan of Action (JCPOA), which offered Iran relief from sanctions in return for limits on its nuclear-enrichment activities. Yet other parts of his speech were consistent with his predecessors' focus on promoting liberal values. He was strongly critical of Venezuela's retreat from democracy and human rights, and he expressed US solidarity with every person living under a brutal regime.

The DPRK's nuclear and missile programmes were a source of rising concern to US policymakers throughout 2017. Trump and Kim Jong-un traded verbal threats as the latter seemingly demonstrated his country's ability to strike Hawaii and Guam with missiles that could carry a nuclear warhead. General Joseph Dunford, chairman of the Joint Chiefs of Staff, said that the US could not allow the DPRK to acquire the capability to hit the continental US. H.R. McMaster, the national security advisor, stated that it was not possible to deter the DPRK in the way the US had deterred the Soviet Union. Preventive strikes on North Korean nuclear and missile facilities were mooted. Yet in November, after the latest in a series of missile tests, Kim announced that the work was concluded. He initiated a thaw in relations with South Korea and in April proposed talks with the US to consider a peace treaty, security guarantees, steps to denuclearisation and sanctions relief. Trump eagerly accepted and, despite the threat of cancellation, the two leaders met in Singapore in June. North Korea made no binding commitments at the meeting but Trump was greatly encouraged and cancelled planned military exercises with South Korea. US sanctions remained in place, pending North Korean progress on denuclearisation.

Trump had entered office deeply critical of the JCPOA and he remained so throughout 2017, although he stopped short of taking any steps to withdraw from the agreement concluded with Iran, France, Germany, the United Kingdom, Russia and China plus the European Union. In January 2018, he gave the other parties 120 days to remedy the flaws in the agreement, under the threat of US withdrawal. Trump sought to make the restrictions on enrichment permanent, to ban Iranian ballistic-missile testing and to allow the International Atomic Energy Agency unconstrained access to Iranian nuclear facilities. The Europeans endeavoured to meet these concerns through side agreements, rather than reopening the JCPOA, but were unable to persuade Iran. On 8 May, Trump announced the United States' withdrawal from the JCPOA and added that, rather than simply reinstating the sanctions previously imposed on Iran, he would extend them further. By extending sanctions, and deterring other states from doing business with Iran through the threat of secondary sanctions, he hoped to coerce Iran into renegotiating the JCPOA or to toppling the regime. European states protested vigorously at the threat of secondary sanctions, but by mid-year it appeared that most European companies had determined to stop doing business with Iran in order to protect their US operations or their access to the US-based financial system.

Together with taming Iran and North Korea, and getting US allies to shoulder more of the burden of their own defence, Trump had campaigned on the notion of improving relations with Russia to further US national interests. His ability to reset ties was constrained by the persistent allegations – and Special Counsel investigation into – Russian meddling in the 2016 presidential election. In August 2017, the Senate voted to toughen sanctions on Russia for election meddling and its military interference in Ukraine. This closed off the possibility for the president to lift sanctions on Russian energy firms and banks; it also made possible the application of secondary sanctions on buyers of Russian weapons. The threshold for sanctions relief was set so high that most observers expected sanctions to be in place for years. In response, Russia expelled some 750 US diplomats. The deterioration in the relationship left considerable doubt over whether the two states would agree to extend New START (the nuclear-arms reduction treaty signed in 2010) and so limit the prospects for a strategic-nuclear-arms race.

In line with Trump's promises to reinvigorate US manufacturing after years of decline that the president blamed on poor trade agreements (rather than automation), the US administration pursued a pugnacious if erratic economic diplomacy. In January 2018, the US imposed tariffs on Chinese solar panels and washing machines, followed several months later by a 25% tariff on imported steel and a 10% tariff on aluminium. Every US president since Jimmy Carter has introduced unilateral tariffs, and these have often involved steel. However, the 2018 tariffs were unique in that they were imposed on grounds of national security. By invoking World Trade Organisation (WTO) article XXI, the US created a problem for any state wishing to challenge the tariffs because the WTO courts will hesitate to become involved and the standard forms of redress cannot be applied. However, the states principally affected – Canada, France, Germany, the UK, South Korea and Mexico – bridled at the protectionist measure and the patently spurious use of the national-security exception. Whether it would benefit the US economy was also open to doubt. Trade Partnership, a consultancy, forecast that the tariffs would create 33,000 metallurgy jobs but destroy 179,000 jobs in metal-consuming industries. EU states responded with a raft of politically targeted tariffs of their own; Trump threatened additional measures against EU automotive imports, although the two sides agreed to enter negotiations before further engaging in trade hostilities. It was possible that the dispute would disrupt US–EU cooperation at the WTO to address some of the trade challenges posed by China and its model of state capitalism.

Canada

Trump's desire to rework or wreck NAFTA posed a particular problem for Canadian Prime Minister Justin Trudeau. The Liberal Party leader remained popular in the year to mid-2018, with an approval rating in excess of 50%. However, his failure to deliver electoral reform and to navigate successfully between the demands of environmentalists and the energy industry helped to narrow his party's lead over the Conservatives, with an election due in October 2019. Canada's economy grew by 3% in 2017 – the highest rate in the G7 – but it was slowing on the back of high household debt and a shrinking workforce; a trade war with the US could be ruinous.

The main engines of the Canadian economy are hydrocarbons and automotives. The former, which by dint of infrastructure is locked into the US market, has suffered from greater competition as a result of the unconventional-oil revolution in the US over the past decade, while the latter is being targeted by the Trump administration, which wishes to bring more manufacturing jobs home. The US tax reform, which brought corporate tax down to 21% (below Canada's 26.7%), was a first blow. Tariffs on Canadian softwood, newsprint, steel and aluminium followed. Three-quarters of Canadian exports go to the US, including 88% of its steel and 85% of its automotive exports.

Trudeau sought to diversify Canada's trade by seeking agreements with other powers. Yet his efforts to defend rules-based multilateral trade by including environmental, human-rights and labour standards in agreements only found favour with the EU and the Asian signatories to the Trans-Pacific Partnership. His visits to China in December 2017 and to India failed to get trade negotiations under way. Trudeau's fidelity to a progressive, values-oriented international agenda created tension in his relations with the Trump administration, which associates the Trudeau administration with the Obama presidency. The Canadian premier also received less support than he might have hoped from European leaders, leaving Canada with insufficient backing to challenge Trump's tariffs at the WTO. This left Trudeau vulnerable to the charge that he was failing to deliver for his population.

North America: Drivers of Strategic Change

- The US government has begun a forcible effort to recast the terms of its trade with major economies, irrespective of their alliance status. Although this is unlikely to deliver net gains to the US economy, it has substantial domestic support and carries the risk of undermining global trade and the position of the US as an upholder of rules and norms.
- A long-standing weariness on the part of the US population towards the country's role as a security guarantor in other parts of the world is starting, inconsistently, to be reflected in US policy towards allies and institutions.
- The withdrawal of the US from the international agreement to curb Iran's nuclear programme signals a departure from a collaborative approach to regional security among the Western powers, in favour of a unilateral posture that appears open to the possibility of fostering regime change in Iran through economic coercion.
- Despite US President Donald Trump's desire to improve relations with Russia, the codification and extension of US sanctions on Russia by Congress will limit economic relations and strain political ties for years, or decades, to come.
- Canadian Prime Minister Justin Trudeau has struggled to mount an effective defence of progressive values within the G7 or of Canada's economy in response to Trump's imposed and threatened tariffs.

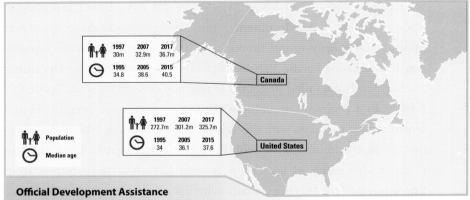

Official Development Assistance
(US$, constant 2015 prices)

	1997	2007	2017
Canada	$3.07bn	$3.73bn	$4.09bn
United States	$9.82bn	$24.94bn	$34.64bn

Defence Budget
(US$, constant 2010 prices)

	2008	2013	2018
Canada	$19.93bn	$18.51bn	$20.22bn
United States	$619.35bn	$599.67bn	$569.45bn

GDP per capita, Purchasing Power Parity (International $, constant 2011 prices)

Country	GDP
1997	
Canada	$33,426
United States	$41,812
2007	
Canada	$41,647
United States	$51,011
2017	
Canada	$44,018
United States	$54,225

Sources: IISS; OECD; UN Department of Economic and Social Affairs (Population Division, 2017); World Bank

The Trump Transformation, Part 1: Domestic Governance

Like a magician, US President Donald Trump uses diversion and distraction to keep his audience from seeing how his tricks work. Much of the media coverage of the White House under Trump has struggled to keep up in the 24/7 news cycle of tweeted personal and policy criticisms and breaking news on supposed scandals. Meanwhile, Trump has made a series of policy decisions that will have a lasting legacy for the United States and its role in the world. Trump has appointed several Republican-leaning judges to the federal judiciary (who will influence the tenor of the federal judiciary long after Trump has left office), and has proposed a broad reorganisation of federal departments in Washington while also granting states greater autonomy. From the very start of his tenure as president, Trump has sought to reverse policies made under the previous administration of Barack Obama. Although Trump failed to annul Obama's signature healthcare bill, he has nonetheless made changes by executive order, the cumulative effects of which have vitiated his predecessor's policy legacy.

Federal-government transformation

Trump does not share the benign attitude of past presidents towards the public service. After his inauguration, Trump learned that the Obama administration had placed him and his campaign under surveillance for alleged links to Russia; that national-security officials had 'unmasked' US citizens under surveillance (i.e., the customary anonymity of US citizens in intelligence reports had in certain instances been removed); that the FBI had attempted to place an informant (Stefan Halper) on his campaign staff; and that the FBI and the powerful US intelligence community had worked in concert in this unprecedented effort, which may have been undertaken with the knowledge of then-president Obama himself.

The non-partisan image of the public service was damaged by high-profile resignations and insubordination by individuals such as Sally

Yates, who as acting attorney general refused to implement Trump's moratorium on immigration from several countries. Then FBI director James Comey broke with policy in an attempt to address questions about email security by Democratic candidate Hillary Clinton during the presidential campaign, and then leaked memos he had made following meetings with Trump to the media. Richard Cordray, the head of the Consumer Financial Protection Bureau, attempted to name his own successor (a progressive activist hostile to the president) when he left to run for the governorship of Ohio as a Democrat.

As the Trump administration entered its second year, members of the White House staff and even cabinet secretaries were confronted in public by civil servants-cum-activists. Allison Hrabar, an employee of the Justice Department, heckled the Secretary of Homeland Security Kirstjen Nielsen, driving her to abandon her meal with a friend. Hrabar later posted about the incident on social media. This trend has led some of Trump's political appointees to federal departments to take note of the social-media posts of public servants who report to them, keeping track of those who are hostile to the administration. In many departments, Trump has yet to name (or secure Senate confirmation for) political appointments, leaving various bureaus leaderless in what may be read by public servants as disregard for their policy areas.

Trump has expressed his frustration with what he judges to be a lack of professionalism in the public service by referring to the federal bureaucracy as part of 'the swamp', in which he also includes the partisan establishment in both major parties which has arrayed itself against him. The resulting atmosphere is prompting a wave of retirements and a loss of institutional knowledge and memory that in the short run will hamper the competence of the federal government. Washington lobbyists, think tankers, journalists and foreign embassies have in the process lost carefully cultivated contacts within many federal departments, damaging the ability of external organisations to gauge what is going on inside the Trump administration.

Another dimension of the Trump administration's transformation of the federal government was his January 2017 executive order to all rule-making departments that they must eliminate or rescind two regulations for every one they propose. (This policy directive is similar to the 'One-In, One-Out' rule adopted in the United Kingdom in 2010, later revised to the 'One-In, Three-Out' standard.) Trump's record thus far has been remarkable, eliminating 22 regulations for every new one introduced in 2017, according to the Office of Management and Budget.

In this bonfire of regulations, domestic-policy departments including Labor, Education, Interior, Health and Human Services (HHS), Energy and the Environmental Protection Agency (EPA) have committed the most arson. At the Department of Labor, rescinded rules include those that made union organising easier and forced workers to pay 'agency fees' to unions even if they did not join them – this in turn funded political activity by unions largely to the benefit of Democratic candidates, which conservatives charged had prompted collusion between Democratic office holders and public-sector unions, to the detriment of taxpayers. At the Department of Energy and the EPA, strict regulations on power plants that were enacted during the Obama years to force electricity generation away from coal use, vehicle fuel-economy targets, methane-flaring limits and federal water regulation of streams, creeks and ponds were all withdrawn. HHS regulations requiring insurance coverage of contraceptives and prohibiting low-cost, low-coverage short-term health insurance have also been withdrawn. Federal Education Department guidance on university adjudication of student sexual-conduct complaints, as well as rules requiring public accommodation for transgender students and restricting for-profit schools, have all been eliminated. The Department of Interior is reversing prohibitions on use of public lands adopted under Obama and making the first major changes to the Endangered Species Act since it was originally passed in 1973. Even the US Department of the Treasury has been involved in efforts to relax regulations imposed during the Obama years on financial planners and large financial institutions. In many of these cases, the federal withdrawal comes in areas that are also regulated at the state level, from health insurance to education policy. Many states will now expand their regulatory activity (or resume it), and to do so will need to acquire new, specialist staff. By reversing a decades-long trend towards federal involvement in state competencies that had accelerated under Obama, Trump-era deregulation may decentralise regulatory action. Some states will become activist where voters support this, but in many states private firms and individuals will experiment with new forms of regulation and unregulated activity. In the short term, the Trump administration's deregulation has sent a powerful signal to markets that has contributed to the increase in private investment and thus GDP growth.

Trump also has ambitions to reorganise the departments and agencies of the federal government. In June 2018, the administration issued a proposal to merge the federal departments of Education and Labor into a Department of the Workforce, and to rename the HHS (which has the second-largest departmental budget in the federal government after the Department of Defense) as the Department of Health and Public Welfare. Trump has also ordered the Defense Department to establish a US Space Force as a sixth branch of the armed services separate from the US Air Force. Such decisions will be difficult to reverse, and they indicate the extent to which Trump aims to build a legacy through changes to the federal government.

The proposed reorganisation of federal departments comes at an important moment when the largest cohort in the federal civil service is the baby-boomer generation (born between 1946 and 1964), which has begun to retire. To date, the most significant downsizing of the federal civil service occurred when the generations born before the Second World War retired under then-president Bill Clinton. Retirees were not replaced one-for-one as the federal government took advantage of information technology to eliminate thousands of administrative professionals, clerks and typists while outsourcing office services – from cleaners to security – to private contractors who did not receive the generous federal-employee pensions and benefits, let alone wages.

The Trump reorganisation is likely to hasten the retirement of many demoralised baby boomers in federal service, and may prompt others to join state civil services (following the decentralisation of their area of regulatory responsibility). New hires will join departments and agencies where the corporate culture is in transition due to the reorganisation. For example, someone interested in education policy will presumably take on a different outlook as part of a federal department of Workforce Improvement than in a Department of Education. Likewise, a new member of the environmental section of the Department of Energy, rather than at the autonomous EPA, will begin from a different perspective.

Over time, the shift of regulatory initiative to the state level and the reorganisation of the federal government may have a combined effect of restoring to the states the role lauded by former US Supreme Court Justice Louis Brandeis as 'laboratories of reform', with greater public accountability and fewer resources in absolute terms than the federal government. Under Trump, states have been given greater latitude for healthcare experimentation under the Medicaid programme (administered by states to provide care for poorer citizens, with a federal match for every dollar spent on the programme by states). Trump's US$1.5-trillion infrastructure investment ended up as US$200 billion in federal funds to match US$1.3trn to be contributed by state and local governments and the private sector. Under the Trump administration, state governments have continued the practice of suing the federal government for injunctive relief from federal mandates. However, it is now liberal states run by Democratic governors and legislatures that are filing cases. Flashpoints have included federal-agency demands for cooperation in immigration enforcement that have been resisted by some states which have adopted 'sanctuary' policies.

In a large, diverse country such as the US, differing approaches to public policy will persist in different states and regions, making national progress on topics of global concern such as climate change more difficult to achieve. As talent and resources shift to the state and local levels of government, future attempts to re-centralise policy responsibility to the federal government will become more difficult since not only would many states resist this re-centralisation, but the federal government would also need to recruit and train civil servants with the requisite expertise and experience (and find tasks for the tenured civil servants hired under the de-centralising phase of the Trump years). If the twentieth century's gradual centralisation of policy authority in Washington DC is a reliable guide, future presidents would need a sustained effort and national emergencies such as the Great Depression and possibly a world war or two to justify this effort and expense.

It is too early to know whether Trump's efforts to reset the balance of US federalism will be sustained; the George W. Bush administration proposed greater decentralisation at the outset, but greatly expanded federal authority over states for reasons of national security after the 2001 terrorist attacks. However, the fact that 33 of the 50 US states have Republican governors, and 31 of the country's state legislatures are controlled by Republicans – a record – provides the Trump administration with willing partners eager to demonstrate policy innovation and garner national attention.

The role of Congress

Trump's popularity has fluctuated, but even at its worst it has not been as low as the popularity of the US Congress during his tenure as president. Public dissatisfaction with Congress is not new: approval for Congress has generally hovered below 40% since 1976; as recently as 2014, it had only 9% public approval. Since Trump's inauguration, approval for Congress has averaged approximately 18%, compared with Trump's average rating of 39%.

In practice, Trump has taken a surprisingly old-fashioned approach to Congress. Unlike Obama, Trump holds regular meetings and consultations with members of Congress and senators at the White House and speaks frequently by phone with the congressional leadership. Trump expects Congress to perform its constitutional function by legislating, conducting oversight, passing budgets and confirming his appointments to key positions.

The landmark achievement of the 115th Congress was tax reform. With no support from Democrats, Republicans enacted legislation that dramatically lowered US corporate tax rates and eliminated a deduction for state and local taxes that benefited high-tax jurisdictions (the deduction had been paid for by an effective subsidy from taxpayers in low-tax states that voted for Trump). The tax reform offered a corporate tax break on repatriated earnings from abroad for a limited period as it shifted US corporate taxes to a locational model like that used by most countries. The reform also raised the standard deduction for individual taxpayers while eliminating numerous deductions for taxpayers that had contributed to the regressivity of the US tax system.

Despite active involvement by the president, Congress tried and failed to repeal and replace the Affordable Care Act, former president Obama's healthcare reform that was opposed by Republicans and which Trump had pledged to eliminate. This defeat appears to have been a learning experience for the president as well as for Republican leaders in Congress; both House and Senate GOP leaders have improved their whipping operations and recalcitrant legislators have been put under pressure by Trump, who has intervened in local primaries in support of rival candidates and ousted incumbents who failed to support his legislative priorities.

A generational shift in Congress is also helping the Trump administration transform the institution. According to the Congressional Research Service, the average age of members of the House at the beginning of the 115th Congress was 57.8 years, while the average age of Senators was 61.8 years – among the oldest in US history. This has been a contributing factor – along with the partisan rancour that has characterised debate in both chambers of Congress since the Clinton administration – to a growing number of retirements of US representatives and senators.

The November 2018 midterm elections, in which all 435 seats in the House of Representatives and 33 Senate seats will be contested, will provide the first indication, apart from by-elections, of the trends in congressional membership. While typically portrayed as a set of contests between Republicans and Democrats, the underlying contest within parties in candidate-selection primaries has been between pro-Trump Republicans and more centrist Republicans, and between progressive activists and more centrist Democrats. So far, it is the centrists in both parties who appear to be losing ground.

In the US two-party system where both parties are big tents (i.e., inclusive of a variety of views), the party that can best control its fringe supporters typically presents its moderate face to voters, and usually prevails in electoral campaigns. In 2018, Trump appears to be better able to control the Republican fringe through a combination of threats and incentives – most importantly of all the attraction of 'winning' – than Democrats. In this, Republicans benefit by holding the presidency during a period of intraparty turmoil, since control of the executive branch provides access to various incentives to win over legislators, and the president is inevitably the highest-profile leader of the party. Democrats are hampered by ageing, centrist leaders out of step with the progressive activists who are becoming the face of the Democratic Party in protest marches and social-media campaigns against Trump. It is entirely possible that Trump as a result will affect the transformation of both US political parties and a realignment of the political spectrum in the US for a generation or more.

Of course, party realignment would occur without Trump. In 2016, US citizens of the so-called 'millennial' generation who were eligible to vote came close to outnumbering members of the baby-boomer generation, and will do so as early as 2019. Perhaps because both parties nominated presidential candidates who would be over 70 years of age if elected, voter participation by millennials was too low to make a difference in the tenor of the campaigns or the issues that were debated. Future elections, however, will increasingly cater to millennial-generation voters. If Republicans can capitalise on clearer leadership and delivery of governance that improves the lives and prospects of millennials, the party may be better positioned to win their support. Trump's use of social media to outmanoeuvre the traditional television and print media favoured by baby boomers is a clear play for direct connection to the youth vote.

The role of the judiciary

As the baby-boomer generation marched through the institutions of American life, it challenged the authority and legitimacy of the institutions of government, the economy, religion, art and culture, and the family. One of the most striking effects of the resulting crisis of legitimacy in the US has been the transformation of the judiciary branch of the US government from a respected arbiter and interpreter in extremis of government and individual rights into a supra-legislature where rights are discovered and policy victories can be won.

This has politicised the federal judiciary to an unprecedented degree, such that the views (real and imagined) of Supreme Court justices and federal judges are the central feature of reporting on legal issues in the media and public debates. Appointments to the federal bench prompt multimillion-dollar campaigns by activist groups hoping to sink or secure individual nominees. Chief Justice John Roberts has frequently lamented the politicisation of the judiciary, and has taken the extraordinary step of chastising fellow justices in writing for the damage that intemperate comments in and out of court have on the legitimacy of the courts and respect for the rule of law.

The current politicisation of the federal judiciary has been decades in the making, and as a result, both parties have developed rosters of potential appointees to judgeships and conducted extensive reviews of each for background, temperament, judicial philosophy and political orientation. Conservatives have an advantage in this effort in that they have a more clearly defined judicial philosophy and temperament they seek to promote: conservative lawyers even established the Federalist Society as a counterweight to the perceived liberal bias of the American Bar Association. High-profile failures of judges proposed by Republicans who were either disqualified due to personal issues (such as Douglas Ginsburg, who disclosed marijuana use during his confirmation hearing and was forced to withdraw) or who turned out to be more moderate than expected have resulted in a finely tuned vetting system for federal judicial appointments that Trump has inherited and adopted.

During the 2016 campaign, Trump published lists of judges he would consider for any vacancies on the Supreme Court. He has stayed true to this pledge since taking office, selecting and securing Senate confirmation for Neil Gorsuch to the Supreme Court in 2017, to the delight of conservatives. The retirement of Justice Anthony Kennedy, a Reagan appointee, has opened a second seat on the high court for Trump to fill. The two oldest Supreme Court justices – Ruth Bader Ginsburg (85 years old) and Stephen Breyer (80 years old) – are among the court's most liberal. Should they leave the court while Trump is president, they will almost certainly be replaced by more conservative jurists, a change which will shift the court in a conservative direction for many years to come.

To ensure confirmation of the Obama administration's judicial appointments when the Democrats formed the majority of the Senate, Democratic senators changed Senate rules to prevent filibusters against nominations, a tool used by senators in the minority to block debates from proceeding to a vote. In April 2017, Republicans extended the ban on filibustering to Supreme Court appointments, giving the Trump administration more surety of his nominations being approved than recent presidents have had.

Like the federal bureaucracy, some members of the federal judiciary have broken with past practice and entered into open conflict with the Trump administration. Prompted by cases launched by progressive activists, federal judges have issued injunctions to block Trump immigration decisions, invalidate Trump actions on healthcare policy and have even advanced cases looking into corruption in the administration.

This has given urgency to the president's responsibility to fill vacancies on federal courts, and the Trump administration has appointed more judges by this point in his presidency than any president before him. At the same time, following the historic decision by the Obama administration's Department of Justice that it would not defend the bipartisan Defense of Marriage Act (which did not recognise same-sex marriages) against court challenges by liberal activists, the Trump administration has announced it would not defend the Affordable Care Act against similar challenges from conservative activists.

This tit-for-tat over judicial appointments reflects the outsized role that the judiciary has in US governance, and presages continuing efforts by activists to attempt to shift policy through legal action rather than through efforts in the elected (and democratically accountable) branches of government. The practice is not new in the Trump era, but Trump's judicial appointments have the potential to tilt the odds in favour of conservative litigants. This will hardly de-politicise the judiciary, and may further delegitimise the courts in the eyes of US citizens.

Trump has not yet taken action on the administrative law tribunals, but conservatives hope he will. Administrative tribunals were set up by federal departments to adjudicate disputes over administrative decisions such as those by the Department of Health and Human Services to reimburse medical expenses, or to deny Social Security benefits. Such tribunals are not authorised by the US Constitution or by statute, and recently conservatives have begun to argue that these tribunals usurp the rightful authority of Congress and the judiciary while giving unchecked power to the federal bureaucracy to police itself (or cover its mistakes with a veneer of legality).

On 30 October 2008, presidential candidate Obama told supporters, 'we are five days away from fundamentally transforming the United States of America'. Republicans never forgot this claim, and as a presidential candidate eight years later, Trump vowed to reverse Obama's policies and 'Make America Great Again'. Trump is on course to fundamentally transform America, countering an Obama revolution with a Trump restoration that could prove more durable due to structural, institutional and demographic factors. Trump may yet falter, but while he has everyone distracted by his Twitter feed, serious work is under way, in plain sight.

The Trump Transformation, Part 2: International Leadership

The hypothesis of American decline is an academic perennial, but US presidents rarely embrace it openly. George W. Bush and Barack Obama sought to prepare for a reduced US role in world affairs, but neither saw the United States as a declining power.

President Donald Trump began from the premise of US decline and has aggressively worked to restore the US primacy that was a hallmark of most administrations since the end of the Second World War. While the US may have declined in power relative to other states in the international system, it retains considerable power in absolute terms. The Trump administration is attempting to marshal this power in a coordinated fashion – encompassing economic, military and cultural pressure – to exert 'maximum leverage' in negotiations with allies and rivals alike.

The credibility of the Trump strategy requires new military capabilities, new global economic policies and the creative use of cultural power through social media and mass communications. Trump is seeking to 'Make America Great Again' with a strategy that Trump believes is worthy of a major power, given a twenty-first-century twist.

Military transformation

Trump proposed and received an increase of approximately 10% in total US defence spending compared to the Obama administration's 2016 defence budget. Trump's realignment of the Department of Defense's priorities was equally important, with the 2018 National Defense Strategy highlighting three areas for improvement in the way that defence dollars are spent: firstly, increasing the lethality of the US military; secondly, developing and deploying new capabilities for US forces (notably in the space and cyber domains), while also acting to improve allied capacity; and thirdly, finding bureaucratic efficiencies to streamline the administration of US defence to devote more resources to the first two priorities.

The objective of increasing lethality – which involves developing hypersonic missiles, rail guns, autonomous systems enhanced by artificial intelligence, integrated manned and unmanned air swarms and a reinvestment in the nuclear arsenal to provide a wider range of tactical options for US forces – represents a subtle shift from the priority of precision. The Trump administration believes that great-power rivalry has returned and is now a more significant threat to US national security than asymmetric threats such as terrorism. Increased lethality is intended to have a deterrent effect by raising the cost of 'grey zone' or 'hybrid' threats that stop short of open conflict that have been employed by China, Russia and other states through proxies. It is also useful against terrorist adversaries, as the use of the Massive Ordnance Air Blast (MOAB) against a tunnel complex occupied by the Islamic State, also known as ISIS or ISIL, in Afghanistan in April 2017 demonstrated.

Trump and his national-security team do not believe that they are starting a new arms race but instead are responding to a prolonged period in which the US neglected defence priorities and unilaterally disarmed while rivals developed capabilities to threaten US interests. The Obama administration had previously invested in countermeasures to address the increased anti-access/area-denial (A2/AD) capabilities of rival states, but these countermeasures have now been transformed into an effort to overleap A2/AD with technologies that will reassert the United States' strategic advantage. Conceptually, the Trump administration is seeking to leverage a public- and private-sector-funded capacity for innovation resulting from a dynamic US tech sector, entrepreneurial start-up culture and ready supply of venture capital. The Trump administration plans to catch up with Chinese and Russian advances (many of which result from stolen US technology) to overleap rival programmes quickly and overmatch and intimidate rivals in the same way that the Reagan administration's Strategic Defense Initiative contributed to the Soviet Union's loss of confidence in its ability to keep up with the US, which led it to abandon the Cold War.

Russia and China are perceived by the Trump administration to have made few original advances in defence technology; rather, both countries are seen to have relied on espionage and the theft and replication of defence technology to improve their war-fighting and grey-zone capabilities. One response to these provocations and threats is economic and trade pressure; another is to leap further ahead, pressing the envelope of military innovation by capitalising on the impressive US private sector and national laboratory and university infrastructure.

The second shift of the 2018 National Defense Strategy involves the development and deployment of new capabilities, but the US will also look to its allies to invest in their own defences in order to add to allied capacity in each area of military capability. Consistent with Trump's 'America First' approach to the economy, this would result in greater allied purchases of US equipment and technology, and the employment of American workers. In response to the general decline in the Western defence-industrial base since the end of the Cold War, the Clinton, Bush and Obama administrations relied on exhortation and rhetoric to encourage allies to strengthen their own defence industries and research. By contrast, the plan of the Trump administration is that the US will position its firms as the defence-industrial base for all its allies. Arms manufacturers in allied countries will invest in the US in order to qualify for orders as the US increases defence spending, and then export to countries whose modest military spending will grow to satisfy US demands for greater alliance burden-sharing.

However, the message from the Trump administration to NATO allies on defence spending (essentially to spend more and buy American) has been resisted in some European capitals. The Trump administration has responded by linking trade policy to defence and threatening to impose tariffs on steel, aluminium and automobiles on NATO member states within the EU, as well as on Canada and Japan, under Section 232 of the 1962 Trade Act (which allows such actions for reasons of 'national security'). This has struck many as an expedient, as Trump's resort to 'national security' tariffs as a way to take a trade action is unlikely to be successfully challenged in US courts or at the World Trade Organisation (WTO). However, allied governments should consider the US invocation of national security as sincere: allied underinvestment in defence and security capabilities since the end of the Cold War has forced the US to cover the security-capability gap while allied states have, from Washington's perspective, chosen to support domestic-welfare programmes and other spending priorities. In the meantime, China and Russia have advanced their offensive capabilities in ways that have exposed weaknesses in the defences of the US and its allies. The Trump administration is therefore attempting to force a re-prioritisation of defence spending by threatening the economies of its allies and trade partners.

Trump's attitude toward alliances is similar to his attitude towards trade: he favours both in an ideal state in which obligations are shared and reciprocal and the benefits mutual or slightly tipped in favour of the largest partner (i.e., the US). Whereas previous US presidents have accepted US alliances (and trade agreements) as an institutionalisation of a past political commitment that must be honoured in perpetuity, Trump sees this as complacency that has permitted – or even encouraged – US allies to spend less on their militaries and spend more on welfare benefits for citizens. Trump sees some alliances, such as NATO, as having continued value, but he wants to renegotiate the price allies must pay to remain in the alliance, and he expects greater deference to US national-security and foreign policy on the part of allied governments that are, to Trump, in arrears on their contributions to collective security. It is noteworthy that Japan, where Prime Minister Shinzo Abe has expanded defence spending and sought to revise the Japanese constitution to allow Japanese forces to aid allies such as the US in conflicts beyond the defence of Japan itself, has been praised by Trump.

The return of great-power rivalry as the focus of US national-security policy has also prompted the Trump administration to question whether US allies are themselves great powers, or middling ones; the answer, for Trump, is revealed by their investments in traditional power capabilities. Russia comes closer to great-power status in this view than does the United Kingdom, and Japan is a greater power than Germany.

The third shift of the Trump administration's defence priorities is a reduction in the bureaucratic costs associated with US defence to free up resources for its other two priorities (lethality and new capability development and deployment). This will eventually result in changes to the Unified Command Plan (UCP). The first UCP was adopted in 1946 to foster an integrated joint command structure across all four branches of the US military. Currently, there are six geographic and four functional combatant commands, each with its own headquarters and supporting staff developing exercises, liaising with foreign governments and undertaking various activities from delivery of food and other aid to contributing to local law enforcement and US diplomacy in various regions. The demand of lethality will require a reorganisation of the US military's operations and could lead to the streamlining or elimination of the current command structure. This may reduce the US footprint in developing countries where the US operates, as well as scaling down US activity that is not directly related to threats to US national security, such as US ground troops in the fight against ISIS and Iranian proxies. For some allies, the need for greater cost efficiencies combined with new technology, such as hypersonic weapons, may lead to the closure of bases and reduced local US expenditure.

Often overlooked in the discussion of US defence policy is the importance of the US Department of Homeland Security (DHS). Since its establishment in 2002 during the George W. Bush administration, the DHS has often been viewed abroad as a law-enforcement agency with a limited and somewhat aggravating presence that adds to the hassles of air travel and passport control. Its most militarily capable units – the US Coast Guard and the US Border Patrol – have been seen in this way, particularly outside of North America. However, the DHS has been from the outset a part of the US national-security complex, much as the intelligence community has been. Trump has captured attention for his focus on building a wall on the US border with Mexico to stop illegal migration, but his policy emphasising border security to reassure the public that he is protecting US citizens first and foremost is consistent with the policies of the Bush and Obama administrations since 2001.

Trump's wall is a highly symbolic rhetorical device, although in reality it will probably be a collection of fences, walls and remote-detection technologies. At the US border with Canada, the technological aspect of border-domain awareness through remote sensors, unmanned aerial vehicles and the provision of ever-greater amounts of information to border inspectors and airport screeners has greater profile. Information sharing between US and Canadian law-enforcement and intelligence agencies is extensive and electronically sifted and quickly disseminated to law-enforcement and DHS personnel. The objective at both borders, at airports and seaports is the same: maximum possible domain awareness and control. To achieve it, the Trump administration is willing to threaten cross-border access to the US of foreign goods, persons and even data – even if that means renegotiating or cancelling the North American Free Trade Agreement (NAFTA). Notably, the 2018 National Security Strategy begins with a discussion of border security, weapons of mass destruction, and biological and cyber attacks on US citizens. The Trump administration's America First security policy puts the security of Americans first in order to maintain the trust and confidence of the public in Trump's leadership.

Economic transformation

To a far greater degree than previous US administrations, the Trump administration is employing access to the US as leverage to force its allies to spend more on defence. It is uncommon for the US to link security and economic issues so directly, and Trump's capacity to do so stems from the organisation of the Washington establishment, where 'career silos' separate experts in domestic and foreign policies from those whose focus is security or economic policy.

Some domestic observers have downplayed the significance of Trump's trade policy, arguing that the administration is transactional and merely seeking to leverage access to the US economy as it renegotiates the deals struck by US leaders following the Second World War. Yet this underestimates the objectives of the Trump administration, which extend to reshaping the future of globalisation on terms more favourable to US workers.

To put the Trump administration's international economic policy into context, a brief overview of the United States' role in the world economy is necessary. Shortly after independence, the US adopted an economic-development strategy that was pushed through the US Congress by Speaker of the House Henry Clay in 1820 and came to be known as the 'American System'. Congress established a high tariff against imports to raise revenue and create protection for US firms so that the firms might grow through sales to the domestic market. Tariff revenue was funnelled into overland infrastructure to connect the east-coast ports to those in the west, adding to the US factor endowment and therefore enabling rapid US economic growth. A central bank – the ill-fated Bank of the US – extended credit to finance westward expansion and settlement. The American System was replicated by Canada and other countries in the western hemisphere.

At the start of the twentieth century, US industry developed expertise in mass production which permitted unprecedented economies of scale and low unit costs (i.e., costs that lowered as the number of units increased). This change to the political economy of the US had international consequences: the United States gradually abandoned protectionism and adopted anti-imperialism and trade liberalisation to open up new markets to US exports. Following the Second World War, the US was confronted with shattered foreign markets and collapsed empires that could not afford US exports. In response, the US shifted policy again, promoting export-led growth as a means for European countries and Japan to rebuild their economies by exporting to the US, and underpinned this with the Bretton Woods institutions and promotion of the US dollar as a reserve currency. Combined with aid under the Marshall Plan, this policy cocktail was successful in rebuilding war-torn economies. However, then US president Richard Nixon believed that Canada, Japan and European allies were manipulating their currencies to continue to rely on exports to the US long after they had rebuilt their economies, and were effectively exporting inflation to the US. Nixon also resented the lack of allied support for the Vietnam War and shrinking European defence expenditures. After failing to convince allies to cooperate in easing the pressure on the US economy, Nixon abandoned the gold standard and imposed a 10% import surcharge.

Calls for new Marshall Plans by American politicians were common during the Cold War for various regions and causes, including Africa, the environment, Iraq and the Middle East, and combating AIDS. The end of the Cold War brought the challenges of incorporating former communist-bloc countries into the global economy and helping them to catch up in development terms with the Western world. At the same time, the countries that were considered part of the 'Third World' were being re-designated as 'less developed countries' and even as 'emerging markets'. The US response in the early 1990s was a return to the export-led growth model that was employed after the Second World War, expanding its application to developing countries through two trade agreements that Trump considers to be the 'worst trade deals ever' in US history: NAFTA in 1994, and the Uruguay Round agreement that led to the creation of the WTO in 1995 on the foundation laid by the 1948 General Agreement on Tariffs and Trade (GATT), which liberalised trade after the Second World War.

Inherent in the NAFTA and the Uruguay Round agreements was a further opening of market access to the US. As intended, this led firms to shift production that required low-skilled labour or was highly cost-sensitive to emerging markets. The immediate benefit was a lowering of the cost of many goods now imported to the US that contributed to improving the quality of life for people in the US. Yet many Americans lost jobs as a result. After the Second World War, the booming US economy generated employment to offset job loss due to imports from Europe and Japan; after the Cold War, emerging markets with access to the US domestic market were more numerous, and so the development benefit spread more widely across multiple economies. This slowed down the development of middle-class consumers in emerging markets, and consequently these countries were unable to import US goods and services in sufficient volume to offset job loss in the US.

While the recovering economies of Europe and Japan were clearly grateful for US support and economic leadership after the Second World War, 50 years later emerging markets were critical of US policy and leadership, and so were European and Japanese leaders and the Russians, still bitter after the Cold War and not as well treated as the defeated Germans and Japanese had been.

Voters in the US signalled their dissatisfaction with trade policy and politicians responded. Running against then-president Clinton in 1996, Republican Senate majority leader Bob Dole called for a 'time out' on new trade agreements until NAFTA and the WTO could be assessed – notably, Dole's trade-policy adviser during the 1996 presidential campaign was

Robert Lighthizer, picked by Trump to serve as US trade representative. Third-party candidates Ross Perot and Ralph Nader were critics of US trade policy. In 2008, Democratic presidential candidates Barack Obama and Hillary Clinton both condemned NAFTA, though Obama's advisers privately told Canadian officials this was just campaign rhetoric. By the time of the 2016 presidential election, both Hillary Clinton and Donald Trump had come out against the Trans-Pacific Partnership (TPP) and NAFTA.

As this history illustrates, the trade-policy consensus that prevailed in Washington following the Cold War was always an elite consensus, and its critics were consistently disappointed by leaders who claimed to share their views. When during the Obama administration polls began to show that a majority of Americans believed that their children would have fewer economic opportunities than they had enjoyed, it was a warning light on the dashboard of the global economy that a change in US international economic policy was coming, a warning light that was either missed or dismissed at the time.

Trump was remarkably consistent in his criticism of US trade policy in the post-Cold War era before his entry into politics. As president, he has sought to renegotiate NAFTA and reform the WTO. Another consistent theme for Trump before he entered politics was his praise for the US economic response to the rise of Japan as an economic rival in the 1970s and 1980s.

Japan's remarkable economic recovery from the Second World War catapulted it to become the world's second-largest economy after the US by 1968. The focused response of the US was to demand that Japan adopt voluntary export restraints, float the yen and open its domestic market to US imports. The US also established a North American regional content requirement in the Canada–United States Free Trade Agreement that was raised even higher in NAFTA for motor vehicles; the regional content requirement prompted Japanese firms to invest in production in North America to satisfy it, shifting production and jobs that might otherwise have remained in Japan. A 25% tariff on light trucks imported to the US led to significant increases in Japanese (and, later, German and

Korean) investment in North America for production of sport-utility vehicles (SUVs), minivans and other popular models. The US response to rising Japanese economic power was broadly effective. US concerns were slowly addressed, and by 2001, Japan was a major investor in all three North American economies. Japan's rise to the status of a global economic superpower stalled, although Japan remained prosperous and successful.

At the time, Trump enthusiastically praised the Reagan administration for addressing Japan successfully. As president, Trump sees the rise of China in similar terms. This has led him to simultaneously renegotiate trade relations with allies and trading partners while orchestrating military, diplomatic and economic measures to manage China's ascendancy, much as the US did with Japan's.

Leveraging culture

The Trump administration's grand designs will, like most human endeavours, fall short of their objectives. Yet it would be a mistake to ignore the strategic picture and conclude, based on the media furore, that the administration will collapse in impeachment and ruin before any of Trump's threats to allies and great-power rivals need to be taken seriously. Trump is attempting a transformative presidency, and this ambition is underestimated by those who focus on daily outrages and Trump's Twitter account.

Consider for a moment that Trump's use of Twitter could be a breakthrough in keeping with the politicians who first mastered radio as a means of mass communication, including Franklin Roosevelt and Winston Churchill, or those leaders – from John F. Kennedy to Ronald Reagan – who exploited the potential of television to connect with voters. Twitter has allowed Trump to communicate with voters without the filter of establishment media, pundits and other critics. Internationally, Trump has used Twitter to communicate directly with North Korean leader Kim Jong-un and Iranian leader Sayyid Ali Khamenei. Hostile media outlets in the US have been unable to resist the president's ability to reset the news agenda through effective social-media use, and as a result, even critical media has amplified Trump's messages and helped them reach people around the world.

The most disruptive effects of Trump's social-media communications are felt by establishment members in countries outside the US. From Justin Trudeau to Xi Jinping, Trump's view of the shortcomings of world leaders are broadcast in 280 characters or fewer. This has energised populists and anti-establishment forces around the world because citizens see Trump saying things that they agree with but cannot say themselves for fear of social or legal reprisals.

The Trump cultural transformation is also politically significant. In democracies, Trump's populism has inspired imitators. In closed societies, Trump's message is even more destabilising. Just as foreign countries have used cyber attacks to sow distrust and political misinformation in the US, the Trump administration is shifting from defence to offence, countering interference in Western democracies with new technologies that open space for dissidents and critics in authoritarian regimes. This follows the path of radio, which led to Radio Free Europe and Radio Liberty; freedom and experimentation in the US leads to early adoption and then mastery of new media for communication and new means to project US leadership abroad.

Trump's argument that the US has fallen into decline is not unique; what is unusual is his belief that American decline can be reversed – albeit with controversial methods – to render the US once again the sole global superpower unhindered by multilateral agreements. Trump benefits from being mistaken for a chaotic toddler with nuclear weapons; low expectations followed by well-promoted successes provide legitimisation for Trump as president based on performance in office, increasing the impact of foreign and domestic policy successes in rebutting critics. Historians will debate the current era on the basis of the changes that emerge from it, particularly those that last longer than present leaders' terms of office. Trump is defying traditions and conventions in his unusual approach to the presidency, but his agenda is similar to that of previous US presidents. Voters, historians and world leaders should look for durable results from Trump's unconventional leadership to determine for themselves whether Trump is a transformative figure in American politics and international relations.

US Climate Policy and the Paris Agreement

The global effort to reduce greenhouse-gas emissions to relatively safe levels is at a critical juncture. Current reduction targets mandated by the landmark 2015 Paris Agreement are inconsistent with the treaty's goal of limiting global warming to well below 2 °C compared with pre-industrial levels, let alone its stricter aspirational goal of 1.5 °C. For most countries, moreover, current policies are inadequate to achieve even these modest targets. The UN Environment Programme (UNEP) reported in November 2017 that 'there is an urgent need for accelerated short-term action and enhanced longer-term national ambition, if the goals of the Paris Agreement are to remain achievable'.

US President Donald Trump's reversal of the United States' long-standing climate policy and his announcement that the US would withdraw from the Paris Agreement have posed even greater challenges. The US is the world's second-largest greenhouse-gas emitter (after China), meaning that the Paris Agreement's attempt to limit rising temperatures will likely fail if the US does not meet or surpass its current emissions targets. Despite vigorous and dynamic efforts at the sub-national level to make this happen, the prospects are uncertain.

Targets and tools

Under the Paris Agreement, countries have submitted their own formal targets (nationally determined contributions, or NDCs) for emissions reductions up to 2025 or 2030. These NDCs must be replaced or updated every five years (beginning in 2020), reflecting increasing ambition in light of dialogue and global stock-takes. This 'ratcheting up' of ambition is key to the success of the agreement, since the UNEP assesses that the initial NDCs cover only about a third of the reductions necessary by 2030 to be on a 'least-cost' pathway to the 2 °C target. If the gap is not closed by 2030, moreover, achieving this goal will be nearly impossible. The Climate Action Tracker consortium (CAT) estimates that implementing current unconditional national pledges (i.e., without further reduction targets being attained) would risk warming of as much as 3.5 °C, well within the danger zone, with high to very high risk of severe, widespread and irreversible impacts globally.

The US NDC calls for a net reduction of greenhouse-gas emissions of 17% by 2020 and 26–28% by 2025 as measured against 2005 levels, to be achieved through federal regulations on vehicle fuel-efficiency standards; carbon dioxide (CO_2) emissions from power plants; and other greenhouse-gas emissions and energy-conservation standards under existing legislation through executive agencies. When the US NDC was submitted at the end of 2015, the US had already achieved a 10% reduction in net greenhouse-gas emissions since 2005, and added a further 2% in 2016. Historical reductions had not been linear, with greenhouse-gas emissions even showing year-on-year increases at times, but the US appeared to be roughly on track to meeting the 2020 target. Meeting the 2025 target would, however, require a near-doubling of the average annual rate of emissions reduction.

A key tool for this purpose was the Clean Power Plan (CPP), a set of regulations that went into effect in December 2015. Under the aegis of the decades-old Clean Air Act, the Environmental Protection Agency (EPA) set incremental state-by-state targets for CO_2 emissions from electrical-power generation, with a national target of a 32% reduction by 2030. How to achieve these reductions was left up to individual states, but the EPA would impose a plan if none had been adopted by 2018. Another important element of the US emissions-reduction effort was increasingly stringent fuel-efficiency standards for cars and light trucks (the Corporate Average Fuel Economy, or CAFE, standards). The bipartisan Energy Independence and Security Act of 2007, signed by then-president George W. Bush, set a national goal of a 40% improvement in fuel efficiency – with a commensurate reduction in CO_2 emissions – by 2025. In

2011, the annual standard was increased for the first time in over two decades, and in 2012 new standards were agreed and implemented for the years 2017–25.

The CPP and the CAFE standards were part of a broader 'Climate Action Plan' (CAP) intended to meet the overall 2025 target. CAP encompassed a range of other regulations, including accelerating and streamlining the permit process for clean energy and electrical-grid improvements; increasing research and development funding for clean energy and energy efficiency; establishing new energy-efficiency standards for buildings and appliances; and reducing emissions of greenhouse gases other than CO_2 in various ways. This would build a foundation for more stringent efforts towards an 80% reduction in emissions from 2005 levels by 2050, a target that was outlined in the Obama administration's 2016 'United States Mid-Century Strategy for Deep Decarbonization' report. This would require an average annual emissions reduction of 2% of 2005 levels to be sustained to mid-century, the same rate needed to achieve the current 2025 target.

In March 2017, however, soon after taking office, Trump signed an executive order formally rescinding the CAP and other Obama-era orders relating to climate change, and mandated a review of the CPP and other regulations with the clear aim of reversing them. This was followed by the expected announcement in June that the US would withdraw from the Paris Agreement, including ending the US NDC. This announcement was mostly symbolic: parties to the Paris Agreement cannot formally announce their withdrawal until 4 November 2019, nor fully withdraw until 4 November 2020, unless they also withdraw from the 1992 UN Framework Convention on Climate Change (UNFCCC) as a whole. Trump's March executive order, however, effectively ended implementation of the NDC, and the US is unlikely to submit a new NDC with a reduction target for 2030, as it is required to do before 2020.

Rolling coal

Gross US greenhouse-gas emissions peaked in 2007 at 7.351 gigatonnes CO_2 equivalent ($GtCO_2e$). By 2009, emissions had dropped by nearly 9% (representing almost the full amount of the total reduction between 2005 and 2015) – mostly the result of the economic contraction that followed the global financial crisis in 2008. As the economy recovered, however, emissions continued to show an overall decline, with only three years showing small year-on-year increases over the last eight years. Between 2005 and 2016, US real GDP rose by 17%, while net emissions dropped by 12%. Meanwhile, total primary energy consumption fell by 5%. Thus more than half the emissions decline over this period was due to a shift towards cleaner fuels, especially for electrical generation. Coal's share of electrical generation fell from 50% to 33%, while natural gas rose from 19% to 33%, and renewables rose from 2% to 7%. A similar shift has been responsible for the United Kingdom's dramatic emissions reductions, where CO_2 levels are now the lowest since the late nineteenth century. Gas is, however, only a temporary replacement for coal, providing time for the development and deployment of renewable capacity to enable the deep cuts necessary by mid-century.

The Trump administration, however, has been actively trying to stem and even reverse the decline of coal. Many prominent members of the administration, including EPA director Scott Pruitt and the president himself, have denied the link between CO_2 emissions and climate change. Trump made reversing the CPP and 'bringing back the coal industry' key parts of his campaign in the run-up to the 2016 election. As president, he signed his March 2017 executive order that reversed Obama's climate policies flanked by coal-industry executives and miners, declaring, 'you know what this says, right? You're going back to work.' As part of his June announcement of intent to withdraw from the Paris Agreement, the US ended payments of the remaining US$2 billion of its pledged US$3bn contribution to the Green Climate Fund. However, the US retained its seat on the board, which it is reportedly using to promote new coal-fired power plants in developing countries, contrary to the intent of the fund. Similarly, Washington's only official public side event at the 2017 UN climate summit in Bonn was a promotion of so-called 'clean' coal as an emissions-reduction mechanism. In August 2017, the administration set in motion a review of CAFE standards. In September, it asked the Federal Energy Regulatory Commission (an independent agency) to guarantee a financial return for any power plant keeping a 90-day supply of fuel on site. This was justified on national-security grounds, but was transparently an effort to subsidise coal (and to a lesser extent nuclear power). (The bipartisan commission unanimously rejected the proposal.) In June 2018, Trump ordered US Secretary of Energy Rick Perry to 'prepare immediate steps' to stop the closure of coal-fired power plants; one mooted proposal is to invoke the Defense Production Act, a Cold War-era law that has not been used on such an industry-wide scale since the Korean War.

Some of these efforts are the political equivalent of 'rolling coal', where owners of small diesel trucks modify their vehicles to produce large amounts of smoke and soot on demand. With roots in racing culture, the practice escaped the tracks onto US roads in 2014, with diesel-truck drivers deliberately and provocatively targeting owners of electric or hybrid-electric cars, cars with liberal bumper stickers and eventually anti-Trump protesters. It has become sufficiently widespread to provoke special legislation in several states, even though the EPA ruled it illegal under the Clean Air Act in 2014. In keeping with his provocative style, Trump's public statements on coal are both deliberately baiting his political opponents and appealing to his electoral base, whose demographics overlap considerably with anti-environmental activists, even if the latter are a small minority. Trump overwhelmingly won 'coal country' in 2016, and his campaign pledges and rhetoric on bringing back coal were important elements in his victory in key swing states such as Ohio and especially Pennsylvania, which had not voted for a Republican since 1988. Internationally, too, many observers in and out of governments consider the US withdrawal from Paris to be sheer provocation. The United States' self-imposed isolation – every other country on the planet has signed the treaty – is attracting more opprobrium than if the country simply failed to meet its NDC targets, which are in any case only enforceable through 'naming and shaming'.

Market forces

Even if Trump's continued promotion of coal has a domestic political upside, its practical effect may be limited. The shift from coal to gas began as early as 2005, with coal production peaking in 2008. The fundamental reasons for the decline in coal production were economic. Coal was badly hit by the global financial crisis of 2008, then the advent of cheap shale gas – coupled with the need to retire and replace a significant percentage of existing coal capacity due to obsolescence – changed the energy balance just as the recovery started. The relatively high cost of building, upgrading and operating coal-fired plants was aggravated, but not caused, by regulations on energy efficiency, levels of renewable energy and non-greenhouse-gas pollution control; tax credits for investment in wind and solar; and the declining costs of solar and wind technology produced overseas. The net result is that roughly half of all coal-fired power plants in the US are now running at a net loss; in many parts of the country, it is cheaper to build new renewable capacity than new coal plants. Over half the US coal plants operating in 2010 had either closed down or announced a closing date by the end of 2017.

Trump's policies promoting coal are therefore little more than futile short-term efforts to hold back the tide. Indeed, the rate of coal-plant closure has accelerated since Trump took office. In the first six months after the Department of the Interior lifted an Obama-era ban on new coal leases on federal land as part of Trump's March 2017 executive order, existing leaseholders suspended eight and cancelled five of the 44 existing leases, and only a single new lease application was submitted. Even the radical step of invoking the Defense Production Act would only delay the closure of some plants by a few years. Reversing the CPP will slow, but not reverse, the decline of coal. Any mines and plants that survive the decline of coal thanks to Trump's policies will, moreover, be the most efficient and automated. Administration policy is unlikely to be able to reverse the decline in jobs, Trump's bottom-line goal.

The market forces that will probably allow the US to meet its overall 2020 NDC target and the CPP's 2025 target for the power sector will, however, likely be insufficient to achieve the 2025 NDC or 2030 CPP goals. Projections suggest that natural-gas prices would have to decline significantly to achieve these targets without the CPP or a similar regulatory regime. Tax credits for renewable energy – which mainly go back in their current form to the economic stimulus package in 2009 – are particularly important in this regard: their reversal or expiration would make the medium-term goals, let alone the aspirations for mid-century, nearly impossible. These credits were mostly revived, retained or extended in the budget act passed in February 2018, although early versions of the act threatened to revoke them. Tax credits are more politically palatable than restrictive regulations, and receive bipartisan if not universal support. Eight of the ten states with the fastest-growing solar-energy industries voted for Trump in 2016, and Republican legislators are reluctant to repeal tax breaks that benefit their constituents. On the other hand, the 30% tariff on imported solar panels announced in January 2018 as part of the administration's protectionist trade policy has already slowed down investment in and expansion of US solar capacity.

'America's Pledge'

Until 2009, most formal policies intended to reduce US greenhouse-gas emissions were adopted and implemented at the sub-federal level: regional consortia, state and municipal regulations, and private-sector initiatives. With the more industrial states tending to have the most stringent policies (only four countries have larger economies than California, and California has some of the most progressive climate policies in the world), these sub-federal efforts combined with market forces to slow the growth in emissions. Their importance continued after 2009, complementing the Obama administration's policies.

Reacting against Trump's announcement that the US would withdraw from the Paris Agreement, state and municipal governments, business, universities and other sub-federal actors expanded existing networks and created new ones in support of the international agreement. As of August 2018, ten states, 277 cities and counties and large numbers of businesses and non-governmental organisations had signed

Falling Carbon-dioxide Emissions in the United States

Despite US President Donald Trump's reversal of Obama-era climate policies and withdrawal from the 2015 Paris agreement on climate change, the United States remains theoretically capable of fulfilling its emission-reduction target for 2025 as outlined in the Paris agreement, aided by the efforts of a consortium of sub-national actors including states, cities and major companies.

A key driver behind the fall in emissions is the reduction of coal's share of energy generation. In March 2017, Trump signed an executive order designed to aid the coal industry, but with the number of coal-fired power plants in decline and shale gas proving a cheaper energy alternative, such efforts may have limited practical effect.

US GDP COMPARED TO CARBON-DIOXIDE EMISSIONS

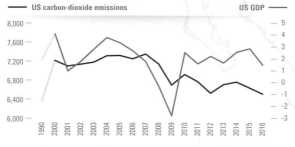

Gross US greenhouse-gas emissions peaked in 2007 at 7.351 gigatonnes CO_2 equivalent ($GtCO_2e$). Emissions subsequently dropped in large part due to the 2008 global financial crisis, highlighting the link between economic activity and emissions. However, emissions have since declined in tandem with a dramatic recovery in the country's GDP. Post-2008, the country's energy mixture saw a pronounced decline in coal consumption, with natural gas becoming a major contributor to the US energy supply and renewable energy showing an uptick.

Sources: *US Energy Information Administration, US Environmental Protection Agency, World Bank*

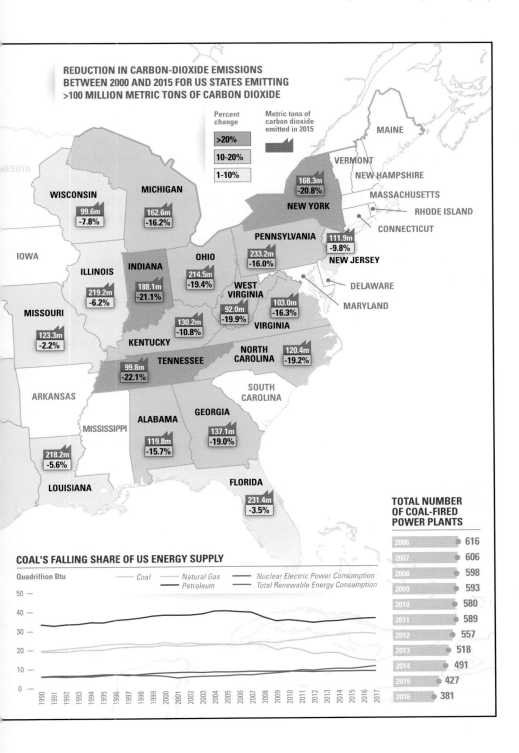

REDUCTION IN CARBON-DIOXIDE EMISSIONS BETWEEN 2000 AND 2015 FOR US STATES EMITTING >100 MILLION METRIC TONS OF CARBON DIOXIDE

Percent change
>20%
10-20%
1-10%

Metric tons of carbon dioxide emitted in 2015

MAINE
VERMONT
NEW HAMPSHIRE
MASSACHUSETTS
RHODE ISLAND
CONNECTICUT

WISCONSIN 99.6m -7.8%
MICHIGAN 162.6m -16.2%
NEW YORK 168.3m -20.8%

PENNSYLVANIA 233.2m -16.0%
NEW JERSEY 111.9m -9.8%

IOWA
ILLINOIS 219.2m -6.2%
INDIANA 188.1m -21.1%
OHIO 214.5m -19.4%
WEST VIRGINIA 92.0m -19.9%
DELAWARE
MARYLAND 103.0m -16.3%
VIRGINIA

MISSOURI 123.3m -2.2%
KENTUCKY 130.2m -10.8%
NORTH CAROLINA 120.4m -19.2%

ARKANSAS
TENNESSEE 99.8m -22.1%
SOUTH CAROLINA

MISSISSIPPI
ALABAMA 119.8m -15.7%
GEORGIA 137.1m -19.0%

LOUISIANA 218.2m -5.6%

FLORIDA 231.4m -3.5%

COAL'S FALLING SHARE OF US ENERGY SUPPLY

Quadrillion Btu

— Coal
— Natural Gas
— Petroleum
— Nuclear Electric Power Consumption
— Total Renewable Energy Consumption

50 —
40 —
30 —
20 —
10 —
0 —

1990 1991 1992 1993 1994 1995 1996 1997 1998 1999 2000 2001 2002 2003 2004 2005 2006 2007 2008 2009 2010 2011 2012 2013 2014 2015 2016 2017

TOTAL NUMBER OF COAL-FIRED POWER PLANTS

2006	616
2007	606
2008	598
2009	593
2010	580
2011	589
2012	557
2013	518
2014	491
2015	427
2016	381

up to 'We Are Still In', a declaration that they remained committed to the Paris Agreement.

At least 20 states, 110 cities and 1,400 companies – including some of America's biggest such as the Coca-Cola Company, Kellogg's, Mars Incorporated, Microsoft and Walmart Inc. – have adopted quantified emissions-reduction targets (California's commitments alone are on a par with those of some individual nations). Together, these actors account for half the US population, over half its GDP and 35% of its emissions. 'America's Pledge', a parallel and complementary effort to We Are Still In, was set up under the leadership of California Governor Jerry Brown and former New York City mayor Michael Bloomberg in order to aggregate and quantify the actions of these sub-federal actors, and to provide detailed road maps to catalyse further climate action.

At the UN climate summit in Bonn in November 2017, America's Pledge released a preliminary report on sub-national efforts, concluding that, given the Trump administration's policies, the currently committed non-federal efforts would be insufficient to meet the US 2025 NDC target of reducing emissions 26–28% below 2005 levels. The report also noted that renewed federal engagement would be critical for achieving deeper reductions after 2025.

The potential actions at the sub-national level mirror those outlined in the national CAP, but using the regulatory and budgeting power of states, counties and municipalities. New and existing networks can help expand carbon markets and provide administrative and organisational support and best-practice guidelines for jurisdictions to use their existing authority to shift to cleaner power sources. Investments in infrastructure (such as the electrical grid and electrical-vehicle charging points) can drive the transformation of energy markets. Stricter regulatory regimes for building codes, manufacturing-energy efficiency and non-CO_2 gases (such as methane and hydrofluorocarbons) can be implemented in a cost-effective way. Businesses and non-governmental organisations, as well as states, counties and cities, can shift to hybrid or zero-emissions vehicles for their fleets. As more such technologies and regulations are adopted, manufacturers will provide more and better options and prices will drop, forming a virtuous circle. With 12 states following its lead on stringent vehicle-emissions policy, for example, California is the de facto setter of industry standards and targets, even in the face of federal efforts to roll them back.

A troubling precedent

Although the US is, on paper, capable of achieving its NDC by 2025 without federal action, the precedent of the 1997 Kyoto Protocol suggests that these sub-national efforts may struggle to achieve the necessary reductions in the face of indifference or hostility at the national level. The Kyoto Protocol was intended as a first practical step towards the goal of reducing greenhouse gases to levels that would avoid dangerous climate change – a goal to which the parties to the UNFCCC had committed themselves. Overall, 52 industrial countries signed up to emissions targets for the period 2008–12, with the US committing to a 7% reduction over 1990 levels.

The Clinton administration signed the treaty but was politically unable to risk submitting it for ratification to the Senate, which earlier in 1997 had unanimously passed a resolution declaring that any agreement that did not impose binding targets on developing as well as industrialised countries would be unacceptable. Within two months of taking office in 2001, the George W. Bush administration announced that it was essentially abandoning the protocol. Nevertheless, by the end of 2006 more than half of US states had adopted climate-action plans, and there were many initiatives at regional and local level.

Despite these efforts, by 2012 US greenhouse-gas emissions had increased by nearly 4% over 1990 levels, a far cry from the 7% reduction which would have been mandated by the Kyoto Protocol. Although US emissions have been falling since 2007, the most recent figures (for 2016) are still nearly 2% higher than for 1990. In contrast, the 15 EU members in 1997 committed to a collective 8% reduction by 2012, and actually achieved nearly 12%. Emissions of the 28 current EU states fell by over 22% between 1990 and 2015. In this case at least, sub-national efforts in the US proved unable to make up for inertia at the top.

2030 and beyond

Although many large emitters, such as China and India, are on track to meet their 2020 and 2030 commitments, CAT calculates that current policies offer only a 3% chance of avoiding 2 °C warming. Even if all countries, including the US, achieve their NDC targets by 2030, the odds improve to only 10%. There is a significant gap, estimated at 11–13 $GtCO_2e$ by the UNEP, between the aggregate NDCs and the reductions necessary by 2030 for a two-thirds chance of success. Put another way, meeting current NDCs would mean a global rise of 2% in emissions by 2030 over 2016, but to avoid a 2 °C rise, global emissions need to peak by 2020 and fall by 20% below that peak by 2030.

Globally, the UNEP estimates that increasing solar and wind power at the expense of fossil fuels, making appliances and passenger cars more efficient, and stopping and reversing deforestation would, without any other enhanced action, suffice to close the gap at a modest or even net-negative cost. Sub-national and non-state efforts, however, will contribute only a modest proportion of this reduction, since much of the potential of these efforts, both globally and within the US, is already accounted for in existing commitments. The sectoral opportunities and policy approaches the UNEP identifies for global emissions reduction closely mirror, unsurprisingly, those identified by America's Pledge for the US. A virtuous circle of supply and demand for low-emission technologies also operates at the global level: the increased cost-effectiveness of solar panels and wind power that has driven the decline in coal in the US has mostly been due to Chinese and European policy and investment.

The UNEP concludes that the level of ambition reflected in new or updated NDCs to be submitted in 2020 is likely to determine whether the emissions gap can be bridged by 2030. With formal withdrawal from the Paris Agreement due in November 2020, the US will almost certainly not submit its own new targets. Sub-federal efforts are at best barely sufficient to meet the earlier and now-abandoned commitments as a stopgap measure, and any incoming administration in 2021 wishing to re-engage with the Paris Agreement will struggle to catch up. If Trump's policies continue after 2020, excessive warming is almost inevitable. The rest of the world would need to make even deeper cuts, while their ability to make even their fair share of cuts would be hampered by the absence of leadership from Washington and a perception that the US is a free rider – the very thing for which Trump has indicted China and other parties to the agreement to justify withdrawal. The accelerated short-term action called for by the UNEP may be feasible, but enhanced longer-term ambition is both increasingly urgent and increasingly uncertain.

Index